CW01306258

In Spite of Everything....

'a Life-story of fear, heartbreak, love, trickery and Triumph'

Pat Coppard ... (PatCee)

authorHOUSE®

AuthorHouse™
1663 Liberty Drive
Bloomington, IN 47403
www.authorhouse.com
Phone: 1-800-839-8640

© 2012 by Pat Coppard . . . (PatCee). All rights reserved.

No part of this book may be reproduced, stored in a retrieval system, or transmitted by any means without the written permission of the author.

Published by AuthorHouse   01/20/2012

ISBN: 978-1-4678-8395-5 (hc)
ISBN: 978-1-4678-8396-2 (e)

Any people depicted in stock imagery provided by Thinkstock are models, and such images are being used for illustrative purposes only.
Certain stock imagery © Thinkstock.

This book is printed on acid-free paper.

Because of the dynamic nature of the Internet, any web addresses or links contained in this book may have changed since publication and may no longer be valid. The views expressed in this work are solely those of the author and do not necessarily reflect the views of the publisher, and the publisher hereby disclaims any responsibility for them.

THANKS FOR THE MEMORY

Acknowledgements

To my Wife Diane, because without her love, help and encouragement, I don't think I would have ever found the courage to put pen to paper.

Courage? Because I have had to open up my inner private self and write about things that I had kept buried deep inside.

Thanks to my lovely Grandsons, Ryan who assisted with the final editing, and Harry who did wonderful work on the front cover. Also to Liz Maguire for her hard work getting my writing onto the computer.

Not forgetting my youngest son Mark for his tireless efforts dealing with Publishers, and to my eldest son John, for the use of his office facilities, and to Claire for just being my daughter.

Dedicated to the memory of my Grand Mother, who preserved my sanity, and to my brothers Teddy and Terry, the best friends I ever had.

Having a lovely family don't arf help. Thanks for the joy you have brought me. God Bless all of you.

Prologue

It was one of those glorious late April afternoons and I had spent the last couple of hours mowing the grass and as I always did, made sure that all the edges were neatly finished off. (I was a fussy old bugger). I looked around in the satisfaction at a job well done. The garden looked a picture. Rosie will be pleased when she gets back from shopping. I thought I deserved a rest so I pulled one of the large cushions from the shed, and laid out on one of our loungers. The sun was shining and apart from an annoying N.E. wind it was delightful. I had obviously chosen a sheltered spot, and could actually feel the warmth in the sun.

I heard it said, that it is a wonderful thing, to be able to lie back and completely relax, and that it's a sign of a contented and clear conscience. I could hear the birds tweeting all around me, and the hum of early bees and wasps, it was very peaceful. I must have fallen asleep, now there's a surprise!!

The familiar noise of an aircraft engine had woken me with a start. I was having a funny dream. I searched the wide open sky, following the direction of the sound, and then I spied it! There it was that unmistakeable shape! It was a "Spitfire". It was effortlessly flying towards the south east, probably headed for the air-strip at Headcorn. The "Spit" still looked and sounded just as I remembered, those 70 years ago. It was a truly iconic piece of flying history.

Dreams are real funny things, because I had been dreaming that I was a very young boy with my two brothers and our Mum, and that we were being bombed by the Germans.

Did the sound of that aircraft set my dream in motion, or was it just a coincidence? The dream was so vivid and lifelike, (as mine always seem to be). It would probably upset me if that particular dream had carried on considering how things had turned out in real life. So, not for the first time in my life, I had something to thank the "Spit" for.

I lay back to drop off again but my mind was in turmoil. Couldn't get those events out of my mind. Was this some weird sign? After a short while I had decided!!

I heard Rosie's car pull up on the drive, then the door banging shut. I had left the side gate unlocked. "Is that you Luv"? "Oo oo darling, where are you"? "I'm sitting in the back garden". She appeared carrying a couple of small bags. "It's all right for some, I'm surprised you're not asleep, the garden looks lovely, I can see you've been busy. Any phone calls"? "I think I heard it ring once, but I was busy". I didn't like answering the phone, and I figured that if it was real urgent they'd ring again.

"Have you made yourself a cup of coffee"? "No, not yet" She smiled "I'll make one for you". Then very sarcastically. "You just relax and have a rest, I'll bring it out for you". She then made a subservient bow.

We were sipping our drinks together, with Rosie telling me about her shopping, and the various people she'd bumped into. These proved plentiful because we, and our family have lived in the Maidstone area for nearly 50 years, and we had ran our own local Pub for 11 of those years. We knew a lot of people.

Eventually I told Rosie about my dream and the sighting of the Spitfire, and then!

"Rosie you know you and the "kids" have been giving me ear-ache about writing my life story, well I've decided to give it a go. I'll buy a couple of writing pads and start at the very beginning then see how far I get". She beamed, "sure you don't want me to get you a small tape recorder, you could speak into that"? "No, honest I don't think so, I'm worried that I might miss bits out if I record the story, no, I'll be better off writing it down. That's always worked for me in the past". "'I'm so pleased, wait till I tell the kids, they'll be really excited".

Rosie rattled on about the various funny stories in the Pub, and the varied incidents, (those she knew about), with my haulage company and the Garage in Bermondsey. Yeah, there was a tale or two! "Don't lets get in front of ourselves, there's an awful lot of traumatic events that occurred during, and straight after the war, I'll have to dig deep into my memory bank for them", I laughed. "I suppose I'd better get on with it, before I get too old". I'm the 'sole' survivor of a very large London/Irish family, so, once I slip off the dish, then it's gone forever.

At least our children, grand-children, and soon to be, great grand-child, and those of my dear brothers, will find out what we all suffered those many years ago.

It's not all doom and gloom however, because there were more good times and many many laughs.

Sit back, make yourself comfortable, you're in for a good read . . . .

Chapter 1

I was down the underground (the Borough) with my Mum, Aunt and two brothers, Eddie and Michael. Eddie was two years older than me and Michael was two years younger. You see, we used the underground as an air raid shelter. I can't remember exact details because I was too young.

The all clear sounded and we all came up to ground level, but when we got to our house in Lant Street, it had been bombed. We all then walked to my grandparents' house, just off St. Thomas Street. I don't think anybody was worrying about Lant Street, they were only too pleased that we were all unharmed.

Our grandparents' house was a very happy and warm Catholic environment. Living there was Granddad Pat, Nanny Annie, Eileen and Johnnie. Although Eileen and Johnnie were Uncle and Aunt, because my mother was the oldest girl of the family there was only seven and nine years difference in their ages and that of Eddie. They just seemed like an older sister and brother.

We all stayed that night, but it didn't seem that long since we had gone to bed when we were woken, told to get dressed quickly because the air raid warning had gone off. I can remember our grandfather getting really agitated and shouting at us to be dressed quickly.

We all ran out of our house and I will always remember the throbbing sound of the German bombers approaching. The shelter, which were the arches under London Bridge railway station were very close, so in just a couple of minutes we were all safely inside. There seemed to be hundreds of people inside the shelters, all obviously local people, so everybody seemed to know some family or other. I remember the enormous gates being closed and the sandbags piled up against them. I wondered what they were for.

There were rows of wooden and canvas bunk beds, and we were each given one to sleep on, surrounded by our family. We, as kids, thought that this was fantastic adventure. The whole place was full of people, mainly women and children. Just try and imagine the noise, and believe it or not, laughter. My granddad had disappeared but the rest of the family were together. Once again, the all-clear siren sounded, but by now all of us children were asleep, so we spent the night in the shelter.

When we emerged from the arches, the first thing I can remember was the smell. It's something I can recall now, even after almost seventy years. The smell of soot and burning and the smoky haze.

We all went back to our little house, and Granddad had already made a pot of tea and a very welcome fire was on the go.

Over the next couple of days some of our furniture and clothing was brought over on a market barrow from Lant Street. We were told we couldn't live there any longer. You are all probably wondering where our Dad was while all this was going on, well he was in the Army.

We quickly settled into living with our grandparents, as well as Eileen and Johnnie. It was obviously very crowded, being a very small terraced house, but we kids didn't notice it very much. It was quite exciting at the time. We soon got into the routine of all going over to the arches every night, and with the evenings closing in, it didn't seem long after our tea that the air raid sirens went off and you could hear the bombers coming over. The noise was like a constant throbbing and the air seemed to shake.

Once we were safely in the shelter everything returned as normal. We played games, the adults played cards and chess. The women seemed to gather in groups, chatting and knitting. Eventually someone started playing the accordion and then before you knew it most people were singing.

Eddie and me used to run around playing with mates. Michael was still a bit too young. There was quite an amount of space, luckily, although we were always being told off for being too noisy and saucy.

I didn't think too much of it at the time, but it seemed that once we were settled, our Mum used to pop off for a few hours, sometimes not coming back until we were in our bunks and asleep.

"Don't worry Paddy," said my Grandmother, "it will be alright" she said, tucking Eddie and me back into our blankets. What had woken us up was the terrible noise and the shaking and rattling of everything. It was like what I imagine an earthquake would be like. We could clearly hear the bombs exploding, they were very close. I could hear fire engines and lots of shouting and screaming going on outside. I eventually went back to sleep.

When I woke up I noticed that everybody and everything was covered in dust, and unusually, most people were very quiet, with some crying. My grandmother was white with shock, but she soon got all of us together and we went to leave the shelter. We had to walk over some planks because a water main was broken and had flooded the road.

The scene I saw when we got out onto the street will stay with me forever. The warehouses were no longer there, and a large section of houses and part of the old Guy's Hospital were also missing. In their place were still smoking ruins, with firemen, police, army and civilian men clambering over them. Further down the street I noticed one of the arches had been blown up. It was Stainer Street.

My grandmother rushed us home, I noticed that Johnnie was not with us and that Granddad wasn't home either. "Where's Mum?" Eddie asked. "Oh, she'll be along in a minute," said Nan, "she's been helping the nuns look after the nursing mothers and the very young babies." She seemed very nervous and tense, something I'd never noticed in her before. With that she started to get our breakfast ready, porridge oats.

"Shall we start getting ready for school?" asked Eddie. "Don't remind her," I told him, since I was never very keen on school. "Didn't you notice when we came up the street that half the school was missing? I don't think there will be any school today" Eileen said. "I'm going down the road Mum, to see if I can be of some help." "Be careful though, and put some stronger shoes on before you go out, and don't be too long" Nan said. "If you see Johnnie tell him to come home."

We sat down in our little kitchen and as usual, finished our breakfast very noisily. We were always skylarking about.

"Eddie, put your coat back on and nip over to the school to see if they are open" Nan said, "Be careful, mind, of all the fire engines and ambulances." It seems real funny while I'm telling you this, could you imagine in today's world, asking an eight year old to go out in all that chaos? It all seemed very different then, somewhat natural. We learned to look out for ourselves very quickly in those days.

Eddie came back indoors after about ten minutes. It was no trouble getting into our house in those days, because the front door key was hanging on a piece of string behind the letter box. Nobody burgled houses then, maybe because we had nothing of value to steal. We lived in a very close-knit community, actually a great percentage of the people living locally were relations, in one way or another. It was always a bit of a joke about there being nothing to steal.

"Father Flanagan said that there is no school today Nan, the bombs last night caused a fair bit of damage. He said that he would make an announcement at Sunday mass. Where is everybody?"

"Granddad, Johnny and Eileen are still helping out over the bombed arches, they'll be back in a minute" Nan said.

"What's it like out there, Eddie?" I asked. "There's a real lot of damage" he replied.

"Can we go out Nan?" I asked, because now that there was no school, I wanted to go out and play.

"Yes, you both can, but be very careful and stay away from any ruins."

We didn't need a second chance, out we dashed. Outside it was complete chaos: police; air raid wardens; fire engines and their crews; men and women scrambling amongst the damaged houses and warehouses.

That's when we saw Granddad, Johnny and Eileen coming up St. Thomas Street. Johnny and Eileen looked upset, holding on to Granddad. His face looked terrible. He was covered in dust and his face, from under his cap, was grey and caked with dirt. But the strangest thing was the lines coming from his eyes, which were as though someone had painted valleys through the grime. They were tears. I had never seen my Granddad cry before, I didn't ever think he could. Eileen came rushing over to us and grabbed us both, she was also crying now. "What's all the fuss about Granddad?" Eddie asked. I was still too shocked to say anything.

"Don't get upset boys, but Mummy has got quite badly injured and they have taken her to hospital, but she will be OK so don't worry yourselves. Where are you off to?"

"Nan said we can go out and play because there's no school today" Eddie said. I just stared at them.

"Well go on then, but don't go down to Stainer Street, go over to Snowsfield and find some mates." We dashed away but I couldn't take my eyes off them for a while before I dashed after Eddie. I felt unusually uneasy, a very strange feeling.

A complete row of houses had been badly hit overnight. It was strange to see some houses with the front walls gone, you could see all the rooms with furniture and wallpaper all on show. They were like dolls houses that the girls used to play with. We were under strict instructions never to enter these houses, it was explained that this was called looting, and both the church and the school had told us that this was forbidden.

We arrived in Snowsfield and upon seeing a crowd of boys and girls we rushed over them. They were all very excited and jumping around. "Have you heard the news?" said Ginger, one of the older boys. "What news?" Eddie asked. "We've all got to be evacuated, whatever that means." "Who told you that?" Eddie said. "Our headmaster, that's why we are not in school." Ginger's school was the Protestant school in Snowfields and this had not been damaged. In those days, believe it or not, we had very little to do with the Church of England schools. We never played football against them, or any other sporting and social activities. We only mixed with other Catholic schools in the area. Now how stupid is that?

It is with little wonder, given our upbringing, we were always at loggerheads with the Protestant boys. We were constantly fighting them, both face to face and at a gang level.

"Eddie!" Our cousin Jim had just turned up and called out to us. Jim was a similar age to myself and Eddie and he was a real scrapper. One of six brothers and sisters, he lived close to our grandparents. "Mum said that you have got to come home to our house at dinner time, and she saw you and Paddy talking to Ginger and his mates—she said no fighting!"

"Let's go over to Weston Street and look at all the ruins," Jim said. So off we went to play. "Have you heard about this evacuation Jim?" I asked him. "Yes, but Mum said it won't apply to us. She said that your Dad is coming home on leave, and should be home tomorrow."

Dad was in the Army and was stationed somewhere in Devon. I didn't know where Devon was, only that it was a long way away. After a few hours clambering over the ruined warehouses, constantly being chased off by the air raid wardens and firemen, we made our way to our Aunt Emma's house. Aunt Emma was Jim's mum. We used to pick up and collect shrapnel, not really knowing what it actually was, there was a lot of it lying around.

In Spite of Everything . . . .

"Don't bring all that rubbish in here," Aunt Emma said. "And dust yourselves down and brush those shoes before you come in." She was a lovely lady and I loved going round their house. Our other cousins were there: Patsy, Sheila, Pat, Eileen and Valerie. Emma's husband, Uncle Pat, wasn't there. There were a lot of Patricks in our family including our Granddad. That was why they called me Paddy. My uncles said it was because I was very fiery.

Aunt Emma did us a nice dinner (it is now called lunch) of fish paste sandwiches and bread and jam. Michael was also in the house, making nine of us, it was bedlam, but Aunt Emma didn't make any fuss.

"What does evacuation mean Auntie?" I said. "Oh, it's nothing for you to worry about, your Dad will be home tomorrow and he'll sort everything out."

"Do you know how Mummy is?" She gave me a long and strange look, then said "Oh she's in hospital, but I'm sure that she'll be out soon, don't worry yourself. By the way, you are all sleeping over here tonight." I loved staying at their house, we would have a great time amongst ourselves and at night all of the boys would sleep in one bed. You can imagine that chaos that caused.

"Are we not going over to the arches tonight?" Eddie asked Aunt Emma. "If there is an air raid tonight, we'll all get in our cellar and under the table" she replied. Their house was bigger than Nan's and it had its own cellar.

Eddie Jimmy, Patsy and me all went out after dinner. "Where are all you lot going?" Aunt Emma asked. "We are all going over Tabard Park to play football," Eddie said, showing Aunt Emma our football. "We are going to meet some mates from school over there."

"Well mind you don't get into any trouble, and be home by five o'clock. Remember, if the air raid siren goes off dash home straight away." She stared at us for a while. "Get going then, Michael's staying with me." Off we went, shortly meeting some mates, kicking the football along the streets as we made our way to the park. A few horses and carts went by, and we all used to jump on the back of them, with the driver yelling at us to get off. It was great fun. We used to run up to the front and try to frighten the horse or horses, but you had to be careful because those horses could be spiteful and also, the driver could flip his whip at you. It was all innocent and childish fun.

Eventually we arrived at the park. There was only one pitch still in use, being cinder of course, not grass. The other pitch had ACK-ACK anti-aircraft guns on it, also a barrage balloon which was tethered by huge wire lines. We used to talk to the soldiers stationed there and give them plenty of cheek, but if they were in a good mood they would let us sit behind the ACK-ACK guns, that was very exciting.

"Have you got a watch mister?" Eddie asked. "Yes, why do you want to know?" the Corporal answered. "We've got to be home at five o'clock and we don't know what the time is." I think it was only Eddie who could tell the time anyway. "I'll give you a shout, just before five then son," he said. "Now piss off!"

It was all very light hearted, and we had been driving the soldiers mad. We played for hours and eventually a soldier yelled out to tell us that it was nearly five o'clock and to get home straight away before it got dark because they were expecting an air raid tonight.

We all got back to Aunt Emma's and the house was in its usual bedlam. Our Aunt Anne was also in the house with her husband Uncle Nathan, I didn't know it then, but a man who would have a great influence on my life.

We eventually had our tea, forever arguing and skylarking about. When the air raid sirens started up, we all helped make sure that all the windows were shut and taped up, putting strips of sticky tape over the window glass. All curtains drawn, then we quickly went outside to make sure that no lights were showing through into the street. This was complete black out. The air raid warden came round to inspect all the houses, giving a rap on the front door of any house where even the smallest chink of light could be seen. They also advised all those families that were going to the arches shelters to act lively.

We all made our way down to the cellar, which actually had two small rooms. It was very crowded, but to us children it was very exciting. Eventually we heard the throbbing drone of incoming aircraft. There must have been hundreds of them. The air seemed to vibrate. This night the bombs were dropping the other side of the river, so they had no effect on us at all. The atmosphere down in the cellar got cheerier and the adults relaxed considerably. The noise amongst us children was considerable. It's worth recalling that we were almost in pitch darkness, with just a single oil-lamp for light. To us kids it was a great adventure. Eventually the all-clear siren went off, by which time most of us had dropped off to sleep. We were ushered up to our bedrooms and all slept on for a few hours.

Aunt Emma and Aunt Anne were preparing breakfast for us, porridge oats. When Granddad called round, he wanted to know how we all were. He told Eddie that we were to stay at Emma's and that he was meeting our Dad at Waterloo Station at dinnertime. He warned us to behave ourselves and not cause any problems for our Aunties (as if we would).

After breakfast, we asked if we could go out to play, and after the customary warnings about our behaviour, we were allowed out. "Make sure you are all back at dinnertime," Emma said. In fact that was never a problem because our stomachs brought us home. When I look back it is quite surreal, when I see how the young ones are looked after today, being for the most part taken to school by car or at least accompanied by parents. When you think of the devastation we were surrounded by, not only partly collapsed houses and buildings, but water and gas mains lying fractured, it's a small wonder that we were allowed out at all. There were no cars however.

As we came back round the back door I saw a big man in uniform, our Dad. Eddie dashed in and jumped all over him, he was holding Michael on his shoulder at the time. I ran up to him as well and he picked all three of us up. We were very excited to see him, but I was surprised that our Mum wasn't with him. "Where's Mummy?" I asked. He gave us all a sad look. "She couldn't come out of hospital yet, but don't worry yourselves" he said. I noticed him glance at Granddad and Aunt Emma. They quickly changed the subject. "We're not being evacuated, are we Dad?" Eddie asked. "No son, you are not. I'm taking you to stay at Aunt Sarah's for a couple of weeks."

Nan and Aunt Emma packed all our clothes, then Nan, Dad and us three went over to the Elephant and Castle railway station, where we caught a train to St. Mary Cray, about 10 miles from London. This was my first glimpse of countryside, I mean with fields and orchards and that sort of thing. We had green spaces, namely Southwark Park, which was a lovely big park with football pitches and large conker trees, as well as an open-air swimming pool, but nothing quite like this!

We all got off the train and there, waiting to meet us, was Aunt Sarah and our cousin Davey, who was the same age as me but a bigger lad. We called him Tarzan. Aunt Sarah was a really lovely jolly lady and she gave us all a big cuddle. "Come on, it will only take us a few minutes to get home. Davey, you run ahead with the boys, I want to talk to Nanny and their Dad."

It didn't take us more than 15 minutes to reach their house, which was in a nice quiet road with all the houses having front gardens, something I had never seen before. Their house was quite small and neat, with a massive back garden. To our great surprise and excitement there was an air raid shelter dug down in it. We dived into this camp as we called it. This was a truly marvellous adventure. "Where's Maureen and Terry?" I asked. They were Davey's brother and sister, both a bit younger. "They're at school. Mum let me have the day off because you were all coming down." I had forgotten about school, ours being closed of course.

"Come on you lot, in you come. I want to show you your bedroom before you get covered in mud and leaves" said Aunt Sarah. Mud and leaves!!!!! That was a change from soot and brick dust!

We were sharing with Davey and Terry. They had one small bed and we had one slightly larger. We used to sleep top and tail, that is Eddie and Michael at the top of the bed, and me at the bottom. We had great larks tickling each other's toes. This usually got us told off, eventually.

Maureen and Terry came home from school and were very excited to see us. We all went out to play, in the road outside. No cars, no ambulances or ruined buildings, it was heaven. We kicked a football about and then a couple of Davey's mates joined in. They were nice lads, not quite as rough as some of our mates, and better dressed. I felt a little sorry for Maureen, being the only girl, but very soon a couple of girls turned up, who were friends, so she was happy.

It was starting to get dark now, then Aunt Sarah called us in to have our tea. "You all seem to be having a nice time out there, boys," said Dad. "How would you like to stay here for a couple of weeks? Aunt Sarah would be really glad to have you. Me and your Nan have got to find somewhere for us to live, because we can't go back to Lant Street!

"Yes, please!" screamed Eddie, and wherever he was, I was certainly going to be. Young Michael didn't have much choice, but he seemed to be more than happy playing with Terry. They were a similar age as well.

"Well, that's settled then" said Aunt Sarah "now, let's get on with eating our tea." We had meat pie, with lots of potatoes and vegetables. It was delicious! We never gave much thought to rationing, which was in place at that time, and it was surprising how much good food we had. The rationing thing only bothered us when we couldn't get sweets.

We finished our tea, then Nan and Aunt Sarah cleared the table and began washing up. Dad suddenly appeared carrying a small snooker table, the first one I had ever seen. He put it on the table, produced the balls and taught us how to play. Davey and Terry already knew what to do. We had a great time, then all of a sudden we heard this noise. I knew straight away what it was, German bombers! We dashed out into the garden and in the far distance we could barely see them, but they could be heard clearly enough. There were searchlights piercing the night sky, and mid-air explosions. It was like watching a fireworks display, although I didn't know about fireworks at the time. We could hear the distant thuds as thousands of bombs dropped on London. Nan was very worried but she had our Dad and Aunt Sarah to comfort her. Sadly Uncle Dave, Aunt Sarah's husband, was away in the army. At that time I didn't quite understand why most of the men were away in the Forces, since it seemed to me that the war was all around us!

We all eventually came indoors, and got ready for bed. Nan and Aunt Sarah made us some cocoa, and off we went upstairs. Dad gave us a kiss, and that's when I asked him "What does it mean to be in the army, Dad? What do you do in the army and what is the war all about?"

"It's a bit complicated Paddy. You're a little too young to understand the ins and outs of it, but we are going to have to stop the Germans from dropping bombs on us, and that's why most of your uncles and me are in the army. Just like you practice playing football, we in the army are practising to stop the Germans." With that he bundled me upstairs to bed.

After breakfast next morning, Davey, Maureen and Terry went off to school. Dad said, "Why don't you boys walk to school with them? It's not far, but you must remember your way back, and don't lark about too much, or get them in trouble. And Paddy, no fighting!"

Eddie and me went with Davey as far as the school gates, all of his mates were shouting at us, saying how lucky we were to be off school. Now it's very funny, because I had no love for school, but they didn't appreciate how grim it had become at home. It was all so peaceful and orderly here.

We left Davey, and as we had noticed the river nearby on the way down to school, we wasted no time in finding it again. The river Cray wasn't much more than a stream, but it was a magnet to us. We larked about throwing pebbles in the water, mainly to see if we could hit the small fish we could see. Fat chance of that. We determined that we must try and obtain some fishing tackle. There were a couple of small shops in the village, and at the general store we spied some fishhooks and line. Sadly our first instincts were to nick some, but Eddie said no. He reckoned we could get some money from Dad.

We crossed the main road, using the underpass, as Davey had said we should, and made our way to some small woods. This was truly magical! Then we ran into a few boys, who were a bit scruffy, not like the other locals. They had real funny accents and were a bit aggressive towards us, saying that these woods were theirs, telling us to scram. They called us "moosh" or something like that. Well, Eddie and me were no pushovers and we weren't frightened or worried about them. Eddie said "we'll come through here whenever we like, so piss off before you get hurt." They looked at us with wide eyes and said "Oh, you're a couple of townies, what are you doing here?" "We're down here to find some fucking Germans, so piss off," I said. They were obviously a bit dubious of us, and they ran off, calling us names and making other threats. We shrugged at each other and carried on towards Aunt Sarah's house. A truly great morning. I liked the country!

Finally we arrived at Auntie's. Michael was playing in the front garden with some snails. I'd never seen so many of them, they were fascinating. Auntie called us in, where there were some sandwiches on the kitchen table for us to eat. "Had a nice time boys, did you? Your shoes look a bit muddy, been playing by the river have you?" "Only for a little while Dad" Eddie replied. "We were really careful, there's fish in there. Dad, can we have some money to buy some hooks and lines with?"

"Well, it's funny, because I've just given your Nan some money and a small amount is for pocket money, so you'd better ask Nan about that." Michael piped up "Can I go fishing with you, Eddie?" "You two can take him with you at some time, but promise me that you will look after him, and never leave him on his own, do you understand? Because he is very important," Dad answered. "We promise that we will Dad," we both answered. We always did. Always!

After finishing our sandwiches, we started making plans to go out again. Then Dad said "Your Nan and me have got to go back to London to find us somewhere to live, and make some arrangements. I've only got 10 more days leave before I have to go back to my unit. You'll all be comfortable staying with Aunt Sarah for a while, won't you?" We all agreed that we would. She was a lovely lady, and this was a nice place to live. "We'll be going shortly, do you want to come up to the station and see us off?" "Yes!" we all whooped.

It was a nice stroll up to St. Mary Cray station, and I do mean up! It was atop of a very steep hill, but it only took about 15 minutes. While we were waiting for the train, Nan kept fussing over us, I didn't think she wanted to leave us. "I've given some money to Auntie, it's for your pocket money, so you had better be very good for her. Don't give her any back-chat or lip, do as you are told." She was not mucking about, when giving them orders.

The train arrived and there were hugs all round. Then they were gone. I felt strangely uneasy, but soon shook that feeling off, once I noticed the woods opposite the platform! I didn't say anything to Aunt Sarah.

Rat-a-tat-tat, the train went as it travelled towards London. "Don't worry Ted," she said, "the boys will be alright with Sarah, and I will look after them while you're away."

"I know you will, Mum, I've got to tell them, but I don't think that I will be able to."

"Please don't worry yourself, you've got enough on your plate as it is. If necessary I'll tell them. They love and trust me. Everything will turn out alright Ted, I promise you!"

We stood outside the school gates, watching them all coming out. It was noticeable how well dressed and tidy most of them were, although not all of them. "Oh, oh, Davey!" Eddie suddenly yelled out. Lots of the other children gazed over at us, though trying not to gape too much. I bet they wondered who we were, and why we weren't at school. "Hi ya, Eddie, hi ya Paddy, what you been doing all day, you lucky beggars?"

"Nan, and our Dad, have gone back to London, so we went up to the station to see them off" Eddie said. "What about Michael? Did he go with them?" "No, they've got important things to do, don't know what that is though. Dad's got to find us a place to live, because we can't go back to our old house, it's been bombed out." "We had a row with some boys in the woods near your house, Davey, who are they?" I blurted out. "They must be the pikeys who live up there. They're a nasty bunch. Shouldn't get mixed up with them." "Well, we told them to fuck off, they didn't seem that nasty to me! What are pikeys anyway?" "Well, they're like vagabonds. They don't live in houses, they thieve, fight and usually go around picking up scrap."

"Eddie," I said, "we must be fucking pikeys." That really made Davey laugh. Davey went over to a group of boys and they were chatting away, sometimes pointing in our direction, very friendly like, though.

"I was just chatting to my friends, because we are playing football tomorrow after we finish school, and they would be more than happy if you wanted to join in. We only play for about an hour because the nights are drawing in and it gets too dark very quickly." "Thanks Dave, I'd really like that." "What about you, Eddie, fancy a game?" "Not really Dave, our Dad left us some pocket money, so I think I'll buy some fishing tackle and have a little fishing in the river. I'll also get some for Michael, he loves fishing as much as I do."

"Well, I'll definitely play tomorrow, I'm not that interested in fishing, I think it's too boring." "That's great," said Eddie, "you're a bloody nuisance anyway, you muck about too much, and frighten any fish away." "There's only little tiddlers anyway, not worth the trouble." Off we sauntered, making our way to the little general stores in the village. Eddie gave me some money, so I dived off to see what I could buy." "I've got some money for you too, Dave. Our Dad gave Aunt Sarah enough for all of us to have a share."

I quickly spied what I fancied, a jack knife. "How much is that, Mister?" "Three and six" the shopkeeper replied. I had an oxford[1] to spend. We did a deal. I can tell you, I was as pleased as punch, like a dog with two tails to wag. I had my first knife. I wonder what the chances would be today for a seven year old to buy a knife over the counter. But, as I've said before, things were different then.

Eddie managed to buy some hooks, floats, weights and line. "Don't buy any rods, Eddie, I can cut some down for you." He smiled back and reluctantly agreed. Off we went home. After crossing the main road, Davey looked over and said, "You're not going through the woods, are you?" "You bet we are," replied Eddie. That really pleased me, because if he didn't want us to go that way, that would have been that! He was my big brother after all!

I couldn't get to the woods quick enough, dashing off and immediately looking for branches that I could make fishing rods out of. While I was busy Eddie and Davey turned up, and straight away picked better branches, or so they thought! I didn't care. I had my new knife and I'd have cut down the entire woods.

"Hoy, what do you townies think you are doing now?" They came rushing towards us, there were about five or six of them. "Piss off!" I screamed out at them. I think that surprised them, and put them off their guard. I think they were used to boys running off scared.

We were certainly not scared of them, and had no intention of scarpering. "Why do you not do yourselves a favour, and stop interfering with us?" Eddie said, whilst staring straight at them. I thought then, that they had better be careful, because Eddie doesn't do his nut that often or very quickly (unlike me) but he is very dangerous. I had never seen him lose a fight. He had a vicious left hook! We used to say that if you want more than one of them, you must be greedy[2].

"Well that moosh shouldn't be cutting down the trees." Davey spoke up, "They don't belong to you, so mind your own business." "Who you calling moosh, you wonky eyed prick?" I said "Fuck off or I'll stick this knife in you."

Eddie jumped between us and they backed off. We thought they'd gone, but suddenly bits of wood and stone were being thrown at us. They were yelling and threatening us with all manner of things, but they went away. I've never been worried about people in gangs making threats, because I've always found that they are usually not that tough. All the bluster is down to the fact that they really don't want to fight.

"You shouldn't have threatened them with that knife, you could get us all into trouble." "Sorry Eddie, but that wonky eyed bastard really annoys me. We'll have to have a fight with them sooner or later. The sooner the better."

"There's a couple of nice branches, cut them down and let's get home." "Will do, Davey boy." As we left the woods, there were still bits and pieces being chucked in our direction. They were a bit clever because they lobbed the logs very high and you couldn't work out exactly where they would land. A bit like those German bombers, the bastards!

"I'll be coming through here with my younger brother tomorrow, so if I was you, I wouldn't chuck any more shit at us. You'd better not hit him," Eddie yelled out. "Why's that then moosh?" Came a call from some distance away. "If you do, you'll find out soon enough."

We were strolling down Davey's road, carrying our new rods, Eddie with all his fishing tackle, as pleased with ourselves as you could get. "Hi Mum," Davey said. "Hi Auntie," we cried. She looked at us, "What have you got there? Been spending all your money I see."

"Only some fishing tackle, I've bought some for Michael as well. Can he come fishing with me tomorrow? Paddy is going to play football with Davey, I'll look after him, you know I will." "And so will I," I said. "How you going to do that whilst you're playing football with Davey and his mates? And, who told you that you could have a knife?! Give it to me now!" "Ah, can't I keep it Aunt?" I pleaded. "When your father comes down, I'll let him decide. In the meantime, give it here." I handed it over. My prized possession! "Come on you lot, sit down at the table, I've got your tea ready."

Even though there was rationing on at the time, we never seemed to suffer any shortages, although I don't think modern day children would agree with that. I was to find out much later why we did have, probably, more than our fair share.

Next morning we didn't follow Davey and the other two to school. We were going fishing! "See you after school, Dave. I haven't got any proper boots though." "Don't worry, our P.E. master has a few spares, he'll fix you up." "I didn't know there'd be a teacher there, are they all right in your school?" "Of course they are, they'll only be too glad for you to join in." "What, even though I'm a Catholic?" "They don't worry about things like that here, see you later and don't worry."

Davey and his family had not been brought up as Catholics, because Aunt Sarah was a Protestant, and she and Uncle Dave married in a Protestant church. The reason for that being that Aunt Sarah, would have been forced to become a Catholic and would have had to promise to bring up their children in the Catholic religion. What a load of nonsense.

The reason I was worried about Davey's school was that it was obviously a Protestant school and, if the roles had been reversed, the Catholic teachers would never allow a non-Catholic to play football, or anything else, that you can be sure, it all seems like the middle ages now.

"Make sure you look after him, and don't let him fall in the river, or get into any further mischief." Aunt Sarah kept a steady eye on Eddie and me. I think she knew more than we thought. She gave us a bottle of tizer and a bag of sandwiches. "Don't let those horrible worms get near your food, Eddie." He'd been digging up worms in the back garden, for bait. "Please can I have my knife, Auntie?" I said, as nice as I could. "No!" I didn't bother to argue, I'm sure it would have been a waste of my breath. "Eddie, finish fishing, and then go and meet Maureen and Terry from school, bring them all home as quick as possible. Don't wait for Davey and Paddy, it's starting to get dark very quickly now. Remember, if the air raid siren goes off, get back here straight away, I mean fast." With that, off we went. We passed by the edge of the woods, not that we were bothered or anything, but Eddie and Michael were in a hurry to start their fishing. There was no sign of anybody! It was going through my mind, however, that now the three of us were together, those pikey idiots probably didn't realise what trouble they could have got themselves into.

Eddie and Michael found a nice spot on the banks of the Cray River. It seemed more like a stream to me. Eddie was really good at this fishing lark and he soon had two lines fixed up with hooks, weights and floats. I was proud of their rods. "Don't break them rods, you two, because I haven't got my knife with me." "We won't" said Eddie and Michael.

I watched them for a while. Sticking worms on hooks and casting the lines into the water. You could actually see the little fish going crazy, the river wasn't deep and it was as clear as tap water. "Can you drink this water Eddie?" "I think so, it looks clean enough, and it is flowing after all." With that I dropped down and scooped up a nice handful of water. It was cool and delicious. "Mind you, don't swallow any fish, Paddy" said Michael. "Well, you'd better hurry up and catch them before I do." "Do you reckon there are any snakes around here Eddie?" "Davey said that they have adders around here, well I think that's what he called them." "I don't really know, but why don't you piss off and see if you can find some, you're spoiling our fishing, making all that noise. You're frightening the fish." I was gone.

I followed the river for at least a mile. It was great. The weather was really warm, especially for late September. I scrambled along the bank. By now I'd found myself a really heavy stick, I was able to smash my way through the stinging nettles and other undergrowth. I thought I was in the jungle. I kept looking over at the opposite side of the river, thinking it looked interesting. Right, I thought to myself, let's have a go! Off came my shoes and socks, we wore short trousers then. Into the river I went. It was cold at first, not too deep, but it came well over my knees. I waded across and scrambled up the other side.

It was no different from where I'd just left, but never mind. I was getting a little bit hungry so I headed back towards Eddie and Michael. I could see them a few yards ahead of me now, they looked quite serious about their fishing I thought. Well, let's liven things up a bit.

I began to chuck small stones into the river in front of them. Eddie looked very pissed off, and Michael started to shout and holler. Then I showed myself. "I knew that was you" said Eddie. "You are definitely one big jacket[3]."

"We've been talking about you, and just waiting for you to show up. You didn't let us down. I had just said to Michael that I bet you start throwing things at us, just like the pest you are." "Did you see any snakes, Paddy?" shouted Michael. I think he was happier to see me than Eddie was. "No, I saw some ducks, but they rushed away." "Yeah, I bet you threw stones at them, didn't you?" "Well, yes I did, but I didn't hit any of them."

Eddie looked at me and shook his head. "You really are a nuisance, Paddy, but glad to see you've come back. We're just about to have a sandwich, want one?" "You bet I do! Caught any fish Michael?" "Yeah, lots." "Well, where are they then?" "We throw them back, don't we Eddie? He gets them off the hook and puts them back in the water."

"That seems like a waste of time to me, but you seem to enjoy it. Do you know what time it is Eddie, because I've got to meet Davey?" "I don't know, but I don't think it's time yet. Have a sandwich and sit down and be quiet for a minute, will ya! When you've finished eating, and by the way Aunt Sarah has put some cake in for us, go up to the street and ask a passer by, and don't be saucy. Now eat!"

"Excuse me, mister, can you tell me the time please?" "You're not from round here, are you?" "No, we're from London, staying at our Aunt's, me and my brothers." "It's half past two, mind that river." With that he walked off. He seemed like a nice enough old man. A bit posh though.

"I'm going over to Davey's school in a minute, the man said that it was half past two. Why's your finger bleeding Eddie?" "Michael accidentally caught me with his hook, and I had to dig it out, it's not that bad though."

Michael looked a bit sheepish, but Eddie laughed it off and reassured him. I took my socks off the small bush I'd put them on to dry out. They'd got a bit wet, then I put both shoes and socks on, and was

In Spite of Everything . . . .

now ready to go. "Any more tizer left Eddie?" "Sorry, Paddy, all gone, there's lots and lots of water though!" I had a drink, it was cool and refreshing. I wonder if you could drink it now. Could you imagine anyone letting you do so?! I couldn't.

"How long are you going to stay down here, Eddie?" "Oh, not much longer, Michael must be getting tired, and we must get back soon, we don't want to worry Aunt Sarah, you know what she's like, a bit of a fuss pot." "I'm off then. See you both later. Mind you don't run into those pikeys." "They'll be sorry if they start mucking us about. I can promise you that!"

I stared at Eddie, I thought yeah, they certainly would be very sorry. He was a very rough handful, and I was champing at the bit to have a go at them. Now for some football!!

"Hello lad! Davey tells me they call you Paddy, are you happy with that? By the way, I'm Mr. Aldridge, Davey's P.E. teacher. I understand your school in London is closed, is that right?"

"Yes sir, it got hit by some bombs last week and we can't go back yet. That's why we're staying down with my auntie."

"Davey tells me that your mother is in hospital and I offer you my sympathy." I didn't quite understand what he was going on about, because it wasn't his fault, and I nodded back at him. "Well, let's get on with it lads. Paddy, here's a blue shirt and try these boots on. There's a couple of pairs here. By the way what position do you usually play?" "Right or left half, sir." "Did you hear that, Kieron? (he was the blue team captain) Off you go and let's have a good practice. We've only got just over an hour."

I got on really well with the other players. I think they liked my aggressive, non-stop way of playing. "Well, thanks for the game sir, it was nice to be able to play on a decent pitch for a change. What shall I do with my shirt sir?"

"Just put it on that pile, alongside the others, and I'll take your boots, once you've knocked all the mud from them. Well played, by the way,

| 21

you looked as though you were enjoying yourself. Will we see you again next week?"

"I don't know sir. I think my Dad is coming down tomorrow to take us to a new house." "In that case, I wish you and your family all the best, and I hope your Mother gets well soon. Goodbye Paddy. Now off you go lads, get straight on home before it gets dark. Remember, you are always welcome here Paddy. Bye now!"

We trudged off home. Going through the village past the general store, I said "You got any money on you Dave?" "No, not a bean" he replied. "Why?" "I'm dying of thirst and could do with a drink." "Let's go into the shop and ask the shopkeeper if he'll give us a drink of water, shall we?"

"Yeah, why not? They can only chuck us out, can't they?" "Mister, any chance of a drink of water? We've just finished playing football and we're as dry as a bone." "Well, I admire your cheek," replied a lady along the counter. "Just wait there a minute, I'll fetch you a glass. Here you are boys, drink it down and be off with you."

To my surprise it wasn't water at all, but a nice cool orangeade drink. It was lovely. What a nice lady, I thought. "Goodbye Missus, Goodbye Mister. Thanks for the drink, it was lovely." "You're welcome boys. Weren't you in here the other day with your brothers, buying up all your fishing tackle?" "That's me, Mister." "Well, get home straight away lads, it's beginning to get dark!" We were home in fifteen minutes, no accidents to report.

Shortly after our tea, the air raid warning sounded. Although there wasn't much chance of any bombs dropping near us, we had to make sure all the curtains were pulled shut, and that there was no chinks of light showing. We ran outside to make sure there was total darkness. In any event the air raid warden went round street by street, checking for light and making sure of complete black out.

"Can we go out into the garden and see the airplanes, Auntie?" We could make out the distant drone of the German bombers, and the anti-aircraft fire, as they headed up the Thames towards London. "Yes, but turn the kitchen lights out before you open the door." Out we shot, all trying to stand on top of the shelter. I was surprised by the number of neighbours who were doing the same. Not only children like us, but lots of adults.

In the dark skies it was impossible to see the aeroplanes, but we could make out the anti-aircraft flashes. The bombers, even at this distance, made a strange throbbing sound, the air seemed to shake. The distant night sky began to brighten up and we could hear the faraway crump, crump, as bombs began to fall.

"Them poor bastards are getting it bad again tonight" I heard a man say, standing a couple of gardens away. "You mustn't swear like that, there's children over there" I heard a lady's voice whisper. Yeah, I thought, some of those 'poor bastards' are my family. Still not fully realising the grave danger they were all in. Eventually we were called in, and after a glass of cocoa, off to bed we went. Tomorrow was Saturday, no school for Davey. I couldn't wait, another day of adventure lay ahead.

"What we going to do today Dave?" "Finish your porridge before thinking of anything else!" Aunt Sarah said. "Then go up and wash your faces. Have you got any toothbrushes?" She directed her remarks at Eddie, Michael and myself. "No, Auntie" said Eddie. We didn't actually possess a toothbrush between us. "Davey, Terry, lend them yours when you've finished."

There was a knock at the back door. Davey answered it, and there was a couple of his mates standing there. "Coming out to play?" "Yeah, in a couple of minutes. My cousins are here and they'll join us, alright?" "No problem, the more the merrier." After a couple of minutes we were ready to go.

"Where are you off to?" Aunt Sarah asked, at the same time looking us over and tidying us up a bit. Straightening our jumpers and patting our hair in place. A fuss pot, but very nice. "We're only playing football in the street, Mum" said Davey. "OK, but don't make nuisances of yourselves."

Now, Davey's road was quite long, with houses on both sides. You must understand that there were no cars around in those days. There were a few motorbikes and cycles, but they had parking spaces in their front gardens. We had the street to ourselves. Coats were put down for goalposts and that was that.

At the end of the road was where the woods started, but we were quite a distance away. "Why don't we play up closer to those woods?" I said. "What do you want to do that for?" said one of the other boys. "Well, when you score a goal at that end, the ball won't run so far away." The ball used to run forever on the hard road surface.

"There's a group of rough boys who play in them woods, we don't have anything to do with them." "Don't they ever play football with you?" "No, they try to muck our game up, they really are rotten people." My mind was buzzing and alive. Could this be the chance to settle with those bastards?

"What do you reckon Dave, I think we should play at the end, it'll get us away from the houses, and Aunt Sarah told us not to be nuisances, didn't she?" Eddie looked over at me, he held my gaze and he knew. He smiled at me with that slightly crooked smile. "I think it's a good idea, Dave, let's go." He picked up our coats and we all followed him. Davey's mates were a bit reluctant, but followed on. I held back for a moment, then dashed round back of Davey's house and picked up my big heavy stick.

It didn't take long.

"Oi, what you lot doing around here? Piss off to your own end." I recognised the bastard's voice. "What, you brought those townies up here to help you out, have you?" "Why do they need any help, we're only playing football. Piss off and let us get on with our game."

In Spite of Everything . . . .

Soon after that stones and bits of wood started to come down on us. This was it! We ran to the edge of the woods, Eddie, Davey and myself. We called them all the names under the sun, and dared them to come out and fight. They came out screaming, about six of them, all with sticks and rocks! I knew I was right to bring my stick. As they came near enough, I smacked the first one straight across the chest, he dropped to the floor, out of breath and blubbering.

They stopped in their tracks. The stared at us. I think it was the first time one of them had been really hurt. Davey's mates had all run away.

"You bloody townies are nothing but trouble. Why don't you go back to London, you don't even fight fair." "Well, there's six of you, well probably only five now" I laughed. "We'll fight you fair, one-on-one if you want. We call it a straightener[4]."

The boy I'd hit was whining a bit, not so tough now I thought. They turned and went away. Afterwards, stones dropped all around us again so we trooped off down the road.

We had only gone a few yards, when we heard a man's voice yelling at us. "Oi, you fuckers, which one of you hit one of my boys with a stick?" Since I was holding my prized possession over my shoulder, I thought that it was fucking obvious. The man came striding up to us. He had dark curly hair and a dark greasy face. He grabbed my stick, went as though to hit me, but then he threw the stick away and clipped me over the head. Eddie jumped in immediately but he got pushed away.

"So you think you're tough, do you? How would you like to take on one of my boys face to face?" "I'd love to, I only hit them because there was six of them and they had sticks and rocks." Not as big as my stick, I thought!

He yelled out some name that I didn't understand and the boys all came out. There were a couple of women amongst them. They looked really nasty pieces of work. In front was Wonky.

"Hey, hold on there!" I heard this loud, menacing voice shout out. Looking round, I saw our Dad still in his uniform rushing up towards us. He looked frightening enough, obviously in a very foul mood, behind him was Aunt Sarah and Eileen.

"Did I see you push my boys about?" our Dad was in a serious rage "One of your boys has hit one of my lads with a great big stick" said Greasy.

"Only because they deserved it Dad, and if they're not careful I'll do it again." "Paddy, be quiet and come over here now!!" I knew he meant it so I did as I was told. Then, as quick as a flash, Dad grabbed Greasy by the neck and lifted him like a rag doll. Greasy's eyes nearly popped out and all the shouting stopped.

"If you ever go near any of my boys again, I promise you that I'll come back and break every bone in your filthy body. That's not a threat, it's a promise." "Right then, now that's sorted, let's have this fight, where's your boy?" With that 'Wonky Eye' pushed his way to the front.

"Let me fight him, Dad" I said jumping forward. But Dad grabbed me. "I told you to calm down and be quiet, will you please do as you're told." "Eddie, the boy is your size, fancy fighting him? No one else will interfere." He glared at the two women who were making themselves busy, Greasy stood back saying "Go on Joe Boy, give that Townie a beating."

Eddie walked towards Wonky "Come on then, I warned you the other day, remember?" Suddenly Wonky rushed at Eddie with arms and legs smashing into him, he was a ferocious fucker and caught Eddie off guard and he went down. Eddie was up immediately and then kept Wonky at bay with a series of right jabs which I could see were hurting and surprising him. Strangely Eddie seemed to be fighting one handed and Wonky was looking as though he might come out the winner, which was both surprising and annoying. The pikey kids were all yelling and whooping and their mothers or whoever they were, were screaming even louder. I'd never heard such a horrible racket.

"Hit him with your left Eddie!" From behind me I heard Eileen call out, she called very loudly so everyone could hear. Whack! Eddie hit Wonky square in the middle of his horrible face, I'm sure his other eye went wonky too! His nose split open and there was blood everywhere. He went down on his knees and that was the end of that.

Remember more than one left hook and you were greedy. He wasn't greedy, it was a good job that Dad was there because I think Greasy and the ugly women would have attacked us. The pikey boys were quiet, and that was a first. They picked up Wonky who was in a terrible mess, and they all quickly disappeared.

"Is it all right, Dad?" I said. "Yes, you can now." With that, I ran over to Eddie and gave him a great big hug. He had a few bruises and scratches but was alright. "I bet you'll have a black eye in the morning, won't you?" "Yeah, I reckon. But it was worth it, they needed sorting out." "Why didn't you hit him with your left?" said Dad. "I cut my hand on a fishing hook yesterday and it was a bit sore, but once I heard Eileen shout out, I thought I'd better use it." Dad nodded. Eileen ran over and gave Eddie a kiss. "Well done, Eddie, I'm proud of you."

"Get your gear and come on in now, you've had your fun, it's all over now and your dinner will be ready soon. By the way, Nan's in doors and she is waiting to see you all." I rushed to pick up my stick and followed them all in. Aunt Sarah looked at me. "You're a rascal, and that's for sure, you just got what you've been looking for." She ruffled my hair and smiled.

We were all excited to see Nan and the small house was in turmoil. The noise was deafening. "Have you been to see Mum, Dad?" Eddie asked. "Have we got a nice place to live yet?" It was as though someone had pulled a black curtain down. I saw the look on Dad's face, I'm sure he went white. "We'll talk about it later, son, get on with your dinner." He glanced over at Nan, and I saw her shake her head at him. I noticed that Eileen went out of the room. I tell you now, I had this odd feeling in me, something I couldn't quite understand. We got on with our dinner, and as far as us kids were concerned, it all returned to normality. Dad, Nan and Aunt Sarah didn't say a word.

"Can we go out and play after dinner, Auntie?" I asked. "Yes, you can, but don't go near them woods and don't you dare get in any more mischief. Davey, take them somewhere nice to play." "Take note of what Aunt Sarah says, don't forget!" Dad said. "How are you feeling Eddie? Let's have a look at you before you go out." Nan came over and rinsed his face and they examined his left hand. "That's a nasty cut you've got there, have you got any ointment and bandage in the house Sarah?"

"Yes Mum, I'll fetch them for you." "Do I have to have a bandage on, Nan?" "I think it would be best, for the time being at least, it will keep any dirt out and stop it becoming septic. It'll only be a small bandage anyway." She held on to Eddie like she didn't want to let go. Well, that's Nan for you, I thought.

"Where're you lot going?" There was Eddie, Michael, me, Davey, Terry and a couple of Davey's mates, who had suddenly reappeared. "I'm taking them up towards the station, nowhere near those woods" Davey said. "Well, ok, but Paddy give me that stick, you won't be needing that where you're going. And remember, behave yourselves, if that's possible! Don't be too late back! We're all staying the night. See you later boys. Eddie, take care of Michael and Terry." "Sure will, Dad!"

Off we went. We hadn't gone far, when Vincent (Dave's mate) dipped into his front garden and came out with this battered old bike. I'd never owned a bike, nor had any of us, so I looked with envy at Vincent. "What we all going to do with just one bike?" Eddie asked. "What we do, Ed, is we take it up to the top of the hill, you know the one by the station, and ride it down as fast as we can, and see who can free-wheel the farthest. It's great fun, you know how steep that hill is, and we haven't got any brakes." Wow, that sounded as much fun as anybody could have. I couldn't get there fast enough.

"Michael, Terry, you two stay at the bottom of the hill and mark out with chalk where we get to" Eddie instructed. "But don't get in the way, I don't want you getting hurt, you'll get me in trouble if you do."

"We'll stay clear, honest Ed" Michael answered. "We've got the chalk ready." We were now at the top of the hill opposite the station.

"What you lot up to?" A station porter was standing at the platform entrance. "Only riding our bike" said Davey. "Well, make sure you all stay away from the railway lines." "We will Mister." Vincent said "I'll go first." Well, it was his bike after all. "You've got to remember it's got a fixed wheel, that means that the pedals go round all the time, so when you're going at full speed, take you feet off the pedals and get them out of the way, or they'll throw you over the handlebars." That sounded painful.

Off he went. Pedalling like mad at first, and then lifting his feet in the air, sticking out like wings of a bird. He went really fast, I can tell you, it was a steep hill. I've seen it, since I've grown up, and it still was very steep, though not as long as I'd thought it was.

He eventually came to a stop. It seemed like miles away. Michael and Terry scampered out and marked the floor. Vincent came puffing back up the hill, he had to push the last few yards.

"You want to go next, Ed?" "Yeah, I wouldn't mind." "Don't forget to get your feet out of the way, that's important." Off he went pedalling furiously, then legs in the air. I could hear him shouting out. I think he went past where Vincent had got to. "He's beaten you, Vinnie boy!" I said. "Well, he is a bit heavier than me, you know! That lets him go faster." "Yeah, but that's the first time he's done it, in it?" I was proud of my big brother. "You looked good Ed!" He was puffed out. "Your turn next, mouthy!" That Vincent had better be careful, he's lucky he's Davey's mate.

Off I went, but I must admit, I was a bit scared. I don't think I pedalled that fast down the hill. I flew, I hadn't been this fast anywhere before. I stopped a good few yards behind both Vincent and Eddie. Now for the bad part, getting back up the hill. I was knackered when I got back to the top. "How did you get on?" "Not so good, I was short of you and Vincent, but you're in the lead Ed." I glanced over at Vincent.

The other boy, John, had his go. He seemed to do really well. I think I was going to be the back marker in this game! When he came puffing up to us, he said "Some of the people in those houses down there told me that we've got to stop racing past them. One of them knows my Mum, so I've got to be careful." "We've only got you to go, Dave, we can't stop now." "You lot go around that other turning so as not to go past those houses. Wait for me for a couple of minutes and I'll ride down. Paddy, don't say anything to anybody!"

We came out at the bottom of the road and we could see Davey at the top. We waved. Then off he went. He came flying down, eventually stopping about twenty yards past what was Eddie's chalk mark.

I didn't mind Davey beating Eddie, remember we called him Tarzan, he was a big boy. Eddie was second and, as I thought, I was last, the back-marker. We all wandered back towards home, it had been a great afternoon. "Had a good time, have you?" Aunt Sarah said. "No trouble?" "No, Auntie."

"Dave, Terry, come with me, Nanny wants to talk to the boys, come on lively!"

"Come in here with us for a minute boys, I need to talk to you." I'd never seen Nan quite as serious before. Dad and Eileen were also in the little front room. Dad sat Michael on his knee, he also was looking very glum. Poor Eileen was near to tears and held me close. I had never felt so uneasy before. "Eddie, come and sit next to me" Nan continued. She looked at us one by one, and when I looked into those blue eyes, I saw a sadness, which throughout her remaining years never totally left her. I must admit, I was scared.

"We've got some really sad news to tell you boys, it's about Mummy." Eddie groaned. I was now getting annoyed, something that always seemed to happen whenever I had bad news, I've never quite understood why.

"Mummy has gone to heaven, God wanted her to help out with all the babies that were killed in the bombing. I'm sorry, but she won't be coming back." Everyone started crying at the same time, that is, except for me. I stared at Nan, looked deep into those eyes, got up and ran outside. I can't begin to tell you what emotions were going through me. I don't know if I fully understood what was happening to us, or the full implications of what had occurred. I remember that I was really angry with everything and everyone. I could have easily just ran away.

The back door opened, and Eileen came out. It was only then that it struck me that she was dressed in black, and come to think of it, so was Nan and what about that black band round Dad's arm. How come I hadn't noticed all of this. Eileen reached out, put her arm around my shoulders and gave me a big, strong hug. Tearfully she said "Please, Paddy, come back in, everyone's worried about you. I promise I will always look after you." "Will I ever see Mummy again, Eileen?" "Yes, one day, when you go to heaven. She'll be waiting for you, I promise." "Why did she have to go to that rotten shelter? It was the shelter, wasn't it, that bastard Stainer Street?"

Even at a young age, I wasn't that convinced about heaven. It was a dreadful scene that confronted me as I came back in. Eddie was in a really bad way. Mercifully, Michael didn't seem to fully understand what was going on, and Dad had a firm grip on him. "Come over here Paddy" he said. Over I went to him, and he literally smothered me. He'd never done that before.

Nan was in tears, a quiet, dignified grief, whilst cuddling Eddie, who was still very upset. Although I was numb with sadness, I still didn't actually cry. I did think of pretending but gave that idea up very quickly. My time would come. "Who's going to look after us Dad?" I asked. "Please don't worry yourselves. Nan and Granddad are going to take care of you, and you are going to live with them, and Eileen and Johnnie too."

"Paddy, come over here" Nan said softly. I looked into those sad eyes, and I knew then what a brave strong woman she was. She was 55 years old at that time. "I'll look after you, darling, and Eddie and Michael, and I promise you that I'll never allow you to be separated.

Never. Now come here and give me the biggest hug ever." It seemed as though that afternoon would never end, it was like a very bad dream, but sadly one that there would be no waking up from.

Over the passing years, sadly, I've been in that situation, and I know how difficult it is to, sort of, kick start normality. Fortunately (it must be in the human make up) it is always easier where children are involved. As we all know, children can be cruel but I think it's natures natural defence.

"Do you want to go outside boys?" Nan said. Eddie said "Yeah, why not? You coming Paddy?" Come on Michael, let's find some worms." Out into the garden we went, and very shortly Dave, Maureen and Terry appeared. Aunt Sarah gave us a brave hug. I have always thought how traumatic it must have been for the adults. Not only had Nan lost her eldest daughter, and Dad his young wife, and poor Eileen, a teenager herself, had lost her eldest sister, all in such a dramatic and awful fashion. But then, they had to face up to the added worry of telling us, not knowing what our reaction would be. What a frightening prospect. We children were all very subdued.

I think that the close neighbours must have known something, because there was nobody in their gardens and it was all very quiet. If anybody is in doubt as to the futility of war, then they haven't gone through what we had to face, alongside, may I say, many millions of other wretched victims. But let's get out of the pulpit!

Eddie and Michael were digging away in a corner of the garden, dragging up worms by the cupful. I just fiddled about, feeling very angry and confused. Even Dave and the others were strangely quiet. I noticed Dad looking out of the back window at us. He made a sad sight. I kept thinking that the pikey was very lucky he never got seriously hurt, especially when you think what my Dad was about to face.

Aunt Sarah called us in for our tea, which again was strangely subdued, with Nan, Eileen and Aunt Sarah fussing all over us. What an ordeal for them.

Shortly after finishing our tea, Dad said "Right, clear that table, let's get the billiard table out." We boys didn't need much encouragement. Dad put the billiard table on top of the, now cleared, kitchen table. Davey got the balls, and cues. The cues were all different sizes because the kitchen wasn't that big and it needed quite skilled positioning to take some of the shots. We had a very good time. Mercifully, the ability of kids to carry on regardless is remarkable. "Make that your last game boys, it's time to get ready for bed." "OK Nan, we won't be long" Eddie answered. After a cup of cocoa and a broken biscuit (they seemed to be the only ones we could get) we gave everyone a kiss, the hugs were deeper and longer.

As usual the three of us slept together. Very shortly we heard the distant drone of enemy aeroplanes. We all jumped up to look out of the windows, but couldn't see anything. The air raid sirens began to wail. Dad came up the stairs. "Nothing to worry about boys, they're miles away and can't hurt us. Now get back to bed and try to go to sleep."

We snuggled back in bed, and after a little mucking about, settled down. My mind was in turmoil. I heard others going to bed and then the house was quiet, dark and still. I was still buzzing. Suddenly Michael woke up and started to cry. Eddie tried to reassure him, but he was very upset. He wanted his Mum! I was devastated, as, no doubt, was Eddie. Soon the bedroom door opened and Nan came in. She came over to the bed. "It's alright Eddie, I'll take care of him. Come on, Mikey, come with Nanny." She scooped him up and took him to her bed. "Try to go to sleep you two, and Davey and Terry." (both of whom had woken up) "Night, night, God bless." She closed the door behind her.

Shortly after, the door opened again. This time it was Dad. "Are you alright boys?" "Yes Dad" said Eddie. "Michael woke up crying, but Nan's looking after him." "You sure that you're alright?" This time we both answered "Yes thanks, Dad." He closed the door and I heard him go downstairs. Eddie said "Paddy, come up here with me." Remember that we used to top and tail. I climbed up beside him, we cuddled and both cried ourselves to sleep. That was a terrifying night, sadly more were to follow.

The hustle and bustle of the morning, with all of us having breakfast and washing and dressing, helped to ease the obvious tension. The adults were doing their level best to make things as normal as possible. They did a great job.

It being Sunday, suddenly Eileen said "Shouldn't we be going to church? Where is the nearest Catholic church Sarah?" "It's on the far side of the village, I'll take you if you want me to." "Yes, please! Are you coming Mum? What about you boys? You should you know." "Do I have to Nan?" I said. I truly was never happy with church services, and I didn't feel like going today. "Well, not if you're really unhappy Paddy. Are you happy with that Ted?" "Look Mum, you're looking after the boys now, remember it's your decision and I'll not interfere. I trust you." "What about you Eddie?" "If Eileen's going, I'll go with her and I'll take Michael. Paddy's a nuisance anyway, he doesn't follow the service." That was settled then. Dad went with them, and I stayed behind with Davey. That made me feel happier already! Off they all went.

"You know that you are a naughty boy, not going to church. You should really, you know." "Sorry Nan, but I've never liked going, and I don't suppose I ever will." "Well we'll see about that. Now off you go and if you're playing with Davey, be good!" I didn't hang about, and scampered out the door. Dave was in the front street with some of his mates. "Paddy for Christ's sake, don't go up those woods, you'll get us all into trouble."

We didn't, although I made sure that I was on the side playing closest. Eventually they all came back from the church. Eddie and Michael seemed very happy. It was then that I noticed that they were chewing sweets. "See what you get for being a good boy?" Eileen teased. But, seeing the look on my face she quickly gave Davey and me a small packet each. She had obviously used some of her sweet ration coupons to buy them for us.

In Spite of Everything . . . .

"You haven't been getting into any mischief, have you son?" Dad said, at the same time eyeing my big stick, which was lying by the side of the road. "No, honest Dad." He gave me a smile, at the same time touching Eddie on the shoulder. "Look after your younger brother!"

Nan came out of the house. "Right, you lot, don't go far away, your dinner will be ready soon, we'll give you a call when it's ready. Eddie, after dinner you boys and your Dad and me and Eileen will be going home to London, so have a nice game with your mates."

We said goodbye to the boys we'd been playing with, and went in for our dinner. Nan didn't have to call us twice, I was starving. We had a beautiful dinner, because although Aunt Sarah was a very good cook, Nan was even better. We were lucky, because we had lots of veg and meat, even though there was strict rationing. The reason for this will all become clear later!

They all came up to the station to see us off. We kids were always dashing off in front. I can remember Dad carrying nearly all the luggage. I thought he was a giant.

We said our goodbyes, lots of kissing and cuddling, not knowing when we'd see each other again. Then off we went, on the 'rattler' home. I loved looking out of the train windows, dashing from one side of the carriage to the other. How soon the landscape changed, fields changed into houses and trees into chimneys. The closer we got to the Elephant & Castle, the more ruined streets could be seen. Although, in truth, this part of London didn't come off too bad. With the exception of Tooting, that is. We had a little game we liked to play. Each train window had a blind, which pulled down and was secured by a small latch, this was for the blackout. We used to pull the blinds down and let them spring back. They were on quite a strong string. Snap and crack they went. Eventually we were told to stop.

As we came out of the station, much to our surprise, there stood Granddad and Johnny. They were very pleased to see us. I couldn't but notice that Granddad was dressed in black and Johnny had that black band around his arm. I'd almost forgotten! The anger welled up in me again. Nan must have noticed because she caught hold of me and held me close. I couldn't get away. Granddad picked Michael up "Come on Mikey boy, let's get you home before it gets dark."

Johnny helped Dad with our luggage, it wasn't actually that much, and off we went. We were walking along Long Lane, and coming towards us were two policemen. As they came closer, one of them stopped Dad and started talking to him. He put his suitcase down and took some papers out of his left breast pocket. They both examined the papers, then handed them back to him. They shook his hand and wished him all the best.

"What was all that about Ted?" "They only wanted to make sure that I wasn't a deserter. I showed them my pass and, as you see, they were happy." "Fucking bastards" he muttered. Nan gave him a look that could kill. I was to find out later that my Granddad didn't like coppers, especially the specials!

We arrived home to our little terrace and as we went in, I stopped dead in my tracks. There stood a blonde lady, and for a glorious moment I thought it was my Mum. It wasn't! It was my Aunt Anne, my Mum's younger sister. They were so much alike. I burst into tears! Kicking out, bashing anything and everything. It took Dad to control me and then he took me for a short walk, I think he was very worried!

"Sorry Dad! I won't do that again, I promise. I don't want to upset you or anyone else." "Don't you worry about upsetting other people, a good cry is good for you. Now come on, we've got to go back, Nan will be worried about you."

It was then that I decided that I wouldn't upset Nan again. I was going to get on with my life as best I could. Not ever knowing what was in front of me. How could I at that age? Mind you, you don't 'arf grow up quick in those circumstances.

We went back indoors. "You alright Paddy?" That was Eddie. "Yeah, you know what I'm like, take no notice." I could see that there had been tears, except Johnny. I think we was a bit annoyed. He was only a teenager himself and a very grown up one at that. He didn't have the patience that the adults had. However, he was very protective of us, as he would prove in later years.

Nan's house was a small mid-terrace, it had three bedrooms upstairs, one of which was really small. Downstairs there was a front room or parlour. That was my Nan's 'best' and, in it, the obligatory piano, some nice furniture and a small carpet. Also there was the picture of the Pope, obviously, and some beautiful glassware depicting Queen Victoria's golden jubilee and various showing coronations of successive Kings and Queens. They were nice, historic pieces. There was a small room facing the back yard, and this served as a combined kitchen, living and dining room. It had a large wooden table and various chairs, an open fire burning wood, coal or coke, in fact whatever was available. Then there was an outside scullery. This housed a big boiler for clothes washing and a range of hobs and an oven, all solid fuel.

There was a small back yard with an outside toilet, behind, which was the stables for the big horses used to pull the haulage carts. Granddad had a small patch of land where he grew some tomatoes and a few potatoes.

Since we were last there, they had changed the front parlour into another bedroom, which Nan and Granddad used. To say it was a bit cramped was certainly no exaggeration. Cramped but cosy!

We all quickly settled down and everyone went out of their way to make us feel at ease. Eileen showed us up to our new bedroom. It was the one facing the back yard. We soon got settled down. She was having Nan's old room and Johnny had the small room. He seemed happy enough with that.

"Come on down, boys. I'm getting your tea ready" called Nan. "It seems a bit early, but we must get finished in case we get an air raid." We weren't bothered, we were always hungry anyway. The front door opened suddenly, and in came our new uncle, Nathan, Aunt Anne's husband. They hadn't been married that long. Nathan, in fact, was an old friend of our Dad's. They worked together, before the war, at

Barclay Perkins, the brewers. He was a likeable and impressive man. After various hellos, he came over to us, gave us all a hug, them produced some chocolate from his overcoat pocket. "Here boys, a little something I managed to find for you." "Oh Nathan, you rascal, you shouldn't have! Boys, don't eat it now, it'll spoil you tea. It was a nice thought Nathan, thank you." Nan smiled and winked at him. "Thank you, Uncle" we all said.

Eventually tea was spread out over the table. Crusty bread, shrimps, winkles, cockles, soused herring and pickled onions. There was the usual game of sticking the winkle eyes on our faces, we all had our own pin in order to get the winkles out of their shells. We had never eaten with so many adults before. It was a lovely experience, one that was repeated for years to come.

"Now boys, it's time to get ready for bed." "Do we have to Nan?" I pleaded. I hated going to bed, especially now. I was enjoying the company. "Yes you do, Paddy and Eddie and Michael as well." She ushered us into the scullery, and made us wash our faces and our hands. I soon realised that there wasn't much point in arguing with Nan. Our pyjamas were already in the scullery, so we changed into them. "Go into the kitchen now and before you go up you can have some of that chocolate. Not too much though, it'll lay on your chest." I never understood what she meant, but I was glad of a chance to have some chocolate.

They were all in the kitchen, chatting away. A bit subdued, I thought. We again thanked Uncle Nathan for the chocolate, remember there was strict rationing at the time. "Come on Annie, we had better be off home before it gets too dark." Aunt Anne got up and gave us all a kiss and a big hug. I'm sure she held on to me the longest, but I might have imagined it. "Good night Mum, night Dad, see you tomorrow." They both said their goodnights to our Dad, Eileen and Johnnie. "See you tomorrow Ted" said Nathan. "Come on then, give Granddad a kiss, I'll see you to your room and tuck you in." We did as we were told, giving Eileen a kiss as well. Upstairs we went. Nan tucked us up in bed, it was a great big one, and that meant that we didn't have to top and tail.

In Spite of Everything . . . .

"Night, night boys, get to sleep quickly before those Germans turn up." We all got a kiss and a hug. "Dad will be up to see you in a minute." Dad crept in. "You all alright boys, nice and comfy?" "Yes thanks Dad!" we all called out. He leant over and gave us a kiss. Then he too was gone.

"Yum, yum, yum, I've got some!" That was me producing a piece of chocolate from my pyjama top pocket. "You crafty sod," said Eddie "give us a little bit." "Me too!" squealed Michael. I very reluctantly broke them off a small taster. Michael slept between Eddie and me, which was just as well, since Ed would have grabbed a bigger piece if he had been able to reach me.

I was woken up by a strange rumbling and stamping sound. It was coming from the stables at the back of us. Then came the air raid sirens. The bombers were on their way. The bedroom door opened and in came Dad. "Lively now, boys, out of bed, it's an air raid. Quickly follow me downstairs." "Shall we put our clothes on, Dad?" said Eddie. "No son, just come downstairs quickly." Down we went.

Things had changed a bit. There were only a couple of oil lamps alight, so it was quite gloomy. (Remember the blackout). "Are we going over to the shelter Nan?" Eddie asked. "No, not any more. Dad and Granddad have done some work whilst we were at Aunt Sarah's." I noticed the small door that led under the staircase. "In there you go, boys" said Dad. In we went. Wow! Dad had installed great big strong lumps of wood to support a big piece of iron plate that formed a snug little shelter. It was a bit cramped, especially when Nan and Eileen squeezed in. We all cuddled up together. "You'll be alright in there. Keep the door open until you hear the bombs dropping. We'll be in the kitchen, under the table." I found out in the morning that they had strengthened that as well. "Can I come in the kitchen with you Dad?" Eddie called out. "No, you all stay together, where you are, you'll be safe in there. Anyway, there's only enough room for Granddad, Johnnie and me." That was that then!

We all crouched there, but this night the raid must have been mainly over the other side of the river. We could hear muffled explosions, but mainly the sound of fire engines and police cars rushing about. And, the rumbling and frantic stamping. "What's that noise Nan?" I asked. "That's those poor horses, they get really frightened by the sound of the bombing. I think we hear it much louder than we do, and it really unsettles them. They are trying to kick their way out of their stables, but they can't. Poor creatures. Now cuddle up and try to go to sleep."

Some chance, I thought, but I did. Bump, bump, it was my head brushing against the staircase wall. I woke up in Dad's arms, he was taking us back to our bed. Eddie was walking in front, half asleep, and Granddad followed up with Mikey, as he called him. The all clear must have sounded. I didn't know how long we'd been asleep, but once tucked in again, I certainly didn't need any rocking.

It was a nice bright morning that we woke up to. A bit chilly, there weren't any carpets on the floor, only linoleum (lino) and no fire. Central heating hadn't been invented yet. Not for us anyway. Eddie pulled the heavy curtains open and the sun came shining through. That was nice, I thought.

"Up you get boys." That was Nan, calling up the stairs. "Down you come, your breakfast will be ready in a couple of minutes. I want you washed and dressed." Eileen and Johnny were in the kitchen. They said good morning, well Eileen did. Johnny was a bit offish. Our breakfast was the usual porridge oats. Hot and warm, lovely. "Where's Dad and Granddad?" "Oh, they went out early to see if they are needed to help with any clearing up. They'll be back soon, finish your breakfast."

"Goodbye Mum, bye boys, see you later." That was Eileen, going off to work. She worked in a local factory, they made custard powder, of all things. Johnny wasn't going anywhere, yet. We had learned that he was starting work next week. Now that he was 14! Could you believe it now? Leaving school and starting work at 14. I don't know if it's because I've got older, but my own grandchildren and their friends certainly don't seem ready for work, but as I've said before, things were different then.

In Spite of Everything . . . .

The front door opened, and in came Dad and Granddad looking grim faced and tired. "They got a right pasting over Stepney last night, poor sods." There wasn't much we could do to help. We couldn't get down Cable Street or the Highway. The police told us to go home." "Do us a bit of dripping toast will you, Annie." Granddad continued "What you up to today John?" "Oh, not much Dad, waiting to start work soon, can't wait for next week to come." "Come on then, you two, sit down and have something to eat." It seemed to me, even after this short time living with Nan, that she was always cooking and feeding everyone. This was confirmed in later years!

"I'm popping over to the school to see if they're open, so you'd better get yourselves ready, just in case." That was like a bombshell in itself, I wasn't looking forward to going back to school. However, I think Nan would be quite pleased to get us from under her feet. Off she went.

"Eddie, I want to talk to you, and you boys. Come over here for a minute." Dad had just finished his breakfast. "Now look. Tomorrow, I've got to go back to my army barracks, and I don't know when I'll be able to see you again." He saw the look of alarm on our faces. "Don't worry, I'm not going to fight the Germans just yet! We are still training in this country. I mustn't tell you where." I couldn't understand the reason for that, not at that time. "I'll write to Nan to check up on you boys, so you better be on your best behaviour." He saved a special glance for me. "Your Nan and Granddad love you very much and they will look after you. Give us a cuddle." Eddie and Michael clung on to him. I joined in, but I was never too comfortable with these moments of affection! Although I did love my Dad!

Nan came back in. "Good news boys, your school is open! Well, not all of it. There are only two classes that are usable." For one lovely moment I thought that I might escape, some chance! "But there are only a few children still living here, so they are able to fit you in." I was devastated. That bleeding evacuation had taken most of the children away. I often wondered where they had all gone, because, as I was to find out, it applied to the big Protestant school in Snowsfields as well.

"You start back tomorrow, so you can go out to play today. But don't go far, and remember, keep off the ruins." Some fat chance of that, I thought. Nearly half of our immediate area was either a pile of rubble or half destroyed. I can't tell you, it was a wonderful and mysterious adventure playground. One of the things we liked doing was collecting shrapnel. Those jagged pieces of bombs that had caused so much death, injury and devastation. We didn't know the significance of what shrapnel actually was. For us kids, it was treasure trove.

"Coming out Paddy?" Eddie said. "Yeah, I'll be with you in a minute." "What about you Mike?" "No thanks, Ed, I think I'll stay in with Dad and Granddad." I think Nan was glad of that, she was a bit worried about Michael going out on the streets with just us two."

"Where do you fancy going Paddy?" "Why don't we go round Snowfields and see if anybody is about?" "Good idea, let's go." Off we went, looking back as I am now doing, what a strange and unreal world we were living in. Half the streets, houses and warehouses were knocked flat, the other half partly damaged. One of the strange things was the lack of windows. Most had been blown away. At the same time people were trying to get on with their lives as normal, or nearly so. Another thing, as we were to soon find out, was the lack of children and young men.

"Where is everybody?" Eddie said, as we both gazed about. There wasn't any boys to be seen. "Snowfields school looks as though it's open, look, I can see people in the ground floor class. There's not even any bomb damage to speak of." "Well, remember Ed, we've got to go to school tomorrow, so even we won't be about. Ed, what about going round to the Vinegar Yard (the warehouses behind our house) and having a look at the horses?" "Good idea." So off we went.

Vinegar Yard was a narrow row of warehouses with a cobbled street down its middle. It was a hive of activity. "Alright for us to watch, Mister?" said Eddie. A big burly man was holding the reins on two big furry footed horses. They were massive. He was making the horses go backwards, and that looked like a very difficult job. The horses were clumping their great legs on the cobbles. There were even sparks

In Spite of Everything . . . .

flying off, now and again. He was managing to do it, however, and his cart, which was full of goods, was slowly edging towards the open warehouse doors, where several men were waiting to unload.

"You can watch, but keep your distance, these horses can be very dangerous." "Thanks Mister" we both chorused. It was fascinating, watching all this going on. There were several other teams of horses, whose carts were either being unloaded or loaded. It was very busy. All this whilst there was a war going on! Very surreal!

I noticed that all the horses at rest had big nose bags hanging round their necks. They were full of food of some sort, and they were mostly chomping away merrily. Every now and again, taking their mouths out of the bags to sneeze or something like that. Great sprays of oats came flying about.

Our cart driver finished putting his cart in the right place and he immediately brought round two feed bags. "Here boys, stick out your hands, you can feed the horses, if you want. Remember to hold your hands flat. Put them up to the horse's mouth, he'll do the rest." He sprinkled some what looked like nuts and oats, into our outstretched hands. Very nervously I reached up to the horse's mouth. Then, hey presto, it was all taken, as smooth as silk, not a sign of those great yellow teeth. The driver dropped the bags and encouraged us to carry on feeding. We didn't need asking twice, this was great fun. We both carried on scooping handfuls, and the horses wasted no time in taking the food, even to the point that they started gently nudging us to hurry up.

"That's enough boys, make way, they've got to have a drink." With that he produced two big pouches and looped them over their heads. The noise they made drinking! Greedy sods. There was this unusual and very strong smell, wafting up the narrow streets. "What's that smell, Mister?" I asked. "Oh, that's coming from the stables at the bottom of the yard." "Well what is it then?" "There's a farrier down there, and he's shoeing the horses. Go down and have a look, but be careful and don't get in anybody's way. Remember I think I know your Granddad, so behave yourselves."

|43

I had never seen anything like it. A couple of horses were tied up in this shed and a man was holding big iron tongs into a big fire. He pulled out some red hot metal and began to bash it about on a big iron anvil. He was making horseshoes. It was amazing to see him shape the metal, every now and again shoving it back into the fire. Once he'd made the shape, he then made holes in it, very clever! Then the real clever thing. Over he went to the first horse. He backed into it, and lifted up its leg.

He placed the red hot shoe on the bottom of the horse's foot, and it sizzled. It didn't seem to bother the horse too much, and that was the strange smell. Away he went, put the horseshoe back in the fire for a while, then bashed it about a little so that it would fit snugly into the horse's hoof (not foot, as I was to find out later). When he was happy, he went back to the horse, grabbed its leg and started to scrape and clean the horse's hoof. Back to the fire, heated the shoe again, returned to the horse, fitted it once more, again the smell.

He seemed happy. Once the shoe was cold, over to the horse he went. This time with a claw hammer and some nails. To my amazement he actually nailed the shoe into the horse's hoof. The horse never blinked, so it obviously didn't hurt. He finished it all off with a big raspy file. Job done. We watched in amazement, it was all done and dusted in no time.

We watched him carry on and repeat the procedure until the horse had new shoes all round. Then his assistant untied the horse and led it away towards the stables.

"You boys looked as though you enjoyed that" the farrier said. He was now pumping up his fire. It looked very hot. "Yes thanks, we did Mister. You don't mind us watching, do you?" "As long as you keep your distance and don't be a nuisance. I'll see your Granddad in the pub later, so I'll tell him that you've behaved yourselves. Go on now, hop it."

I thought 'everyone seems to know our Granddad, and they seemed to know who we were, creepy! We'd better be careful.' The next

In Spite of Everything . . . .

really amazing thing was the stables. They were on two floors, and the horses were led up a spiral wooden walkway. Where all the stalls were. We could hear them stamping now. Little wonder, we heard them during the air raids, when they were excited and frightened.

We made our way back home, I was getting hungry. You could set your clock by my stomach, and still can! Nan was in alone, as usual, in the scullery. We excitedly told her all about our adventure. She seemed pleased that we had enjoyed ourselves, but again reminded us of the dangers, and told us to promise to be careful. We did.

"Where's Michael, Nan?" Eddie asked. "He's gone out with your Dad and Granddad. They'll probably be back shortly, because of Michael's dinner." The front door burst open, and in raced Michael, very excited. "Look what I've got!" In his hand he was holding several silver coins, sixpences and shillings and a two bob piece. "Where did you get all that?" Eddie asked. "Well, I was outside the pub, where Dad and Granddad were having a drink, and men were coming out and just giving me money. I don't know why."

"They are friends of mine" said Granddad. "Very generous friends, and anyway, the money is for all three of you to share. Michael, give the money to your Nan, she'll take care of it for you" he continued. "Had a nice time boys?" Dad said. "What have you been up to?"

"There weren't any of our mates about, so we went round Vinegar Yard and saw a man putting metal shoes on horses. It was brilliant!" Eddie answered. "You didn't make a nuisance of yourselves, did you? Especially you Paddy." "No, honest Dad, it was really smashing. The man who was putting the shoes on knew Granddad, so you can ask him yourself." He grinned. "After you've had your dinner, I want to speak to you boys, but eat your dinner first. I think Nan is ready for you."

We finished our dinner, which once again was delicious, Nan was a very good cook. We always had plenty of potatoes and veg, and always a small portion of meat, usually with some bread and margarine. Dad sat down with us around the kitchen table. "Do I have to share my money with Eddie and Paddy, Dad?" Michael squeaked out. "Yes, that's one of the things I want to talk to you about, amongst others." He continued, "Now, look here boys, I've got to go back to my army unit tomorrow." "Do you have to?" Eddie asked. "Yes, I'm afraid so son! There's a war on, and I don't have any choice in the matter. I'll write to you, and try to get some more leave, but I can't be sure of anything at the moment."

I noticed Nan standing in the doorway, looking very serious and worried. "You know that your Nan and Granddad will be looking after you, therefore I want you to take notice of everything she says, and I want you to help her where possible. I'll be keeping in touch with Nan, so I'll know exactly how you all are, and how you're behaving yourselves. Now, this is very important. You boys must stick together like glue, look after each other and share everything." He glanced at Michael, who was wide eyed. He had never heard Dad talk this way before, and neither had I. It was very unnerving! "When I go away, I know that you are in the best hands possible, so look after your Nan, she's precious." Over the coming years I was to find out exactly how precious she was.

"I won't be leaving until dinner time tomorrow, so I'll see you all before I go. Come on, give me a big cuddle." We did, but I was very uncomfortable, I couldn't help thinking that the last time I saw Mum, she said she was only going away for a short time. Well, I don't know about heaven, but that seems like a long way away. A place that you certainly don't come back from. I was very worried, and strangely, again very annoyed.

"Come on you boys, why don't you pop out for a minute, and let Dad and Granddad eat their dinner. Dad's not leaving until tomorrow, remember!"

"Here's some money for you. Eddie, take them round to Sonny's (that was a general store in Snowfields) ad you should be able to buy a few sweets that are not rationed." With that Nan gave Eddie a six pence piece (a spratzy). "Don't go too far! Remember you've got Michael with you." Off we went.

"Now Ted, I don't want you to worry about the boys. Me and Dad are capable of looking after them, and remember I've got Anne and Eileen to help out as needs be. We can cope. They seem very settled here and once they get back to school it should take their minds off things. You have to concentrate on what you are doing, and make sure you don't get hurt."

"I know you will Mum. It's such a heavy burden. Three boys! I'm a little bit worried about Paddy, he acts very strangely at times. What do you think?"

"You know he's always been a bit of a handful, but he'll be ok, I'm sure. Don't worry, I know how to handle him. Remember as well, Ted, I've got Eileen here and he really adores her, so please, you mustn't worry yourself. That's an order! What time have you got to be off tomorrow Ted?"

"I'll see the boys at their dinner time and say goodbye. I hope I can do it without breaking down, that would really unsettle them. I'm dreading it."

"Listen, I know them boys. After a morning at school, they'll be so full of stories that your leaving won't affect them too much. Annie, Eileen and Johnnie have promised to be here when they come back in the afternoon. We'll all look after them when you go away Ted. You must go with a clear head and conscience, you deserve that after all you've been through. Anyway, the war can't go on forever!"

"We'll all look after them son, that I promise you!" Granddad looked over at him from the corner of the kitchen.

"Where you lot been? We thought that you'd been evacuated." A few boys and girls were dribbling out of our school gates. There weren't many of them. A few mums were hanging around, talking, and I think they were talking about us, because there were lots of nervous glances in our direction. I realised that I was jealous, because I couldn't help thinking that I'd never have a mum meeting me from school. The dreaded anger started welling up inside of me. It must have shown because Eddie came over to me. "Don't let anyone upset you Paddy, nobody means you any harm." "Ed, I just don't like people talking about us, it really pisses me off." "Let's get out of here then! See you tomorrow Pete, we're coming back to school in the morning. Come on Mike, and you Paddy!"

We followed Eddie down Kipling Street, where there was a small park with some swings and slides and things. Michael loved it playing on the roundabout with the youngsters. He particularly liked it when I used to spin it very fast, jumping on and off. Sometimes I managed to get it going so fast that it threw me to the ground, Michael used to squeal with laughter. I think Eddie liked talking to his mates and the young girls. He was always one for the girls!

Suddenly the whistle went, it was the park keeper, Mr. Wood, as they were all called. "We're closing the park in five minutes, so you lot had better scarper off home." I noticed that he only had one arm, with the sleeve of his jacket tucked in. He probably lost that in the first war. There were a lot of men around with legs and arms missing. One man in particular, who had no legs, used to wheel himself about on a sort of trolley. He used to help out at the tea bar at the front of the shelter on Weston Street. I was always fascinated by him, and could never stop staring. I was always told that it was rude to stare at such an unfortunate man, and that I should feel sorry for him. I remember saying to my Mum (there I go again) that it wasn't my fault that he had no legs, so why should I be sorry! There's no answer to that!

We got home, let ourselves in. We were able to do that because the front door key was hanging on a piece of string behind the letter box. Could you imagine that today! Over the years we have always laughed at that, because my theory, shared by many in my family, was that people weren't necessarily much more honest in those days, but the plain fact was, that there was nothing in anyone's houses that was worth nicking. There is probably a bit of truth in that, but also you must remember that all of our neighbours were either close relations or family friends.

In Spite of Everything . . . .

"Had a nice afternoon?" Nan said on hearing us come bundling in. "Yes thanks, Nan, we got a few funny sweets, met some mates leaving school and went over to Kipling Park. Michael and Paddy seemed to be enjoying themselves." "And Eddie was talking to some girls" piped in Michael. Nan, Granddad and Eileen all laughed at that. There was a nice fire going in the little kitchen, it was just starting to get chilly, now the nights were drawing in.

"Where's Dad?" Eddie asked. "Oh, he's just popped over to see your Aunt Anne and Nathan. I think he wants to say goodbye, he's off tomorrow remember." How could I forget!

"Johnny's gone with him. I think your Dad is his hero, he hangs round him most of the time. I'll have some tea ready for you soon, so sit down and settle down, Granddad's trying to read his paper." With that, Granddad peered over the top of his paper, glasses perched on his nose. He nodded, smiled and stuck his face in the paper.

Eileen said "Do you want to play cards Paddy?" "Yes please, I wouldn't mind, but you'll have to teach me how to play." "What about you Ed, fancy a game?" "Yeah, I wouldn't mind, but you'll have to show me as well." "OK, let's wait until after tea, and then we'll get the cards out."

"You've got to make up sets of three or four cards, say 3 x 6s or 4 x 7s or runs of three of four." Eileen was explaining the simple rules of rummy. She'd already showed us the four suits, how to shuffle and other basic rules of cards. I was hooked immediately. Playing cards was something I would enjoy throughout my life, and still do! Once we had mastered the basics, we played a few hands, it was a noisy and enjoyable time. Before very long, Nan said "Come on Eileen, finish up your game, the boys have got to get ready for bed. Come on boys, get washed and changed into your pyjamas, you can stay up for a while and wait for Daddy to come home."

This done, we asked Eileen to play some more cards. She willingly agreed. Then just as we got started the air raid siren started wailing, and you've guessed it, the rumbling and crying started up in the stables.

"Can I go out into the back yard and see the searchlights Granddad?" I blurted out. "Well, very quickly then, you can't stay out very long." Eddie said "I'll go out the front and check our blackout is OK." "Hurry up then."

Outside, the noise of the horses was really loud, and now that I knew what was going on, I felt very sorry for those poor animals. I never gave a thought for our discomfort and imminent danger. I could hear that distant throbbing, which I knew were German bombers. There was the thud of distant anti-aircraft batteries, searchlights and barrage balloons lit up by all the activity around them. Chaos. And to think I didn't really understand the danger all around us. I bet the adults did!

"Paddy, in you come, go to the toilet if you need to, but hurry up. Eileen, you and the boys get under the staircase immediately, I'm just going to make a pot of tea." That was Nan, as cool as a cucumber. We were all soon in our little cubby hole, which, by now, even had a bit of carpet on the wooden floor. It was just like a little camp.

The front door opened suddenly and in dashed Dad and Johnny. Both panting and out of breath. "Nearly got caught out that time" Dad said, "they're a bit early tonight, ain't they?" "I think they must be enjoying themselves that much that they can't get here quick enough" quipped Johnny, in his sarcastic way.

"Dad, can I come under the kitchen table with you tonight?" said Eddie, obviously aware that this would be his last chance. "Yeah, that'll be ok son, we'll make room for you. Alright with you, Dad?" "We can always make room for a little'un," Granddad replied.

It was a while before the bombs started dropping closer. Then the adults finished their tea and Dad said "Right, out you come Eddie, and dive under this table, get right in the corner. I'm going to shut the door on you lot now, is that ok with you Mum?" She nodded, but didn't seem to want to talk. Michael and me cuddled up to Nan and Eileen. Then, as usual, Eileen began to hum some songs, very quietly.

The bombs again seemed to be falling quite a way from us, and very shortly I was asleep.

Again, head bumping against the stair wall and then our comfortable bed. This routine was to be repeated over and over again. To us, this was normal life. How strange is that?

"When you've finished your breakfast, I'll walk round to your school with you. You've got to take your gas masks with you this morning" Dad said, at the same time reaching into the understairs cupboard and taking out three dreaded gas masks. They were hideous and frightening pieces of equipment. I hated putting my one on, not only because I disliked having anything over my mouth, but also because of the dreadful smell of the things. They made me feel sick. I supposed there would be a gas attack drill at school today. I knew that, sadly, there was no escaping these drills.

"Bye Nan, bye Granddad, bye John." We had to shout up the stairs to Johnny, he was still in bed. Eileen had already gone off to work. "See you at dinnertime, remember be good." I'm sure Nan gave me an extra stare. Could have been my imagination, although I wasn't happy!

It was only a few hundred yards to our school. Off we went. Michael was on Dad's shoulders and Eddie was hanging on to Dad. I lagged behind a little. "Come on Paddy" Dad said, smiling back at me, "you'll enjoy it once you mix with some of your mates." I don't think I agreed with that, but I didn't show it too much! There weren't that many children in the playground, and the few adults all seemed to know Dad. Some of them came over and hugged him and shook his hand, at the same time glancing over in our general direction.

I suddenly spied my best mate Peter, and off I dashed. I forgot to say goodbye to Dad. I knew I'd see him at dinnertime, so I wasn't that bothered. The school bell suddenly was rung, and all the adults left. We all formed a couple of lines, the headmistress directing us to where she had decided we should be. There could only have been 50 or 60 pupils in total, probably just a quarter of the entire school.

There was the usual assembly, and, as normal, one of the local priests said prayers, all of which we had to repeat with him. The Church was actually attached to the school, therefore unfortunately the priests were ever present. Then the headmistress took over. Much to my surprise she actually welcomed us back to school alongside one of our cousins. I don't think it was a coincidence that Rose had lost her mother in the bombing also. I wasn't very happy, I don't know what stopped me walking straight out! Possibly it was Eddie staring at me. Anyhow, I didn't.

The headmistress explained, that due to the war, and the evacuation of many children, there would only be two classrooms open, and they would be mixed age groups. She explained that there had been damage to the school, and that we were not to use the stairs that led to the top classrooms. They were taped off anyway. She also advised us that an air raid warden would be calling in explain gas mask drill. That's when she asked if we had all remembered to bring them to school. As usual, on this occasion, a few had forgotten.

Assembly finished, we were shown to our classrooms. I found myself in the same class as Eddie. Michael was in the other. He seemed very comfortable with that arrangement. There were luckily quite a few of his mates in school.

Our class was arranged as such, that the youngest were in the front few rows, with the oldest in the rear. That's where Eddie was sitting. Our teacher, a lady (in fact they were all ladies) was a very nice person and she soon put us all at ease. I can't actually remember the way in which she organised our lessons, but we all seemed to get on alright. I had always found learning easy. Not, I hasten to add, because I'm anything special, but because I have a very good memory. I only have to read, and then write things down, and it seems to create a picture in my head. A picture I can usually recapture when needed. Over the years I was able to pass exams, when I know the cleverer people actually struggled. One of the failings of exam culture I'm afraid.

The warden came in, with his tin helmet and uniform and took us through gas mask drill. Luckily, as awful as the gas masks were, we had a really good laugh looking at each other. It was a riot, one which the teacher soon brought to order. She was such a nice lady, that I and others didn't want to fall out with. Order was soon resumed. The school bell rung, it was dinnertime. Eddie collected Michael and off home we went.

We rounded the corner, and the first thing I noticed was the big kit bag standing out by the front door, nice! The little house was crowded: Nan, Granddad, Aunt Anne, Uncle Nathan, Eileen, Johnny, Dad and a few other relations. They all made a big fuss of us, it really embarrassed me, I don't know why, but I hated too much fussing about. They meant well, and I always was able to understand that.

"Mind out of the way, these boys have got to have their dinner" Nan called out, at the same time putting our dinners out on the kitchen table. I then noticed the bottles of beer. They had obviously been celebrating, seeing Dad off, that is. Our family drank beer at every conceivable occasion. It was a tradition! It was then that I also noticed that one of our local priests was in the room. I suppose he was having a sup as well! (What the XXXX is he doing here?) I thought. I knew that my Granddad was not very keen on the Church and priests, but they were always making themselves busy. I suppose they thought they were doing good, they brought some comfort to a lot of people.

"Finish your dinner boys, because I've got to get away very soon. Will you all walk to the end of the street with me before we say goodbye?" The house went very quiet. "Can I carry your kit bag and go to the station with you Ted?" Johnny broke the silence. "That will be nice, thanks John." "Come on boys, put your coats on. Dad's got to get away, or he'll be in trouble with the army." Nan started fussing round us, with a little help from Eileen. There was a lot of kissing and hugging and a few tears. I noticed Dad whispering in Nan's ear and then we were outside. Johnny had Dad's kit bag on his shoulder.

"Can I walk with you to Waterloo Station?" Dad grinned. "Do you think you'll make it all the way carrying my kit? It'll start getting a bit heavy." "I'll give it my best, if you don't mind." "Come on then, let's be off." Dad turned and waved to all the family that were now standing in the street, then we turned the corner. As we approached the top of Melior Street, Dad stopped. "Come here boys. You've got to leave me now and get to school." I thought "Leave him? He's leaving us!"

First he picked up Michael and gave him a big hug. "Remember, behave yourself for Nanny, and be good." Then he put him down. He grabbed me and I thought that he would crush me to death. "Make sure you look after Michael, take notice of your big brother and be as good as you can." Then Eddie, another enormous hug. "Eddie, you're the eldest, you've got to take care of your brothers and help Nan and Granddad as much as possible. I love you all, but I've got to go back to my army unit." "Will you come back Dad?" Eddie asked. "Yes, yes, I promise! Come on Johnny, let's be off, now get to school boys." With that, he turned and marched away, with Johnny following closely behind.

As I watched him going down Maize Pond. I thought "Will I ever see him again?" In my own mind I could not understand why he was walking away from us, just like that! I wondered if I would ever solve that particular puzzle.

We rounded the corner into Snowfields, only a few yards from our school gate, and I don't know why, but I just said to Eddie "I'm not going to school this afternoon." Eddie gave me a long thoughtful look. "Alright, Paddy, I won't make you, but please tell me what are you going to do? You're not going to do anything silly, are you? Like running away, for example. Please promise me you're not!"

"No, Ed, promise! I just can't face anybody, I feel very uneasy and strange. I'll just wander around for a couple of hours, and then I'll come back, promise." "OK, see you later."

They went through the gates, and I walked the other way. I noticed some parents watching me as I trooped off. I just walked the streets, my mind a complete blur. I didn't know where I'd wind up, but eventually I arrived at Tabard Park. I watched the soldiers, men and women, who were just hanging around nearby the big barrage balloon. That was boring, so I made my way up towards the Borough, then along to

In Spite of Everything . . . .

Lant Street, our old house. It was hard to take in, what changes had happened to my life in such a short amount of time. The old house, well actually the row of houses, were in ruins. The wasn't much point in hanging about here, so off I went in the direction of London Bridge. The main road was very busy, lots of horse and carts, some buses, trams and the odd van or car. Just short of London Bridge there was a big bronze statue of a soldier, it was a war memorial from Great War. Looking at it, I thought, "That's my Dad!" We were to visit that particular statue many times over the coming years.

Suddenly a voice called out. "What do you think you're doing Paddy?" I nearly jumped out of my skin. There by the side of the road, his head hanging out of a small van, was Uncle Nathan. "Nothing, just walking about. I'm not doing anything wrong." "Shouldn't you be at school with Eddie and Mike?" "Yes, I suppose so, but I just didn't fancy it. It's not any of your business anyway. What do you want?" "Slow down son. I'm not having a go at you. I was just a bit worried. Your Nan would have a fit if I hadn't stopped to talk to you. Want a lift?"

I'd never been in a car (van) before, and I didn't have to be asked twice. In I jumped. He was a nice man, really, was Uncle Nathan. "I'm just going over to the market to see some people I know. I think it will interest you son. Slam that door shut, I don't want you to fall out, your Dad would kill me."

I felt very comfortable with Uncle Nathan. The market was nearly deserted. He explained to me that all the activity took place early in the mornings, that was, if the bombing was over. I once again thought how life goes on regardless.

He introduced me to a few very tough looking characters. They all made a fuss of me, however. There seemed to be a lot of whispering and close contact chat. Then a few handshakes and we were off. "Want me to take you back home to Nan's?" "No, thanks Uncle, but could you drop me off in front of our school? I've got to meet Eddie and Mike. I promised Eddie I would." "Jump in the van then, I'll do just that."

Once we were in Snowfields, the van pulled up and stopped. Nathan leant over and roughed up my hair. "Off you go, son." Soon all the children started pouring out. Michael appeared first and came running over to me. "Where've you been all afternoon? You're going to get into trouble." "I don't care. I've just been walking about, but guess what? I went for a ride in Uncle Nathan's van!" "That's not fair, you lucky sod!"

"You're going to get yourself in a load of trouble, Miss Batone is looking for you." Eddie had just appeared. "I don't care about her, or anybody else. I wasn't doing anything wrong. I just went for a walk, and guess what? Uncle Nathan took me over to the Borough Market, it was great."

Eddie ushered us away from the gates. "Come on, we'd better get away from here before the teacher sees you. Anyway, Nan likes us to go straight home." Off we went. I had to turn around! That's when I saw Miss Batone glaring at me. I just looked her in the face, turned away, then followed Eddie and Mike.

We rounded the corner at Melior Place and walked past the Horseshoes Pub. That's when I saw Uncle Nathan's van parked outside our house. Oh shit, I thought. We let ourselves in, that's when I heard what would become a very familiar call. "Paddy!!! Come out here, I want to see you. I'm in the scullery." She sounded very serious! I went straight down the narrow passage and walked into the scullery. Nan was standing over the stove. She gave me that rueful look. She was obviously very mad, but I could feel that she had already forgiven me. She bent down and grabbed me by the shoulders, stating straight into my eyes. I looked straight back at her, blue eyes vs. blue eyes.

"Paddy, you are a very naughty boy. You shouldn't just walk away from school like that. You'll make us all so worried. If I'd have known what you'd done I would have had fifty fits. Promise me that you won't do that again." "I'm sorry, Nan, I wouldn't harm you for the world. I didn't think I was doing anything wrong. I just didn't want to talk to anybody, sorry!" I promised myself there and then that I would never do anything to upset Nan again. She gave me a big hug. "Off you go then, everyone's in the kitchen. Get out of my way now, I'm doing some cooking." "What you cooking Nan?" "Uncle Nathan brought home a nice piece of lamb and a few vegetables, so I'm making a nice lamb stew for tomorrow."

Off I went to the kitchen, thinking "stew!" Nan made a lovely stew. I couldn't wait for tomorrow's dinner, yum, yum! They were all in the kitchen—Granddad, Aunt Anne, Uncle Nathan who gave me a sly wink, Eileen and Johnny. Eddie and Michael were sitting at the table, eating what looked like chocolate. Where on earth did they get that from? "Look what Uncle Nathan's given us!" Michael piped up, all smiles.

"There's none for you, my son, you've already had your treat today." Uncle Nathan looked around, waited a few moments for that remark to settle in. Then smiled, dug into his jacket pocket and threw me a large piece of chocolate. I caught it greedily and smiled at everyone. "Thanks Unc." Running through my mind was "How does he do it? Where does he get all these things from?" I'd have to find out.

We didn't bother going out. It was always interesting when the adults were together. In spite of all the terrible things that were taking place all around, there was always laughing and joking. Another thing was the constant flow of visitors, various relatives and friends, who mostly seemed to be nice people.

Eventually, we had some tea. "Dad, fancy a pint?" Nathan glanced over to Granddad. "Now that's a great idea, let's get me coat and hat." Granddad popped into the scullery and I heard him tell Nan that he was going for a couple of pints. As they were leaving, Eddie said "Can we come with you and play for a while out front?" "If Nan says it's ok, then yes, you can." Eddie dashed in to ask Nan. He came rushing out. "Yeah, it's ok, but only for a short while. What about you, Mike? Do you fancy it?" "No thanks, Ed, I'm playing with Johnny." They were building a wooden aeroplane, so off we scampered.

The pub was, literally, only a few yards away, and it was at the end of a cul-de-sac, with a decent area in front. Eddie poked his head through the pub doors, and called out to Granddad to ask if we could have a lemonade or tizer. I loved peering into pubs, there always seemed to be a mystery about the place. Maybe it was because we weren't allowed in. Also, there was always a buzz going on, sometimes the piano would be playing, with lots of laughter, and now and again, a singer. Tonight, however, it wasn't that busy, I suppose it was a bit early.

Granddad came out with a couple of tizers and a biscuit apiece. "Here you go boys, get that down you, and once you've finished you'd better get back home. It'll be getting dark soon. We don't want to get Nan worried, do we?" He held on to my glass of tizer as he said that! "Thanks Granddad, we will. I'll shout you when we've finished so that you can take the glasses back." "Good lad, Eddie." We didn't rush ourselves, but eventually Eddie returned our empty glasses and off we went.

"You going to stay in school tomorrow?" "Yeah, I promised Nan! It's not that I don't like the school Ed, it's just that when Dad went away I wasn't very happy, and I just didn't want anybody around me. I don't mean you, of course. I didn't want to mix with anybody else." "I understand. I would have probably come with you, but I had to make sure Michael was ok." I didn't think of things like that.

We could hear the comforting and warm noises coming from Nan's kitchen. As we appeared, Nan said "Had a nice time, have you?" We both smiled and nodded. Mike and Johnny were getting on really well with their aeroplane, it was actually beginning to take shape. Even at his young age, Michael was very good with his hands, I think better than Johnny.

We hadn't been in long when the blasted air raid siren started. God, they were even earlier tonight! "Shall we have a wash and get in our pyjamas, Nan?" "Not tonight, Eddie, there's not enough time. Nip upstairs and make sure all the curtains are drawn tight, and make sure the windows are closed. John, clear that away quickly, and help Eddie." "I'll make sure your front room curtains are closed properly, Mum." I'd forgotten that Aunt Anne was still here.

There was a rat-a-tat-tat at the front door. Eileen went to look. It was the air raid warden asking if everything was alright. They always checked to see if you were going to the arches, and, if you were, to give a hand if necessary. "Thanks, Albert, but we're all ok." The next minute the front door flew open and in dashed Granddad and Nathan. "Hurry up, get under those stairs, and Anne, you'll have to squeeze in as well." It's a big raid tonight, there's lots of bombers coming over. We could hear them as they were coming down the street. But don't worry, you're all safe in your little cubby hole. I'm going to close the door now."

He wasn't making it up, when he said it was a big one. The windows were rattling and the whole house was shaking. We snuggled up close to each other, and for the first time, I could hear Nan actually praying, with her photo of the Pope right beside her and Michael. Eileen gripped me as hard as she could. I couldn't see Eddie and Aunt Anne. I could feel them through.

That night the bombers were dropping very close, I could hear the thuds and feel the tremors, but they weren't that close. Certainly not on top of us. I must have dozed off, but, even as I awoke, the air raid was still going on! It was a terrible night. At last, the all clear. We were safe. The strain on Nan and Granddad's faces was clear to see. I don't think that having to look after us three was that good for them, but they certainly coped.

Nathan popped out to check on his van. As he came back in, he said "Just a bit of dust on the old girl, no damage." "What's it like outside, Nath?" "They must have missed our little area, but someone local must have got it. I can smell the smoke."

There wasn't any point in going to bed, because it would have been time to get up soon. "Boys, have yourselves a wash and I'll start cooking you some breakfast. Johnny, in a short while I want you to pop over to the boys' school (which incidentally was still Johnny's school, he wasn't 14 yet) and find out if there will be any lessons today. That bombing last night was very close."

"We'll be on our way home in a minute, Mum" Aunt Anne said, whilst bringing in a pot of tea. I learnt at a very young age that, whatever the occasion, tea was always on the go! "The water tap's not working, Nan," Eddie said, whilst leaning over the sink. "It must have been cut off! Johnny, take that bucket, and nip over to Weston Street Arch. If they have cut the water off, they usually have a tanker standing by." He dashed out straight away. "We'll wait until he gets back, before going home, Mum. Nathan might be able to sort something out if needed."

We didn't wash, but Nan had made our Quaker Oats, so we sat down and gobbled our breakfast. Like kids today, washing was not high on our list of things to do. "Here you are Mum. You were right, the water has run out and they don't know when it will be back on. They used all the water, trying to stop the fires last night. The A.R.P. told me that they dropped a lot of incendiary bombs, and set the City alight."

He handed Nan a full bucket of water. "Come here boys" Nan said. She had poured a little of the water into a bowl and then dipped a flannel and soap into it. She then proceeded, one by one, to wash our hands and faces. "It's a cat's lick today, boys, I can't spare too much water. We don't know when we'll get any more."

Annie and Nathan went home. "I'll call back later this afternoon Mum, and see how you're getting on" Anne called out as she left. Johnny came back in. "The school's open, Mum, but only until dinnertime. I think it's to do with the water shortage." I thought "Lovely, only a half day, and the smell of Nan's stew spread all around our little house."

Granddad suddenly said "After you've had your dinner, I'll take you boys out for a walk. I want to go up to London Bridge, so you can come with me." "Yes, please Granddad" we all chorused. Off to school we went.

"I want to talk to you, Paddy." Miss Batone picked me out as soon as I walked into the playground. "I know that you have had a very bad time lately, but you can't just hop off from school whenever you feel like it. If you have any problems, please come and talk to me. I'm sure that I'll be able to help you. Are you alright with that? And do you understand what I am saying?" "Yes, Miss." I wasn't too worried about her, or the school for that matter, but she was a very nice kind person, so I was nice to her. However, I thought "I don't need your help, and if I don't fancy school, then I'll hop the wag[5]." She patted me very tenderly on my head, and told me to run away and play. That was the end of that. Morning soon passed. We were told that there had been a very serious air raid last night, and that the City had been badly damaged.

Nan's stew was indeed delicious, and we made pigs of ourselves. Nan liked us to eat big massive dinners, and we certainly didn't let her down. "Ready, boys?" Granddad has his coat and cap on. "Can you spare some crusts for the boys, so that they can feed the pigeons?" "Well, only a little bit, I am going to make a bread pudding with any stale bread, but I'll try and find some." Nan gave Eddie a small bag with some pieces of crusts. "Off you go, and enjoy yourselves, but stay close to Granddad. No running off."

We were walking up St. Thomas Street, all close together as instructed. There was lots of activity. There was a water tanker on the corner of Weston Street, with a long queue of women and children, all carrying various buckets and containers. They looked a sorry bunch, but then again I suppose we didn't look all that bright, either. We turned into Borough High Street, and it was then that I could smell the smoke, and what I now know was the smell of cordite and TNT. We were now at the corner of Duke Street Hill and London Bridge itself. There was a sight, that I had never seen before, or since, thankfully! There, in full view of St. Paul's Cathedral, at least half of the warehouses and office blocks were just piles of rubble, some still smoking. Cannon Street station had been almost obliterated. It was carnage and chaos. We all just stood and looked, it was an amazing sight.

Police were stopping anyone going over the bridge. The fire engines were all standing about, with the odd ambulance dashing by. "Come on boys, get that bread out, and let's feed the birds." It will always amaze me that, with all this going on, as soon as Eddie opened the bag of bread, hoards of pigeons swooped around us. The birds were not aware of, nor cared about, any silly old war. For them, life carried on as normal.

Michael was squealing with delight as the birds took bread out of his hand. I, on the other hand, was doing my best to catch one of the birds. No chance! Granddad was chatting to the two paper sellers. They had a pitch on the corner of Duke Street Hill. I noticed, as usual, one man had an arm missing, though not all of it, because he had a bunch of newspapers tucked under something. The other man was in a wheelchair. They were chatting and pointing. Granddad seemed to know them very well. The man is the wheelchair suddenly called out to Eddie and beckoned him to come over. I noticed that he put something in Eddie's hand.

The bread was all gone. "Come on boys, let's be getting away." We followed Granddad down the hill until we came to a pub, called Moonies. "I'm just popping in for a pint. Don't go away and don't run into the street." In he went. Very shortly a man we didn't know came out with three glasses of tizer and three packets of crisps. "Here you are lads, get this down ya." We thanked him and set about removing the little packets of salt that were in every crisp packet. Duly salted the crisps, and then munched our way through them, at the same time drinking our tizer.

The pub door opened, and another man came out, we didn't know him either. "You look like the eldest, here son, take this." He put a couple of pieces of silver into Eddie's hand. He patted him on the head, smiled at us all and disappeared back into the pub. There was someone playing the piano, I could hear it each time the door opened. What mystery!

Granddad came out after a short while. "Give me your glasses, boys, I'll pop them back into the pub, then we'll be off." He was out straight away. "Granddad, those men gave me lots of money, why do they do that?" "It's because they are old friends of mine, and they are kind and generous people. You know it's for sharing, don't you Eddie?" "Yes, I do. I'll share it out once we get home."

In Spite of Everything . . . .

We made our way down the hill, then into Tooley Street, past the bottom end of Stainer Street, which was all boarded up. Granddad was careful not to have taken us past the other bombed out end. I don't think he ever walked past it for the rest of his life.

What was amazing, was, how little damage had been suffered by the dock and warehouses lining Tooley Street. This was known as the Pool of London. I suppose it was because big ships could go no further than London Bridge and Tower Bridge had to be raised, so that large cargo ships could get into this area of the river. When you compared it to what had gone on north of the river, it was nothing short of a miracle. I would have thought that the Germans would have concentrated on destroying the great iconic landmark that was Tower Bridge, which incidentally, most foreigners actually think is indeed London Bridge. But they didn't.

Tooley Street was busy and bustling, with a great number of horse and carts, as well as petrol powered lorries. Granddad seemed to know most of the dockers who were milling about. When we arrived at Bermondsey Street we headed off home. "That's where we go sometimes, Granddad" said Eddie, as we came upon Vinegar Yard. "Will you take us down to where the horses are having their shoes put on?" I asked, smelling that unmistakable odour. "Yes, certainly, but we mustn't be a nuisance. Old Albert is a friend of mine, so he won't mind."

Albert was indeed busy. He smiled and waved at us. "Brought your boys round to see me, have you Pats? They're good lads, no trouble at all. Are you going to have a pint later?" "Yeah, see you later. We'll be off now, out of your way." We all slowly trundled off home. It had been an interesting afternoon.

"Where did you get all that silver from, Eddie?" "Some of Granddad's friends gave it to us, Nan." She took it off him, and started counting. "My, you've got six shillings here, you are very lucky, I hope you said thank you." "Yes, we did, Nan" we all chorused. "I'll take care of it for you, I don't want you going out wasting it on a lot of junk. If you need any money, just ask me. Do you all understand?" "Yes, Nan!" We already knew that we could trust her.

Thankfully the water had been turned on, but it was only a dribble. We were told to pee in the garden and only use the toilet for number 2s. Eileen and Johnny soon came in, and Granddad popped out, to the pub, I suppose! "You've just missed Annie." Nan was talking to Eileen. "They showed their faces, but, as the water was back on, they didn't hang about. She said she would see you tomorrow." Same old routine!

Just as we all got settled, the air raid siren went off. Huddled together again. This night the main raid was quite a way off. It sounded ferocious. Eventually the all clear! We managed to get some sleep in bed!

The next few days went by without any major incidents as far as our little area was concerned. But there was no let up! Water was short, and the gas kept going off. We had gas lighting in our house. There were these very fragile mantles that was our only form of light. It was always very dingy. Luckily Nan did all her cooking and washing on a solid fuel range and boiler. We mostly used coke, only using coal to get the fire started. Remember, all this fuel was rationed, and scarce.

Granddad showed me how to get a fire started. I loved doing it, so it became my job. I used to get a lovely little fire going in our little kitchen. It made it very warm and cosy. The nights were drawing in fast.

The warning siren wailed. I didn't know it then, but my life was about to take another defining twist.

"Hurry up Anne, get yourselves into your cupboard. Don't forget to take a drink in with you." Granddad was fussing about. "Johnny, quickly make sure that all the curtains are pulled tight, and turn those gas mantles off." With bombs likely to be falling around you, it was essential to make sure the gas was off!

In Spite of Everything . . . .

The stamping and screaming of the horses got louder, but, more seriously, so did the sound of aircraft. That strange throbbing sound was making everything shake. Boom, bang, crash. The noise was all around us. Then came enormous explosions. The house shook. The back windows blew in and there was a terrible crashing noise upstairs. Our little cubby hole shook. It was as though some giant had us in his hands, and was shaking us.

Nan's beautiful glass plates and ornaments came crashing to the floor. The noise was frightening. We huddled together, and, for the first time, I was very frightened. We were covered in dust, coughing and spluttering, totally helpless. The bombs were still exploding all round us. I thought it would never stop, and that we would all end up like Mum and Aunt Mary.

It felt like it had gone on for hours. Suddenly the door was dragged open. Granddad was standing, holding an oil lamp. He looked like a ghost, covered in brick dust. "Thank God! You're all safe and sound in there." I then noticed Johnny standing behind him. "We've got to get out of the house smartish. Come on boys, and you, Eileen, mind the debris as you come through the passage, quick now."

As we crawled out, I saw the damage to our house, I think part of the chimney had collapsed. There was bricks and plaster all over the place. Granddad had the front door open, and since it was now getting light, I could see the total carnage in the street. Added to the mayhem out front, I could now hear the terrible din coming from the stables behind us. Those poor horses.

There were fire engines charging around, their bells clanging frantically, police, fire wardens, some soldiers and civilians. What a sight. The remaining warehouse had now virtually disappeared, still a smouldering ruin. Then, as we were herded towards the Weston Street arches, we hurried past where no.9 and no.11 had been, just a pile of ruins and, even more startling, the warehouses at the front of Vinegar Yard were a pile of burnt out ruins. Although our house was badly damaged, we were probably saved by the large wall that backed on to us, where the farrier and stores once were. It had been a very close call. I think Nan's praying with her rosary might just have helped. She thought so anyway, so that was good enough.

The arches were packed with people. Most covered in dirt and dust. Some had blood on them, and there were nurses and doctors bandaging many people. The noise was deafening. The Salvation Army had a tea and cake canteen going full pelt, and Nan soon had us sitting down on canvas beds, with a warm cup of tea and large lumps of fruitcake. I thought this was really exciting!

"Where's Granddad and Johnny, Nan?" Eddie asked once we were settled down. "Oh, they've both gone to help the fire and ambulance crews. There has been a terrible amount of damage last night, so they need all the help they can get."

With that, Nan went over to where there was a large group, of mainly women. They were all talking in an excited way, first pointing this way and then in another direction. They mostly looked in total despair. Some of them were crying, and being comforted by others. It was a really desperate scene.

Some very nice, well spoken ladies, came over to us and asked Eileen if we needed anything. Eileen asked if it was possible to get hold of some blankets, since it was quite chilly and damp under the arches.

They wanted to know who was looking after us. Eileen pointed out Nan. They said goodbye and headed over to Nan. Very shortly a Salvation Army man dropped off a few blankets, which we quickly wrapped around ourselves. "That's better" I thought.

Nan eventually came back to us. "I don't know when, or even if, we can get back home. It's too dangerous to go outside yet, we will have to stay here for a while. Do you boys feel hungry?" "Yes Nan" we all called out together. "Does that mean that we don't have to go to school?" She smiled "No, not today Paddy, has that made you feel happy?" I grinned back at her. You bet it had.

In Spite of Everything . . . .

I thought "What happens now?" There seemed to be this continuing uncertainty. It was very disturbing. Nan came back with a plateful of hot sausage rolls. I had never tasted anything like them before. "What are these sausages, Nan?" "They are called saveloys, why, don't you like them?" "No, I don't mean that, Nan, they're lovely." They were very tasty! Certainly a different kind of breakfast than we were used to.

Suddenly Aunt Anne appeared. Upon seeing her, and only for an instant, thoughts of my Mum. It was as though someone had stuck a sharp knife into me. Then it was gone. Her face lit up once she'd seen Eileen and us three all huddled together. She spied Nan at the same time. She hurried over to her and they hugged. Of course, they had tears. As they approached us I could hear her saying that they knew that our area of London had been badly bombed, so they had rushed over as soon as the all clear had sounded. Nathan and a couple of his mates had also come over, in case they could be any help. Aunt Anne gave us all a big hug. She was very happy to see us, knowing that we were safe and well. They (Nan, Annie and Eileen) were all in deep conversation. Suddenly, Nan looked over to us. "Boys, I want you to stay here a bit longer, Eileen will stay with you. Me and Aunt Anne are going home to see what state it's in. I'll be back soon, so behave yourselves and don't annoy Eileen too much." That would have been hard to do, she was an angel!

It didn't seem that long before Nan came back. This time Johnny was with her. He looked a mess, covered in soot and dust. There was blood on his hands, they were cut to pieces. He went over to the first aid post and they immediately started clearing him up. The bandages and tape soon appeared. He looked over at us, shrugged his shoulders and smiled, well almost!

"The roads are a bit clearer now boys, so I'm taking you back home. You might as well know now, however, that we won't be able to live there anymore." Shit, I thought, here we go again, where the fuck are we going to live now? I was getting seriously pissed off!

Nan, ever watchful, must have noticed the expression on my face. "Don't worry Paddy, everything has been taken care of. We are all going to live together, so please don't worry, and that goes for all three of you. This will put a smile back on your face—no school for a while!"

That certainly brightened things up! As we all trooped out of the shelter, Eddie said "What about these blankets, Nan?" "Oh, don't worry Eddie, someone will bring them back, once we have all finished with them."

It was a frenetic and chaotic scene that we faced. The rubble from the roads had been mostly pushed in piles to either side by a small army of volunteers and professionals. The dust hung around like a fog, with the now all too familiar smells. We could see directly over to the stables. That was indeed carnage! Some of the horses must have been killed. Although, their side of Vinegar Yard hadn't actually been hit. Damaged maybe, but still standing. The few windows had obviously been blown in, but otherwise ok. That's indeed what saved us. We soon appeared at our house, and it didn't seem that bad to me. Granddad was outside with some other men. Other than Uncle Nathan, I knew none of them, or thought I didn't, until I noticed a man who had been chatting to Uncle Nathan in the Borough Market the other week.

"Are some of the horses dead, Granddad?" I asked, as we got closer. "Yes, unfortunately son." "But the bombs never dropped on them, did they, so what killed them?" "You do ask a lot of questions, don't you Paddy? Well, I'll explain. Apparently, in their blind panic, a few horses got free of their stalls and I think they actually kicked each other to death. They must have been in a right state. You happy now? I've got more things to worry about than a few fucking horses!" Nan gave him a real dirty look, but I think he really did have more on his plate. That satisfied me anyway.

"Go into the front room boys" Nan instructed us. It was quite amazing because the front of the house was hardly scratched, but as we entered the passageway, what a mess! There was a great mass of bricks lying on the staircase, a big hole in the roof above and the scullery, at the back, was virtually split in two. I was thinking that it was a good job

In Spite of Everything . . . .

that our Dad had made that strong shelter for us. I think we might have been in trouble if he hadn't.

The men had climbed up the stairs and were in the bedrooms. They were trying to salvage as much as they could. "Johnny, get as much of the boys' clothing as you can, will you? If you take everything to the front, you can drop it out of the front window. But for gawd's sake, be careful." Uncle Nathan and his mates were up there as well. The old house was now very draughty and a bit creaky.

In no time at all, Nan had us dressed and tidied up. "Granddad has gone over to the police station, because he knows they will have a telephone that works. He is calling Aunt Sarah's neighbour, she's got a telephone in her house and has kindly said that we can call her, so that we can get a message to Aunt Sarah whenever necessary." I knew those people were rich, but I never knew anybody who actually had a telephone. I was thinking that I'd never used a phone, and didn't know how! What a change from today!

There was bashing and crashing coming from the upstairs rooms, I think they were moving whatever they could into the front of the house. Nan was looking at all the broken glass plates and ornaments. They had been collected over the years, to celebrate Queen Victoria's Golden Jubilee, and various coronations and marriages. Poor Nan, she was in tears. Eileen and Anne were comforting her she looked very sad. Now, I don't know why, and I could never understand it, but I was so angry. There was a rage inside of me that almost drove me mad. I didn't like to see Nan cry, and for some strange reason I got very agitated. "It's alright Paddy, calm down, everything will turn out OK, you'll see." That was Eddie, but he looked upset too!

Granddad turned up at the front door. "I've managed to get a message to Sarah, firstly to let her know we're all alright, and to arrange for the boys, Eileen and Johnny to go down there today, as long as the trains are running."

"So that's what's happening! Why ain't you coming with us Nan?" I blurted out immediately, not very happy at all! "Don't worry Paddy.

Granddad and me have got to find a new place to live. We can't live here anymore. You can see that, can't you?" "Well, how long have we got to stay with Aunt Sarah then" I asked.

Nan could tell that I wasn't too pleased about the arrangements. She could read me like a book. She just smiled and said "It won't be long. You like it in the country anyway. You'll all have a good time and it will be nice to get you all away from all this." She spread her arms out and looked around.

I just didn't like all this uncertainty. We were soon packed and ready to go. We didn't have a great deal, anyway. A couple of Nathan's mates said they would go with us to the Elephant & Castle railway station.

"Eddie, make sure you take care of Michael, and Paddy, be good for Aunt Sarah." "Don't worry, Mum, I'll see that they will be alright." With that, Eileen took hold of Michael's hand, and we were off. We had to go down Weston Street, because the whole of Maize Pond had been obliterated. The water mains had been smashed, and I presume the sewage as well. There was water everywhere. As you can understand, at my age I didn't even know about sewage and such things. However, it all added to the smells and general mayhem.

"We've got a two hour wait for the next train, boys. But at least they are providing a service." "Eileen! There's a cafe round the corner. If you like I'll treat you and the lads to a drink and a sandwich, or some cake." Uncle Nathan's mate smiled at us with that remark. "They make a really good bread puddin', fancy that John?" We were on our way in a flash! Eileen spoke to the porter before we left, I think to let him know what we were doing. What a day! And night I suppose!

Sarah and Cousin Dave. They waved and Davey dashed up to our carriage. He was definitely pleased to see us. As we made our way to Davey's house, Eileen was giving Aunt Sarah all the news and giving the details of last night's raid. Funny, but it all seemed so far away and strange. This place was as though there wasn't even a war on. The only sign being, they had to observe the blackout, like everybody else. It was so peaceful.

In Spite of Everything . . . .

"How long are you going to stay, Ed?" "We don't know. No doubt we'll find out soon enough. I don't worry about it, not like him." He glanced over to me. "I just don't like being fucked about." "Paddy!!! Enough of that!" "Sorry Aunt Sarah, it just slipped out, sorry!" Oops, I thought, what did Nan say?!

In the event, we had a nice few days. I was geeing Johnny up, telling him about the pikeys, but they had gone. I would have liked to have seen Johnny taking them apart. He was a tough bastard!

We got back to Aunt Sarah's after an afternoon playing and larking about. Much to my surprise, she had let me have my precious jack knife, so obviously, I had a lovely big stick!

"Granddad's been in touch and they have been given a new house to live in. There's a bit of work to be done, and any salvaged furniture to be moved. Johnny's going home straight away, to give a hand, and we should be going in a couple of days. What do you think of that, then?" "Yeah, yippee!" we all shouted. I don't know why, since it was fantastic staying here. But you know what kids are like! "I imagine Nan will be happy, and no doubt also be happy to see you boys, and of course, you Eileen." "Thanks for looking after us Sarah." "Anytime, anytime, Eileen. You know that you are always welcome."

"Tea's ready!" We didn't need a second call. We were at the table in a flash. "I think you should at least give your hands a wash before eating your tea." She was a fusspot, was that Aunt Sarah.

"Once you have eaten your breakfast, say goodbye to Davey, Maureen and Terry, because I've received a message from Granddad. He's coming down this morning sometime, and you are all going home to your new house. Granddad said that it was much bigger than your old one. Will you make sure, Eileen, that you've got all the boys clothes and things? Paddy, that jack knife please!"

I thought she would have forgotten about my knife. "Please, Auntie, can't I take it home with me? I promise that I'll behave." "Sorry Paddy, your Dad left me with strict instructions that you mustn't take it with you from this house. Hand it over!" Yeah, I thought, my Dad's pissed off somewhere and left me and my brothers, what right had he got to lay down the law? However, I had promised Nan that I would behave myself. I fished in my pocket, which had plenty of stones in it (I loved throwing stones). "Here you are Auntie, make sure you look after it, won't you!" She took my precious knife and gave me a sarcastic smile.

"Can we go out and play?" Eddie asked. "Yes, but don't go away, remember Granddad will be here shortly." We just mucked about in the street and in the front garden. Michael found plenty of snails to play with. Eddie and me played with a tennis ball, just chucking it at each other. Then we thought of a good game. I went into the back garden and Eddie stood in the street. We threw the ball to each other, over the house. That was fun.

"I think I can see Granddad down the end of the street" Eddie suddenly shouted. I dashed out into the road. Sure enough, our Granddad was getting closer and closer. He had a kind of saucy gait, and he walked quite fast. Totally dressed in black, as usual. Even his flat cap. He waved at us.

"Nice to see you, boys. Been behaving yourselves, have you? Not driving your Aunt round the bend?" "No, honest Granddad" Eddie replied. Michael ran and jumped all over him. "Nice to see you Mikey, what you got?" "Only some snails, Granddad." He ignored me, but then he did that sometimes. I didn't give a fuck! "Ain't you happy to see me Paddy?" It must have been the way I looked. I didn't mean any harm. "Yeah, not 'arf. We've got a new house, ain't we?" "Yes, you'll like it. Lots of rooms and, above some shops." I thought "That sounds interesting." I couldn't wait to get back to London. Now how silly was that? Swapping the peaceful country for war torn London. But, it sounded exciting.

We all piled indoors. Granddad gave Eileen and Sarah both a hug and a kiss. Obviously they were all glad to see each other. "What's it like Dad?" said Eileen. "Oh, I think you'll like it, six bedrooms and two kitchens, and right above the shops, with Bermondsey Street market opposite. Nathan and his pals have been a great help. They managed

In Spite of Everything . . . .

to salvage quite a lot, and the council have given us beds and crockery, so we will be quite comfortable. Mum will be pleased to see you!" A slight hesitation. "And the boys, of course!" Then he grabbed hold of his favourite, Michael, but he was the youngest, so I didn't mind a bit. To be really honest, my Nan made a fuss of me anyway, and so did Eileen. That was enough for me.

"I'm sorry Sarah, but we'll have to hurry. The trains are barely running, and we must get home before it starts getting dark. You ready, boys?" "Yes, Dad" said Eileen. Aunt Sarah walked with us to the station and she asked Granddad to try and keep in touch. That wasn't easy to do, in those days. There were public phone boxes, but a lot had been damaged and didn't work. He asked her to thank her neighbour, saying that he was sorry that he hadn't seen her himself. He promised to keep in touch.

We had a long, boring wait for the train, but it eventually turned up. Kisses and hugs, frantic waving out of the train window, and we were off. Another new phase of my life! It didn't take that long to get to our station, Elephant and Castle. We dashed down the stairs, with Granddad frantically calling for us to slow down and wait for him. Shouting at us not to run in the road. We didn't!

"Well, boys, let's cross the road, because we are going to catch a bus." What excitement! "Can we go upstairs, Granddad?" said Eddie, our spokesman. "Yes, of course you can! But wait till the bus gets here first." "What number bus is it?" Eddie again! "Believe it or not, no.1!" I thought he was pulling our legs, but we wasn't. What about that, I thought, the first bus! There it was, a no.1 came into view, and we all scrambled aboard, dashing upstairs immediately. Then, luckily, because the bus wasn't full, right up the front we went. Eileen and Granddad followed, struggling with a couple of suitcases. Off we went. A lady bus conductor turned up, and Granddad bought a couple of tickets. He didn't have to pay for us. I didn't know if we went free, but the lady didn't seem to bother. There was a war on, remember!

Chapter 2

"There it is!" Granddad was pointing at the shops in Tower Bridge Road. "There, above those two shops." Granddad pushed the bell, and down the stairs we all scrambled. We hadn't been on the pavement more than a couple of moments when, from behind the shops, appeared Aunt Anne, waving and shouting at us from across the road. There was quite a bit of traffic. It was a main road after all. And there were hundreds of market stalls, for as far as I could see. It was bustling! It turned out that Nan and Aunt Anne had been looking out of the front windows, waiting for us to show up. Eventually we crossed the road. "Come on, this way" she said. We followed and passed two paper sellers on the corner who shouted out to Granddad. There was an alleyway that ran behind the shops, and then to our front door.

Nan and Johnny were waiting for us. Nan's smile was a picture in itself. She was so pleased to see us again. She grabbed us and pulled us close to her. I didn't think that she was ever going to let us go! "Come on, up you all come."

After entering the front door, there was a steep flight of stairs, once up them, there were three rooms off the landing and yet another four steps going off to the right. Turning left were yet another flight of stairs, and they took you up to a mirror image of the floor we were now standing on. We followed Nan up the four stairs and there was a large kitchen, with a toilet next to it. An inside toilet, what luxury!

In Spite of Everything . . . .

The kitchen had Nan's big old table standing in the middle, with half a dozen wooden chairs around it. They had managed to salvage a great deal. Another feature was electric lights. No more gas mantles, and the dinghy light they provided. Things were looking up!

"Come on now, boys, I'll show you the upstairs, and your bedroom." We followed Nan up the stairs. Another landing, three rooms and another kitchen. This kitchen was empty, though. She opened the corner door, opposite the banisters, and there was our big bedroom. Our old bed was sitting there, and there was also a smaller bed in the corner.

"Paddy, I thought you could have that single bed, as long as it's alright with you. I think that Eddie will be better sharing with Michael. You know that he can look after him, much better than you. But" she turned to face me "if you are not happy, you can all sleep together. Whatever you want! Do you understand? I just thought you might be more comfortable sleeping in your own bed. Please, understand, it's entirely up to you." I thought it was a great idea. My own little bed. I smiled at Nan. "Thanks, Nan, it's the best idea ever, honest."

I thought that I'd have to explain to Eddie, later, that I wasn't having a go at him, or Michael. That was settled then. We actually had two sets of windows in our bedroom, and they looked over Tower Bridge Road, where we could see all the market stalls. How brilliant was that!

We soon got settled in, exploring our new house. Johnny had the bedroom next to ours, the other one was empty, just like the other kitchen, but we had our own toilet. Nan and Granddad's bedroom was directly below us, with Eileen's next to them.

Nan had made the lower spare room into what she had before we came on the scene (a front room). They had salvaged the piano (how they got that up those stairs, I couldn't imagine) and some nice old furniture, although there were gaps, and of course, all her lovely glassware was gone forever.

Nan soon had our tea ready, I'd forgotten how hungry I was. We made short work of our tea, in our lovely new kitchen. We seemed to have so much more space. There was a great big fire grate, and even though Nan now had a large cooker in the corner, the grate also had a couple of hobs and an oven.

Then, just as we were about to settle down for the evening, the air raid sirens started to wail, and off we went again! We were in for a bit of a surprise. Obviously the arrangements had already been made. Nan told us to hurry up and make sure we had an outdoor coat on and had our gas masks with us. Then off we all went, following Granddad who was fussing about as usual, down the stairs and out into our alleyway. There was a door open to the right of ours, and an elderly couple were waiting for us.

"Come on, children, quickly now, in you come." The lady, who I was later to know as Kit, was speaking to us. I noticed straight away that she had a funny accent. In we all went. We were in a large room which had some chairs and a couple of sofas, plus big piles of boxes. There were no windows in this room at all. I found out later that it was the storeroom for the front shops.

"Hurry up, and make sure you close the door tightly behind you. They do come down here and make sure there's no light showing." That was the man talking to my Granddad. He also had an odd accent. His name turned out to be Michael. So we had two of them in the room.

"Now please make yourselves comfortable. Would anybody like a cup of tea?" said Kit. They were very friendly people and she soon began to fuss over us. She actually had some lemonade and cake. I took an instant liking towards her. This certainly was the best air raid shelter I'd ever been in.

That night went by very peacefully. We were now a few miles away from the river, and although we could still hear the muffled sound of explosions, combined with the sound of fire engines and ambulances, I suppose because we were now on a main road, I soon made myself comfortable on one of the sofas, snuggled up next to Eileen, and fell asleep.

In Spite of Everything . . . .

"Come on, sleepyhead, we can go home now and get you into bed." Eileen helped me up and we were soon in our new bedroom, and in a new bed. I was asleep again, almost immediately. I woke up to the sound of trams clunking by and buses, and almost every kind of transport you could imagine. It took a few seconds to work out where I was. Eddie and Michael were still asleep, that was until I had run to one of the windows and started describing things to them.

It was a magical scene. Most of the market stalls were already in place. It was very busy. It came into my mind once again, how people seemed to get on with their lives in spite of what was going on, amazing!

Nan must have heard us, because she called up the stairs, telling us to come down to the kitchen, breakfast was ready. Down the stairs I scrambled, two at a time, and dashed into the kitchen. "Paddy, take your time coming down those stairs, you'll break your neck if you're not careful." Nan's always seemed to worry about something! There on the cooker was a great big pot of porridge oats, nicely steaming away. I loved my porridge! She told us where to sit, and immediately filled up three bowls. They were big bowls, and Nan expected us to finish them all up. She did however give Michael a smaller portion.

"Once you have finished breakfast, I want you all to use the upstairs toilet and wash basin. Eileen is using the one down here. Get washed and dressed because I'm going to take you to school. One of the reasons is to show you the way, and the other is to make sure they are open." Ugh, I thought. I don't know why, but I wasn't expecting the school to be open and I had thought that we might change schools, now that we had moved away. I should have realised that there weren't that many Catholic schools around. Nan brought up a big kettle of hot water for us to wash in. We only had cold water taps, so the hot helped a great deal.

"Michael, hold my hand, Eddie, make sure you hold on to him. Paddy, don't let go of Eddie's hand until we are on the opposite pavement." With that, Nan led us across the busy Tower Bridge Road. Off to school we went. Once we were safely across, Eddie and me dashed in front of Nan and Michael, and off down Bermondsey Street we went. We knew that we were heading towards Snowfields, even though we had never been this far before. "Don't get too far away" Nan called out. After about fifteen minutes, we arrived at the top of Snowfields, and we were soon at our school gates. Sod it, they were open.

Miss Batone was standing at the school gates, and she seemed so happy to see us. She even gave Eddie a little hug. Her and Nan were having a long talk. She was constantly looking in our direction. Soon it was time to line up.

"Now remember, make sure you all leave school together, and stay together all the way home. You know the way don't you, Eddie?" "Yes, Nan, I do. Don't worry, I'll take care of them." Take care of us? He was only a kid himself! But as I've said before, we grew up very quick in those days. "Don't forget, when you get back to the main road, wait there and someone will be there to see you across." "We won't, Nan" we all called out. Then Nan was away, and into school we went.

We were the centre of attraction at play time. Most of the older kids wanted to know how we managed to survive the bombing of the other night. Sadly, there were a few who didn't. It seemed very strange, and almost natural, that people simply disappeared. That awful tragedy, mercifully, didn't register on our young minds.

Dinnertime came, and I made my way to the gates. There was Miss Batone, holding Michael's hand. "Wait here with me, Paddy. Eddie will be here shortly." So that's what they had been talking about. Once Eddie turned up, Miss Batone actually walked with us until we were in Bermondsey Street. Then, and only then, did she let us go on our way. "Take care now, remember what your Nan told you, see you after dinner and don't be late!" She was still a bleeding teacher I thought. It didn't take us long to get to Tower Bridge Road. We stopped on the pavement. There wasn't anybody we knew. "I thought Nan would be here." "Don't worry. Someone will be here in a minute. Hold my hand, Michael." With that, Eddie calmed him.

I then noticed one of the paper sellers, the one with the bad arm, dashing across the road towards us. "Alright boys. I promised

In Spite of Everything . . . .

your Granddad that I would see you across." Well, now I knew the arrangements. He must have been a reliable man. Across the road we scampered, down the alley, pulled the door open and up the stairs we scampered. I could smell our dinner, it was rabbit. The front door system was in operation here too, i.e. the key hanging on a piece of string behind the letterbox. Which was just as well, as it meant that nobody had to keep running up and down the stairs.

"Sit down, boys. You haven't got that much time before you'll have to be back at school. Is everything alright, Eddie? Are you happy with the arrangements?" "What do you mean, Nan?" "Well, the extra journey to school, and you having to look after Paddy and Michael. I realise that you will have less time to play with your mates." "Honest, Nan, that's no problem." "When you come home this afternoon, one of the family will see you across the road. The paper man will have gone. They don't come back until later." With that she gave him a hug. I was jealous!

It didn't take long to scoff our dinner down, and before we knew it, we were back in school. We even had some playtime. The paper man had seen us across, by the way.

End of school, same routine, no time for sky larking, home we went. There, standing on the pavement, was Eileen. She smiled when she saw us, took hold of both Michael and me, and over the road we went. Aunt Anne and Aunt Emma were in the kitchen, and with them were some of our cousins, Sheila, Pat and Jimmy. The place was bedlam. We quickly showed them around our new, enormous house. We now even had our own play room, the empty upstairs kitchen. Even though we didn't have any actual toys, we were still able to play games and enjoy ourselves.

It seemed no time at all before Aunt Emma called up the stairs, ordering our cousins to come down as it was time for them to go home. They lived at Brockley, which was a few miles away, and they needed to be home in case of an air raid. They all left together, Annie catching the no.1 bus to Kennington, and the others catching a bus in the other direction. It was really handy, this new house, the bus stops were all around us.

Very shortly, Granddad came in and sat down reading his paper at his usual place in the kitchen. Every now and again he peered over the top and made a soft "tut tut." I think we were a bit noisy for his liking. Nan always rounded on him, telling him not to be so miserable. As I look back, I can sympathise with him. He thought he'd brought all his family up, and now, he had us three to contend with.

Suddenly there came the cry "Star news, Standard." It was the two paper sellers who had returned to their pitch and were trying to sell their papers. It was a very busy corner and they seemed to be doing very well. "I'm going to make the paper sellers a cup of tea in a minute. Would one of you boys like to take it down to them?" Nan looked straight at Eddie and me. There was no way that I would take anything down to them or anyone else for that matter. Good on you, Eddie! He knew that I would not go on any errands. He immediately volunteered, so that was taken care of. Nan, as she always did, certainly looked after the two sellers, tea and sandwiches. No wonder they didn't mind seeing across the road.

Nan busied herself getting our tea ready and soon, we were all around the table eating bread and jam and homemade cakes. Johnny had come home, so with Eileen and Granddad we had a full kitchen. It was noisy and happy. Things were looking up!

Talk about bringing you back to earth with a bump. The cards had just come out when the wail of the siren went off. Another fucking air raid. I don't know about the others, but I was getting seriously pissed off.

We all slipped into the now well practiced routine. Granddad fussing around, geeing us up to get all the curtains pulled tight, get our heavy coats on, don't forget your gas masks. We always had to have them with us, but, other than practice, we luckily never had to use the horrible things. Now we had electric lights, and not gas as in our old house, we turned all but a couple of lights off.

In Spite of Everything . . . .

I heard that odd sounding voice of Michael calling out. He was telling us to get into the storage room. In no time at all, we were down the stairs and into the storeroom. The sound of bombing and gun fire could already be heard in the distance. The raid didn't seem to last as long as some nights, and the all clear sounded. Maybe they were running out of bombs, or getting fed up, I thought to myself.

We managed to get a reasonable night's sleep in bed. It wasn't long before the road and market outside started bursting into life. Carry on regardless, that definitely seemed to be the motto. We all easily slipped into a daily routine, even managing to meet school mates on our way to school. Every day, however, there seemed to be more and more damage. There were ruins everywhere. The weather was closing in, getting colder and darker. Then, almost as it had first started, the air raids stopped. Apart from a few false alarms, there was no more bombing. We went to bed and slept through the night without being woken up.

It would be Christmas soon, and our lives were becoming very settled. It felt strange, because at first it was difficult to remember before the bombings had started. All I knew, however, was how our lives had been ripped apart, never to be the same ever again. It made me sad and very angry. I suppose, now, remembering as I do, it was a bit of self pity, but I did feel very hard done by!

Nan bought some paper chains (well, let me explain). They weren't chains at all. Just strips of coloured paper, which we stuck and interlinked, using flour and water. They did, however, look quite good and they were certainly Christmassy. Uncle Nathan was round our house all the time, he even managed to get us a small Christmas tree. I think it was actually, a piece of a tree, but Nan decorated it, and it looked good.

Being Catholics, the down side, was the amount of holy events going on at school. I didn't get too involved, if I could possibly help it, but Eddie and Michael loved it. They actually sung in the choir at Church. Eileen got very involved, but luckily Johnny wasn't too keen either and he helped me to get out of most things. There was one job that

I was captured for, and that was manually pumping the big organ at the back of the Church. The cunning priest had found a way of keeping me in Church. I think Nan must have had a twinkle in her eye when she agreed with the priest that it was alright for me to do the job. Well, I fucking hated it. There was a real old fat bastard who was playing the organ, and he was forever yelling at me to keep pumping. I wasn't going to stand this for too long. I put my mind to work!

So what happens if I stop pumping? I didn't understand how the organ worked, but it didn't take me long to work out that if I didn't pump too hard, the old bastard made a right mess of the hymn. That was that then! I fucked them about, like you would never believe. I pumped like mad for a little while, then stopped, then started again, it was a scream. The priest, who was taking choir lessons, came tearing up the stairs. He was raving mad. He couldn't believe that I was unable to understand that I had to keep a steady pumping action in order to keep the pressure up. I played it dumb for a short while, then I started fucking about. There was chaos. The old fat bastard was doing his nut, luckily he didn't realise that he was close to having the pump wrapped around him. Enough of this shit. I just stopped altogether, walked down the stairs and out of the Church, that was their lot!

I waited at the front of the Church. The priest appeared. "Get back there at once! Do you hear me?" I looked him in the eye. "No, Father, no, I will not." He didn't know what to do. He hesitated, stared at me for a few moments, then about turned and went back into the Church.

I heard him talking to Eileen. "That child is out of control and completely impossible!" "In actual fact, Father," I could hear Eileen's voice, "he's a very nice boy! But if he doesn't want to do something, nothing will change his mind. I'll go out and have a talk to him."

I thought, good old Eileen, she'll stick up for me. Eileen appeared. She tried very hard to look angry, which was impossible as she had the face of an angel. She could hardly stop herself from laughing. "Oh, Paddy, what are we going to do with you?" "Well, one thing's certain, Eileen, I'm not going back in that Church to pump that fucking organ." She gave me a soft clip on the head. "Now, don't get excited and stop that language, Nan would kill you if she heard you. Look, you are still in part of the Church." "Sorry, Eileen, I didn't want to cause any trouble, I'd just had enough. I don't know what came over me." "Oh, OK, don't worry. You'll have to come back in Church and just sit at the back, and be quiet. I'll let the priest know what's going on. He, or anyone else, won't bother you, I promise."

We went back in, and I did as Eileen has asked. The choir sounded quite good and I'm sure I could hear Eddie's voice above all the others. Young Michael was standing in the front. He looked great.

On our way back home, Eddie, Michael and Eileen were all laughing about the organ. Eddie said that he didn't know how he'd stopped himself from collapsing with laughter. He'd actually sussed that I was mucking about. "When the organ actually stopped, I said to one of my mates 'I bet Paddy's had enough and probably walked out.'" We all burst into laughter, so the evening had turned out alright.

"You sound like you've all had a nice time" said Nan, as we piled into the kitchen. "There's a few biscuits and cocoa for you boys. Finish it up and start getting ready for bed. You look like you've enjoyed yourself as well, Eileen. What are you smiling about?" "I'll tell you later, Mum!"

Once we'd had a wash and put our pyjamas on, we went down to the kitchen so say goodnight. As we went into the kitchen, Nan gave me an old fashioned look, but she couldn't hide the smile in her eyes. Granddad had his face covered by the newspaper, and I could see it shaking. He daren't look at us.

"I've had a letter from your Dad, and he's getting a few days' leave, which means that he'll be home for Christmas." I could see how happy Eddie and Michael were. It didn't seem to bother me, one way or another. I was quite happy with things as they were.

"Come on, give us a kiss and off to bed with you. Eileen will take you up and tuck you in." Granddad called out "night, night" from behind his paper, and I'm sure he was in tears with laughter. "Do you think there will be an air raid tonight, Nan?" said Eddie, as we were going up the stairs. "Well, I hope not. There hasn't been any for the past few weeks. They may have stopped for Christmas. Now, just go to sleep and stop worrying. Goodnight, God bless, see you in the morning."

Christmas was soon upon us. We'd broken up from school and had plenty of time on our hands. The bombings seemed to have stopped, and most things were getting back to normal. It was great, living where we did, the buzz of the market stalls was really exciting. Eddie and me spent most of our time wandering up and down the Tower Bridge Road, and it didn't take long before most of the stallholders knew who we were. They mostly seemed to be friends of at least one member of our family. It had it's own energy, lovely! We wound up doing little jobs for some of the stallholders, and made a bit of spare pocket money. I was surprised when we came across Michael and Kit, our next door neighbours, who we hadn't seen since the bombings had stopped. They had large stalls and looked very busy, they sold ladies' clothes and shoes, and items of underwear that I have never seen before!

They looked genuinely pleased to see us. "Hello Eddie, hello Paddy, lovely to see you. How's your little brother?" "Nice to see you both, yes, Michael's very good thank you. We've missed you, now that the air raids seemed to have ended" Eddie replied. Kit came from behind the stall and surprised me by giving us both a big hug. "You boys mustn't be strangers, why don't you come up and see us sometime? We would love to see you, but remember, ask your nanna first." "Thank you, yes we will, honest." Then we were off.

We were just going past the wet fish stall, when the man, who we later found out was called Waggie, stopped us. "Your Nan told me to give you these herrings to take home, here you are, get them home as soon as possible." With that he plonked a great package into Eddie's hands. I noticed he had a large bucket full of water, in which there were live eels, wiggling away. He noticed me staring at them. "Ain't you ever seen eels before, son?" said Waggle. "No, I've had jellied eels, but I've never seen them alive." "Watch this, then." A lady had just arrived at his stall and ordered a pound of eels. It was magic. He dipped his hand into the bucket, and using a couple of fingers and his thumb, he yanked out this long slithering eel, placed it on a large wooden block, sliced its head off, slit it down the length of its body and scraped out all the innards, which flopped into another bucket. It stunk a bit, I can tell you! There were a lot of cats hanging about. The eel was still slithering about. He chucked it into an old newspaper and continued until he'd prepared enough for the lady. He wrapped them up, and they were still moving. She paid him and off she went.

I was fascinated. This was indeed a very interesting place to be. We took the herrings home and Nan was pleased to see us. We heard loud footsteps coming down the stairs, and then our Dad appeared. Eddie, as usual, jumped all over him, even though he had Michael on his shoulders. I was pleased to see him and he grabbed hold of me, nearly crushing me at the same time. I don't think he realised just how strong he was. We were all talking together, telling about all our adventures, which made him smile.

"Have you killed any Germans yet, Dad?" I asked eagerly. "You're a bloodthirsty so and so, aren't you! The answer is no, not yet anyway, but if it will make you happy, I intend to, very soon." I couldn't wait! "Come on, boys, I'll take you down the road, and see if we can find any sweets." We didn't need any encouraging. Firstly sweets, like everything else, were rationed, and very scarce. But I was soon to find out that there was a thing called the black market, which meant that if you knew the right people, extras were available, and our family knew the right people!

Half way up Bermondsey Street we came across a small shop. It was owned and run by Italians, and obviously sold ice cream, sometimes. We went in. One of the little fat men from behind the counter came out front and warmly shook Dad by the hand. They laughed and chatted, then they disappeared into the back of the shop. When they returned Dad was holding quite a large bag of various sweets, magic! As we were leaving, the chubby Italian grasped Eddie and me by the shoulders and told us to come in now and again, and he would look after us. We thanked him and left.

Dad gave us all a handful of sweets, and we didn't waste any time polishing them off. "One of your teachers, Miss Batone, is actually their sister. Don't say anything to her about what's gone on here today. It's none of her business anyway." Dad smiled as he told us that. I couldn't have agreed more, it was nobody else's business. Things were looking up, definitely.

As we got to our front door, Dad suddenly looked at me and said "Oh, I forgot to ask, how's your pumping arm?" He had a broad grin on his face. I don't think he expected an answer. I thought that everybody must have had a good laugh at my expense!

Christmas soon came and went. We didn't have many toys, hardly any in fact. Some toy soldiers, jigsaw puzzles and odds and sods. We were lucky. Lots of children weren't even at home and most of those that were, had very little indeed. But that was the norm, so we didn't expect much. We didn't see that much of Dad. He was out and about with Uncle Nathan most of the time. , or with Granddad and sometimes Nan, having a drink in the pub.

There was one important item I had forgotten to mention previously, our cat! When we had been bombed out, Nan's cat had gone missing, and both Granddad and Johnny had returned to the old house. They both, in fact, had seen the cat, called Tabby. How original was that! But they seemed unable to capture it. One day, shortly before Christmas, Granddad had asked Eddie and me if we'd mind going around to try and fetch Tabby. I wasn't interested, because although I would never harm an animal, I couldn't give a rat's arse for any of them. Once Eddie had agreed to go, then I was going with him. Two's better than one! Granddad gave us a coal sack to put the cat in, should we catch it. He also gave us a couple of sacks to wrap up in, reminding us that cats can scratch you very badly, and bite, by the way! Final instructions: get a few fish heads off Waggie, be careful in the old house and, if we were stopped by the police, explain what we were doing. We weren't looters.

Off we went. It felt very strange, getting into our old place. We had to push hard on the front door before it would open. It seemed so odd, standing in our old passageway, what a mess. There was dust, and old wallpaper, and debris, everywhere. It was hard to imagine that it was only a few weeks ago that we had lived here. Hardly any of the windows weren't broken, very odd!

Eddie called out for the cat, then, much to my surprise, there she was, mewing and purring. I made a grab for her. No chance. "Give it a chance, Paddy, don't be too anxious. Anyway, you had better wrap your arms up, like Granddad told you." With that, he put the fish on the floor directly in front of us. He held the coal sack open. I wrapped up! Very slowly, and I mean very, Tabby came towards us. Now, you see, that's why I'm not keen on animals, the fucking time it took. Two steps forward, one step back! She greedily got hold of the fish heads. That was my cue. I made a lunge at her and managed to pin her to the ground. She went berserk, spitting and screaming. She was stronger than I thought, and was very hard to hold down. Wasn't I glad I was very well wrapped up. Luckily, she was her own worst enemy, because her claws became all tangled up in the sacking and she couldn't get away from me. I flung her into the sack. Eddie helped me with my sacking, and it all went into the coal sack.

That cat was something else, it was going mad. The coal sack was alive, it was a good job that it was strong. I reckon that if that cat had escaped, it would have scratched us to pieces. Now we had to get it home. Eddie tried to put the sack over his shoulder, but the fucking thing managed to dig its claws into him. "Eddie, we'll have to drag this bastard home. If it scratches me, I'll kill it." So that's what we did. There was lots of sacking between the cat and the ground, so it came to no harm.

We had a bit of luck, however, as we were passing the ruins on Leathermarket Street, we spied an old burnt our babies' pram. It still had wheels on it, well the iron frame anyway. I tested it. Yes, it would get us home. We chucked Tabby into our pram, and off we went. I'll never forget the sight of this heaving bundle in the bottom of a burnt out pram, wonderful.

Eventually we arrived at the main road opposite our house, there were no paper sellers around. We waited, getting some strange looks, the cat was still squirming and screeching. Suddenly, from out of the front of the shops came a man we knew as Victor. He signalled to us, crossed the road, looked at the pram. Eddie explained what was going on. He looked amazed but he did see us safely across the road. We thanked him and arrived home. We called up the stairs, and Nan and Granddad came dashing down.

"Well done, boys. Was everything alright, you didn't get hurt, did you?" Granddad looked quite concerned. "I like the pram, that was a good idea. Leave it to me now, I'll take care of the cat." Granddad lifted the sack very carefully! There was a fierce and angry animal in that sack. It also stank quite a bit. I think the cat had, at least, pissed itself. Granddad let the cat out in the big spare room, and I think it literally climbed the walls. Nan put a saucer of milk out for Tabby, but closed the door very quickly behind her. A few hours later Nan looked in on the cat, and it was asleep. No harm done there then. Nan was really pleased, and therefore, so was I!

The new year started. Nan, Granddad and the rest didn't celebrate too much. Remember, they had recently lost their daughter and had four sons in the Forces.

These were uncertain times, even though the newspapers kept on about us smashing the German Air Force and bigging up our Navy, no one was sure of the future.

We were still on school holidays, when one morning Dad got us together. I thought "Oh no, what now?!" "I've got to return to my army unit, boys. I'll be leaving about dinner time. I don't know when I'll be able to get any leave again, but I'll keep in touch with Nan, so she'll let you know." He gave us all a big hug. He looked very sad.

We did our usual tricks, playing up and down the market. By now, we'd made a few new friends and we were quite rowdy, sometimes getting told off. Most times followed by a quite friendly "piss off."

Home we went, we'd crossed over further up the road and someone had seen us across. At the top of the stairs, there was Dad's kit bag,

In Spite of Everything . . . .

with his tin helmet and gas mask. He was obviously ready to leave, and, as usual, Johnny was waiting to go with him. "I was getting a bit worried about you two boys. I thought that I might have had to leave before you got back. I've got to get away pretty sharp or I'll miss my train. I've got a long way to go, and daren't be late." He grabbed Eddie and hugged him close, then the same to me. Michael was sitting on Granddad's knee. He gave Nan a peck on the cheek and waved to Michael. "Come on, John, off we go." We dashed down the stairs and ran to the main road. We waited by the bus stop and I was amazed by how many of the passers-by called out "Good luck, Ted, God bless you!" It was quite a close community in those days. "Are you going to fight the Germans now, Dad?" I blurted out. "I don't think it will be too long, Paddy. Why, do you want me to kill one for you?" He had a broad grin on his face, it was nice to see him smile. "And one each for Eddie and Michael." "You'll never change, will you Son." With that, he tousled my hair. Then the bus came along, more hugs and kisses and then he was gone! "When will I see him again?" I thought.

Our lives really started settled down now. Thankfully there were no more air raids and we slipped into a steady routine. The winter wasn't that bad. We had a bit of snow, but not much. School wasn't that bad. I found it easy to understand the lessons, but couldn't make out how I managed it. The school was still probably only a quarter full, so in a funny way, the teachers had more time for us. They were all women and they weren't that bad. Unfortunately, the parish priest was always on the scene, making himself busy. I don't think he was that fond of me. The feeling was definitely mutual. I ignored him most of the time, although I was never rude. Nan wouldn't have like that. I just wanted him to leave me alone! What made matters a little awkward, was the fact that Eddie and Michael were in the fucking choir. Eddie used to tell me not to wind him up, and preferably to stay out of his way.

There was real excitement in our house at the news that Johnny had left school and had a job, as a van boy. He, in actual fact, had not been back to school ever since the bombing had started. He was 14 years old. I always thought back at that when I saw my own grandchildren at that age. Where have all the years gone!

Johnny had only recently gone into long trousers. There again, how different from today! Kids wear long trousers from a very young age whereas we wore short trousers right up to the start of our teens. It was strange seeing Johnny going off to work. He only worked locally, in Tanner Street actually, so we took to coming home from school that way in the hope we would see him. We did, once or twice, and he was very red-faced when we started shouting out at him.

We were now settling down nicely and our lives entered a steady period. Whilst telling my story, many lost memories have come to light. For example, I suddenly realised that our numbers in school now stayed pretty steady. In other words, not so many absentees at morning roll call. I can understand now, that most of the absentees were in fact casualties of the bombing. The poor sods had been blown to Kingdom Come. Now that's a sobering thought!

Our Aunt Emma came round with four of my cousins, including Jim. They were all very excited because they were going to be billeted near a place called "Burnham-on-Sea". That was miles away. For a moment, I felt a little bit jealous, but only for a moment. I was very happy where I was. Jim's Dad, my Uncle Patsy, was a professional soldier at the time. He had joined the army as a boy soldier. Many young men in the late 20's and early 30's had joined the army because of a lack of jobs. They were also able to send a bit of money home, and this helped feed the younger members of the family. Patsy was the eldest of nine and times were very hard indeed. He had been amongst the men who got back from Dunkirk and had a tale to tell!

Off they eventually went. Hugs and kisses, with promises to keep in touch. Now that the bombing seemed to have stopped, the goodbyes weren't so heart-breaking. We all assumed we would see each other again, some day! That day was to be much sooner than I thought!

Nan used to get letters from our Dad on a regular basis and, even though there was strict censorship, he was able to let us all know that he was fine. And Nan, in return, used to tell him all about us.

In Spite of Everything . . . .

There sadly was a dark side to all this peace and calm. It gave us boys time to think about our Mum! It started with Michael. He had difficulty settling down at night and getting to sleep. He used to get very distressed and Eddie couldn't calm him down. However, Nan, who was always alert and very sensitive to our moods, took charge as usual! She came upstairs and scooped Michael out of bed and he slept with her and Granddad. This was a routine that was repeated for many years. It certainly worked for Michael, which was good for all of us.

I had my own demons. Some nights I was unable to sleep and my mind whirled around until I just had to get up, or I think my brain would have burst. I used to creep down the stairs and sit at the bottom, listening to the murmur of chat going on in the kitchen. It seemed that most evenings, Eileen and some of her friends or Johnny and his, enjoyed themselves playing cards and "chewing the fat". Eventually, as though by some sixth sense, the kitchen door would open and I would be taken into the kitchen. I was treated like royalty. Everyone seemed to be concerned about me. Never an order to go back to bed. That's how I learned how to play cards, sometimes for money, only half pennies and pennies however. Now, this is the thing, I used to win most times and you cannot imagine some of the stick I took from Johnny's mates, although, to be true, it was very light-hearted. The main point however, is that this always seemed to clear my head and enable me to calm down and relax. I think it stopped me from going insane.

These dark thoughts went through my head for many years, but fortunately I managed to overcome them. I did this in my own special way! I completely erased the memory of my mum from my mind. She was gone, never to return, so I forgot her!

Now this might seem pretty extreme, but it was the ONLY way I could handle it. My Nan was now my Mother and that was that!

Eddie had his own demons, but luckily he was a romantic and was able to cherish our Mum's memory, and the way she died. He was completely absorbed in our now larger family. He, being the eldest, was treated almost as an adult and he loved it. He grew up very quickly under these conditions. Because of his loving nature, Annie adored him, as did Eileen and our many other Aunts: Eddie would do anything for them, he was very obliging. I think sadly he clung on to the (I thought stupid) hope that somehow our Mum would return one day. Eddie was forever worrying about me. He understood, like nobody else, with the possible exception of Nan, how my mind worked. I've often thought back to those times and regretted some of the problems I caused him. The really funny thing is how that scenario reversed itself in later years. But that's a long way off just yet!

Although Michael was very badly affected by losing his Mother, luckily he was young enough to absorb the gallons of love he received from all the family. He probably came out of this tragedy the best.

To finish this sad part of my story, we all, by staying close, managed to go forward and have very happy and enjoyable lives. It's worth mentioning however that, because I refused ever to mention the word "Mum", we did have a couple of bad disagreements. But that was much later, when we were all adults. Or was it sooner than that when this caused a bit of conflict? There was another unknown surprise for me in the not too distant future.

We galloped up the stairs and dashed into the kitchen. Nan, Eileen and Granddad were there. "Look Boys, I've received a letter from your Dad." Eileen had just read it out fully for her. Nan could read a little bit, which made me laugh, she missed out all the big words. I used to help her read the paper sometimes, but only if she got stuck and asked. Nan was born in 1886, and when she became a young lady at about thirteen, her Father would not let her leave the house without her Mother or much older Sister. School was definitely out. But to be honest, at the end of the 19th Century, there wasn't much schooling for poor working class kids. I remember when Nan had told me this I couldn't really understand why. I do now! I suppose one of the plusses of being brought up by Nan was the many and detailed chats we used to have. You see, I was always a curious kid. I remember asking Granddad what was in the newspapers before the war. Simply because they were virtually full of war news, from front to back. He had a little trouble explaining, but I was to find out for myself once the war had ended.

"I've got some good news. Your Dad has arranged for us to go down to the West Country and stay for a few weeks on a small farm. That way he can see you most days. Now, what do you think about that?"

"Cor, smashing!" Eddie yelled out. I wasn't really that bothered. I had never heard of the West Country before. Now, all of a sudden our cousins and now us were off there.

"You'll be staying near the sea at a place called "Woolacombe," Eileen continued, "and there's enough room for five." The kitchen was buzzing. Granddad said that he couldn't be coming, because he'd only just started up his fish stall and he couldn't afford to lose his pitch. "What about you, Eileen?" Nan asked. "Well Mum, I will if I really have to, but jobs are scarce and I don't think my bosses will give me time off. They're short staffed as it is. What about Johnny?" Granddad looked over: "I'd be happier if Johnny went with you. It's a long way away and he can look after himself and you lot", glancing in our direction. "Why don't we wait until he gets in from work and talk about it then." That was settled then. There remained an excited buzz in the kitchen. "I'll have some tea ready for you shortly", Nan added. "Anyhow, it's a couple of weeks away yet. Around Easter-time. Off you go and play, but don't go far. I'll be calling you in a minute."

We were playing down our private alley, amongst the empty market stalls. I heard Johnny coming towards us. "Hiya John! We're all going to the sea-side to see Dad. Want to come with us?" He smiled and looked a bit confused. "Nan will tell you all about it." "Thanks, Eddie!" Indoors and up the stairs he went. In a short while the bathroom window opened "In you come! Tea's ready!" We didn't hang about. Nan didn't like us being late for our meals. That was something we quickly learned.

The kitchen was noisy. Eileen was telling Johnny all about the letter. We were rowdy and excited and Granddad was trying to read his Evening Standard. "I don't mind coming with you Mum, but I'll have to straighten it out with my boss. Remember I've only been there for a couple of months. But if you need me, I'll go with you anyway, fuck the job." "Johnny, mind your language in front of the boys!" If only Nan had known. I was certainly no stranger to the "Eff Word". He apologised all the same, smiling in my direction. Now, even after a couple of months, Johnny had decided that him and hard work were not going to be the best of companions. "Don't worry John. I know Tommy Hatcher very well. He's a drinking mate of mine. If it's alright with you, once I've explained the situation to him, I'm sure he'll understand and I doubt if he'll object." "Okay then, Dad, I'll go with them. I've never been to the seaside. Where are we going again, Eileen?" "It's a place called "Woolacombe". It's miles away. Ted says in his letter that he'll send the railway tickets in the next few days."

As I gobbled my tea up, I thought that this could be quite an adventure after all! Once again, I could never imagine how it would turn out! Woolacombe!

Chapter 3

Suddenly the day had arrived. Johnny was coming with us. Granddad had straightened that out then! Nan had been busy over the past weeks. Dad had sent her some money, so she had gone out and bought us some extra clothes, using up all the family's clothing coupons. It mainly consisted of wellington boots and rain-proof outdoor stuff. And some extra woollen jumpers.

The house was in turmoil. Aunt Anne had turned up and Eileen had stayed away from work for the morning. And of course Granddad was fussing about in his usual way. We couldn't keep still and were driving Nan mad. "Boys, go outside and play for a couple of moments! You're getting in my way. But only in the alley, no further because we will be off in a short while."

"Toot, toot!" There, driving down the alley, was Uncle Nathan in a much bigger van than the one he usually drove. "All ready to go, are you lads?" he called out before going indoors. That was a surprise! I didn't know we were going by road! We weren't. Nathan and Johnny appeared with a few suitcases, only a few! We didn't have that much clothing between us. "Nan wants you lot upstairs now!", Johnny called out. Through the front door and upstairs we dashed. Nan had her coat and hat on. "Come on, boys, put your coats on and don't forget your gas-masks. We've got to be off now or we'll miss the train. Uncle Nathan is taking us to Waterloo Station."

We didn't need telling twice! Granddad was busy talking to Nan. They were checking that she had everything. Tickets, money, identity cards, ration books. She had, and she told Granddad to stop worrying. I don't think he could!

We were all soon outside in the alley and I was surprised to see Kit and Michael standing alongside Nathan. They seemed to know him quite well, by the way they were chatting. Kit approached Nan and put something in her hand. I was later to find out that it was some money! I knew they were nice people.

There was kissing and hugging and a few tears. Then we bundled into the back of the van: Nan in the front, Johnny, Eddie, Michael and me in the back and we were off! It didn't take long to get to the station. I had never seen a place as big as that. It was enormous! There were people everywhere, all dashing about, many of them in uniform. I was completely bewildered. Luckily, Nan and Uncle Nathan weren't! Eddie and me carried one of our cases between us, Nathan and Johnny took care of the other two. The noise of the place was frightening. There were whistles going off all over the place and the noise of the great big steam engines was something else. I held a fear of those engines for many years. Eventually, we came to some gates, which was where our platform was. Nan showed our tickets and the guards let us through. Uncle Nathan came on the platform and helped us find a carriage. Once he had done that, off he went, waving and telling Johnny to look after us. (Now there's a thought: a fourteen year old, the war on, looking after other people! We grew up pretty quick in those days.)

We settled into our carriage alongside a couple of people. They helped Johnny to lift our cases onto the luggage racks. "Can I look out of the window, Nan?", Eddie asked. "Me too!", I quickly butted in. "If you like. Just let the window down, but don't lean out too far." There was a loud whistling and the train jerked and clanked a bit, and we were off. "Close that window now, and come and sit down, and stay away from the door!", Nan commanded. We settled down. Very shortly, we were going through countryside and the train was bumping and swaying. It was going quite fast.

In Spite of Everything . . . .

We were on the train for hours. Luckily, there was a corridor, which meant we had somewhere to move about. The place was full of soldiers, mostly standing beside their kit-bags and smoking. They didn't seem to mind us scampering around. Nan had made some sandwiches and had a bottle of lemonade so we didn't go hungry. There was even a toilet on the train, how good was that!

Time went by and we had a nice sleep. Then, suddenly we arrived at a large station. I didn't know what it was called, but I think it was Exeter. Off we got! Nan showed a porter our tickets and he directed us to another platform. In actual fact, he helped us with our luggage. We had to climb some stairs and cross over the main line. There was another train waiting. It was a bit smaller than the one we'd just got off, but almost completely full of soldiers. They helped us with our luggage and we soon found some room in a carriage. A couple of soldiers gave up their seats for us. Nan had a chat with one of the guards. She came over to us: "The train won't be leaving for another hour, but there's a cafe on the platform, so we'll have time to get something to eat and drink."

She asked a couple of the soldiers to look after our belongings, then off to the cafe we went. "Keep an eye on that clock, Paddy", Nan instructed me. "We don't want the train going without us." I did. We had some really nice pies and some hot tea. I shouted out, "Time to go, Nan!" We bundled out onto the platform and made our way to our carriage. Nan thanked the soldiers for looking after our things and produced a pie for both of them. They thanked her very much, saying that she shouldn't have done that, but you see they never knew my Nan.

Whistles, shouting, clanking and shaking, we were off again. The train was a bit slower than our previous one and it slowly made its way through some pretty wild and isolated countryside. It stopped a couple of times and a few soldiers got off.

End of the line, Woolacombe. It was a tiny station. Our journey had ended. The light was just beginning to fail. We were helped off the train and very soon the soldiers were all lined up and climbing into lorries. We were soon almost alone. Nan spoke to the railway man and he showed us to (would you believe it) a horse and cart. Nan spoke to the driver, a big red-faced man with a funny hat and an even funnier voice. She showed him an address. He smiled and nodded, then told us to climb on the back of his cart and chuck our luggage along beside us. I couldn't actually understand what he was saying. Anyway, on we climbed. This was very exciting. He gave his horse a slap with the reins and off we lurched. It started raining. Luckily, Nan had made sure that we had our raincoats handy. We climbed up a steep hill and very shortly we had passed all the houses. There weren't that many, it was a small village. It only took another ten minutes when he pulled into a farm yard.

There was a small brick house with various barns and outbuildings around it. The lady inside must have been expecting us, because as we pulled into the yard, she appeared at the front door. She looked like a dumpling with a red tomato stuck on it. She did appear very friendly. She chatted to Nan, thanked the driver and ushered us into the house. "Come on in, out of the rain, and make yourselves comfortable", she said, although in an odd accent.

We were now in a fairly large kitchen, with a stone floor and an enormous wooden table and various chairs. There was an open fire on one side with a great big oven. She told us to take off our coats and sit at the table. She then brought out masses of pies and potatoes. "Get that lot down thee, yo muss be tired and ungreee."

We didn't need much encouragement, it was delightful. "Mr. Gartree is in the parlour, I'll take you to meet him once you've finished yo's supper." There was a jug of milk on the table and Nan told us drink some, which we did, and once again, it was lovely! Very different from any milk I'd drunk before. Once we'd all finished she showed us into "the parlour". That was another word I'd never heard before.

There he sat, in front of another fire, a fat gruff old man, smoking a funny pipe and lying next to him a large black dog (I found out later that it was a sheep dog). At that time, I didn't know much about dogs, or, for that matter, cared. He didn't get up, but mumbled something

In Spite of Everything . . . .

to Nan. He eyed us up and down, not in a very friendly way, I thought. The signs between us were not that encouraging. Mrs. Gartree very quickly ushered us back into the kitchen.

Once there, she appeared very sorry, but told Nan that us children weren't allowed to go into the parlour. But other than that, we had the run of the place. "What about me?", Johnny asked. "Oh, I think it will be alright for you! But not the youngsters. I'm sorry but my husband will not allow it!"

We were shown up to our bedrooms. Nan and Michael were in one room, Johnny, Eddie and me in another. There were two beds in our room, which was a bit of luck, because Johnny would not have shared with Eddie and me. It was a very tiny room with a low sloping ceiling, but very clean and comfortable. "Where's the toilets?", Nan enquired. "Oh, they be outside, just by the back door from the kitchen." "Right boys, get down those stairs and make sure you go to the toilet before getting into bed", Nan said. "And be quiet doing it, quick now."

We were soon in bed. Johnny came to bed the same time as us. "Goodnight Eddie, Paddy, see you in the morning." I think I was asleep as soon as my head touched the pillow.

Jesus Christ! What a noise! It was only just getting light when all hell broke loose. There was the noise of horses and the jangling of machinery. There was chickens crowing (I was to find out later that it was the cockerel that crowed), the sound of men shouting and cows mooing. It was a hive of activity. Eddie was up and peering out of the little window. He was very excited. "I'm going into Nan's and see if we can get up", he said. He was gone in a flash. Johnny wasn't too happy. "Nan's awake and said we can get up. We've got to go downstairs to have a wash." Down we went in our pyjamas. We piled into the kitchen. What a smell!

"Morning lads, did thee sleep well?" "Yes, thanks Mrs. Gartree", Eddie replied. "Just pop outside and have a wash. There's soap and towels out there for you." She pointed us towards a small scullery. A bare stone room with just a sink with a tap. It was very chilly and the water was of course cold!

We quickly washed ourselves. Then Michael appeared, very wide-eyed. Eddie helped him get washed and dried. It was very cold, so we didn't hang about. We scrambled upstairs. Nan was up. "Make sure you put on your wellington boots and your thick clothing. I'll see you downstairs in the kitchen once you've dressed yourselves. Come on John, time to get up for you as well.", she called out. Johnny groaned. We were soon in the kitchen. What a breakfast! We had fried eggs with bacon, hot creamy milk and great big slices of bread. I thought that they couldn't have had rationing down here. "Come on up to the table you boys, I've spoiled you today. I'll leave your Grandma to look after you tomorrow. We mustn't overdo your welcome", said Mrs. Gartree with that lovely round red face. We didn't need much prompting. The breakfast was eaten in a flash. Johnny turned up just in time.

After breakfast Eddie asked "Can we go outside, Nan?" Nan glanced at Mrs. Gartree. "Yes of course you can, but be careful. This is a small working farm. You can help out if you wish but don't get in the way." With that Nan said "Don't go far, because I would imagine that your Dad will come up to see you some time today. Put your coats on before you go out."

Eddie went into the barn where they were milking some cows, Michael helped Mrs. Gartree feed the chickens, and the last I saw of Johnny he was off with one of the farm workers alongside a couple of enormous horses. I just wandered around exploring. I wasn't interested in animals. I was rummaging around in some old barn with bits of machinery. That's when I found the old rusty knife, wonderful! I took it to another barn where an old man was working. I noticed the charcoal fire and various tools. They were familiar to me because of the man in Vinegar Yard.

"Ore, ore there lad, what thee be wanting?" He was a friendly man. "Just exploring, Mr. Am I alright in here?" "Thee arrre, as long as thee don't touch anything." "Can you clean this knife up for me Mister?" "Where thee get that?" I pointed to the other barn. "Give it here. Be careful with it mind. Anyway, what do you want it for?" "Oh, just to cut down a bit of wood, so that I can make a stick." He shrugged then put some oil on the knife and used a lathe to clean it up.

When he gave it back it was almost like new. "There thee go, but be careful mind." Off I went. I could see Michael amongst the chickens. He waved as I strolled by. I rounded a corner and there, waddling towards me, were (as I was to find out later) half a dozen geese. They flapped their wings and stuck their necks out in a very unfriendly way. I just ignored them. They were very aggressive and noisy. The cottage window popped open and Mrs. Gartree shouted out "Don't you go upsetting them geese, they can be dangerous!" "I'm not upsetting them, I'm just walking about", I called back. I glared at the geese and couldn't quite understand how these big birds could be "dangerous". They didn't have teeth or anything like a dog has. Then I was in the woods. I soon found a nice branch to make a stick with. I was soon swooshing myself a path through the brambles and ferns. I didn't go too far away and I was soon back in the farmyard. Eddie was helping by leading the cows into a nearby field. Johnny had disappeared and Michael was larking about with a couple of dogs. I heard Eddie call out. Then Dad appeared. He was in uniform. I noticed straight away that he had a stripe on his arm.

"Hi Dad, what's that stripe for?", I called out. He grinned. By now, Eddie was jumping all over him and Michael had stopped playing with the dogs, but they were having none of that, they wouldn't leave him alone. "I'm now what they call a "Lance Corporal"!" "Is that because you're the best soldier, Dad?" "The very best, Son. How have you been boys? Enjoying yourselves?" He looked at me. "Where on earth did you manage to get that stick?" "I've just cut it down from those woods over there." "Where did you get a knife?" "I found it, honest Dad, and that man in the barn cleaned and sharpened it for me." "Well, let's have a look at this knife." With that, I took it out of my pocket. Dad winced. "Look Son, you shouldn't be running around with a knife like that, and certainly not in your pocket. If you had fallen over, you could have cut yourself." He took the knife away. "I'll give it to your Nan. She'll let you use it now and again." With that he went into the kitchen and I could hear him chatting away to Mrs. Gartree and Nan. He came out after a few minutes. "Can you take us down to the sea, Dad?", Eddie asked. "Not today I'm afraid Son, I'm only here for a flying visit." Eddie looked very sad. "But I've got a 48 hour pass at the weekend and I'll take you then." Eddie brightened up. We all piled back into the kitchen where there were great lumps of bread and jam. This was indeed a nice place.

Dad left and as soon as we had finished eating, Eddie and me went exploring in the woods, following my paths. Those fucking geese had a pop at us again. I was now getting seriously pissed off with them. Something had to go! Eddie told me to try and avoid them. "The trouble is, Ed, that they turn up wherever you go." "Well, just ignore them Paddy, they're trouble." I thought about that. Yeah, so am I!

The days went by and we were now getting into a routine. The boys helping out and me exploring. One morning, Mrs. Gartree suddenly asked me to bring some logs into the kitchen for her. There was a massive pile up against one of the sheds. I didn't mind helping her out. She showed me where a wheelbarrow was and I went to work, quite happily. It took a few trips to get the logs into the kitchen, where I piled them very neatly next to the fire grate. "There you are, Mrs. Gartree, is that alright?" "Oi yes young Paddy, but now will you do the same in the parlour? You've done a lovely job." I stared back at her. "We aren't allowed in the parlour." "Oh, don't worry, it will be alright." Nan was in the kitchen and as I've said before, I think she could read my mind. She fixed me with that gaze of hers. "Well it's not alright with me, you can't have it both ways. I'm not going into the parlour." She looked shocked, I walked out of the kitchen and put the wheelbarrow where I'd found it. At the same time, those geese came screeching at me. I lashed out with my foot and that sent them scurrying away.

Nan followed me out. "Paddy! Calm down! Come here!" I went over to her. "Paddy, you were a bit rude to Mrs. Gartree, you'll have to apologise." "I didn't mean to be rude Nan, but I'm not taking logs into the parlour." "Now, calm down! You don't have to if you really are unhappy about it, but please go in and say sorry." I went into the kitchen and, even though I didn't agree that I had been rude, apologised. She accepted my apology and luckily never asked me to take logs into the parlour. I think Nan had told her that it would be a waste of time.

Later on that afternoon, Eddie took care of that job. He just smiled and shrugged at me. "Ed, if Nan had asked me, I would have taken those logs into his fucking lounge." "Not so loud, Paddy. Nan knew that you weren't happy. I don't give a fuck." That's my big brother for you!

Things were never quite the same again with Mrs. Gartree and me. "Nan, do we have to do work and help around the farm?" "No Paddy, of course not! Why do you ask?" "Well, that thing the other day, with Mrs. Gartree, and that old pig of a farmer, he gives his orders out and I don't think he likes me strolling about." "Now, don't worry yourself. You must keep out of mischief and out of everybody's way. By the way, I saw you lash out at his geese. Now keep away from them, understand?" "I will Nan, but they're horrible!"

A couple of days passed, without incident. I was able to wander about, sometimes with Eddy and sometimes bumping into Johnny, who was enjoying himself. I noticed that there were a couple of girls helping out. I think that's why he smiled a lot. Before we knew it, the weekend had arrived. We hung around and waited in anticipation for Dad to arrive. He didn't let us down. Eddie saw him first. He was strolling up the hill, coming towards us. We all dashed out to meet him. "Hi Dad!", shouted Eddie, with Michael scrambling close behind. He scooped Michael up in one arm. Then Eddie in the other. He stooped down and I climbed on his shoulders and he walked into the farm with all three of us, screaming and whooping. The dogs rushed out to meet us. They were as excited as we were. "Can we go down to the sea, Dad?", said Eddie. He spoke for all of us. "Yes, but let me go and see your Nan first, then once I've got rid of this pack, we'll be off."

The old farmer made an appearance, no doubt curious about the row going on. He just about showed out to Dad but completely ignored us. I didn't take my eyes off him, horrible ignorant bastard. I don't think he was very happy with the way his dogs made friends of us, especially Michael, they loved him. Dad appeared shortly. "Come on boys, let's be having you, we're off to the sea."

Off we strode. "It's alright for me to take my stick Dad, isn't it?" "Yes of course you can, Son." "What about my knife?" "Noooo!"

I was surprised how close to the sea we actually were. It only took us about half an hour. All downhill. Michael was on Dad's shoulders for most of the way. We soon came across houses, all made of stone with big front gardens and stone walls. Even though it was a Saturday, there weren't that many people about. Mind you, those that were seemed friendly enough and waved at us as we walked by. I remember the smell and then the roar of the sea. I'd never seen the sea before. It was almost frightening. There were great big waves crashing in against the rocks. One big wave after another and it stretched for as far as the eye could see. When we got closer to the actual beach, we were in for a bit of an anti-climax. The beach was a no go area. It had barriers and barbed wire across the entry point, with a couple of soldiers guarding it. Dad showed out to the guards, they obviously knew each other.

"Sorry boys, you're not allowed on the beach area, but you can certainly play on the rocks, but not in the sea. It's too rough and cold anyway." I didn't hang about, nor did Eddie, we scrambled over the rocks and got as near to the sea as possible. "Not too close, you two", came a cry from Dad. The sea was relentless and, even to this day, I love rough sea. We found little pools, which were full of tiny fish and small crabs. This was heaven.

I could have played all day but eventually Dad called us in and we reluctantly made our way back to the farm. It was a much tougher walk back. It was a good job Dad was with us, because Michael wouldn't have made it. We all told our Nan about our adventure and she seemed pretty impressed. Johnny had returned to the farmhouse and he was in deep conversation with Dad (his hero). Very shortly dinner was ready. Great piles of potatoes and vegetables with stewed rabbit, it was delicious. It got even better, there was an apple pie for afters. She was a good cook, was Mrs. Gartree, but Nan had helped out as well.

Dad popped into the parlour to have a chat with Mr. Gartree, but he wasn't very long. We all sat around playing cards and dominoes, with the big open fire making the kitchen nice and warm, also adding extra light since there were only oil-lamps providing the lighting.

"Johnny has allowed me to sleep in his bed, which means someone has to sleep on the floor. Any suggestions?" "I'll sleep on the floor, Dad," I blurted out. I preferred to sleep on my own anyway. "That's decent of you, Son. Don't worry, I'll make a comfortable bed for you. You won't be sleeping on the actual floor boards." He chuckled at that. It would have surprised him to know that I hadn't actually thought that one through.

Eventually we were packed off to bed. Usual routine, wash, toilet, "Good night Mrs. Gartree, thanks for the meal!", "Goodnight, God-Bless Nan. See you in the morning", then off we went. My bed was cosy and warm and I was asleep as soon as my head touched the pillow.

Although it was Sunday, the farm carried on as usual. Well, the start of the day anyway. Another windy, damp morning, but I didn't care. I was enjoying myself. After breakfast, Nan gave out a good bit of news, as far as I was concerned anyway. "There isn't a Catholic church nearby, so no church today. Dad's going to take you for a walk. We got ourselves ready, but before we started out I got the wheelbarrow out and filled the fireplace with logs. I made sure there was plenty. I piled them as close to the parlour as I could. Mrs. Gartree thanked me, then I put the wheelbarrow away.

Off we went. Michael on Dad's shoulders as usual. Eddie and myself leading the way. "Where are we going today, Dad?", Eddie called out. "Let's make our way to the woods. You know the way, don't you Paddy?" I nodded and led us to one of my favourite places. We followed the trails that I was proud to point out I had made. Dad called out "Hold it there boys! I'll make you some bows and arrows!" Dad produced "my" knife and showed us how to slice the best branches for the bows and those for the arrows. Once we had three suitably sized branches, he showed us how to tie the strings in a way that they wouldn't slip. I remembered those tricks for the rest of my life, as my grandchildren can confirm. We had a whale of a time, but as usual time flew. "Come on boys, we'd better be getting back." Reluctantly we followed Dad back to the farm. What a great day we'd had.

Once we'd eaten our lunch, the rest of the day quickly passed. Eventually Nan called us in. "Dad's got to go back to the barracks, so you'd better come in and say goodbye." Dad was ready to leave. He gave us all a great big hug. He whispered in my ear "Don't aggravate the farmer", giving me an extra hug as he did so. "When will you be back to see us, Dad?", Eddie asked. "I can't say for certain at the moment. There has been a lot of activity lately and the army doesn't tell me everything. But it will be as soon as humanly possible." More hugs, a kiss for Nan and a handshake for Mrs. Gartree. Then, with Johnny by his side, he was away. He wasn't to know that he'd be seeing us sooner than he thought!

The next few days passed without incident. I had a wonderful time with my new bow and arrow. Nan made sure that I kept well away from everyone, always telling me to be careful and not shoot at any of the farm animals. Although, I must say, I was sorely tempted.

It was mid morning, quite a bright and sunny day. I was behind one of the barns (out of everyone's way), when I heard this terrible racket. For a moment I froze, because it was Michael screaming in terror. I could also hear those fucking geese going mad. I dropped my bow and picked up my stick, dashed round the corner and there, to my horror, was Michael, being attacked by that big fucking goose. I yelled out and went crashing into the geese, but my eye was on that big fucker, who was really having a go at Michael. It never knew what hit him! I smashed it right across that big beak of his. The stick shook in my hand. It made a funny sound as its stumpy legs gave way and it virtually collapsed. Its wings were flapping wildly and that stopped it totally collapsing. I wasn't finished yet. It is hard to describe how angry I felt. I jumped on the goose, got my arm around its neck and forced it to the ground. I didn't realise how strong this bird was. It was squawking and flapping its wings and at one time I thought that it might take off, with me still hanging on. But it didn't. I had it in an arm lock, which was one of my favourite positions. Not many people got away from that. Added to that was the fact that I don't think I'd ever been quite that mad before. It was the first time in my life that I actually wanted to kill something. It became a desperate struggle, but I could feel the goose weakening. It was then that I became aware of the noise going on around me. I could hear Nan calling for me to stop and Mrs. Gartree screaming. There was all sorts of mayhem. But it made no difference to me. This thing had attacked Michael and, as many people would find out in the future: "That was a mistake!"

Suddenly I felt a strong pair of arms dragging me off the goose. I looked up. It was the farmer, Mr. Gartree. His face was redder than ever. He managed to drag me off his bird, then began to scream abuse at me. He then made a silly mistake: he raised his walking stick to strike me. In a flash, and I hadn't even noticed him, Johnny stepped forward and yanked the stick out of the farmer's grasp, pulling him over as he did so. The farmer was now on his knees, still shouting abuse. Johnny stood over him. "Don't you ever raise a stick at my nephew!" With that, he snapped his stick in half and flung the pieces at him. "Come here Paddy, get away from these people." I closed in on Johnny. Nan was holding Michael, who was still sobbing, and Eddie was standing next to her, in a very menacing way.

Once it had calmed a little, the farmer started to scream at Nan, telling her that we all had to leave. Johnny told him to keep his voice down and told him that he could stick his farm up his arse. That certainly calmed him down. He stomped off. He looked fatter and redder to me. "I'll make the necessary arrangements and we'll leave you in the morning, if that's alright Mrs. Gartree. I'm sorry that it had to end this way. Remember, I did tell you that those geese were proving to be a problem." She than looked over to me. "Paddy, now calm down. It wasn't your fault. I want you to come into the kitchen." I followed her in. "Sit down and calm yourself, it's not very good for you to get that excited." I did as I was told, but couldn't calm down, not for quite a while. Nan had sent Johnny, with Eddie in tow, to the barracks to get a message to Dad. I bet he'll be surprised, I thought.

| 107

I played snakes and ladders with Michael and tried to teach him how to play cards. He actually picked it up quite well. Eddie and Johnny came into the kitchen. "We actually saw Dad, Nan. Johnny will tell you what he said." Johnny then proceeded to tell Nan that Dad would make arrangements for us all to be driven to Burnham-on-Sea, where our Aunt Emma was. Apparently, they were staying in a very large house right on the sea front. Nan and Johnny chatted together for quite a while. There was a very awkward atmosphere in the kitchen. Mrs. Gartree was very quiet, but still friendly. The food however was great. Remember, our Nan was involved as well so it would be, wouldn't it!

Next morning after breakfast Nan told us to get all our things together, because as soon as Dad arrived, we would be off. "Can I take my bow and arrow and my stick, Nan?" "You'll have to ask your Dad. Johnny threw your stick away." Nan glanced at Mrs. Gartree as she said that. Mrs. Gartree looked at Nan, very nervously. "I'm very, very sorry, but Mr. Gartree has insisted that nothing can be taken from the farm. The wood belongs to us, that means you cannot take that bow." Nan walked up to her and put her arms around her shoulders. "Don't worry yourself. I understand. You've been very good to me and my boys. Please don't get upset. He'll soon make himself another."

"Well, the string ain't his!", and before anybody could stop me, I was out of the kitchen. I was soon in the barn, busily untying my string. I then noticed the farmer eying me. He said nothing. I think he was curious at what I was doing. I soon had the job done. Once I'd finished, I broke the bow into as many pieces as I could and threw the bits outside. I pocketed my! string. I dashed into the kitchen. "I'm ready Nan."

Eddie came dashing in excitedly. "Dad's outside, Nan, with a couple of mates in a great big lorry. He's on his way down." "Come on you lot, John, you can carry a couple of suitcases, hurry now." Nan ushered us out, at the same time giving Mrs. Gartree a hug. She was in tears and kept apologising. I was off, but as I left the cottage, I couldn't help but look for those geese. They were gone. The two big dogs chased after Michael, they would miss him, and he would them. Dad, who

In Spite of Everything . . . .

was in uniform, was in deep conversation with the farmer. They both kept glancing in my direction. The farmer didn't have much to say for himself, he just listened. He wasn't that silly then!

We were soon at the farm's gate and Eddie was right: a big lorry and two big soldiers. I noticed one of them had two stripes on his arm, as opposed to Dad's one. They were very cheerful, quickly throwing our luggage in the back of the lorry, then helping us up. There were two rows of seats down each side of the lorry. Finally they helped Nan up and Dad quickly followed. The tail gate was closed and in a few moments we were off. Dad looked over to me. "Are you alright, Paddy?" I didn't quite understand what he meant. "It was my fault, Dad. Those geese attacked Michael and I ain't gonna stand for that!" "No, no, Paddy, it wasn't your fault. You did the right thing. You protected your brother. As I've told you all many times before "Always stick together and look after each other"". "I wasn't there Dad, or I'd have helped Paddy out", Eddie butted in. "I know you would have, Son, but from what I've heard, he didn't need any help!" He couldn't hide a faint smile.

"Now, this is what's happening. I've had a chat with Nan and you may, or may not, know that Aunt Emma and your cousins are only about 50 miles away, so we thought you would like to see them and stay with them for a few days. We can't take you all the way, but as it happens, we've got to go to a place called "Taunton" where you can catch a train to Burnham. So settle down, because these trucks are a bit bumpy and it'll take us a couple of hours.

It was a bumpy old journey and we could only see out of the back, but we did eventually arrive at the railway station at Taunton. They didn't hang around for too long. Dad said a hurried goodbye and they were off. As usual, we waited around and Nan sorted out our tickets, then, before we knew it, we were on the train and off we went. We were certainly having an adventurous time. We woke up in the farm, had breakfast, then in the back of an actual Army Lorry, an exciting road journey, all chatting and laughing together, and now on a train. At the same time there was a war on.

It didn't take that long to get to Burnham and as soon as we were outside of the railway station Nan showed the porter a bit of paper with an address on it. He pointed towards the sea, telling Nan that it wouldn't take us that long to walk. "Come on you lot. John, you take the biggest case, Eddie, you and Paddy carry that one. I'll carry the last one. Hold my hand, Michael." Off we went. We followed Nan just like those geese used to do, behind that big fucker!

We were getting closer to the sea and, as we turned a corner, there playing in the street alongside the sea-wall was cousin Jimmy with his big sisters Sheila and Pat. Jimmy noticed us first. They were gobsmacked. They came running towards us. They were excited to see Nan—remember, it was their Nan as well. They were firing questions at us, ten to the dozen. Pat dashed off to get Aunt Emma. We were at the front door before she appeared. She looked shocked to see us and furiously began to ask Nan how, where and why we had turned up here. Nan said "Emma, make me a cup of tea and I'll explain everything!"

The house had three floors and it was at the end of a row, right next to the beach. "What a spot!", I thought. Once all the excitement had died down and Nan had a chance to explain all to Aunt Emma, we were taken up to the top floor and shown a bedroom. It actually faced the sea. There was even a couple of small beds in it, although not a lot else. Johnny was going to share with Jimmy, whose room was next to ours. We very quickly settled in. I heard Aunt Emma ask Nan if she had our ration books with her, and upon being told "yes", she and Nan trooped off to the local shop to buy some food. This was going to be a bit different from the farm, I thought.

Jimmy was excitedly showing us around the place and we put him in the picture as to how and why we were here. Nan soon returned. "I'll just make you some bread and jam for now, you must be starving. You'll have a cooked meal later." We all sat around eating. The bread was lovely, very similar to what we had at the farm. The jam was nice as well. "I'll show you the beach once we've finished", said Jimmy excitedly. A new adventure was about to start . . .

Chapter 4

It was an amazing place. The sand was only a few yards away. We all dashed onto the beach, which seemed to go on for miles. It was empty, except for an old run-down building, about half a mile away. That's where we headed. There were other children playing about and I was very surprised to actually recognize a few of them. They were from our neighbourhood in Bermondsey. They were equally amazed to see Eddie and me. It was explained that they were evacuated very close by. I thought that this was turning out wonderful but there always seemed to be something to upset the apple cart. We dashed into this old barn type building, only to be confronted by about a dozen boys and girls, all very hostile and, judging by their accents, "locals". They all screamed and yelled at us to get out. This was their camp! Jimmy wanted us to leave them alone, so we about-turned and followed Jim and the girls, Sheila and Patricia, away from the barn. "There's lots more beach to play on. Aunt Emma doesn't want any trouble!" We trooped off down the beach, wiggling our toes in the cold water as we went. That sea was cold and very rough and as we ambled along, throwing pebbles into the sea, Eddie glanced over to me. He gave a slight nod and a shake of his head. "No trouble, Paddy, you heard, didn't you." "Why can't we play in that barn, Sheila?" I asked. She was the oldest, by the way. "Well, those locals don't actually own it, it's been abandoned long ago, but they consider it their camp and don't like us evacuees taking over. They are not bad people really and we get on with most of them." "So, they can't stop us then?" I asked. "Paddy, you are a nuisance! Listen, they aren't there all day. Remember, they all have to go to school in the week, so we can use the place while they are in school, OK." That was that then. We carried on our way, sky-larking about as usual.

We were all crammed in around the table and stuffing a lovely dinner down our throats. The noise was deafening. There was, with Johnny, ten of us. "Have you all had a nice day?" Nan said. "Haven't got into too much mischief, have you all?" She saved a lingering look for me. "No Nan," we all chorused. I gave Nan a huge smile. She looked right through me, as if reading my mind.

Very shortly we were in bed. After some initial rowdiness, off to sleep we went. We could hear the sea from our bedroom, also smell the salt and sea weed. They are smells and sounds I can never forget and even today, nearly seventy years later, whenever they occur I'm back immediately to this place and time. The sense of smell is indeed a wonderful thing.

I suppose it was inevitable that there would be a confrontation of some sort. This morning we turned left from the house, taking us towards town, still going along the sea-front. There was a big stone built paddling pool and we had some fun in that. Remember, we all wore short trousers then. We boys just had to take off our shoes and socks and we were paddling. The girls tucked their dresses into their knickers and they were away also. There were other kids playing also and I immediately recognised a couple of boys. They were in that barn. They eyed us warily but we stayed away from each other. It was a large pool. We were having a great lark, then unfortunately a couple of the local lads soaked poor Patricia. She had wandered away from our main group. She screamed and began to cry. Sheila (no shrinking violet by the way) dashed, or I should say, waded over to them. She started to scream and shout at them. Eddie and I followed very quickly. Eddie was fastest. He grabbed hold of one of the biggest boys and pulled him down into the water. He held him for a moment, then let him go. He was saturated and spluttering for breath. Jimmy and me made our way towards the other lads, but they quickly retreated and got out of the pool. The drowning rat got out as quick as he could, but it wasn't over yet. Sheila was like a wild cat and she carried on attacking the boy. She was screeching and scratching him then before we knew it, some adults came between us all and broke up the fighting. We were being shouted at by the local kids and in turn we were shouting back, chaos! Suddenly two policemen showed up. They told us all to be quiet, which we did. They chatted to the adults and very shortly said: "Come on you lot, take us to where you are staying and no trouble." We followed them home, all very subdued. They had a long talk with Aunt Emma, but before they left they warned us to behave ourselves in future, or else we would find ourselves in serious trouble.

I thought it was a bit unfair of them not to get our version of the events. Looking back, I realise that we were the strangers and there was a bad reputation hanging over evacuees from London. Not, always totally unfair, to be honest. For once, I wasn't the cause of this particular bit of trouble and once Sheila had given her side of the story, all was well but we were warned to be careful.

Obviously, the old barn was like a magnet and sure enough we took it over. It was a dump, but there was one small golden nugget. There was an electricity supply to the barn and it was still live. We used to chuck lumps of wood at this box on the wall, which caused it to spark. We loved it! We even discovered a better game: once the girls were out of the way we used to line up in front of it and piss on it, to see who could get the highest. That certainly made it crackle and spark. What fun!

We usually were long gone well before school had finished. Not that we were worried about the locals, but we had been told time and time again to avoid trouble. Well, this particular afternoon we must have lost count of time. There, coming down the beach were a gang of boys and girls. We stood outside and, if only they had known, we would have scarpered, but they started yelling and jeering at us. That was that then! We challenged them to come and force us out, but they kept their distance, then disappeared altogether. We thought that was the end of that little incident! It then started! Stones, large and small, and all bits of bric-a-brac came raining down on us. This gang of boys and girls, which had got larger, were in the big sand dunes at the back of the barn. They were throwing everything at us. Unfortunately for us, there wasn't much of the roof left. We were therefore getting hit. "Fuck this!" I said, "I'm not standing too much of this." I picked up some heavy stones and dashed out and started throwing them back. They never knew it, but I was one of a few boys who could throw a stone onto the roof of our local Guinness buildings. I soon hit a few of them. Eddie, Jimmy and a mate from London called Tommy and his brother Bill all started chucking stones back. We got hit a few times, but kept going back into the barn for more "ammunition". I was on my way back when, thud, I felt this terrible pain in my back and I dropped to my knees. I knew I was in trouble. Eddie dashed over to me. "Don't move, Paddy" he said. I could tell he was worried. "You've got a big bit of slate stuck in your back." I heard Jimmy screaming at the locals to stop throwing because one of us was badly hurt. Yes, it was me!

Suddenly, there was a big crowd of boys standing over me. They all seemed very concerned. Someone dashed away, calling out that they were going to fetch a doctor. Eddie told me to lie still. My back was now beginning to hurt. Somebody said "Shouldn't we pull that slate out of his back." But Eddie told him to mind his own business. Then, just before it started to get ugly, I heard a grown up voice call out "What's going on down there!" Two soldiers were on top of the sand dunes and making their way over to us. They were standing over me in seconds. "What the hell has happened here? Now, all stand back and make some room." One of the men knelt over me and ripped my shirt open. I heard him tut tut. "We'll have to get you to the clinic, without any delay. That's a very nasty wound." He looked over to Eddie. "It's a good job you left him alone, Son, because if you'd pulled that slate out, he could have lost a lot of blood. The slate's stuck tight and is stopping most of the bleeding."

Another soldier called out from the dunes. "What's going on down there, corporal?" "We've got an injured boy, Sir. He's badly cut on his back. Permission to take him to the clinic, Sir." The officer was over in no time at all. He looked at my wound. "Right, you two men, get this boy some medical help straight away. Rest of you boys, stay where you are. I want to ask you all some questions. Eddie explained that he was my older brother and wanted to be with me. Jimmy told the officer that he was my cousin and this seemed to satisfy him. "Off you go then, hurry Corporal. You do know where the clinic is, don't you?" "Yes Sir, we'll have him there in about five minutes."

In Spite of Everything . . . .

With that, I was picked up and the bigger of the two soldiers put me over his shoulders and off we dashed. My back was really starting to sting. The other soldier was pushing some material quite firmly into the area where I had been hurt. Luckily the clinic was only a couple of hundred yards away, but we had to go right past the house where we were staying. One of the girls saw us go past and with a startled gasp, she ran into the house calling out for Nan and Aunt Emma. The soldiers didn't hang about, we were at the clinic in minutes. A nurse took one look at me and instructed the soldiers to place me on a large high bed. She hurried away and a doctor soon appeared. He started to examine my back, at the same time firing questions at the soldiers, then quizzing Eddie. The nurse came back with a tray of instruments. She had a white gown on. They were all asked to leave the room. I heard Eddie thanking the soldiers, who left as quick as they'd arrived. The nurse started dabbing my wound and it made it sting like mad. I thought they were torturing me then the doctor came back and he was all dressed up as well. I heard a commotion in the outer room, then the door opened slightly and a lady called out "The boy's parents are here." The nurse popped out to see them. She was back in seconds. "Your Mum is outside and we have told her not to worry. We'll have you fixed in no time." MUM! She couldn't understand how mad that made me. I started to get a bit agitated. The doctor thought it was because of my injury (it wasn't). I could have got up and just pissed off. Mind you, with what was to come, I think it was a blessing that I was as mad as hell.

"We will have to remove this slate and clean up the wound. It will sting a bit but you look like a tough lad. The nurse will put something on to ease the pain." I didn't like the clinking of instruments, nor the horrible smell but the nurse put some liquid on me and it cooled my back down. They then went to work. It did hurt, but not that bad. "The wound is nice and clean now, but we'll have to stitch it. Are you happy with that?" Before I could answer Nan's voice said "You're the doctor, do what you think is necessary. Are you alright Paddy?" I hadn't realised that Nan was actually in the room. "Yes NAN!" I emphasised those words "It's a bit sore, but I'm OK." I had never had stitches before, but I had heard all about them. I had fifteen in all. Apparently, some of the cut was very deep. I still carry the large scar to this day.

They had me bandaged up quite quickly. I was wrapped up like a mummy. The doctor turned to Nan: "We would like the boy to stay here for a couple of hours. Just to make sure he settles down. Are you happy with that?" Nan nodded and said she'd come back to get me later. With that, she came over, gave me a kiss and with a slight shake of her head said "I think the devil seems to find you, Paddy. I'll be back in a couple of hours. Now, please do exactly as the doctor or nurse tells you. Bye." Another kiss, then she was gone.

The nurse came over: "Paddy, you have been a brave boy. I want you to stay on your stomach and try to get some sleep." Some chance of that, I thought. I hated the smell of disinfectant, but fall asleep I did. I woke up and at first didn't know where I was. It was beginning to get dark outside but I could see the garden through the windows. I felt a bit groggy and my back really hurt. It was worse now than when I had a dirty great bit of roofing slate stuck in it. I called out and a lady came into the room. "You're awake then?" I'd never seen this one before. "Your Nan has called in a couple of times, but the doctor wanted you to rest. How do you feel? Do you feel sick? Have you got a headache?" I said no to all her questions. "My back feels a bit sore, that's all." "Well, it will feel sore for a couple of days. You had a very nasty wound. Now, let me help you off the bed, then you can come out into the reception and sit in a chair. Your Nan will be along shortly."

She sat me in a chair, then she turned up with some cake and a large glass of milk. What a bonus! I made short work of that. Shortly after that, Nan turned up with Eddie. He looked very worried. "How are you, bruv?" "Me back's a bit sore but, other than that, I feel alright. Have you found out who threw that slate?" "Now, now, boys, remember Eddie, I told you to forget all about those local lads. It will only cause more trouble. You were all throwing stones and things and it's a wonder someone else wasn't hurt" She looked me straight in the eye. "Now, listen well to me, young man. Get yourself better and forget any ideas you might have about getting your own back. I am really serious, Paddy, so please, please do as I say." Well, there was no way that I could disobey Nan, not with that sort of plea. Nan certainly understood my mind. Revenge! You bet. I had it all planned out. Now I would have to forget those ideas and that was more painful than the injury. What annoyed me most of all was that I'd been hit in the "back". People could imagine that I had been running away, and not going back for more ammo! Now I wouldn't be able to put it right.

We strolled home once I'd said goodbye to the lady at the clinic. She gave Nan instructions about how to look after my wound and told Nan to bring me back in the morning. There was great excitement as I entered the house. I was being treated as a hero. Aunt Emma gave me a cuddle and showed a great deal of concern, seeing all the bandages. In those days, even though there was a war on, they didn't muck about wrapping you up. A bit over the top, I think. The girls were all fussing around me, wanting to know everything. Nosey cows, the lot of them. Michael was almost in tears but once I'd given him a wink and a pat on his head, he was happy. I hadn't noticed Johnny, but he came over to me. I think he was worried because he was our minder and it was a bit of an insult to him that I had been injured because he felt that he should have been around to protect us. "You alright, Paddy?" "Yeah, honest John, I feel OK." "Eddie and me went looking for that gang of lads, but we couldn't find them, or anything about them. The locals look after their own." "Nan has told me to forget all about them, John." "Yeah, I know. There's nothing we can do." He gave me a crafty wink.

Not long after having our tea, I felt strangely tired. Nan noticed and I was in bed and asleep in no time at all. I woke up once or twice during the night. It must have hurt me as I twisted and turned. I was always a restless sleeper, and still am!

Whilst having breakfast the next morning there was a knock at the front door. Aunt Emma answered it and I could hear a man's voice. I knew that I had heard that voice before. Then right behind Aunt Emma, walking into the kitchen, was a soldier. I recognised him straight away. It was the officer from yesterday. He smiled at me and seemed genuinely concerned. He asked me how I felt and was interested to hear that I had all those stitches. Nan and Aunt Emma thanked him very much for his help and then asked him to thank his soldiers. I also thanked him and gave my regards to the two soldiers who helped me. "They were just doing their duty, Sonny." He held out his hand and I shook it. I felt very grown up. "You are aware that you shouldn't have been fighting in that manner, aren't you?" I nodded. Nan assured him that it wouldn't happen again. Before he left, he took some particulars from Nan. I heard him tell her that he would make sure our Dad was told about the incident. Nan thanked him and then, with a smile and a nod in my direction, he was gone.

Now came the boring part. Whilst all the others went out to play, I had to stay in. One thing I did notice, was that Eddie and Johnny went out together. Eddie couldn't help but glance in my direction as they went on their way. I wished that I could have gone with them!

Nan took me back to the clinic, which was quite busy. Eventually, a nurse took a look at my back, prodded around a bit, asked plenty of question, then seemed happy. She wrapped me up again and told Nan to bring me back tomorrow. With instructions to make sure I had plenty of rest. She also asked Nan not to get the bandages or my wound wet. On our way home, we called into some shops for groceries and what surprised me, was that most of the people we met knew all about the fracas and all seemed very worried about "little old me". I wasn't very happy with all this attention, but it seemed that I couldn't do much about it.

I just sat around, mostly playing games with Michael and Patsy. There wasn't much I could do about it. During the afternoon we had a visitor. It was a policeman and he was very serious. He asked Nan all about my injury and then wrote down everything. He eventually got to me and fixed me with a serious look. He wanted to know what we were all doing and if I'd seen the person who threw the slate. I wasn't scared of him, with his serious manner. I looked him in the eye. "I was hit in the back! How could I tell who threw the fucking thing!" He looked a bit shocked. Nan scolded me for swearing, telling the policeman that it must be the pain I was in. He grunted, took a few more notes and then went away.

Aunt Emma had to take Eddie and Jimmy up to the police station, but they couldn't give any more information. They were, however, given a stern lecture and warned not to go near the old building again and

In Spite of Everything . . . .

to keep out of trouble with the local boys. Later that evening, Jimmy told me that they had roped off the old building along the beach and there was a big notice which said "Keep Out".

The days went by very slowly. I was totally bored. Nan had let me go outside but warned not to go far away or start running around. Then, just before tea-time, Dad showed up. His first "port of call" was to come over to me. He was quite relieved, I think, to see that I was in fine shape. I can't imagine what kind of message he got. He gave me a big hug but couldn't resist a little shake of the head. "Paddy, my son, you'll be the death of me. Trouble seems to search you out, like a sniffer dog but you look alright. How are you feeling?" "It doesn't hurt very much now, Dad. It just feels a bit tight as I move about. Other than that and being bored stiff, I'm OK, honest. And by the way Dad, I wasn't running away!" "I couldn't imagine you running away from trouble Paddy. That your problem. You always run TOWARDS it." With that, he ruffled my hair and patted me softly on the head.

Nan made Dad some dinner, which he was just about able to eat, considering the fuss Eddie and Michael were making. I could hear Dad, Nan and Aunt Emma chatting away. What's that all about, I thought. One thing I did hear Dad say was that he was going out to meet uncle Patsy and have a few drinks with him. They never knew when that opportunity would happen again, or if . . . !

Dad had stayed the night, but next morning he had to go back to his unit. He wasn't very happy about that, but there was nothing he could do about it. He gave all us boys big hugs, making sure that he didn't hurt me, at the same time hanging on to me a bit longer. As he left us, he said: "Nan's got some news for you. Don't forget, be good for her." As usual, an extra glance in my direction. Then with a broad smile he was off again.

"What's the news, Nan?" "Well, your Dad's battalion are leaving this area and returning to their HQ, which is near Reading. Therefore, once Paddy has had his stitches out and the doctor gives us the all clear, we'll be going home." Eddie just nodded. Once again, I noticed that

Eddie and Johnny went out together, keeping away from the others. I'm gonna ask him what's going on once they get back.

That evening, I button-holed Eddie. "What's going on with you and Johnny?" "Shush, be quiet, you'll get us all in trouble. Now, you don't think I'm going to let them get away with what they've done to you, do you? Me and Johnny have been trying to find out which one of that gang threw that slate. We now know that it was one of the older ones. So, what we're trying to arrange is a straightener, and the good news is, I think it's nearly sorted. Jimmy knows about it, but not any of the girls. Sorry to tell you Paddy, but you can't have any part of it. Just keep your mouth shut." Good old Eddie, I almost felt sorry for the bloke who chucked that slate. He didn't know it, but he'd have more pain than me. I knew that Johnny would be going along to make sure nobody else interfered. "Well, you'd better hurry up, Ed. When I was at the clinic today, they reckoned that my stitches will be out in a couple of days." Eddie looked worried. "Yeah, and then we're off, back to London."

It must have happened! Eddie, Johnny and Jimmy slipped into the back door. Aunt Emma gasped. "What you been up to Eddie, your face is all bright red and you've got a cut on your ear. And look at your shirt! That's blood, isn't it? "We've been climbing trees in those woods over the back there and I just fell into a bunch of brambles. No damage really." "Well, take that shirt off. I'll have to wash it and sew it up because you've badly torn it. It's a good job Nan's not about. Luckily for you, she's taken the youngsters for a walk." She paused for a moment. "You haven't been fighting, have you?" She'd definitely tumbled, but she was a lovely lady, so she wouldn't make a fuss. Eddie winked at me, just before he stripped off his shirt and dashed upstairs for a clean one. You must remember this was war-time, with rationing, food and clothing. Luckily, Aunt Emma was a wiz and mending and sewing, with six kids, she had to be. Eddie had to suffer the third degree from Nan at tea-time. She just made that humming noise of hers but I think she had a good idea of the truth.

That night, I'd never been in that much of a hurry to get to bed. "What happened today, Eddie?" "Be quiet. I know you won't stop until I've

In Spite of Everything . . . .

told you. I sorted it out today. It was payback time." With that, Jimmy butted in. "Let me tell him all about it, please Ed!" "Go on then. I know that you're dying to tell him." Jim started. Apparently, they had made a meet. It was at that small housing estate on the edge of town. There were about a dozen of them, boys and girls. Luckily, Johnny was there and they had the sense not to tangle with him. The lad who had thrown the slate actually apologised for injuring me so badly, but they were all still very aggressive (it got better). This lad said to Eddie that, in spite of that, he'd still give him a "pasting", as he put it. Eddie told them all that it was probably a good thing that I was unable to be there, because, as he said "I was a very nasty little bastard". Then they had a fight. Everybody stayed out of it, just one on one. It turned out that this was a really tough lad and Eddie took a fair bit of punishment. But, as I've said before, this boy may have been good, but Eddie was "seriously good". Jimmy carried on, very excited. Once Eddie had got his range, and those damaging left hooks began to land, it was only a matter of time. The boy was knocked to the floor several times. Eventually he'd had enough. He was well beaten. Eddie was now happy and he could relax. They walked away from the crowd and it wasn't until they'd got to the end of the street before they were yelled at and called all sorts of names. Johnny smiled. "Eddie, remember, stick and stones may break your bones, but names will never hurt us." They gave them "V" signs, then walked away. Jimmy was as proud as punch. It was a story he remembered all his life.

"Thanks Eddie", I said. "I still wish I could have been there. How do you reckon I'd have got on with him?" "He was a couple of years older than you. It would have been hard for you to handle him, but I'm glad you wasn't there, because you can be a right pest." "Thanks again, are you alright?" "Yeah, of course I am. Shut up and get to sleep." I noticed Michael lying there, his big blue eyes almost popping out. "Keep quiet about this Mike, and you get to sleep as well."

Another couple of boring days went by, for me anyway. Then I was off to the clinic to have my stitches out. I didn't know what to expect and I wasn't looking forward to it cos' I figured that they hurt going in, so they must hurt going out. I recall watching Aunt Emma stitching up Eddie's torn shirt. I asked her if that was how they'd sewn me up. She said "Similar". They were very nice people in the clinic and the nurse soon had me in the treatment room. I was a bit scared, but I wasn't going to let her know that. She asked if I wanted Nan in the room whilst she took the stitches out, but I said that wasn't necessary. I don't think Nan was too pleased! After taking off the bandages which, thankfully, had decreased a bit over the past weeks, she put something on my back that cooled it down. Then the horrible smell of disinfectant, the clink of metal instruments. Much to my surprise, it didn't hurt too much, more like a stinging feeling. She made some very encouraging noises, then it was over. "You are a lucky boy, it's healed up nicely, but you'll have quite a nasty scar. It was a very ragged and splintered cut." I wasn't bothered. After all, I couldn't see it. I had to do some stretching exercises, then she seemed satisfied. "I'm going to put some gauze and plaster over the scar, just to protect it for the time being." With that, she gave me a couple of sweets, then out into the outer room to see Nan.

The nurse very carefully gave Nan all the necessary instructions about how to look after me. Giving her a small pack of bandages and sticking plaster. We thanked everyone, then got on our way. I was bombarded with questions at tea-time. You see, at that time, none of us had been stitched up before.

The very next day, we were off. We said our very sad farewells, none of us knowing when we would see each other again. It didn't bother me that much, because I was looking forward to being back in London. In truth, because of my accident, I hadn't been able to enjoy the seaside as well as the others. They all came to the little bus station, then the journey home. We were getting old hands at this sort of thing. Bus, two trains, this time arriving at Paddington Station. Then a couple of buses to Tower Bridge Road. I enjoyed the familiarity of the place. It made me feel secure and it was nice to see Granddad and especially nice to see Eileen. They had some exciting news: Aunt Anne had given birth to a baby boy. Nan was very excited and asked a million questions. The boy was called "Walter". I didn't know it then, but our lives were to be very involved in future years. But then all that is another story.

Chapter 5

It didn't take long to get back to our normal routine. Off to school we all trooped every morning. It was now getting lighter and warmer. Johnny got his old job back, which pleased him because, although he wasn't that keen on work, he liked the money. There was a slight increase in the school attendance. Some of the children were actually coming back from being evacuated. There were a few false air-raid alarms, just to keep us on our toes I think, but other than that, the war seemed far away. We did hear of other places being bombed. However, although the bombings had become more and more haphazard, there were a couple of enormous raids during the early part of the year. Most were over the other side of the river, but there was one terrible incident, only about a mile away, where a school and shelter took direct hits. There were many deaths. Amongst them were a few distant relatives and friends.

Weekends came and Eddie started to work on Kit and Michael's clothing stall. He was actually selling. I helped, but only re. stocking the two stalls, one in Tower Bridge Road and the other in the "Blue Anchor" market at the other end of Grange Road. Michael had got me an old bike for the job. We also helped the other stall holders in their packing away, we then pushed the empty stalls down our alley-way, the one behind the shops. Even young Michael helped with that. We soon became well known in the market. I noticed that a few of the local lads weren't too happy about that. There was an uneasy standoff between us and a few of the chaps. "If those three fuckers don't watch out, I'm gonna do something about it." "Now calm down

Paddy, they're alright. Just a bit jealous. They're too stupid to get any work and too wary about tangling with us. All they want to do is thieve. Do me a favour and ignore them." "Yeah, I know you're right Ed, don't worry." I somehow knew that some day it would be off.

Well, the summer was drifting away, nothing very special happening. Our lives were now very settled. I still had these dark thoughts in my head and, try as I may, couldn't get thoughts of my Mum out of my head. Nan was wonderful. She seemed to be able to second guess me and as soon as I felt a little disturbed, she was there to comfort me. Living in our busy house was brilliant. I think that living with older people made us grow up quicker.

"I've had a letter from your Dad. He's coming home in the next few days. He's got some important news. Do you want to read it, Paddy?" "Yes please Nan." I knew that Nan couldn't read that well and this was her way of making sure that she hadn't missed anything important. The letter was very odd indeed! Half the sentences had been crossed out completely. But yes, he was coming home shortly.

I was coming out of school, skylarking about as usual. Then I spied him, Dad, with Michael on his shoulders. I yelled out to Eddie: "Quick, Dad's outside, waiting for us." Most of the other kids all seemed to stop and stare. There, standing on the pavement was this big soldier. I dashed over to him and he gave me a big hug. He held on for a bit longer than usual. Then Eddie arrived. We were all very excited. I sensed that Dad was a little bit uncomfortable. "Come on boys, let's be getting home. I'll try to get you some sweets or ice-cream on the way home." We soon arrived at "Nastri's" shop in Bermondsey Street. They knew Dad straight away and began shaking his hand and generally making a fuss of him. They were two little fat Italian brothers, both a bit scruffy and dirty, but they certainly made a fuss of us. Then soon produced a few sweets from the back of the shop (no ration coupons needed). They didn't have any ice-cream (no eggs, apparently). We were happy, though. Before we left they told us that we were welcome to come in and they would find us some sort of sweets. "Don't come in with any of your mates, only you three." They had very strange accents.

In Spite of Everything . . . .

We continued up Bermondsey Street, all busily chomping on our treats. Suddenly Dad said "Now listen boys, I've got to go abroad and do some fighting against the Germans." "Oh no!" cried Eddie. "When have you got to go, Dad?" "I'm sorry boys, but it's this evening. I have no choice. I was very lucky to get here to see you. I was given special permission." "When will you be back, Dad?" Eddie asked. He hesitated for a short while. "I honestly don't know, but I promise I WILL be back some day." I saw Eddie's eyes begin to well up. "Will you kill some Germans, Dad?" I asked eagerly. He looked at me with a strange half smile on his face. "Yes Paddy, I'll try, just for you!" Well, that was alright then, my immediate thoughts were. Here we go again, just as things were getting settled, another bombshell. I thought "Will it be like this all my life?". I was really pissed off again!

When we got home, the house was crowded: Nan, Granddad, Eileen, Johnny, Aunt Anne with her new baby, Uncle Nathan and a couple of the Fitzimmons (Dad's cousins). The place was in turmoil. Dad, Granddad, Nathan and the cousins went out over to the pub. I didn't think they opened this early, but they had their ways. Nan made us our tea. I was very quiet. "Come on Paddy, don't worry. Your Dad will be alright, he can look after himself." She could read me like a book! What she didn't realise was, I wasn't worried about him. Just truly and completely pissed off! He shouldn't be leaving us!

We finished our tea and Nan said that we couldn't go out to play because Dad wouldn't be that long. She popped over the pub for a short while and Johnny went with her. We could actually see the pub from our windows. That just left us, Eileen, Annie and Walter of course. Suddenly they were all coming back. Chaos! There were lots of good-byes, cuddles, handshakes and tears. Then Dad grabbed Michael and hugged him close, whispering in his ear, he then handed him over to Nan. He seemed confused by all the excitement. Then my turn. I shall always remember the beer smell on his breath. He cuddled me. He did look very sad, told me not to worry and be good for Nan and Granddad. Then Eddie! Eddie did not want to let go, but it had to end. Alongside his cousins, Nathan and Johnny, he was gone. We watched him disappear round the corner. He turned and waved, there were tears in his eyes. "Daddies and heroes don't cry, do they!" Alone in my thoughts. I'll probably never see him again. Will everybody leave me one day?

That night in bed, I called over to Eddie. "Are you still awake?" "Yes", he whispered, "but don't talk too loud, Michael's gone to sleep at last and Nan won't be very happy if you wake him up. Anyway, what do you want, you pest?" "Do you think Dad will ever come back again? What about those Germans, they won't kill him, will they?" "Don't be stupid. You know how strong Dad is, don't you! I shouldn't think any German could kill him! Don't let Nan hear you talk like that, because she'll get really annoyed. Now please, Paddy, stop worrying and go to sleep. Goodnight, God bless." "Well, if they know what's good for them, they better not! I owe those bastards one, anyway! Goodnight, God bless, Ed. See you in the morning." You see, I always liked to have the last word!

As usual, I couldn't get to sleep, so down the stairs I crept. I could hear muffled sounds coming from the kitchen. It was pitch black, I could hear my own heart beating. All of a sudden the kitchen door opened and a shaft of light brightened up the stairs. "Is that you, Paddy?" Eileen whispered. "Yes, I couldn't sleep." "Be quiet and come over here, quickly now." There were two other girls sitting round the kitchen table, one of whom I recognised as Patty Bygraves. Her older brother was to become very famous in future years. We of course never knew that then. I think he was in the air force. They all made a fuss of me and we played some cards. Probably Pontoon and I probably took money off them. Only "pennies and ha'pennies". Eventually, Eileen ushered me off to bed. I slept.

Life settled down once more, school, weekends, warmer light summer evenings. It didn't get dark until 11 o'clock, because we had double summer-time. The clocks went forward 2 hours. Nan had an awful job, getting us to come in for our bed-time. It seemed like the middle of the day and we just wanted to play outside with our mates. Nan was very strict about us going to bed, so we didn't get away with much. If she couldn't actually see us, she would come out into the street and call out our names. (She had a very powerful voice and was a very beautiful singer).

In Spite of Everything . . . .

We came home from school, this particular afternoon, and there was Uncle Nathan fixing a shelf up in the kitchen. Nan was very excited. "We've got a wireless and your Uncle is fitting it up for us." Now, this was exciting, because we had never had a wireless before. There were two reasons for this. The first, we never had electricity in our old house and, even if we had, secondly, we had no money. Apparently Dad had given Nathan some money to buy a wireless and Uncle Nathan knew where he could lay his hands on almost anything. The only time I had listened to a wireless was next door in Kit and Michael's house. They had everything, including a gramophone and a refrigerator. However, Michael was always sad over the fact that they had no children. That was something I could never quite understand (I can now). It wasn't long before we had the wireless going. This was really exciting. That evening, Granddad was reading his paper, as usual, but now he was able to listen to the news as well. There was soon the old familiar "Tut tut" coming from behind his paper. Unfortunately, we were still as noisy. Then, as usual, Nan would have a go at him, at the same time telling us to finish our tea and go out to play. "Not too far away, mind!"

A wireless! When you think of all those famous war-time rallying speeches by Churchill, we, and millions like us, never actually heard them at the time. We read about them, but I think that millions of Londoners and others didn't. I sometimes wonder whether Mr. Churchill was aware of that.

The year drifted by, the nights drew in and it got gradually colder. Christmas was approaching. "We've got a letter today from your Dad", Nan told us excitedly as we came in the house. "How is he, Nan?" shouted Eddie. "He's very well and wants to know how you all are." "Here, Paddy, you read it out for everyone." I took the letter. It was written on funny paper and it was very short. There had been crossings out. He couldn't tell us where he was, but he was in the "Royal Berkshire Regiment" and part of the eighth army. He sent his love, wished us all well and, once again, reminded us to behave ourselves for Nan and Granddad. He hoped that Nan was receiving money from the army and asked her to get some photographs of us three and post them out to him. B.F.P.O. something, was the address.

Well, we were all very excited with the letter. It was hard to realise that he'd been away six months already. Very shortly our lives were to change once more.

Granddad was listening (yes, listening) to the evening news, when a literal bombshell occurred. The Japanese had bombed America at a place called "Pearl Harbour". We didn't know where that was in America, but it was frightening news. They were a worrying lot, those Japs. Nan was very worried because she knew that her son George was in the Far East somewhere. Another son, Jim, who was in the navy, was also somewhere out there. Not a nice Christmas present. We all went to church that Christmas. Yes, even me. Eddie and Michael were in the choir but they didn't ask me to pump the organ.

Christmas came and went. Nothing like the Christmases of today. No turkey, very few sweets, no toys. Our main treat was an apple and an orange. Courtesy of Uncle Nathan. We did also have a chicken. We were lucky, many millions had much less. I was sitting alongside Eddie in the kitchen of Kit's house since she always invited us for tea on Saturdays, once we'd put their stalls away. She made a wonderful chicken broth, with lovely soft rolls. It was delightful! They were talking about the war and seemed very glad that the Americans were now fighting the Germans, as well as the Japanese. They seemed to think that the war wouldn't last very long now. I was going on about how much I hated the Germans and that I would kill them all, if I had the chance. Michael quickly changed the subject. "Have you heard from your Papa." (strange accent). Eddie told them about our letter. We finished our broth and then Kit gave us a frozen orange afters (dessert). Again lovely. We thanked them both. "Don't forget to give your Nana our blessings. Have you given the boys their money?" "O yeh, to be sure I have. Thank you Eddie, thank you Paddy, be good."

Once we'd got outside, Eddie pulled me by the arm: "You're a real dope, you are. Don't you know that they are both from Germany?" "I thought they were Jewish!" "Well, of course they are, but they are also German. But to be honest with you, from the way I've heard them talk, they are not very happy with the German people. They still have

In Spite of Everything . . . .

relations living in Germany and they are very worried about them. But Paddy, from now on, mind your tongue, OK." "Sure Eddie, sure."

The year was already racing by. Nan had taken all three of us up to a photographers in the Old Kent Road and had some photos taken. She made us all put a short message on the back and then posted it off to Dad. Things were really settling down. Granddad had his "cockle and whelk" stall going flat out every Friday, Saturday and Sunday. I loved helping him getting his fish prepared, but Granddad preferred young Michael to help him (his Mikey). Well, he was the youngest and he would do everything Granddad wanted (without question), unlike me. His stall was outside the Horseshoes Pub, which was only around the corner from our old smashed up house. Most Saturday nights, Nan would walk down to the pub for a couple of drinks, so we went with her. We used to play outside, sometimes helping Granddad, but I think, more often than not, we were a nuisance. Especially when some of our old mates turned up. Granddad used to treat all the kids to lemonade and crisps. I think that was part of the attraction. Crisps! There was only one flavour then: salted. The small bags of salt were in each packet. Now and again, if you were lucky, there would be two packets. These were happy times. Even so, at unguarded moments, I could detect the worry in Nan's eyes. The War.

It gradually came to our notice that, during the summer, Americans started to appear. There were a lot of them posted in the Tower of London and we soon got the message! We used to stand on Tower Bridge and call out "Got any gum, chum." And usually some of them would appear on the actual tower walls and throw chewing gum over to us. And sometimes, if we were lucky, great big bars of chocolate. Now, obviously we were not on our own. There were hundreds of us. This caused a great deal of scrambling. Sometimes we came out on top. Other times we were unlucky. It was exciting though. We had never seen actual Americans before. The all looked very big and smartly dressed. I don't know what impression we gave, but unfortunately, a lot of children looked in a bad way. Not very well fed and dressed in not much better than rags. I think we were all a bit pasty faced.

There was always a great deal of activity in our house as the year went on. Since we now had a wireless, we were all able to listen to the news and we were very aware of the fighting going on around the world. Our particular point of interest being Egypt. We knew that's where our Dad was, somewhere in that area, and there were reports of very heavy fighting. I could only imagine our Dad killing lots of Germans. I never realised the mortal danger he was in. Nan did however! At last a letter arrived. Good news! He was safe and well and, apart from sending his love and asking for another photograph, that was that. "Censorship."

We saw more and more of Uncle Nathan. He and a few friends seemed to spend a great deal of time with Granddad in the upstairs kitchen. They were up to something, I thought. Then, one day, Michael and Kit paid us a visit. Upstairs they went with Nathan. Eventually we found out what was going on: "Nylons". Uncle Nathan and his mates were doing deals with the "Yanks". They supplied the nylons in return for petrol coupons (forged of course). I had already heard Uncle Nathan telling Granddad about the "coupons" one Saturday night around the cockle stall. Apparently, they were a "nice little earner". Now, there was the extra earner from the nylon trade. You see, women could not get hold of proper nylons, even with their clothing coupons. Therefore, within reason, they would do anything for their precious nylons! It soon became known that Kit and Michael's two market stalls had nylons for sale, but only to a few special customers and at a price. Eddie soon became very popular and I earned extra money for running a few pairs up to the "Blue".

"Now, listen to what I'm going to tell you." Uncle Nathan was in the upstairs kitchen facing us. "I'm going to let you both have a couple of pairs of nylons for you to sell privately. You pay me once you've sold them. The reason I'm doing this is that I don't want you getting tempted into becoming "tea leafs". If you've got any brain, you don't need to pinch things. Certainly not off people you know. That's a "mugs" game. You should be able to earn yourselves an extra bit of pocket money in an honest way! Yeah." [Honest!! That was stretching it!!]

He had a great wisdom, that Nathan! Well, our standing around the "manor"[6] and all over the market was now about as good as it gets. We didn't have to queue for much, most times walking straight through to the back of the shops, where we were able to get almost all we wanted. Johnny had grown into a very powerful teenager and had soon got a reputation for fighting. There weren't many who would tangle with him. Eileen (beautiful Eileen), had a string of boyfriends, but nobody that special. I was always slightly jealous when she brought blokes home. I didn't like sharing her affections. I didn't know then, but I do now, she was acutely aware of this.

The summer soon passed, without any major incidents, other than the fact that Aunt Anne had another baby, a boy. They called him Seamus and they seemed to spend most days round Nan's. Uncle Nathan was very active, sometimes just one step in front of the law but to be honest, because of his activities, most of the family were well looked after.

Christmas came and went, and another year started but there was no sign of the war ending. Quite the reverse, apart from the fact that all was quiet on the home front (no bombing), there seemed to be vicious fighting going on in the Middle East (Dad's area) and the Far East, where Uncle George was. The Americans were engaged mainly against the Japanese, although many more were appearing here. Uncle Nathan loved them. And I now know why! The shortages however got even worse. The war in the Atlantic was a big worry. We were losing tons of shipping and even bread was becoming harder to get. The dreaded queues. We used to take it in turns to wait in line, spelling each other after about an hour. I hated standing around doing nothing, listening to the idle chatter of the women. So, I had a great idea. I paid one of my cousins to take my turn in the queue. Eddie wasn't very happy, but I'd got in first! Thank God for Uncle Nathan.

One of the bonuses of the lull in the bombing was that the picture palaces opened up. That meant we could go to the pictures and also a lot of the boy's clubs reopened in the evenings. I really enjoyed playing football and doing some boxing. I loved the training and the sparring in the ring. Eddie was a brilliant boxer and it didn't take long before most lads wouldn't get into the ring with him. One of our trainers one night suggested that I should spar with Eddie, although he was bigger than me. I was very hard to hit. But before we had a chance to put it to the test, the head of the club put a stop to it. "I made a promise to your Nan that you must never, never fight each other. She'd have my guts for garters." That was the end of that then. Eddie loved joining things. He joined the boy scouts. Now, that went down like a "lead balloon". Granddad went "ape-shit". He hated the boy scouts. I can hear him now "Fucking grown men going around in shorts! Something very odd about that. You don't want anything to do with them!" He therefore had to very quickly "knock that on the head". Not to be deterred, Eddie went and joined the sea-cadets. Granddad gave that the seal of approval. The sea cadets used to march down Tower Bridge Road most Sunday mornings. Eddie loved it. He looked really smart in his navy blue uniform and, in no time at all, there he was at the head of the band, swinging the mace. (He really looked the part). I used to help him with the white blanco on his "spats and trimmings". We all used to turn out to watch them go past and Nan was bursting with pride! From my point of view, because of Eddie's interest in the cadets, he stopped going to Sunday mass. Remember, sea cadets are a Church of England thing. I had, for a long time now, been skipping mass, so now Eddie was no longer interested, Nan didn't bother sending us off to church. That pleased me no end and took the pressure off. I was never entirely comfortable deceiving Nan. I found out later however that she knew exactly what I was up to.

Most Sunday mornings now, I could help Granddad get ready and go down the pub with him. Whilst there, I would usually bump into Uncle Nathan and some of his "colourful" friends: Smuggler, Joe Diamonds, Waggy, Tom Thumb, The Iron Duke, they were all great characters. Uncle Nathan once said to me: "Paddy, all these people are thieves and thugs, they are never to be completely trusted. They might be friends of mine but they are all low-life, filth, remember that." That startled me. "The only people to trust are your own!" There ended the lesson. I never forgot!

As the year wore on and summer was fast approaching, we heard that Aunt Emma and all our cousins had come home to Brockley.

In Spite of Everything . . . .

This was only a couple of miles away so I looked forward to seeing Jimmy again and the rest of them of course. We carried on in our now comfortable and contented routine. Eddie was very popular with all the local women because he was a very good nylon salesman but I was only interested in getting my cut for my delivery service. Added to all this, was the hidden bonus of our popularity with Michael and Kit. They adored us, probably Eddie most, although Michael had a lot of time for me. There was a glaring example of his fondness of me, which came about in a couple of later years. There was a certain very popular Irish Tenor and we all whistled and hummed his hit songs. I was sitting in Kit's kitchen one Saturday evening, having finished taking down and putting away the stalls. Their wireless was on and there he was, singing away, in what I thought was a very powerful and delightful voice. "Titch, titch", Michaels mumbled. "Do you like that kind of music, Paddy?" "Well, not bad, he's a very, very good singer", I replied. "Come into the parlour (that's what they called the living room—we called it the "front" room), Paddy. If you like I'll play you some really classy music." "Oi, don't you go pestering young Paddy with your music", Kit looked over at him sternly. "No please, he's not bothering me, honest. I don't mind at all, as a matter of fact, I like music. I prefer to hear that American stuff. Eileen is always playing nice music. We've even got a wind-up gramophone now. Nan likes to listen to Bing Crosby but I prefer a new singer called Frank Sinatra."

Michael sat me down in one of his big armchairs. He put this record on. After a short while, really wonderful music started to play. Then this rich powerful voice, it was truly magical. The record stopped. Michael looked over at me. There were tears in his eyes. Even Kit had come out of the kitchen. "Paddy, that was a singer called "Gigli", a famous Italian tenor. I hope you can agree with me. Remember please, he is class! The Irishman is a "good" singer. I hope you can tell the difference." I could! And, thanks to Michael, I've always been able to. My appreciation of good music was also influenced by Eileen mainly and to a lesser extent in later years by Uncle Jim.

Arriving home from school one day, we were greeted by the news from Eileen that she was going away to join the "land-army". Young girls were recruited to work on the farms to gather the harvest to provide the much needed food. We, and certainly me, were not very happy. The thought of losing Eileen was frightening. She took great care to explain that it wasn't a proper army and that she would be in no harm. She would only be away for a few months anyway but I still felt very uncomfortable.

Then another bad bit of news. Nan had received a letter from the navy. Uncle Jim was in hospital in Calcutta, India. He had contracted tuberculosis! Apparently, it was in its early stages and quite mild. He was being very well looked after. Nan made me read the letter again and again. Luckily I was able to stress the good parts. We played on the fact that at least he wasn't fighting the "Japs". Now, this brings me to an amazing and very true and quite miraculous occurrence. One of Nan's other sons, George, was actually fighting the Japanese on the Burmese/Indian border. Now, he WAS in mortal peril. It is well to remember that, to ordinary people in Bermondsey, S.E. London, India/Burma/Japan, all these places were in the "Far East" and we were not aware of the distances.

George's wife, Lil, did receive very occasional letters from her husband, only of course when he was on leave. Now, this is the thing: She (Lil) had only been round home the other day to let Nan know that George was fit and well. He had been on leave, would you believe it, in Calcutta. Upon receiving this news, Aunt Lil dashed round to a branch of the Red Cross to see if they could be able to arrange for Uncle George to get to see his younger brother Jim. They (the Red Cross) were very excited and assured Lil that they would be in touch with the War Office. They did and, although it was many months later, Lil received a letter in which was a photograph of George standing alongside his brother Jim, he in his hospital whites, with George in his jungle greens. That photograph is still in existence today. Nan always had it standing atop of her piano.

Aside from the near miracle of the meeting of two London brothers on the other side of the world, was the worry over the wellbeing of George. We were all aware of the gigantic and terrible battles taking place against the Japs and of the terrible casualties. The picture of George and Jim was over three months old when we received it. It

In Spite of Everything . . . .

was a weird and strange feeling. Granddad and Nan never uttered a word. I thought, will this ever end? There seemed to be dark news around every corner. How the adults carried on, I'll never know!

I popped home for something to eat one Saturday dinner time. The house was buzzing. Besides Aunt Anne and her two young boys (they were there every day except Sundays) was Aunt Emma with all six of my cousins, Jimmy included. We were all very excited and pleased to see each other. The girls made me take off my shirt so that they could see my scar. They were impressed. I quickly gobbled down my food. "Why don't you take Jimmy down to see Eddie? He's dying to know all about your shenanigans" Nan said with a wink and a smile. "He's also got news for you." Off we went. "What's this news then, Jim?" "Well, Mum hasn't been very well lately, that's why we came home from Somerset." I did think then that Aunt Emma did look quite pale and drawn and strangely subdued. "Nan said that I can live with you lot for a while, at least all through the summer holidays." I don't think I'd smiled as much for a long while. "That's terrific, we'll have a smashing time. Wait till we tell Eddie. We'll be there in a minute." The extra plus for me was Jimmy's love of sport, which matched my enthusiasm. You could hear the market before you laid eyes on it because the market sellers used to yell out a great deal in those days, telling all and sundry about their particular "bargains"!

"There he is, Jim." Eddie was at the stall serving a lady. I hasten to add, not nylons but other ladies items. The nylons were definitely undercover. Jimmy was eager to dash over to Eddie, but I held him back. "You can't disturb him while he's serving, Jim. The guv'nor (Michael) will be a bit pissed off." Eddie noticed us anyway. He gave a smile and a nod and, once his punter had gone, he mumbled something to Michael, who looked over to us. "Good day, Paddy, nice to see you again." I'd already made a delivery this morning. Eddie slipped off his money bag, gave it to Michael and came over to us. "Hello Jim, what you doing here? I thought you was in Somerset. Let's pop over to that cafe, I've only got fifteen minutes, we're pretty busy. You can tell me all about things whilst I'm having a sandwich and a mug of tea. I've got a little bit of business over there, anyway." Jimmy looked puzzled.

The cafe was busy, but the moment the boss-lady spied Eddie, she signalled for him to come round the back. He returned very quickly, sat down and gave me a wink. Mugs of tea and great lumps of homemade bread pudding soon arrived. Jimmy quickly told Eddie the news, which pleased him also. "In that case Jim, I'll put you in the picture once I get home this evening. There's too many "ear-'oles" around here and we don't want to educate anybody, do we!" We wolfed down our food and were away. "See you later, Ed", we called as we left the market. "I think I'm going to enjoy this!"

"Let's go over the park (Southwark) Jim, before going home. There's usually some lads playing cricket. You still play, don't you?" "Yeah, but not for a while. How far is it?" "It'll take us about five minutes to get there, come on, be lively." With that, I started to trot. Jimmy followed. Sure enough, there was a bit of cricket going on.

"Oh, oh, can we have a game, lads?" I asked. "You'll have to be on different sides because we've got even numbers" one of the older lads yelled out. "What do you want to do Jim? Field or bat?" "I think I'll be on the batting side, are you ok with that?" "Sure, I love fielding anyway." I jogged onto the pitch. "Do you bowl or bat?" I was asked. "Well, to be honest, I haven't done a lot of either, but I like bowling best." With that, I was directed out onto the leg side.

We had a great afternoon. Jimmy got a few runs and I got to bowl a few balls. At the end of the game, a man who seemed to own the bats, stumps and balls came up to me. "Hey sonny, how long have you been playing cricket?" "Hardly ever, Mister. Why?" "Well, you look a natural with that ball in your hand. When you get older you should play a bit. Don't forget! You and your friend are welcome to a game anytime. We play here most Saturday afternoons. Goodbye!" "Thanks Mister. By the way, he's my cousin, not a friend!" There's a difference! "But thanks for inviting us, it's been a good afternoon." With that, we started off home. On the way I explained to Jimmy what we were getting up to. He was all ears. "I'm sure Eddy will agree, Jim. So I think we'll put you in it." "That'd be nice" he replied with a wide smile.

In Spite of Everything . . . .

"Where have you two been all afternoon?" Nan enquired as we appeared in the kitchen. "Your Mum and the girls waited as long as they could, but they had to get home." I had noticed how quiet and empty the house was. "Paddy, you had better get over the market, they are starting to pack away. Take Jimmy with you."

Off we went. We started to break down the stalls, pushing them away down our back alley. I was getting fed up with explaining who Jimmy was, but everybody seemed happy with him. We soon finished our jobs, then home we went. Eddie was in by now, as was Michael. He'd been out with Granddad. The tea table was noisy, with everyone talking at the same time. "When you've finished your tea, take Jimmy out and show him around, but don't go too far" Nan instructed. Granddad looked very pleased as we dashed away. "Oh, by the way, I've got some interesting news for you all when you get back. Don't forget, not too far!" "OK Nan" Eddie called as we galloped down the stairs.

"Wonder what the news is?" Eddie looked puzzled. We took Jimmy around "the buildings," where lots of our mates lived and played. Jimmy, as always, got on with nearly everybody. There were always a few assholes who thought too much of themselves. "They don't count, Jim" I said in a very loud voice. I didn't like them, and they didn't like me. I liked it that way! We didn't hang around too long. We were all curious about Nan's "news."

"I was just going to ask Johnny to fetch you lot" Nan said, as we all trooped in. "Had a nice time, Jimmy?" "Yes, thanks Nan." "What's the news, Nan?" Eddie blurted out. "I'm going to write to the farmer and book a bin and a hut to go hopping (hop-picking) during September." Now that was a good surprise. We had been hopping for a short while in 1940. But there was a certain "air battle" going on at the time. We came home as soon as we could, just in time for the Blitz. The short time we were there was indeed exciting, and I couldn't wait to go back. It was only after all the excitement had died down, when we were all in bed, that it dawned on Eddie. "What about my job and Uncle Nathan's sideline?" "I hadn't thought about that" I answered. Now, there was a puzzle, if ever there was one.

|137

Sunday morning, Eddie off to his sea cadets, Jimmy and me helping Granddad get his fish ready. Nan was very excited, she loved her four weeks in Kent, picking hops. Lovely fresh air, and a chance to earn a bit of money. Nan had explained to us how much she was paid for every bushel she picked. "Paddy, I want to speak to you as soon as you've finished helping Granddad." "OK, Nan." Wonder what she wants!!

"What is it, Nan?" I thought I was in trouble again, but I couldn't for the life of me remember why! "I want you to help me write a letter to the farmer, a Mr. Larkin. They won't allow us on their farm without permission." Help, I thought, now that's a laugh. Nan fished out the address. Horsmonden in Kent. Spring Farm. She asked me to write some funny things. Nan thought that the farmer was a very important man! He's only a fucking farmer, I thought! Obviously, I wouldn't say that to Nan. I shortened the letter, kept it very formal and to the point. Nan was happy and that's all that mattered to me. "Thanks, Paddy, you're a good boy. I'll go over to the post office and put a stamp on it first thing Monday morning. Are you going with Granddad?" "Yes, Nan, is that ok?" "Of course it is, but take Jimmy with you. Michael's going with Granddad." Jimmy was very happy.

When we arrived at Granddad's stall, he was already doing a fair bit of trade. He nodded at us. Granddad was a man of few words, especially when he was taking money. Jimmy's old bombed out house was only around the corner, as was ours of course. He had to have a look, so round we trotted. There, coming down St. Thomas' Street, was Uncle Nathan with Smuggler. I bet you can imagine how he got that name! As they passed us, Nathan gave me a friendly tap on the back. "What you doing round here, young Jim?" he smiled. "Hello, Uncle, I'm going to stay with Nan for the summer. Got any nylons?" Nathan was obviously a bit annoyed with that last remark. "Keep your tongue between your teeth son, and don't be a silly boy! Paddy, I'll have a chat with you a bit later on." They passed us by, heading for the pub. "I think I've upset him, haven't I?" Jimmy looked worried. "Well, yes, just a bit! Uncle Nathan doesn't like people knowing his business. He's always told me to be careful, because there's a lot of "grasses" about. Don't worry too much, Jim, I'll straighten it out. There's a bit to learn, however!"

Nathan called me to one side, just a few yards away from the stall. "Have you been telling people about our little bit of business?" "No, no, honest. Jimmy came with me to the market, he had to know. You know that I wouldn't breath a word to anybody. I'll straighten him out. He's only been with us a day. He's very sorry and worried." "In that case, I'll leave it to you to 'educate' him. I'll send you out some crisps and lemonade in a minute. Be careful!"

Now, here's the thing. Uncle Nathan was always impressing upon me that information is precious, it's 'education.' "Son, education has to be paid for, don't give it away for nothing. The best thing is not to educate anybody, because then they'll know as much as you! And that could be very dangerous, and costly." I have never forgotten that piece of advice.

Chapter 6

*I*t was dark as we all trudged up to London Bridge Station. Granddad and Johnny pushing a big ship's trunk, which was fixed on to pram wheels. We were off hopping.

It was about the second or third of September and already the nights were drawing in, but the mornings were even darker. I think double British Summer Time was to blame for that. We approached London Bridge via Long Lane and Borough High Street. I don't think Granddad wanted to walk up past Stainer Street Arch. What was left of it, that is. We were getting closer to the station, when we noticed a rag-tag army of families like us, all travelling to Kent to pick hops. There were a few familiar faces, but many more strangers. We looked a sorry bunch. Not like today's travellers, with their designer luggage. We were lucky with our sea chest, some had old tea cases, others old sacks, some with blankets, all holding their belongings. There were special trains laid on by the railways. These were packed full of us harvest workers. Our train took us to Paddock Wood. In later years, Johnny used to laugh and reminisce over this event. He used to say jokingly, that the reason our trains were so early (6am-7am) was so that the commuters coming in from the suburbs wouldn't have to come into contact with us, the great unwashed. This was always a point of amusement, but the reality was that the fares were very cheap for the adults and children went free. As I look back, I marvel that all during the war, the City gents and workers, most with their bowler hats and briefcases, poured into London Bridge, and like a tide, passed over London Bridge itself. We thought they were all posh and rich, but I doubt they

In Spite of Everything . . . .

all were! One thing's for certain, the Germans couldn't put them off. It's a pity that Adolf Hitler couldn't witness this. He probably would have worked out that you can't push these sort of people about!

Granddad waved us away, this was fast becoming a common experience for him. So, there was Nan, Johnny, Eddie, Michael and me. We were old hands at this train lark. Although, I was never relaxed when those great steam engines started roaring and hissing. The whistles sounded, and with a clanking and shaking, we were off. Rat-a-tat-tat, rat-a-tat-tat. Soon we were leaving London behind. We stopped several times, shunting into sidings, to allow other trains past. Some had military equipment, some going into London, just people. By mid-morning we arrived at Paddock Wood. End of the line. Again, in a siding. It was the usual, mad, manic scramble to get us, and our belongings, off the train. Women were screeching at their kids, and kids shouting and crying back. God knows what the local people thought of us lot. Much the same reception a train load of poor illegal immigrants would probably get.

Nan had a chat with a railway porter and I noticed him pointing towards another platform. "Come on boys, we've got to get over to that other platform. There will be another train along in a minute. Johnny, you and Eddie will have to take care of our luggage (the sea chest)." "No trouble Mum. Come on, Ed." "I'll give a hand as well" I volunteered. Nan had hold of Michael tightly by the hand. He was going nowhere. We managed to get to our train, which had just pulled in. There was only one carriage, being pulled along by this great belching steam engine. There were now only half a dozen families, one of whom we knew quite well. We were soon settled and off. It didn't take very long before we arrived at Horsmonden Station. Off we scrambled, the train only went as far as Goudhurst, the end of the line. Then about turned and came back. This time the engine pushed instead of pulling. You see, it was only a single line track. Sadly, no more, a certain Mr. Beeching took care of that many years later.

There, waiting for us in the station yard, was a big horse and cart. The horse reminded me of those lovely animals in Vinegar Yard. The driver was a big, red faced, ancient man, or so I thought at the time,

|141

anyway. He had an unfamiliar twang to his voice, but he was very polite, and very helpful. We were all soon in the back of the cart, then off we went. We were totally uncovered. Thank God it wasn't raining. I enjoyed this experience, but Spring Farm was only two miles away and we were there in no time.

The farm, or more accurately, the area set aside for our dwellings, comprised of a large area of grass, which was known as 'the common,' surrounded by wooden or iron corrugated huts. That was that! There was fresh water coming from out of a pipe in the side of a hill. It must be said, that this was the coolest and best tasting water I have ever, and I mean ever, tasted. There were a series of smaller huts set aside as toilets. These sat over deep holes that had been dug in the ground. Not much privacy there! There was a quite large shed that was used by the women to cook in, or get their washing dried, when it rained, and boy, did it rain!

Nan had her favourite hut, and luckily, this had been assigned to her, thanks to my letter, I thought. Nan's hut was locked by a small padlock, over a hasp and clasp fitting. She then produced a key, which she gave to Eddie. He had it open in no time. It was just an empty shell, with a flat wooden board over various apple boxes. "What a dump!" was my immediate reaction. As usual, Nan must have noticed my looks. "Just you wait and see, Paddy. I'll have this looking like home in no time. Right! Let's all get to work. Paddy, go over to those woods and cut me five pieces of stout wood, about six feet tall and as thick as your wrist. You know how tall six feet is? Well, it's about as tall as your Dad." With that, she produced my jack knife. I was now like a dog with two tails to wag. I was gone in a flash. The woods were brilliant. There was no shortage of good stout branches. I didn't know what it was then, but I do now. It was chestnut. Just what the doctor ordered. In no time at all I was back at our hut. By this time, it was a hive of activity, other families arriving and unpacking.

While I'd been away there had been a delivery of bales of fresh straw. Eddie and Johnny were tearing a bale apart and were helping Nan stuff out these big palliases. They were to be our beds. Whilst this was going on, Michael was bringing out of the hut the big old cooking

In Spite of Everything . . . .

pots and the irons for them to hang over a fire. Nan then gave him a broom. "Paddy, fix that broom to one of those poles of yours!" That didn't take me too long to do. Just a bit of shaving, and job done. Johnny knew what to do with my remaining handiwork. He made two cross frames, about five feet apart. Screwed them into the ground and lashed them together with some strong string, that Nan had brought along. Out of the hut came a big long metal bar, and before long all the pots were hanging over the ground. "What next, Mum?" said Johnny. "First, help me with these bed spreads. Then dig a hole where the fire's going to be. Not too deep, remember." Johnny had done this before! He started to work. There was a spade amongst Nan's things as well. She hadn't forgotten anything!

"Eddie, see that big pile of wood over there." About a hundred yards away was this pile of cut wood, about as big as a house. It had been tied up in big bundles, they called them faggots. "I want you and Paddy to go and bring me over three bundles, only three, no more, remember." Off we went. By now a few other boys, and women, were scrambling about on this moving mass of wood. Some were struggling a bit. That's when Eddie took charge. He climbed on to the top of the pile and started chucking the faggots to the ground. He was instantly very popular, he loved it. I ferried three bundles to our hut. By now, Johnny had a two foot round hole, only about six inches deep, and he'd compacted the sides down. The soil was mainly clay, so it made a very neat job. Nan was in the hut, busying away. She appeared. "Now, Paddy, Granddad has shown you how to get the fire started, hasn't he? He told me that you are good at it. Well, now's your chance." With that she chucked me over a box of matches.

I think I like this hopping! The faggots were tied together with twine but I soon had that cut. Luckily there was wood of all different thicknesses. I went to work cutting off the thinnest of twigs, then slightly thicker and so on. Soon I had a big pile. Nan gave me some old newspaper. Hey presto, in no time at all, a blazing fire. Michael was sent down to the spring for some water. He came back soaked, he'd been mucking about. He did manage to bring back a pot full, however so Nan hung it over the fire, and we had a cup of tea in no time. She produced a big pile of wrapped up sandwiches and we greedily tucked into them. Eddie must have smelt them, because he showed up very smartly.

After a short while, a lady turned up in the next hut. She was alone with two girls of about our age. They didn't have a clue, but Nan was on hand. Nan had been told that there was a bus that went to the village every couple of hours. There was a bus stop just outside the farm entrance. Well, it was just a pole really, but it did have a timetable on it. I was sent to find out the times. "Nan, there's a bus going by in about twenty minutes, what do you want to know that for?" "I need to buy some food for you all, you want to eat, don't you?"

Nan had given our new neighbour a nice cup of tea and a couple of our sandwiches. She was like that. "I'm going to catch the next bus into the village. Eddie, I want you and Michael to come with me. Johnny, you stay here and keep an eye on Paddy. Will you give Dol (that was apparently the lady's name) a helping hand if she needs it?" "Yes, sure will, Mum."

They walked up to the main road, and very shortly a bus appeared. It was a single decker. This seemed odd to me, us being used to the big London buses and trams.

Johnny asked Dol if we could help her, but she didn't want a fire built. She would use the facilities in the public cookhouse. She did, however, ask me to fetch her a couple of faggots. She just fancied a small fire of her own as it got dark. This I did. "Want to have an explore and look around, Paddy?" "Yeah, not 'arf." We didn't bother locking our hut, most people were like us, poor but relatively honest. Well to each other, anyway! We strolled past the two rows of huts. Women and children were busying themselves, getting their lives together. Not many were as organised as us, but there were five of us. Then we came across the spring! There was a metal pipe sticking out at the bottom of a hill, and this cool tasty water was just pouring out non-stop. What wasn't used, fed a small stream. There was a massive archway, over which the single track railway went so we carried on, under the arch. The ground sloped away quite sharply, and it was a tough climb all the way to even more woods. In the woods we went.

This was really exciting. Very shortly, the woods ended, and there in front of me was an apple orchard, full of lovely red apples. There was a fence however.

"Wow, John, do you see those apples?" "Of course I can, but two things Paddy: they may not be ripe and I don't think the owner wants you to start nicking them! Do you?" "Leave off, John, there's fucking millions of them, he won't miss a few!" With that, I was over the fence. I quickly picked as many as I could carry, actually stuffing them down my shirt front. I then heard dogs barking, luckily quite a way off. I quickly got back over the fence. We then retreated into the woods. The big black dogs soon appeared. They were barking like mad and were clearly agitated then a red faced man eventually appeared. He looked around, but couldn't see us hiding amongst the trees. He did shout out however "I know you buggers are in there somewhere, the dogs can smell you. Don't you be coming into this orchard, it's private property." We just grinned at each other. "Silly bastard," Johnny whispered "I told you to be careful." After a short while, the man and dogs went on their way. "Come on Paddy, let's get back. I'll take some of those apples, you'll get your collar felt[7] with them sticking out like that." He then bit into one. "Mmm, they're lovely and sweet."

On our way back, we discovered another large pile of wood. This time, cut into thick logs. "We'll get shot of these apples, Paddy, and then come back here for some of these thick lumps of wood. They'll be ideal for keeping the fire going. They look nice and dry, as well." That's just what we did. I was busy picking out the thickest and driest lumps, when a man appeared from out of the nearest hut. "Hey, what the fuck do you think you're doing? That wood belongs to us, now fuck off." He hadn't noticed Johnny! "Oi, who do you think you're shouting at, you dope. This wood's for everyone to share. There's a big pile of faggots up the top, which is much thinner wood, so that you can get your fires started. That's for all to share as well. Now piss off!" He glared at Johnny but, luckily for him, turned and went back in his hut. There was a lot of families taking notice of the incident. "Take no notice of that burk[8], I don't think he'll bother you again Paddy!" He didn't. I returned another three times to get more logs. "That's

|145

enough wood, Paddy." Johnny had worked out that I was only going down there to annoy that bloke.

"I think we should get a fire started, Paddy. Nan will be home soon." It was getting a bit chilly all of a sudden. I went to work, breaking up small bits of dry wood, then with a little amount of paper, I had the fire alight in no time. I placed some of the thick logs, making a circle around the main fire. We had a blaze in no time so we sat down on Nan's old wooden stools, of which there were four.

The bus pulled up, and very shortly Michael and Eddie came running down. Eddie was carrying a heavy bag. "Nan needs some help, she's got two bags to carry." Johnny jumped up, met Nan and took the bags from her. "Now, that's a nice fire. Did you do that Paddy?" I was proud to say that I did.

Eddie told me all about the village. He was most excited because there was a shop that sold fishing gear. I told him of our adventures. "Where did these apples come from?" Nan had discovered them on her small sideboard. "I picked them in the orchard, Nan." "Well, you mustn't. The farmer will fetch the police and throw us off the farm. We can buy them from the farm shop really cheap. There's no need to scrump them. That's a country word for thieving. You understand, Paddy?" "Yes, sorry Nan. Nice fire though, ain't it?" With that, she laughed "You cheeky little sod."

Nan had brought loads of food, mainly vegetables, but a little meat. She had all of our ration books with her, including Granddad's, so we weren't that bad off. In no time at all, she had a tasty stew boiling away. Dol looked on enviously. "Want me to start you a fire off?" Nan said. "I don't want to trouble you Anne." Now that always fascinated me, when I heard people call my Nan by her proper name. "Don't be silly, you're no trouble! Paddy, be a good boy and get Aunt Dol's fire going." Everybody was called Aunt or Uncle, although they weren't actually related in any way whatsoever. I did as I was told, and she soon had a fire going. "Where did you get those logs from, Paddy?" Eddie asked. "Oh, there's a great pile of them down the bottom, why?" "I'll go and get some for Aunt Dol." (What a creep!) There was

In Spite of Everything . . . .

no way, however, that I was going to let him go on his own. I wanted to see old grumpy bollocks, so off we went. He peered at us while we were cherry picking our logs. But he kept his trap shut. I'd told Eddie the S.P.[9] so he was fully prepared. "Don't wind him up, Paddy, I know what you are like."

We had a delightful dinner sitting around our fire. Nan made the best stew I have ever tasted. I knew that she would. She had made an enormous amount, enough to feed Aunt Dol and her girls. Nan would look after the whole country, if she could. After our dinner, Nan shooed us off to get out of her way. She had work to do. The evenings were still light because of double summertime, a war-time invention. "Don't go too far, don't get into any mischief." Those blue eyes pointed in my direction. "Get back before it gets dark." This time looking at Eddie. "We will, Nan" he said, as we scampered away. Obviously, we made for the woods. Eddie wanted to make a camp.

We soon found a suitable site and set about clearing away the shrubs and ferns. It was a magical time, very different from Bermondsey. "Come on, it's time to get back. We don't want to worry Nan." We did as Eddie said, no arguments. Our fire was still burning as we got back to our hut. Johnny was sitting on one of the stools, lightly prodding it. "Had a good time, lads?" "Yes, thanks John, we're making a camp" Michael replied, very excitedly. Nan popped up out of our hut. She looked as though she had been working hard. She had. It is hard to describe how she had turned this simple, barren hut into a comfortable living space. The beds were all made up, well actually one gigantic bed. She had managed to curtain off her private bit, and had hung large curtains, so that the bed was divided from the rest of the hut. There was a small piece of carpet, sitting in front of her small dresser. She had all her knick-knacks placed on that. There was a picture of the Virgin Mary and the Pope. Well, she would, wouldn't she! This was all shown off by the light of an oil lamp. It was quite amazing, what women could do with such a little. It's a shame we didn't have a camera, but I've tried to paint the picture.

"You can sit outside for another half hour, boys. Then you've got to get to bed. It's been a long day, and we've got to be in the hop garden by eight o'clock. Work starts tomorrow. Johnny, once they're in bed, I want you to go into Horsmonden and bring me back a couple of Guinnesses from the pub. The nearest one is The Gun."

I stoked up the fire, and we sat around chatting excitedly. The smell of those fires will stay with me forever, even today. After all these years, whenever I smell a bonfire (well most times anyway), I am back immediately to hopping.

In to bed we clambered. I was surprised how comfortable our straw mattress was, that is, once we'd. We were asleep in no time, but for the fact of Johnny getting into bed, I went into a deep sleep. Then, there was this banging on our hut door, this was our alarm call. This, apparently, was a job done by one of the farm hands. There was certainly no chance of overlaying. He didn't stop knocking until Nan called out. I could hear the same routine being carried out all over the farm.

"Come on boys, rise and shine. Paddy, get a nice fire going and I'll get your breakfast on." We jumped all over Johnny, getting out of bed. He wasn't very pleased. I stayed in my pyjamas, just putting on my shoes, then out the front door I went. It was only just getting light, and surprisingly, very chilly and damp. Damp! I hadn't thought of that. All my twigs were wet. This was going to be a challenge! "Have you got any old paper, Nan?" I called out. I was worried. She produced the paper I needed. It was a good job that she had used a lot of paper when packing all her crockery. It was then that I spied smoke coming from the cookhouse. I dashed over, carrying a bundle of twigs. There was a nice blaze on. "Can I put these twigs next to your fire, just for a couple of minutes? I need to dry them out. They're wet, but I never heard any rain." "Yes, of course you can, young fella," the old, weather beaten man answered. "Push them alongside the flames, they'll dry in no time. It's not rain, by the way, it's dew." What in the hell was dew? I thought to myself. He must have noticed how puzzled I looked. "Overnight in the country it gets cold and damp, and this settles on everything, like a wet blanket, and I mean everything, mind."

My twigs were soon dried so I gathered them up, some very hot, and thanked the old man. With my dry twigs, and the paper Nan had supplied, I soon had the fire going. I was very careful to only put the underlying wood on. Eddie then started to interfere. Now, the trouble with Eddie was that he was totally impatient. He would have piled as many logs on the fire as he possibly could, and that would have put the fire out. "Ed, will you do me a favour, and stop interfering? Nan, would you tell him please?"

Nan gave him a job. "Take that bucket, and go down and fill it up with water. It's no good Michael going, he can't carry enough." Off he went, and in no time I had a roaring fire going. "Paddy, you and Michael go over to the washhouse, take a bar of soap and a towel, and give yourselves a nice wash." Washhouse—a couple of standing taps, with some wooden slats, all covered by a tin roof. No sides. The water was freezing and there was no privacy. We waited our turn, stripped to the waist and gave ourselves a good sleush. This was a wash down, probably derived from sluice. We were cockneys, after all!

The whole place was now a hive of activity. Nan soon had the water boiling and was now able to make our breakfast, porridge oats. Made with water, by the way, not milk. We ate outside, whilst Nan washed and dressed privately.

We were now ready for our first day actually picking hops. A couple of farm hands and a smart tall lady appeared at the top gate and instructed everyone to follow them. We crossed the road, went up a narrow track and after just a couple of minutes, there it was. This enormous field, you couldn't see the end of it.

The hops grew on bines, about 12ft. tall. They were attached to overhead wires by string. Four hop bines grew from the same clump of earth, which in turn were about six feet apart. They all sloped towards each other, making long arches, each (in this garden anyway) stretching for a good quarter of a mile. Placed inside each pair of bines was a hessian covered bin. The bins actually resembled stretchers, which were about three feet high, the hessian reaching to the ground. They were about six feet long. Each picker had their own "alley," which meant you picked from both sides.

The farmer, an elderly man dressed in plus-fours and a tweed jacket, was standing on a big cart. Alongside him were a bunch of farmhands. The lady crossed over and stood below the farmer. We were all welcomed and wished well. He then proceeded to spell out what he expected from his pickers. We were warned to be on our best behaviour, no swearing or fighting or taking fruit that didn't belong to us. He pointed out that he didn't want to find too many leaves amongst the hops, and then, crucially, he announced that he would be paying 10D. (10 pence) for every bushel picked. That is about 4p of today's money. I didn't understand whether that was good or bad, but Nan didn't seem to be too bothered. Nan then got into a queue, and very shortly the smart lady, who Nan called Elsie, gave Nan a tally book. One of the farmhands then showed us to her bin. We were now ready!

"Now settle down, you boys, and I will show you how to pick hops." With that, Nan tugged hard at one of the bines and it came crashing down. She draped the bine across the bin, which was about three feet wide when fully opened. "Now, watch, look and learn." She tore off the lower longer branches, turned the branch over. The hops then dangled from the branch. She then very quickly stripped the hops, and a few small leaves, into the empty bin. "Now, Michael, go round the other side and start taking those hops off and drop them in the bin. Eddie, you and Paddy, start just as I have, at the other end." With that, Eddie dragged down a bine. We started picking hops. It was awkward at first, but it was surprising how quick we mastered the art. "I'll pull the next bine down, Nan" Eddie said. Which he did, with great gusto. Now Eddie, being Eddie, had a good idea. "I'll pull three down at a time, Paddy, and that will make us quicker at it." Well he did, and it was a disaster. Once he'd flung them across the bin, it left no room for actually picking. That was Eddie for you. Ever impatient. We abandoned that idea, but it seemed like no time before we had picked our sixteen bines. Nan showed us how to tidy up the now stripped bines. We were ready to move into the next row. Eddie and me got hold of a handle each, with Nan at the other end. We carried it forward. At this stage, it wasn't too heavy but we didn't take that long to realise that with more hops in it, it would become heavier. We whirred away for the next couple of hours, making good progress along our lane. From the air, it must have looked like slow moving locusts that were gradually devouring the hop garden.

Another amusing thing was the way the bins moved up each row. It was like a boat race. Different people picked at varying speed, so therefore the bins were no longer in a straight line, as they were at the start.

Eddie was most concerned at being left behind, so he devised another strategy. Michael was finding it difficult to pick at the bin. He wasn't much taller than the sides. Eddie went off and came back with a wicker basket. "Come on, Mike, come up here." Eddie had gone forward a couple of rows, he quickly pulled down a couple of bines and lay them on the floor. "Here you are, Mike, fill this basket up and when you have, give us a call and I'll empty it into Nan's bin." Now, that proved to be a good idea. Shortly after that, Johnny arrived. He had brought a tin container with some hot tea, and another containing some Tizer. Nan was grateful of that, so were we. Johnny didn't particularly like hop picking, but he set to it and we were soon starting to fill our bin. Nan, every now and then, would dip down and fluff up the hops at the same time removing as many leaves as possible.

"What happens when it's full, Nan?" I asked. That had started to puzzle me. "Don't worry, son, it won't get that far. They come round during the afternoon and empty out our bins. That's when the 'measurer' does his work." With Johnny with us, we were having spectacular results. I had gone up to help Michael, because he was getting a bit frustrated trying to fill his basket. With my help, we soon had not just one, but a couple of basketfuls. The added advantage being, that when our bin arrived in this lane, it was half picked. Which meant, in no time, we were moving forward again. Eddie was chuffed.

"Boys, I'm going back to the hut to make some sandwiches. Give me about 20 minutes, and then come back for some food." Off she went. We carried on picking, whilst all around us people were gradually sloping off for a break. The farmer didn't like people taking too long over their dinner break. I noticed his eagled eyed manager making mental notes. Surprisingly, that made me feel uncomfortable!

"Come on, let's go, Nan will be ready for us now." We didn't need any encouragement. I was starving. We stopped picking and followed Johnny. The Manager stared at us, I stared back at him! "Paddy, what's your problem? He's only a local carrot cruncher[10]." "I don't care what he is, I don't like him staring at us!" "Behave yourself, you're too sensitive, now be lively!" Off we went.

When we arrived at our hut, Nan had a great pile of sandwiches ready for us. They were all piled in a great heap on one of Nan's little tables. She'd made a pot of tea by making use of the fire in the cookhouse. Most of the other women were doing the same. There were cheese and pickle and luncheon meat sandwiches. Courtesy of Uncle Nathan.

It is difficult to explain, but, when you pick hops, your hands get stained by the pollen, and even though Nan made us wash our hands, the stain and taste stayed on them. Now this gave our sandwiches a unique taste. The memory of this taste has stayed with me forever. If you ever get the opportunity to get to the Kent Life Museum, take a nice thick cheddar cheese sandwich. Pick some hops, then taste the flavour!

It didn't take us long to demolish the pile of food. We then became restless. "Sit still for a minute, and let your dinner go down. I'll be getting back to our bin in a short while. You can stay and play for a bit. Then come up and give me a hand. I know you're interested, Paddy, don't be too long, because the measurer will be along during the afternoon." She was soon off. Michael and Johnny went back with her.

"What do you want to do, Paddy?" Eddie asked. "Why don't we go to our camp for a little while? I'm certainly not going to rush back, that fucking local is annoying me!" "You heard what Johnny said! Behave yourself. I think you imagine things sometimes." We locked the hut and sauntered over to our camp. "I'm gonna cut myself a nice thick stick,

In Spite of Everything . . . .

do you want one Ed?" "No, thanks, but cut some thinner branches so that I can make a bow and arrow for Michael. I'll make one for you, if you want." Eddie made a mean bow. He had a great knack of tying the string by 'whipping,' a skill he learned in the sea cadets. "Yeah, yes please, Ed." These woods were magic. I could have cut enough wood for hundreds of bows. I also managed to cut myself a really nice branch. This will make a great stick. Eddie soon got fed up. "I'm going back to help Nan, you coming?" "Not yet, Ed, I'll be with you a little bit later." "Make sure you're not too long. See ya." With that, he was off. I cut a few more nice branches, and eventually dropped them off outside our hut. Eddie had the key with him, so I couldn't get in. I walked up to the garden, busily shaping my stick. There he was, staring at everyone, at the same time chatting to one of the pickers, a lady. I strolled over to Nan's bin, swishing my new stick as I walked past him. "Oi, you haven't been cutting down all our trees, have you?" "No, mate, there's still millions of the fuckers left." "Hey, mind your language, you cheeky townie[11]." Johnny glared over at him. He didn't say no more. Nan gave me that steady stare of hers. "Mind your language, Paddy. Don't annoy that man, he's the measurer. Come on, whir in and pick some hops for me." She actually used to say "wire in," maybe because she wasn't able to read much, and it sounded the same. Johnny smiled at me. "You're enjoying yourself, ain't ya." "Not 'arf" I said. "I'll go up the row and help Michael." This pleased Michael and we set about filling the basket. Suddenly, Elsie appeared at the first bin. Alongside her was the measurer. Plus two more hands, carrying big hessian sacks. The measurer dipped his bushel basket into the bin, filled it with hops. He then tipped it into the open sack, which was being held by the farm hand. "One!" he called out. "Two." And so on, until he'd emptied the bin. 12 was the final count. Elsie then marked that down in her register, and wrote it down in the lady's card. They were soon onto us. I watched eagerly at proceedings. This is a joy to relate!

Every time the measurer, who turned out to be called Russell, plonked his basket into the pile of hops, thereby crushing them, Nan would dip on from the other side and fluff them up again. It was like a Laurel and Hardy film. I don't know how I stopped myself from saying something to Russell, but I didn't. But I helped Nan fluff them up. Nan showed me how to grab hold of the far end of the bin and tip them forward towards Russell. He stopped at 22. Eddie was delighted, not because he was greedy or anything, but because he wanted us to have more than anyone else. Unfortunately there were a couple of bins that had more than us. Elsie marked Nan's card, smiled and said "Good afternoon, pleased to see you again. Are these all your boys?" "One son, and three grandsons." "Well, they are a credit to you, lovely boys. Now, don't forget, send one of the lads over to the farmhouse this evening. There will be fresh milk and eggs. Just get them to bring your book along and I'll lay it off against your earnings. Have a good afternoon." With that, she was off to the next bin.

There is nothing worse than looking down into a great empty bin. It seemed to take forever to get a layer of hops again. But we pressed on and the bin started to very slowly fill up again. Nan was always one step ahead of the game. She must have sensed that we were all getting a bit fed up with sticking around the bin. "You can all run away and play for a while, if you want. I'll be alright, remember Johnny's here to keep me company. Don't go too far though. I need to go into the village to buy some fresh food. I'll need to get away early to catch the bus that goes by on the half hour. Now, take care of Michael and stay out of mischief. Paddy, you be careful what you do with that stick! Last thing, be careful around that lake. Now off you go!" Lake? What lake? "Ed, do you know where the lake is?" "How the fuck do you think I know! I've been here the same time as you! But, I'm about to find out!" He spied one of the farm hands who had a great big pole with a wicked looking hook on it. They used it to cut down any branches that had broken off as the bines had been pulled. They were able to cut the strings that were stopping the branches from falling. "Hey, Mister, do you know where there's a lake round here?" "There'll be a few lakes arounds about, but the biggest and best is just yonder behind those line of trees." He pointed out the trees in question. "Mind, you be careful, the water is very deep. Make sure you look after the nipper[12]. Is that your Grandma over yonder?" He pointed towards Nan. "Yes, why do you want to know?" "Ho, ho, don't panic, young man. She's an old friend of mine, and your Uncle Pat's a good friend also. Now, be off with you, I've got work to do."

In Spite of Everything . . . .

We were soon beside the lake. It was huge. You could tell it was deep, by the dark colour. I lobbed some big clods of earth, into the water, they went splosh. We were shouted at from over the other side of the lake because some people were fishing. Eddie and Michael were really excited, they both loved fishing. We made our way round to the other side of the lake. I, very willingly, cleared away any obstacles, any nettles. My stick came in handy.

"Be a bit quieter, will you! You'll scare all the fish away." The voice came from a small clearing by the lakeside. A couple of blokes, probably Johnny's age, were fishing. "Sorry fellas, my brother gets a bit carried away. He's not a fisherman." "Well, if you're gonna stay here, please be quiet." "Have you had many bites?" Eddie whispered. "Yeah, the lake's full of fish." "Can anyone fish here?" whispered Eddie. "You have to have a permit from the farmer. What farm are you on? I presume you're down here hop picking?" "Spring Farm." "Well, you're in luck. This lake belongs to the owners of Spring! You just have to go round to the main farmhouse, and you can buy a permit. Have you got any fishing gear with you?" "Thanks for the info, but no, I haven't." "There's a good shop in Horsmonden that sells a lot of tackle and bait, do you know it?" "No, but I was in town last night, so I know where Horsmonden is. Thanks for your help. We'll get out of your way and let you get on with your fishing. Bye!" With that Eddie strolled off, and beckoned us to follow. "Be a bit quieter, Paddy, for a couple of yards at least! Fancy a bit of fishing, Mikey?" "What about fishing tackle?" he asked eagerly. "Don't worry, I've got money. I'll buy some for both of us. You interested, Paddy?" "No, thanks Ed, I've got me own Nelson's[13], but I ain't gonna spend it on fishing."

Eddie was making his plans. "Let's get back to Nan. I'll ask if I can go with her to the village. She'll need a hand anyway, then I'll get all we need, Michael." It was easy finding our way back. We only needed to be opposite where the fishermen were, and Bob's your uncle. "Blimey, you weren't away too long. What, were you missing the hops?!" Johnny smiled warmly at us. Eddie went on to explain what had gone on. "Funny thing, Eddie, I was going to ask you to come with me. Have you got any money with you?" "Yes, Nan, I always carry money in my "sky[14]." "You shouldn't carry too much on you. You might wind

| 155

up losing it" Johnny said. "Don't worry, I've got deep pockets and I'm very careful."

"Paddy, nip over to Mr. Russell and ask him the time, will you." Nan knew that I could already tell the time. She also knew that she was the only person that I would run errands for. "Don't forget, be polite." "Hello Mister, can you tell me the right time, please?" He looked at me like I was a piece of dirt. His 'kettle'[15] was neatly tucked in his waistcoat pocket. He slowly pulled it out, flicked it open and shoved it in my face. He was shocked when I glanced at it, and read the time "quarter past four." I kept that to myself, however. "Ta very much, Mister." I about turned and dashed back to Nan. "You've got just over a quarter of an hour, Nan, before the Bus comes by." "John, will you look after Michael and Paddy until we get back?" "Sure Mum, no trouble. We'll stay and pick you some hops for another hour. It'll give you a good start for the morning."

Tomorrow was Saturday, a half day, but you had to wait until you'd been measured out before you could leave the field. Any hops left in the bin over the weekend would be ruined. "I'll get you a nice fire going, Nan, by the time you are back. Bye!" They were soon on their way. We went to work with gusto! I was getting pretty good at this hop picking. Nan said it was because I picked left handed. I never did work out why that was!

"I should think that Granddad will pop down tomorrow, and I wouldn't be surprised if your Uncle Nathan didn't make a show as well. I hope he comes down in his van, then I can get a lift back. I've got to get back to work on Monday. If I'm not back soon, I'll get the tin-tack[16], and I don't need that." "We'll be alright, John, we'll take care of Nan." With that, he burst out laughing. "Honest, Paddy, I'm not taking the piss, but it's Nan who looks after you, remember! But I know what you mean, and I've no doubt you will!" With that, he chased round the bin, and we had a playful fight. Michael joined in as well. The people near us couldn't make out what was going on. It was none of their business anyway!

In Spite of Everything . . . .

I had a nice fire going in no time. There were fires going all around us, I've said it before, the smell, plus now we had the strong smell of the hops with all that pollen flying about. I was learning quick. I kept a nice bundle of very small twigs in a corner of the hut, in the dry. We were now just sitting around the fire. I was breaking up the smaller twigs, to replace what I had used. Johnny had gone down to bring up some big logs, Michael had gone with him. I could just see the top of the Bus, it was only just visible over the tall hedgerow. People started to appear at the top of the farm gates. Yes, there was Nan and Eddie. Nan was carrying a couple of shopping bags, and Eddie had, what looked like, fishing rods. I rushed up to meet them. "Got a nice fire going for you, Nan, and we stayed late and picked you loads of hops." "There's a good boy. Can you help me with this shopping?" I grabbed one of her bags. "What ya got there, Ed?" "What do you think it is? Fishing rods, you dope. Where's Mikey?" "Oh, he's down the bottom, helping Johnny." Nan was soon unloading the shopping. I could see fresh bread, potatoes, cabbages, carrots and a few tins. There were other packages as well.

"Since you've all been such good lads today, we've got a special treat tonight. I was able to buy some homemade sausages and a nice piece of lamb for tomorrow." "Ain't there no rationing here in the country, Nan?" I asked. "Yes, of course there is. This lot used up all our rations. There is definitely more vegetables and bread available and I think the local butcher gets hold of a few extras, but don't you go worrying about that. Concentrate on your fire, I'll want it blazing shortly."

Just then, Johnny appeared, carrying a great pile of large logs. Michael dashed over to Eddie and they excitedly started going through their fishing gear. "Eddie, once you've got Michael settled down, will you go and fetch a bucket of water. I want to start your tea." "OK, Nan, just give me a minute." "Do you want some faggots?" Johnny asked. "Yes, please John. We could do with a couple of extras to sit on." Off he went. I gradually built the fire up. Nan, amongst her many things, had an old iron self-standing griddle.

"Paddy, when I tell you, I want you to place that griddle into some hot embers. Not too much smoke. Think you can do that?" "Course

I can!" I wasn't really sure if I could, but I started experimenting with the thicker logs of wood. After a while, it seemed to be working.

Johnny and Eddie started peeling potatoes and Nan cut them into nice chunky slices. "You ready, Paddy?" I was. "Take this damp cloth and put the griddle over your fire. It looks like you've done a nice job." I gave the fire a good poke, and then very carefully put the griddle over the red hot embers. Nan produced a big frying pan, unwrapped a packet of lard, then placed a great lump in the frying pan. On the griddle it went. It was sizzling and spitting in no time. Out came a large pack of the biggest sausages I'd ever seen. They looked delicious. She plonked half a dozen straight into the pan. They were sizzling in no time. "Eddie, watch those sausages and turn them over from time to time, try to stop them from sticking." She dropped the pile of cut potatoes into a boiling pot of water, then a tin of baked beans into a smaller pot. "Keep that fire nice and hot, Paddy." Eddie was prodding away, while I busied myself with our fire. Nan then produced a large loaf, and cut it up into great thick slices. She very quickly emptied the potatoes out into a wire basket. "Out of the way, Eddie" she said, taking charge of everything now, except the fire. She seemed happy with the sausages, that by now had begun to split open, and transferred them to a plate, then dropped the chunky potatoes into the frying pan. I wish I could describe the smell to you, talk about make you starving, unforgettable!

There we were, two of us sitting on big bales of wood (faggots), the rest on small wooden stalls, all eating sausage, beans and chips, with fresh bread to dunk up all the gravy. We were in the middle of a world war, eating like kings! Even today, with all our fancy advances, I don't think you could eat any better.

We had finished our meal, when Nan said "Paddy, keep that fire going, I will want some hot water to wash up with. Eddie, will you take my "book" and go over to the main farmhouse and bring me back some milk. Take these two jugs with you. Get going a bit lively, before it starts to get dark." "Can I go with him, Nan?" piped up Michael. "Of course you can. Stay close to Eddie, mind."

In Spite of Everything . . . .

Johnny had drifted off. I could see him chatting to some girls, over near the pile of faggots. Which, of course, were slowly disappearing. Nan looked over to me. "Paddy, after tomorrow's measure, I want you to tell me how much we have earned. Can you do that?" "Course I can! You're getting 10 pence a bushel, ain't you?" "Yes." "Well that's gonna be a piece of cake Nan, leave it to me."

Eddie and Michael returned in no time at all. They had two jugs of lovely fresh milk. We all had a cup before going to bed. Nan said "In the morning boys, well just you two (Eddie and me), I want you to get up to the hop garden as sharp as possible. I need to tidy up around here, because Granddad might pop down tomorrow. I'll be with you as soon as possible, is that OK?" "No trouble, Nan." Eddie spoke for both of us. We were in bed, listening to the murmured conversations going on around us. The next thing I knew was the shouting and rattling going on outside. Morning!

Nan was up straight away. "Come on, up you get. Paddy, get that fire going as fast as you can. Here's some dry paper and matches. Eddie, Michael, go down and get washed. Eddie, once you've dressed, go and get some water please!"

As I picked up my bundle of dry twigs, I very smugly went outside. It was damp and quite chilly, just getting light. Crash, bang, wallop, I had a fire. There was a stream of people going to and fro to the toilets and the wash taps, some of them looked quite amazed at my fire! I looked over to the cookhouse, no smoke! I just couldn't resist dashing over there. The old man was just getting his (though I must admit, larger) fire started. "Mornin' guv, beat you this morning." He just looked at me, touched his forehead, and smiled. "Thanks for the advice though, ta!" Better get back and build up my fire, 'cos Eddie will be here with water very soon. "Well done, Paddy. Now take this bar of soap and towel, and go and get washed and dressed." Nan held out both for me.

After our breakfast, a big bowl of porridge (what else?), washed down by a cup of creamy milk, Nan packed us off to the hop garden, not before running a comb through our mops of hair. Nan always wanted us to look smart.

Now, I had a little trick up my sleeve! Eddie was always rushing headlong into things. He never gave himself time to think, he was reckless! Remember, I was told all about "dew."

"Quick, Paddy, let's get to Nan's bin and tear off a few bushel of hops for her before she gets up here!" "That's a great idea, Ed. Start pulling those bines down and we can get started." I hung back, just a little. Now Eddie, being Eddie, didn't fuck about. He tore into the row and pulled down two bines at a time. Well he got completely soaked. It was like having a cold shower. I fell over laughing. "You rotten bastard. You knew what was going to happen, didn't you?" I couldn't stop laughing, but kept out of his reach for the time being. I didn't think it was wise to push him too far! We certainly got a move on with our picking, and soon had a fair few hops in the bin. Johnny showed up. "Nan will be here in a short while, how you getting on?" "Look and see for yourself." Eddie pointed at the bin. "Your Nan will be pleased!" There were now three of us picking. It was great, chatting away, Eddie telling jokes, a lovely atmosphere. It was even getting nice and warm. A nice, sunny, September day.

Michael showed up first, closely followed by Nan. She had a drink for us, and, a big surprise, some cake. Apparently a baker's van had visited the farm, and as well as some fresh bread, they had some homemade cake. What a luxury. We soon all settled down to some serious picking. The usual format, Michael and me ahead, and now, Nan, John and Eddie around the bin. "Thank you boys, you've been really good. I don't know how long we'll be here today, but I've made some sandwiches, just in case. Johnny, will you go over and find your pole-puller mate, and try to find out when they are going to measure out the hops." Johnny was back in no time. "They're starting the measure in about an hour, they want to be finished by midday, that gives them a chance to get all the hops to the oast houses, so that they can get them dried out." "Come on then boys, let's wire in." Nan's hands were a blur. It was now our turn. Nan handed Elsie her book and Russell started measuring out, with Nan fluffing up the hops

In Spite of Everything . . . .

after each dip. I'd swear that bastard was pushing down extra hard. Something would have to be done eventually! Eddie was jumping up and down. "24 Bushells," our new record, and only half a day. Elsie marked Nan's book and bade her good afternoon. "Send one of your boys to the farmhouse, we have some fresh eggs. You can have six. Goodbye."

With Nan's say so, we scarpered back to the farm. We now had the weekend to look forward to. There was a real buzz about 'the common' (as we called the hutted areas), it had a fairground feel to the place. Most people had settled in nicely to the strange lifestyle and the weekend was upon us. There was talk of a gypsy fair on the green in Horsmonden this Sunday. That sounded interesting. These were proper gypsies, unlike the pikeys that had sprung up. A couple of gypsy families were picking on our farm, and they were nice, interesting people.

"Wot ya gonna do this afternoon Ed?" I asked. "I think me and Michael will go fishing. Fancy coming along? But if you do, no fucking about." "I dunno, I might just have an explore." Nan appeared with Johnny, looking pleased with herself. "Paddy, before you run off, will you tell me how much I've earned? You've all been very good boys." Johnny smiled "She's just an old money grabber, you know!" Nan clipped him behind the ear. All jokingly though, Nan was quite delighted when I told her that in 1.5 days she'd earned £1=18-4D. (One pound, eighteen shillings and four pence.) Now that's not bad, when you realise that a good wage in those days was four pounds a week. I can assure you that there weren't too many getting that sort of money. No wonder she was pleased.

Eddie and Michael, after digging up worms and Nan giving them some old bread, went off to their fishing. They told me where they'd be, so I could find them if I wanted. Johnny set off for Horsmonden, with a couple of blokes and some young girls.

"Nan, will you want a fire tonight?" "Oh, yes, definitely son. Why don't you go with Eddie and Michael?" Nan was always a bit concerned when we split up. "Oh, I might join them after I've had a look around."

|161

I started chopping up one of the faggots, and soon had a nice pile of twigs. It was a beautiful warm sunny day, no danger of the wood getting wet. "I'm gonna be off in a minute, Nan. You alright down here on your own?" "Course I am, you silly sod. Now be off and enjoy yourself. Two things Paddy. Don't get up to any mischief and don't be too late coming back. If you do see Eddie, tell him not to be too late as well." With that, she playfully roughed up my hair. I made sure I had my knife with me, and my faithful stick. I made my way to the road, and just as I got to the gate, a brown van turned up. The window wound down, and out popped Uncle Nathan's head. "Hello, son, nice to see you. Open that gate for me, I've got ya Granddad in here with me." I then noticed Granddad waving at me. I did as I was told, and with that, Nathan drove his van in. "Where's your Nan's hut, Paddy?" I jumped on the running board. "It's just down there, I'll show you." "Hold on tight, it'll be a bit bumpy." Uncle Nathan drove down, and as he spied Nan, he tooted his hooter. There were lots of staring eyes, all around. We pulled up in a clear space between huts and they all climbed out. There was one of Nathan's mates with them, Harry 'The Horse'. I knew him from the market, he actually had a face like a horse. His nickname didn't seem to bother him.

Nan was very pleased to see them, hugs and kisses all round, even Granddad. I thought I'd hang around for a bit. There was the usual adult chit-chat going on. Nan was wanting to know how Auntie Ann was, and all about her two little boys.

Nathan opened up his van, and brought out a big parcel. Granddad had something as well. He'd brought some fish, smoked haddock, herrings, and, what a delight, jellied eels. There was also a crate of beer. Nathan took his large parcel and placed it inside Nan's hut. "There's a few bits in there for you, Mum, for you and the boys. Don't bother now, open it up later. There's nothing that can go off. Now sit down and I'll pour you a nice Guinness! Sorry son, but I've got no drink for you." "Oh, don't worry about me, I'm ok." They sat round, very relaxed. There was a nice, happy atmosphere. Nan telling them all about how we'd all been getting on.

"Have you been getting enough food down here?" Nathan asked. "Well, it's a bit in front of things in London. We can get fresh milk, plus fresh eggs have been promised. A small baker's van calls by, with lovely fresh bread, and, believe it or not, even fresh cakes!" "That sounds sweet! What about meat, are you getting your ration?" "There's a nice butcher's shop in Horsmonden, in actual fact, there are two. I managed to get some really nice sausages yesterday. There are also a couple of gypsy families here, and I've been promised some rabbits. So, all in all, we're not doing too bad." "I think your eyes will pop out when you see what Nathan has brought you. Those Americans certainly know how to live!" Granddad seemed pleased with himself.

"Anyway, want some jellied eels, Paddy? We've got to eat them a bit lively." "Yes, please, Granddad." I loved eels. Nan popped into the hut and brought out some chunks of bread, as well as vinegar and pepper. Granddad passed me over a carton of eels. I didn't take too long getting rid of them! "You didn't have to bring any fish, Granddad, Eddie and Mikey have gone fishing, so no doubt there'll be plenty of fish!" "Don't take the piss, Paddy" Nathan said, laughingly. "I'll go and tell them you're here. They'll probably come back with me. Thanks for the eels, see you later." I dashed away. What did he mean by 'The Americans', I thought!

It didn't take long to find them, and for a lark, as I got closer, I started to bash and crash my way towards them. There were a few nasty remarks coming across from various directions. I was in stitches! "I knew it, absolute dead certainty. What did I say Mike? There's only one fucker who'd muck about like you." Even Eddie saw the funny side of it. I am sure that because other fishermen (strangers) were getting a little aggressive, Eddie immediately closed ranks and became protective.

"Where's all the fish then?" "We've caught a lot, but we put them back" piped up Michael. "Well don't worry, Granddad and Uncle Nathan have turned up, and guess what? Granddad has brought some fish. To eat! The jellied eels are all gone." That last remark I said with a wide smirk. They quickly packed up their gear, and we all made our way back to the common. Guess what? I made a lot of noise. The more they yelled, the more I enjoyed myself. Eddie made me quieten down!

Granddad was excited and pleased to see us all return to the common, especially Michael. Well, he was the youngest in Granddad's extended family. Michael enjoyed being fussed over by his Granddad, and rightly so. There was a genuine buzz all around. Nan asked me to get a nice fire going, so that she could get some food cooked. We were all going into town this evening, which we were all excited about. Eddie was sent for some milk. "Don't forget to collect six eggs, they've been promised, and here, take my book with you." "Sure thing, Nan" he replied. As soon as he'd picked up the empty milk jugs and the book, he was off. Not surprisingly, Michael stayed playing with Granddad. I soon had a good fire on the go, with Granddad giving me reassuring glances. "You're doing a good job there, Paddy. I see that you've remembered all I taught you, good boy." I smiled back. Of course I had remembered!

"When you've done your job, Paddy, come over here. I want a chat with you." "What about?" Uncle Nathan gave me one of his looks, and shrugged. "You'll find out soon enough. How many times have I told you not to be so aggressive?" He smiled at his mate Harry.

Once Nan was happy with the fire, I sat down alongside Uncle Nathan. "When we're in town tonight, if you see the butcher, the one that Nan gets her meat from, I want you to point him out, but, be a bit slippery, I don't want everybody to notice." "Sorry Uncle, I've never been shopping with Nan, so I don't know him from Adam. Eddie'll be able to do it, he knows all the shopkeepers." That made Nathan smile. "Yeah, I forgot you won't go on any errands, will you? Never mind, I'll button-ole[17] Eddie when he gets back." Eddie came back with milk and eggs which pleased Nan because they were great big, brown, fresh eggs. We hadn't seen too many of those over the past few years.

Nan went to work at her cooking, while Granddad skilfully gutted the fresh herrings he had brought with him. I loved herrings, both hard and soft roes. I can still recall the smell of that evening, it's actually making me feel hungry, just the thought of it.

Once we'd eaten, I made sure the fire was completely out. We then had a rinse under the cold tap, there were no others. Then off we all trooped up to Horsmonden. Eddie and me strode ahead with Uncle Nathan, Johnny and Harry The Horse. Yeah, he walked, just the same as us, he didn't trot!! Nan, Granddad, Michael, and, by now, Aunt Dol with her two girls, followed a few yards behind. We made a happy bunch, that nice, warm evening. There was still a couple of hours of daylight left.

We stopped outside 'The Gun.' There was a big outside barn, and the hoppers were restricted to that area. They didn't want all these rough Londoners in their nice pub but they wanted their money! "Go and play on the green, we'll bring you out some crisps and a lemonade in a minute. Remember, not too far away. Eddie, you're in charge. Keep an eye on Dol's girls as well." "OK Nan, will do."

I was surprised how busy the whole place was. There were three pubs in the village, all spread around the green, and they were all very crowded. There were a crowd of gypsies gathered at the top end. They had a few horses with them. Every now and again, they galloped across the green. It was very colourful. Johnny brought us out bags of crisps and some biscuits, plus a jug of some sort of lemonade. We were happy.

I noticed that Uncle Nathan flitted from one pub to another, him and Harry. They seemed to know lots of people. At one time they called Eddie over, and he pointed to this big, fat faced man. In no time at all, Nathan was in deep discussion with the man, and at one time Nathan pointed Eddie out. Now what was he up to?

It started to get dark, so Eddie told all of us, including the girls, to stay close to the pub barn. We could hear a piano playing, and before long, the voice of our Nan singing. She had a lovely, strong voice. "Give me your smile, the love light in your eyes." That was one of her favourite songs. That was quickly followed by "I'll take you home again Kathleen." People loved to hear Nan sing, and boy, you could certainly hear her! Not a dry eye in the house!

They all piled out of the barn, all very noticeably merry, and we made our way slowly back to the farm. The adults were a lot noisier than on their journey up to the village. Nan asked me to run ahead and get a fire going. Luckily, I'd remembered to place a bundle of twigs inside the hut. It was already starting to get chilly and damp. Eddie went ahead with me, he had the key to the padlock on our hut. It was a race to get the fire going before they all got back. I could hear them getting nearer. It was as much as I could do to stop Eddie shoving too much wood on the infant fire, he was an impatient sod. By the time they all arrived, we had a nice blaze. "Ed, I know what you can do, why don't you make yourself busy and get some more faggots. We'll need some for the morning and we can sit on them now, anyway." He nodded, and was gone.

We all sat around chatting, well, mainly the adults. We listened a lot. Uncle Nathan could certainly spin a yarn, as could Granddad. There was also Johnny's wicked sense of humour. Suddenly, Nan appeared with a plate of sandwiches. She had disappeared into the hut the moment they had got back. The sandwiches were smashing. "What kind of meat is this?" Johnny asked. "It's thanks to Uncle Nathan, it comes from America, in tins. It's called spam." I didn't care what it was called, it tasted delicious. We didn't feel any shame in feasting ourselves, although, looking back now, there was severe rationing going on at the time. We were having more than our fair share. Many years later, when talking to Nathan about those times, he would say "Now don't be a dopey bastard, your Dad and Uncle were away fighting hard for their country, that's why I was left here, to look after you all. You don't think for one minute, that those lucky rich bastards living in Belgravia and the like just survived on ration books, do you? How many times have I told you, look after your own[18]!"

We were packed off to bed. I went to sleep, listening to the murmurings outside. I woke up. No shouting or rattling, it was Sunday. Eddie, Michael and me clambered over Johnny, who grunted. Nan wasn't up, I could hear her and Granddad's deep breathing from behind

In Spite of Everything . . . .

the curtains. They weren't about to be getting up in the near future. We went out, had a wash, and got ourselves dressed. The place was deserted, except for the old gypsy man in the cookhouse. He already had a fire going, I could see the smoke, and smell it. "I'll get a fire going, Ed." "That's a good idea. Don't make too much noise, let Nan have a lie-in." Unfortunately, no one thought to tell Michael. (He was a noisy bugger.) Nan's voice came from the hut, she sounded a bit croaky. "Eddie, be a good boy and make us a pot of tea. I've got a splitting headache. I'll cook you a nice breakfast, but you'll have to wait for a while."

"You get busy with that fire, Paddy, and I'll go and fetch some water. Michael, stay out of Nan's way for the time being." Eddie was in charge. We soon had a pot of water bubbling away, and Eddie made a big pot of tea. Then Nathan and Harry showed up. They looked a bit dishevelled. They had slept in Uncle Nathan's van. "Gor, blimey lads, is that a pot of rosie[19] you've got going on? I'm gasping, I've got a mouth like I've been chewing cardboard. Nan not up yet?" "No, not yet Uncle, she's got a headache. I'm just about to take them in a nice cuppa." Uncle Nathan smiled upon hearing the word headache. I was to find out in later years that alcohol seemed to have that effect. "Make sure you use the tea strainer, your Granddad hates leaves in his tea." Eddie did as Uncle Nathan had suggested. He then took tea in for Nan and Granddad. I heard Nan "Ooh, you lovely boy. Put the mugs down there, I'll be up in a moment and cook you a really lovely breakfast. No porridge today, my lad."

Nathan and Harry sat around, enjoying their tea. They had two mugs. The whole place was gradually coming to life. People hurrying to and fro between the toilets and the taps. The ladies filled bowls and washed inside the huts, the men and the boys stripped to the waist and washed. Most making shivering noises as the cold water hit them. The place was buzzing. "You'd better stoke that fire up, son." Uncle Nathan was always full of advice. In later years, him and I had many a barney[20] on that subject.

Nan wasn't lying when she promised a good breakfast. There was another gem that Nathan had supplied. Powdered egg. There was

|167

this great big cake, tin with the American flag painted on it, which contained dried, powdered egg. Nan mixed it up with water until she had a paste, then she poured it into a frying pan, over my fire, and in no time at all made a massive omelette. Eddie had been toasting thick slices of bread, and Uncle Nathan had crept away to see the old gypsy, and came back with great big mushrooms. This breakfast was as good as it gets. However, for Granddad, Johnny and Nathan, and of course, Harry, Nan produced the eggs that Eddie had got. She dropped four of them into boiling water, and then produced some smoked haddock. There was no doubt where that had come from, Granddad of course. "This will settle your stomachs, get it down ya." They didn't need any encouragement. Nan had certainly brightened up.

Elsie, the farm owner's daughter, showed up with a tractor driver and a big high sided wagon. She was taking all those that wanted to, to Sunday morning Church. Nan politely declined, it was for Protestants, not Catholics. I certainly wouldn't have gone anyway!

Uncle Nathan and Granddad wanted to be shown about, so Eddie and me took them on a long walk. The weather was very hot and sunny, by now. We made our way back to the huts. "There'll be open soon, Dad, fancy a livener[21]?" "Are there any thieves in Bermondsey??" "Fancy a pint, John?" He smiled and nodded. He was underage, but hell, we were at war! "I'm going up in the van. I've got a little bit of business to take care of." Granddad looked Uncle Nathan square in the face. "Mind yourself in that village, they're funny people, these locals, and the plod[22] do keep an eye on all of us Londoners." "Thanks for that, but I've already straightened[23] a couple of people." "We'll be off shortly, Anne. Are you coming up later?" "Yes, I'll bring the boys up with me. Do you want to go up to Horsmonden, boys?" We nodded enthusiastically.

Nan busied herself, preparing vegetables for our dinner. Michael helped her pod the peas, Eddie scraped carrots, while I cut and broke up twigs so that I could make Nan a good fire when we got back. Nan was satisfied with her preparations, so off we all strolled up to the village. There was a definite Carnival feel in town. The pubs were crowded, mostly men, and most of them outside the pubs in small

In Spite of Everything . . . .

groups, sharing jugs of beer between them. There was a noisy buzz about the place. Granddad made a fuss of Nan as soon as he saw us. Her favourite Guinness was soon in her hand. We dashed around on the large village green, rushing up to where the gypsies and their horses were mingling together. I wouldn't say that they were unfriendly, but they did tend to ignore us. There were a mixture of young children like us. I thought that a couple of the boys were a bit flash, but Nan had worded[24] us, and as usual, stressed upon me not to get involved. So, we didn't! Uncle Nathan called Eddie over to him. "You boys want a drink of lemonade and some crisps?" The answer to that question was a foregone conclusion. "Eddie, see that bloke over there?" He pointed to a couple of locals. "The man with the trilby on." Eddie glanced over. "Yes, he's the local butcher, I've seen him when I've been shopping with Nan, why?" "Make sure you go with Nan next time she goes shopping, he'll have an extra bit of grub for you. Take it, and don't make a fuss. You can handle that, can't you?" Eddie didn't ask any questions. "You know I can."

More and more people were arriving, amongst them were a few of our relations, and the atmosphere and general hubbub were getting very excited. I heard someone moaning because there were no spirits. They had forgotten there was a war on and spirits were severely rationed! That fact was to have an effect on my life in the not too distant future. I didn't know it then!

Nan called us to walk back to the huts with her. We'd gathered a few extra for dinner. We left the men, but Nan told us that the pubs would be closed very soon. Immediately we got back, I went to work on the fire and we had a blaze in no time. Nan was pleased, she was humming away to herself. The magic of a couple of glasses of Guinness! Eddie made sure that I had plenty of wood, and Nan soon had great big pots on the boil. I dodged off to play with my bow and arrow, but didn't go far. I returned at regular intervals to stoke up the fire. Uncle Nathan's van appeared, and out jumped Granddad, Johnny, Harry the Horse, and three of their cousins, the O'Sullivans. They were all laughing and joking. I found it very funny when they spoke to Nan, they were very respectful! [Because she was their Aunt] At the time I didn't give much thought to the fact that none of them was in the army. They all looked pretty fit to me!

Nan made a lovely dinner, and everybody got a decent portion. It was a very happy and funny dinnertime. The conversation was very witty. The men all seemed to have a joke to tell. The amazing thing is that, even today, some of their jokes stand the test of time. The men strolled over to the adjacent field, the common and fell asleep under a beautiful, warm, sunny September day. Nan went into her hut and had a peaceful afternoon's sleep, she deserved it! Eddie and Mike gathered up their fishing tackle, and headed off towards the lake. I had made friends with a boy of my own age, called Peter and we sloped off towards our camp, with me armed with my bow, arrows, jack knife, and of course my stick. They were from Battersea. He was alright! A bit flash and fond of himself. He kept bragging about how well developed his body was. I had noticed his Dad this morning, stripped to the waist and he looked like a body builder. He was in the army, but on leave. Peter told me that he was a PTI (Physical Training Instructor), and it was his job to get our soldiers fit to fight the Germans. We got on reasonably well, both liked to explore and give our eyes a chance[25]. But he was a bit bossy and I could sense a falling out! Nevertheless, we busied ourselves, improving our camp. We even dug fairly deep holes in front of our entrance. I don't know what we thought we'd catch but we had great fun. After a few hours we returned to the huts. Peter was continuously pushing and shoving, in a playful and friendly way, I might add. But I was never keen on being man-handled. I didn't react!

They were all back, sitting around, drinking mugs of tea. "Shall I stoke up the fire, Nan?" "Oh no thanks, Paddy, we've had a nice cup of tea, and Granddad, Johnny and Uncle Nathan have got to make their way back home soon. I'm going to make some sandwiches with the rest of the bread. Once we've eaten we're going into Horsmonden for an hour or two. We can see them off from up there."

Even though we hadn't had any major air raids for a long time, the black out was still in force. This meant that Uncle Nathan needed to get home before dark. Headlights were forbidden, and it's fucking dark in the country! I heard Granddad say that it only took 1 ½ to 2 hours to get home. They wouldn't have much time in the village.

Nan produced a big plate of sandwiches. She always managed to do this, and many years later, when I was a young man, I always marvelled at this. I stamped out the fire, made sure I put dry twigs inside our hut, then off we all trooped. As we neared the village, our men could be seen standing around outside The Gun. We got closer to them, and, Eddie called out "Any chance of some lemonade? We're dying of thirst." Granddad answered "Well you'll have to die then, son, they're not open until seven o'clock. Won't be long now though." We played some football on the village green. Sadly, no proper football, just a tied up bunch of rags. The village was slowly coming to life again. There was quite a crowd at the top end of the green because there was an evening church service going on. The sound of hymns being sung wafted across the village. I didn't like the church and wanted no part in it, but, I must say, the sound of people singing was very pleasant.

"Come on over here, boys, there's some drink and a bag of crisps for you to share." We stopped our game and dashed over to Granddad. In no time at all they were saying their goodbyes. I was sad to see Johnny go, but he had to get back to work. He wasn't keen on work, but he liked the money. He knew that he'd be called up in a few months. A very uncertain time! "Be good for your Nan, and Eddie, you're in charge now. See you all next weekend. Stay out of trouble." Granddad fixed his eyes on me at that last remark! They all piled into the van, not the O'Sullivans, they made their own way home. Then, with a puff of exhaust smoke, they were gone. "You can play for a bit longer, boys, I'm just having another Guinness with those ladies. I'll call you when it's time to go." We larked about for a while and it was getting a bit dusky. The local policeman, on his bicycle, appeared. He was checking out the blackout. He popped into each pub in turn, and although you couldn't see a chink of light from any of them, I noticed someone inside fiddling around with the curtains. It would be dark soon.

We heard Nan's voice calling us, so we went to her straight away. "We've got to be going back now boys. We've got an early start in the morning. Those hops won't pick themselves. Eddie, take my arm, I don't want to slip over in this dark, and Paddy, hold Michael's hand."

I grimaced. "Do I have to, Nan? You know what a nuisance he is." "Yes, you do!" Now don't moan, and do as you're told. Michael, you behave yourself as well. You know what Paddy's like." We made our way back without incident. It was pitch black. I had never seen so many stars. There were quite a few creepy noises coming from all around. Michael clung on to my hand. He didn't try to run off, like he usually did. "What's all those noises, Paddy?" he whispered. "No trouble, Mikey, only some lions and tigers." "I heard what you just said, Paddy, stop trying to frighten Michael, he'll have nightmares." We all laughed. We were soon tucked up in our bed then I heard Nan saying her prayers. The next thing I heard was the early morning wake up call, and the banging of his stick on the hut doors. Nan called out and he moved off. A new week had started. Same old routine: fire, wash, dress, breakfast (porridge of course, forget the eggs) and before we knew it, Eddie and me straight up to the hop garden to give Nan a good start. Eddie had wised-up about the dew, giving the bines a good shake before pulling them down. All the now familiar noises, people talking, singing, laughing, and some crying, from young children. In all, an atmosphere never to be forgotten. There was also the wonderful smell. If you've never experienced it, it's impossible to describe. I only have to get the slightest whiff of hops and I'm back almost 70 years in a flash. On the downside, there were millions of insects of all descriptions. They crawled all over me. There was a nickname lousy 'oppers, and I soon found out what was meant by that.

Eventually Nan turned up with Michael alongside. "Ooh, you've done well boys, you've picked me at least a couple of bushel, that'll give me a good start. I've brought you some lemonade and a few biscuits." Biscuits were a rare treat, but we were very fortunate because we lived near Peek Freans, the big biscuit makers. We only managed to get hold of broken biscuits of various varieties. Luckily, one of Dad's sisters worked there and, with a little help from Uncle Nathan, we had a steady supply.

It didn't take us long to gobble up our biscuits and down our drink. "Give me a couple of hours more picking boys, and I'll make you some nice sandwiches out of that tinned meat that Nathan and Granddad left us, then you can go and play for a few hours. Eddie, I've got to go to Horsmonden a bit later, and I want you to come with me, but don't worry, that's later this afternoon. Come on, let's wire in for a while and get some hops picked." We steamed in, usual ploy, me and Mike up the row, Eddie and Nan round the bin. After a short while, a strange thing happened. One of the pole-pullers, who didn't have that much to do between measures, came over to our bin, and whilst chatting away, started picking hops in Nan's bin. I had noticed that he had been talking and joking with Johnny and the others, whilst they had been outside the pub at dinnertime on Sunday. He certainly helped us out. He only left our bin to give help to the other pickers, mainly to help cut down bines that wouldn't be pulled, or to help shifting the bins into fresh rows. He wasn't a bad bloke, but as usual, I was a bit wary of him. "I'm going back to our hut to make you some sandwiches, give me half an hour and follow me down. Do you want me to bring you back a nice sandwich, Jim?" "That would be really kind of you, Mrs., are you sure you don't mind?" "Of course not, you've been a great help."

We followed Nan in about half an hour, in truth probably more like 20 minutes. We were starving! "I'll keep an eye on things for you whilst you're at dinner." As I dashed off, I turned "I bet you will! There's a nice sandwich at the end of it." He smiled back, but it was a weak smile.

Nan had boiled a kettle from the fire in the cookhouse. We had a nice cup of tea to go along with our spam sandwiches. Nan returned to the hop garden, and we went off to play. My mate Peter had to stay with his Mum and pick hops. I, therefore, hung around with Eddie and Michael. We had great fun, and the odd quarrel, nothing unusual. Believe it or not, we actually heard Nan's voice calling out for us. She had a very good pair of lungs. "Come on, we'd better get back to Nan quickly!" Eddie said and immediately dashed off. "I was getting a bit worried, where you all were. It's getting time for us to catch the bus into town. Paddy, do you want to come with me?" "No, thanks Nan, I'd sooner stay here. Do you want me to look after Michael?" "Do you want to stay Michael?" Nan asked. "Can I come with you and

Eddie, please Nan? He'll only keep moaning at me to pick faster." I very quickly chipped in "I don't mind being on my own, honest Nan." "Are you really sure you don't mind being on your own for a while? I don't like the thought of you alone." I gave Nan a very broad smile. "Honest, Nan, don't worry, I can look after myself. Do you want me to leave and get you a fire started?" "Yes, please son. You don't have to, but I'd like you to pick hops for a while, because the farmer isn't too happy if we knock off too early." She gave me a little cuddle. Then they were off. I noticed that she said a few words to Jim before she left. I was happy enough in my own little world, picking away merrily. I was never alone, anyway. The other bins were only a couple of yards away, all with women and children around them. They were all very friendly. I don't know if people have changed over the years, but in those harsh, hard times, most people would help each other out for no reward except a smile or a thank you.

There was a bin a couple of rows away, which had three women around it. All of a sudden one of the women came over to my bin. "Been left all alone, have you?" "Yeah, Nan and me brothers have gone shopping. I don't like shopping, I'd prefer to stay here and pick some hops. Anyway, I'll be going in about half an hour to get Nan's fire started. I'm honestly not bothered." "I'd like to keep you company, and pick a few hops for her. You don't mind, do you?" "No, no, that's very kind of you." She was a very pleasant lady, and we got on fine with each other. She could pick hops as well! Sadly, after a while, dark thoughts began to rear up in my head. This could have been my Mum. There was no escaping the fact that I would never be able to erase my Mum from my head. I couldn't stand it any longer. I knew it was rude, but, I just stopped talking and picking, picked up my jacket and walked away. There must have been something in my manner that alarmed this nice lady. She carried on picking without saying another word. As I hurried away, I saw Jim the pole-puller out of the corner of my eye. "Hey there, you're leaving a bit early, ain't you?" I didn't even look at him. "Fuck off and mind your own business." He didn't reply.

I'd got a nice fire going, then I saw the bus pull up. Then I heard Michael calling out to me. I waved at him. Eddie and Nan quickly followed, both carrying bags of shopping. "Have you been alright on your own,

Paddy? I've been really worried about you. I won't do that again, never mind what you say." "No trouble Nan, honest." "Well, look what I've managed to get for you, some sweets. They're not much cop, but the best I could do." "Thanks anyway, Nan, I'll build your fire up when you want."

Eddie said to me "You'll never guess what happened in the butcher's shop. Nan managed to get a fresh rabbit and a few sausages on our ration books. When, out of nowhere, the butcher handed me a wrapped parcel. 'These is some bones for your dog' he said, and gave me a sly wink. It was the same man who had been drinking with Uncle Nathan and Granddad. When we left the shop, Nan had a look. Bones! There was a fucking great pile of pork chops! Nan's eyes nearly popped out. She was going to take them back. Then I told her about Sunday on Horsmonden Green. She just nodded her head whilst muttering 'Crafty so and sos.'"

Nan took her shopping bags into the hut. When she came out she was carrying a couple of small parcels. She walked over to the next hut, calling out for Dol, who appeared almost immediately. "Here you are, love, cook these for you and the girls." Aunt Dol was speechless! "I won't take no for an answer." She then went over to another hut, where the lady had six children with her. I saw her giving the chops to her. The lady was almost in tears. She couldn't stop thanking Nan. We had a lovely bit of grub. No pork chops, however! I learnt a right lesson about Nan. She was very generous, and apart from us, she'd sooner go hungry herself, than see others less fortunate go without. It did, however, take me quite a while to understand! Luckily, I did eventually!

We dashed off to play for a short while before it got dark. When we got back, Nan was sitting just inside her hut. She must have heard us. "Paddy, come in here for a minute. Eddie, you and Michael go and fetch me some more faggots. Did you have any trouble while I was away?" "No, why?" "Kate, a lady I've been talking to, was very worried that she might have upset you. You swore at Jim, she said. What was that all about?" "Sorry, Nan, I don't really know. I just got a bit fed up, that's all." "I had a bad feeling about leaving you on your own. As I said before, it won't happen again." "Nan! Really, I don't mind being on my own and I know the lady was only helping. She's a very nice lady. I'll go over and straighten her out." "Well that will be nice. She's very worried about you. Now come here you soppy sod." With that she gave me a big hug. It was hard for me not to cry.

The funny thing is that I can stand a great of physical pain, but very difficult to handle that sort of affection. I've never altered. "Hello, lady, Nan said you're a bit worried about me. There's no need, honest. I'm sorry that I worried you. I didn't mean to. I just have funny moods now and again. I wasn't being rude, and by the way, thank you for helping Nan out." I was about to run off, when the lady grabbed me and gave me a hug! Talk about being embarrassed, this was far too much. There must have been half a dozen pairs of eyes on me. I squirmed away, and was gone. Fuck that! I won't be going near that lot in a hurry.

The week went by very quickly. The weather still fine and warm during the day, cool at night and in the morning. We heard the sound of aeroplanes from time to time, bombers! Not sure whether ours or German. A reminder that the war was still going on. Everybody was friendly and helpful. Even Jim came round regularly and picked hops for us. He couldn't stop grinning at me! I still wasn't sure of him!

The weekend arrived again, and Nan was really pleased with herself. I reckoned up her tall book for her, she'd made just over eight pounds! A small fortune! When we got back to our hut, Granddad was there, so was Johnny and a couple of his mates. They had come down by train. The whole place was buzzing again. Johnny and his mates had been in the pub for a short time. They were very relaxed! Granddad had a couple of large parcels, mainly fish.

Nan soon had food on the go. After we'd all finished eating, the men strolled over to the common and lay down on the grass. My mate Peter's dad was larking about and wrestling with him. "Hey Johnny, fancy a wrestling match? You look fit and strong." Eddie gave me a knowing look. "No thanks, Frank, I don't like wrestling." Johnny's mates began egging him on. It was all very light hearted. Frank wouldn't let it rest, nor would Peter. The upshot was that in the end, Johnny gave in. "Come on then, I'll have a lark with you." They both stripped down to their waist. Peter's dad was very fit, but Johnny had a magnificent physique as well. By now, there was quite a crowd gathered around. Nan wasn't happy! They circled each other, and it was obvious that Peter's dad had the better technique. He had Johnny on the floor time after time, but Johnny was stronger. This meant that Frank started to tire, and wasn't getting it all his own way. He eventually called a halt. They shook hands and there were smiles all around. Then it happened! "Hey, young Paddy, that's your name, isn't it?" He was looking straight at me. "Yeah, what's it got to do with you?" That quietened them all up. "Fancy a wrestle with Peter? You're the same size." Peter had a smirk on his face. I always felt he was a bit big for his boots. "No thanks, I don't wrestle." "Come on, it's only a bit of fun. You're not scared, are you?" "No, but I don't fight anybody for fun. Leave me alone!"

Eddie chipped in "Mr. Philips, I don't think it's a good idea. They're mates." "Oh, what a lot of nonsense. Come on, please." By now, Peter was swaggering about. I'd had enough. "Alright, but I don't like wrestling." We stripped to our waists. Peter was well built. We shook hands, and as we faced each other, I heard Nan's voice saying to Granddad "You shouldn't have allowed this fighting, you know what he's like." "Don't worry Anne, it's only a bit of fun." The next thing I heard was the thud as I hit the floor. He'd turned me over in a flash. I was back on my feet just as quick. We grappled. On my back again! Fuck this for a lark! Peter came charging back at me (that smirk again). He didn't smirk when my left hand smashed into his nose. There was claret everywhere. I smashed a right and a left hook into his face, all on target. He went down. His father screamed at him to get up and fight. He stupidly did! I hit him, one, two, three times. He eye split open and his mouth was a bloody mess. Granddad grabbed me and pulled me away. He knew that I wouldn't stop. Peter had!

"You fuckin' horrible little bastard, you were supposed to just wrestle!" I stared back at him. "I told you! I don't wrestle!" His face was almost purple with rage and, he advanced towards me. Eddie was up before anyone else, closely followed by Johnny. "This wouldn't be a good idea, Frank. It was your silly idea. Lay one hand on Paddy, and I'll show you a real fight! Now piss off and look after your boy. He looks like he needs help." Peter was covered in blood, snivelling on the ground. The smirk had gone! I felt Nan's arm on my shoulder. "Come away, son. I want you to sit down and calm down." She stared at Granddad. "Are you stupid or something? I told you it was a bad idea. That boy (Peter) could have been seriously hurt. Come here Paddy, now!"

Once Nan was satisfied that I had relaxed and quietened down, she went over to the Philip's hut to make sure Peter was alright, and to help in anyway she could. When she came back, she said to Granddad "That boy has got to go to the first aid clinic in the village. He needs stitches in his eye, and they are having trouble stopping that bleeding in his nose. I blame you for allowing it to happen. You can't say that you don't know what he's like. I've now got to settle him down." I felt alright, but I must admit that I found it hard to relax. Eddie never left my side. "I told them it wasn't a good idea Nan." "Yes, I know you did Eddie. It wasn't your fault!" She was glaring at Granddad and Johnny. Johnny was finding it difficult not to look too pleased!

Eventually things settled down and normal order was restored. I saw Peter, his dad and mum head off to the clinic. His dad didn't look too happy. Peter didn't look at me, well he was wrapped up like a sore toe. We had jellied eels and herrings for our tea, with fresh crusty bread and margarine, we couldn't get butter. Saturday night was spent in Horsmonden, which was very lively, as usual. There was the odd argument and a couple of fights. Normal service being resumed.

Sunday morning was grey and quite chilly. After breakfast, about mid-morning, Uncle Nathan's van turned up. We had a nice surprise when Aunt Anne got out of the van. She had her two little boys with her, Walter and Seamus. Wally was now running about, so the moment he saw Michael, he dashed towards him, unfortunately falling over a couple of times. He was now covered in dirt. So much for his Sunday best. Uncle Nathan couldn't stop laughing. Aunt Anne didn't share the joke. Nan was pleased to see Aunt Anne and the kids, so there followed lots of hugs and kisses and non-stop chat.

It was then that I noticed the Phillips family were taking all their stuff from out of their hut. Another man was helping. He looked a lot like

In Spite of Everything . . . .

Mr. Phillips, probably his brother. "Excuse me a minute, Anne, I want to go over and talk to Mrs. Phillips, I won't be too long." Aunt Anne turned to Granddad. "What's that all about?" Granddad related the full story. Aunt Anne was shocked, but Uncle Nathan roared out laughing. "I've told you all not to muck about with that boy, he's dangerous, like a wild dog!" He walked over to me and gave me a big hug. "Serves that fucker right. I thought he was a bit flash! Are you alright, Paddy?" "As good as gold, Uncle." Nathan was bouncing about like a dog with two tails!

Nan came back after a couple of minutes. "Everything alright, Mum?" Aunt Anne asked. "It's a shame, but they're leaving the farm and going home. Their boy is still a bit shaken, but otherwise alright. They are a nice family. The dad's a bit silly though. Like some other people I know!" Her deep blue eyes were levelled on Granddad and Johnny, who had just made an appearance.

Uncle Nathan was in deep conversation with Eddie. I'd find out about what later on. We all had to keep an eye on Wally, mainly to make sure that he didn't fall into any open fires. The farmer's wife, Elsie, appeared, offering a lift to church. Quite a few people took her up on the offer, and scrambled onto the open cart. They were soon off, as were the Phillips. Not a glance in my direction. It was soon midday, still very gloomy, trying to rain. Couldn't remember the last time it rained properly. Nearly everybody scrambled into Nathan's van, and they were Horsmonden bound. I stayed back with Nan, Michael, Aunt Anne and the boys. I made sure that Nan had a good fire because she was boiling a great big piece of pork, that Uncle Nathan had provided. It wasn't very long before I got fed up. "Is it alright if I go up to the village, Nan?" "Yes, of course you can. You've been a good boy. Don't get into any mischief and remind Granddad to fetch me back a couple of bottles of Guinness." Aunt Anne, bless her, gave me a warm smile, but she knew that I was never entirely comfortable around her. It wasn't her fault that she looked like my Mum. I dashed off, and luckily, by the time I reached Horsmonden, I'd got over my dark mood. I was pleased to see Eddie. He called me over to where he was hanging about with a group of children of about our age. It was a very pleasant atmosphere. "Paddy!" Uncle Nathan roared out "Over here son." He

|179

was outside the "Town House" chatting to a group of men. One of them was our butcher. They all looked very pally. A couple of the men looked a bit pikey. "Bill, this is the boy I was telling you about." Now Bill, known as Big Bill, was enormous. He looked fearsome. I was to find out that he was once a wrestler, the Iron Duke. "I'll think I'll have to keep an eye on you, young man. We'd better be friends!" With that, he stuck out an enormous hand, and we shook hands. Well, he shook me. Nathan laughed. He turned to the butcher. "That's his brother over there." He pointed at Eddie. The butcher nodded. Nathan then added "You won't see this one in your shop Butch because he won't go on errands, he's an awkward fucker." They all roared out laughing. I scowled at them. "There, see, look at him! Come over in a minute, I'll get you and Eddie some crisps and something to drink. Now piss off, we've got some business to talk about." Nathan was still laughing! As soon as I saw Granddad I reminded him about Nan's Guinness. He hadn't forgot. "She's unlucky today, no Guinness, but I've got her a couple of bottles of stout. Have you and Eddie had anything?" "Yes, thanks Granddad, Uncle Nathan has looked after us." He looked across the green and smiled. "I bet he has" he muttered softly. "I'll give you a shout when we're ready to leave, so don't go far. Have you seen anything of Johnny?" "Yes, he's at the other end of the green with his mates. Me and Eddie are over there." I pointed Eddie and friends out.

I could hear the shouts of "Time, Gentlemen, please." We'd be off back to the farm shortly. Eddie turned to me "Come on Paddy, let's get back before Granddad and let Nan know that they'll all be back soon." "I'll let Granddad know, and take Nan's stout back." I popped my head round the pub door and called out to Granddad. Children were forbidden by law to enter a pub bar. I took the bottles off Granddad, then we were off. Nan was pleased to see us, and her beer. "They'll be back soon, Nan, they've called time." "Do you want me to liven up the fire?" "Yes, just a little if you don't mind, Paddy." Whatever Nan was cooking smelt wonderful. Michael appeared, with Wally toddling behind. He was filthy, but happy. Aunt Anne thought it was quite funny.

"Toot, toot," Nathan's van appeared. Granddad, Johnny, Ron and Alfie all dived out of the van, giggling and laughing. They were all great characters. I didn't know it then, but I would get to know them all in future years.

It was threatening rain, and luckily, after dinner, it did. Nan, Aunt Anne and the babies sheltered in our hut. The rest of us took cover in the cookhouse, alongside many others. It was very smoky, but great atmosphere. Eddie and Michael put on raincoats and went fishing. It was supposed to be good fishing in the rain but I never found out why, then again I didn't fish. They all decided to go home earlier, so Nathan drove Granddad, John and friends to the railway station. He was back in no time. "I think they've got a long wait for a train, but they're in the dry. Come on Anne, let's be 'aving ya, we've got to get back before dark." Aunt Anne soon had herself and the kids ready, they were soon on their way. "Paddy, well done son. That boy was a bit cocky. He needed a good lesson. Remind Eddie to make sure the butcher looks after you." With a big wink, they were off. "Paddy, get in out of the rain, I'm going to have a lie down for an hour. What are you going to do?" "I'll bring some wood inside, Nan, to keep it dry. Then I'll go over to the cookhouse for a while." "I don't think we'll be lighting any fires tonight, son. It'll be sandwiches for tea." By now it was raining very hard.

That night the noise of the rain bashing down onto the tin roof sounded like Fred Astaire tap dancing. It didn't stop us from getting to sleep though! Pitter, patter, the noise was still there when we woke up. No early wake up call today! Outside, the ground was drenched, there was mud everywhere. Luckily we had brand new wellington boots, and boy, did we need them. I helped the old gypsy with the fires, and Nan was able to cook our breakfast porridge oats. It was none too warm, so porridge was very welcome.

We didn't pick at all that Monday, but thankfully the weather improved and picking commenced. Time flew by. A couple of colourful weekends, and it was time to go back home. The hop gardens now looked very sorry for themselves. Where once stood these giant fields of rows and rows of golden hops, now just rolled up and stripped empty bines. It looked quite sad. After a month living like we had been, it will be strange to get back to London.

The last day, Johnny had come down to lend a hand. We cleared the front of our hut, and put away all of Nan's pots, pans and cooking hooks and stowed all her furniture. We emptied out our straw palisades, piling the straw onto a giant bonfire. Then the farmer arrived with Elsie, and his foreman and other hands. They had a couple of big open carts, one filled with apples and all types of vegetables, the other with chickens. They were big chickens and alive.

Nan got into a long queue in front of the farmer, and one by one they were paid out in cash. Elsie checked everyone's book (tally card actually) against her own ledger. I had brought Nan's book up to date by adding up all the deductions for milk, eggs, butter and cheese. Nan had sworn me to secrecy not to tell anybody how much she had earned, especially not Granddad. She promised us three a little present once we were back home. Nan collected her cash, a little over £36. Believe me, that was a considerable amount of money in those harsh times. We helped her carry apples, both eaters and cookers, she didn't bother too much with the veg. Then she picked out a nice chicken. The farm hand promptly wrung its neck and dropped it in a sack. We said our goodbyes, and two families at the time were taken by horse and cart to the railway station. Johnny and Eddie pushed our own big sea chest on pram wheels to the station by themselves.

The station was crammed with people, all carrying their produce. Children running around, with frantic mothers trying to keep track of them. People were only interested in getting home.

Eventually the big steam engine, pulling just two carriages, pulled into the station. With a great deal of pushing and shoving (most of it good humoured), we were loaded on. The train stopped at Paddock Wood, where it met the main line. Three more carriages were attached. Nan let me and Eddie stand on the platform while they did that. It was quite fascinating, the great engine going back and forth, its wheels spinning at times, with great clouds of steam, and the clanking of the carriages being locked together. The other carriages were also full of 'oppers. Amid lots of shouting, whistles blowing and flags waving, we were off home! Hoppin' was over!

Chapter 7

Before getting to London Bridge we had to pull into sidings a couple of times, to let goods train go by. There were lots of guns and army vehicles on these trains, a timely reminder that the war was still on.

It must have taken us five hours to get to London Bridge so we were glad to get off the cramped train. London Bridge was very busy, as usual, but now at least half the people were in uniform. Army, Navy, R.A.F., with quite a few being Americans. You could always recognise the Yanks, they wore much smarter uniforms and were normally bigger people than us. They also stared at us in a surprised and confused way. I think I know why! They probably thought that we refugees from Europe. To be honest, we must have looked pretty shabby!

It felt strange being back in our house. A proper kitchen and proper beds to sleep in, and even though, by today's standards, it was a bit spartan, it was home! Granddad was pleased to see us, and there was an added bonus, Eileen was home from the Land Army. I was to find out later that there was a dark side to that. She hadn't been very well. We had a lovely evening, one of the talking points being how much Nan had earned. Mind your own business was her friendly and slightly mischievous reply. "Paddy will tell us, won't you darling?" smiled Eileen. I just put my finger up to my lips. Nan smiled at me. "Does anyone know how to pluck this chicken?" Nan was looking at Granddad. "Don't ask me" was his reply. We all stared at each other.

"I bet Kit does, you know, Kit next door. She's always got chicken." "I think you're probably right, Eddie, what a good idea. I wanted to let her know that we were home." "I want to see her as well, Nan. Come on, I'll carry the chicken." With that, Eddie scooped up the sack containing the chicken, and him and Nan went next door. They were back after twenty minutes or so. Nan said "Well, that's sorted. Kit is going to prepare it for me. She reckons that it's a first class chicken." Eddie turned to me to tell me that Kit and Michael were really pleased to see him, and that they needed us in the morning, it was Saturday, and that they had missed us. That was handy, I've still got a job.

Granddad suddenly said to Nan "Haven't you noticed that letter on the mantelpiece?" We all stared at this letter! Luckily Granddad was smiling. "It's a letter from your Dad, boys. He's fit and well!" There was a sigh of relief all round. We were all aware of the massive battle of "El Alemain" and we knew that Dad was fighting in that area. We used to talk about this battle because it was a famous victory. We told everybody that we had beaten the Germans because our Dad was there! Eileen read his letter out loud, mainly because of Nan and Mikey. He was now in Egypt on leave. He'd written one special sentence to me: "Tell Paddy that I had so many Germans stuck on my bayonet that Montgomerie gave me a day off!" It was quite a long letter, even with the blacked out bits. They didn't black that bit out! I could tell by the look on Nan's face that the joy she felt over Dad's news also highlighted the plight of one of her other sons, George. He was fighting in Burma, and there was serious action going on over there, with very heavy casualties. We were all very aware that according to the news the conditions over there were truly atrocious. There had been lots of telegrams from that area. She also had Jim, another son. He was in the Royal Navy and the last we heard, he was in Indian waters. It was still a very worrying time, but our lives were to settle down for a while, that is until the next crisis!

It was strange, and took some getting used to, walking down the drab streets, with more and more bombed ruins, going to school again, after spending the last month in the country. There were a few more children at school, although still only two full classrooms.

In Spite of Everything . . . .

The teachers seemed to be glad to see us. You never knew what could become of people in these traumatic days. The school term had been running for about three weeks, but our absence didn't seem to cause any problems. This coming year was when Eddie would take a scholarship exam and, if he passed, he would move to another higher school. During the first playtime break, we met up with our mates and swapped stories.

We soon got back to our old routine, soon forgetting the countryside. I was still in Eddie's class in school and our teacher asked me to help Eddie with his arithmetic. Apparently, that was one of his weak subjects. Of course, I agreed. Surprisingly, Eddie didn't mind either because he was very keen to get to a higher school.

Nathan was also pleased to have us back, where all the action was taking place. There were more and more Yanks wandering about in London. They all had plenty of money (man with plenty of money and little brain, is made for man with plenty of brain and no money). Enter Nathan and his band of rogues. Eddie went back to selling on Kit's stall in the Blue, but I wasn't interested in working all day like that. I helped out doing various jobs and dodging around for Uncle Nathan. That suited me; I didn't like being tied down. Eddie went back to his sea cadets, leading the band on Sunday mornings. He always looked very smart. He used to spend most of Saturday evening blancoing his kit and pressing his blue uniform. Michael used to give him a hand and even I joined in occasionally. Granddad was now well established at his fish stall and I loved helping him on Sunday morning. I used to poke my head into the church, always made sure I was seen, then immediately do a runner[26]!! Eddie and Michael were trapped, they sung in the choir. I didn't. They certainly didn't want me at the organ pump!! I dashed round to Granddad's small yard. He didn't mind me bunking off from the church because he hated the priests and everything about them. Nan knew what I was up to but she turned a blind eye. Anyway, Granddad could do with some help. It was a smelly job but I enjoyed it. Granddad always insisted that the worm in the whelks was taken out. It was a messy time-consuming job. I had to break the back of the whelk and pull out this worm (if you ever get to eat whelks, make sure the back has been broken).

There's a great story attached to this that happened 30 years later. I was in our local pub on the outskirts of Maidstone. It was Sunday lunchtime. There were about eight to ten of us mates drinking together. Over the past couple of weeks, a travelling cockle and whelk stall had started appearing outside the pub. One of the lads had decided to pop out and buy some whelks for us to eat in the bar. He'd Okayed it with the landlord, then plonked them on the bar and the lads immediately dived in. I waited until they all had their mouths full, then very slowly and deliberately, I chose a nice fat whelk. The back had not been broken!! Then with as much fuss as possible, I pinched open the back of this whelk then, hey presto! Up popped this worm (it was dead, of course) and I very slowly pulled it out from the back of the whelk. The look on my mates' faces was a picture. They were shocked!! They couldn't spit the things out of their mouths quick enough and since some of the greedier fuckers had already eaten one or two, they were nearly sick. It was hilarious!! It was even suggested that I had planted the worm as a sort of windup (in truth, I had pulled a few fast ones in my time). To convince them and the landlord, I picked out another. They watched me closely as I broke its back and produced another worm. Nobody ate any more whelks or anything else, for that matter. When the van driver heard about what had gone on, he bounded into the pub and started to have a go at me about ruining his business.

He started off very aggressive but soon realised that he had bitten off more than he could chew. I fucked him off, telling him that he should find out how to prepare his food before selling it to the public. He was a dirty, unwashed fucker anyway!!

The rest of the year passed by in a flash. There were still the isolated air raids, as there had been throughout the year. Luckily, we hadn't been too badly affected. The queues for food and coal weren't getting any shorter, even bread was becoming scarcer. We, as a family, were well off, as compared to many others. Granddad was making a living, both Eileen and Johnny were working and Nan was getting regular money coming from the army. We also had Uncle Nathan and friends.

In Spite of Everything . . . .

We had a nice Christmas and even managed to have a chicken at Christmas dinner. We also had a letter from Dad. Thankfully, he was well and had been promoted to sergeant. Nan had heard from Jimmy (not such good news). He was safe and well, in hospital, in a place called Durban. He had contracted TB. It seemed that if the bombs and bullets didn't get you!!

Her other sons, Dave and Patsy, were both stationed in the north of England. They were safe and well. We hadn't heard from Uncle George following big battles in the Far East. In those days, no news was good news. The last thing you wanted was a telegram.

There was, however, one incident at school. This would annoy dear Eileen until the end of her days. We had been getting food and clothing parcels from people in Canada and the US. Parcels containing sweets and small toys, as well. Ours, being a Catholic school, received parcels from Catholic families in those countries and, being Catholic, the priests took charge. Before we broke up for the Christmas holidays, these goodies were handed out.

Eddie received a parcel, as did Michael, but I didn't. They called all the names out, one by one. The vengeful bastards dropped me out!! It would be a lie to say that I was not, at first, very unhappy and a bit jealous, but worse things had happened to me, so it didn't take me long to shrug my shoulders and ignore their stupid games. I can still see our headmistress (who, incidentally, I got on with very well) in huddled conversation with the parish priest. They were glancing in my direction. My only, and I mean my only, regret is that they didn't change their mind. I would have loved to refuse any gift.

On our way home, Eddie said, "I don't know what they were up to in there, but you know that we will share everything between us, don't you?" "Of course I do, Ed. What about you, Mikey?" He pretended to pull his parcel close to him then smiled, "I'll give you one guess." We walked into the kitchen. They were in there, Nan, Granddad, Eileen and Johnny. When Eddie told Nan what had gone on, Eileen went mad. I'd never seen her like this before!! She was normally such a calm, placid girl. It was a good job that the school was closed!! Nan said, "Eddie, Michael, don't open your parcels. I'm taking them back to the church." She turned to Granddad, "Men of God!! They should be ashamed of themselves. We don't want their charity."

Eddie and Mike gave up their parcels without a second's thought. The next day, Nan set off to the church. Eileen was right beside her. "Can I come with you, Nan?" She gave me that piercing look (deep into my soul). "I think it's best not, don't you? Anyway, I'm surprised that you know where the church is!! Run off and play with your mates."

We never saw the parcels again and Nan never ever mentioned it again. Eileen, however, must have told that story hundreds of time during her lifetime. She never got over it. It didn't matter how many times I told her that, genuinely, I didn't give a tinker's cuss. In actual fact, it quite amused me. Just confirming how really stupid some people are. I've always thought that all fanatics, whether they be religious or political, are really funnily stupid!!

We returned to school in January and I could sense that the headmistress seemed to avoid me. Once or twice, Eileen met us from school. None of the teachers (there were only four women) would go anywhere near her. They had made a rod for their own backs!!

Nothing of great consequence went on for the early part of the year, except for the increasing amount of soldiers all around us, both American and our own.

Great convoys of troops and big lorries, with guns and small tanks, started to travel down the Old Kent Road. As soon as we got wind of this, we all dashed up to watch. It was mainly British troops, all waving and shouting. People, mostly women and kids, waved and cheered back at them. Some had flags to wave. If we were lucky, an American or Canadian (we couldn't tell the difference) convoy would pass by. Why lucky? They would chuck great bars of chocolate out into the crowds and, sometimes, they held out precious nylons. The women went mad for them. It was all a bit dangerous!!

I don't think there was much thought given to that small fact. Not when you think where they were soon to be going (although we didn't know, of course). It was obvious something was going on. The newspapers and wireless were full of stories about possible invasion. I will always remember the posters that were stuck all over the place, reminding us that careless talk could cost lives and of the possibility of spies in our midst. I always found that to be amusing. What could we possibly say that a spy would be interested in anyhow!! Spies in Bermondsey although, sad to say, with my background. There were certainly some Irish who would have done our country harm, if they possibly could. Thankfully they were very few and kept a very low profile.

Spring came and the days were getting longer. There were only a few air raids during this time and, apart from the rationing and the endless queues, life was easy and enjoyable. Uncle Nathan had hit onto another moneymaking scheme. He had me going round to various pubs and rummaging through their waste bins for empty scotch and gin bottles. He had managed to straighten someone out, who worked in one of the local bonded warehouses. They were managing to smuggle out raw spirits, mainly rum, I think. Now here's the rub! Nathan and my dad worked at Barclays Brewery before the war and Nathan, being Nathan, knew the brewing staff, so he had a man who was able to rig up a makeshift still. They were then able to break down the raw spirit into a drinkable commodity. That's why he needed all these empties. He sold the product mostly to Americans. They had scotch if in a scotch bottle, gin or brandy, as available. Now this was a very lucrative and dangerous business. Spirits, like everything else, were severely rationed, hence good profits were made. Nathan had this operation taking place from our top spare kitchen. Two things. It was essential that the police were ignorant of these capers, for obvious reasons. Secondly, where money was concerned, other villains in the area would have liked to muscle in and take over. Nathan, however, was a very hard man and he had some very tasty[27] friends. He was also very intelligent. He knew that to operate in the West End, he had to deal with the Italians and Maltese. He had to put them in it[28]. He did!! That also turned out to be a blessing because then he supplied a couple of their clubs. They didn't care what type of bottle the booze was in!! I used to take bottles of lemonade and Tizer over to them on my bike. Nathan wouldn't let me collect any money. "Much too dangerous, son," he would say. He knew that I wouldn't nick any money but he knew that I could count and reckon up very quickly. Then, I'd have known as much as him. "Don't educate people, son. Education has to be paid for." I can hear those words, even now!!

Good news, bad news.

The good. Aunt Lil turned up one day with a letter from Uncle George. He had been in some very serious battles on the Indian-Burmese borders (we didn't know then, but they were the victorious battles of Imphal and Kohema). He was well and uninjured. Now resting at a base camp. Exact details were, of course, censored. That mattered little. He was alive!! Nan and Granddad were visibly overjoyed, as were all of us.

Then came the bad news!!

Our dad had been wounded. He had received a bad leg injury at a place, in Italy, called Monte Cassino. He was now in hospital in Egypt. We really didn't know how badly he was hurt. His letter didn't go into to many details. I had a dreadful foreboding. It just wouldn't get out of my mind, those few years ago (Mum's been injured, she's in hospital). Well, we know how that turned out!! Nan said not to worry, "He can't be that badly hurt or he wouldn't have been able to write this letter." Yeah, I thought. Thanks Nan but the letter wasn't written in his handwriting. I knew what his writing was like. I'd read enough of his letters!! Will I ever see him again?

"We'll write back to him. Eddie, you and Michael can write a few lines each. He'll just love that and I'll bet it'll make him get better much quicker." "That's a great idea, Nan," yelled Eddie. "I'll help Michael. I can tell Dad that I've passed my exams and that I'm going to a new school later in the year." Michael was very excited, jumping up and down, as usual. "Mikey, slow down a bit, you must have St Vita's dance." Granddad chirped up. Nan gave him one of her serious looks. "For God's sake, Pat, leave the boy alone." Granddad buried his face

In Spite of Everything . . . .

in his newspaper. Nan was seriously protective. That night was a mixture of joy and worry, but we didn't know there was more to come very soon.

It was now mid-summer. The weather was very drab and wet. I had started to play cricket for our borough but we didn't get to play much. We mostly sat around waiting for the rain to stop. We then heard, yes heard, remember, we now had a wireless. We had invaded France and us and the Americans had gained a foothold. Church bells had been rung and everybody was happy and optimistic. We had been led to believe that once we had landed on the continent. The war would soon be over. The military traffic on the Old Kent Road was now almost non-stop and it had become so commonplace that we hardly bothered to walk up there. War nearly over!! Now there's a joke. One night, the air raid sirens again. Granddad woke us up and we all huddled together in the kitchen. We couldn't hear any bombers and because the air raids were more sporadic and not so concentrated, we were getting a bit carefree. Obviously, we made sure that we were well blacked out. We could hear anti-aircraft fire coming from far away down river but no bombers!!

There were a few muffled explosions from over the East End. Then nothing. We drifted off to sleep. The all clear sounded and it was now light and morning time.

Our day started as normal but when we arrive at school, we were sent home. The air raid last night had been carried out by a new type of weapon and nobody was sure when the next raid would take place. The school was shut. It was nearly end of term anyway, so home we went. Nan was surprised but happy to see us. The news was full of it!! The Germans were sending unmanned rocket bombs over to London. These were very powerful so people were advised to take shelter during any raids. Most were not only worried but also annoyed because we thought the war as nearly over!! Nothing seemed to happen for a couple of days. Then it started they came over, night and day, and you never knew which part of London or the suburbs they would hit. We used to sit and listen to this peculiar sounding short stubbed rocket with flames coming out of it. Then silence! It had run out of fuel and dropped to the ground. The explosions were enormous. They would knock down a complete row of houses unlike the blitz of 40/41, when you knew which area was being bombed. These things landed anywhere. The terrifying seconds between the rocket motors stopping and the wait, between life or death, was even scarier than the utter chaos and bedlam of the concentrated bombing. I was a bit older now and therefore more aware!!

These rockets, Londoners soon christened them "doodlebugs", caused utter confusion and fear. There seemed no defence which made them very frightening. Meanwhile, our armies were gradually winning the battle for France. We were never told of the heavy casualties. The air force had pinpointed where the doodlebugs were coming from, so they attacked them causing many air force lads to lose their lives. This war will go on forever, I thought.

"Right, boys, after your breakfast, get yourselves ready. We're going to Aunt Sarah's. I can't stand this any longer." Nan looked tired and drained. We were soon on our way. Granddad and Eileen came with us. Aunt Sarah was pleased and relieved to see us. As was Dave and the others. "We've been really worried about you, Mum. We can see and hear those flying bombs going overhead. It's terrifying." Apparently, a couple had dropped not that far away in Sidcup and Eltham.

Early that evening, shortly after the air raid warning (remember it was June), we first heard the strange rattling. We dashed out into the street. There they were: one, two, three, four; all belching flames and headed for the heart of London. They were being chased by Spitfires but they were not shooting at them!! What were they doing? We were all out in the street with the neighbours but poor Nan was extra concerned because granddad hadn't stayed because of Johnny. He wouldn't leave London. Someone had to keep an eye on the operation going on upstairs!!

We stayed all through the rest of June, going on into July. The local schools had broken up, therefore, the whole bunch of us used to go fruit picking in the nearby fields. We picked raspberries, strawberries, cherries and peas. We all managed to earn a bit of pocket money even though the weather was shit! We had our daily sideshow of doodlebugs whizzing by, with the occasional close explosion, always followed by the fire engines clanging their way along the main Sidcup road.

Granddad came down one Sunday afternoon in July and, that evening, we all went down to the big pub on the main road, quite close to St Mary Cray station, The Bridge House. It was a lovely sunny and warm evening so we were all playing around at the front of the pub and even though there had been a warning, by now we weren't that over concerned. Suddenly, Eddie called out, "Look that doodlebug is coming towards us." I looked up. Yes, it was, and it was much lower than all the others I'd seen. "Fuck me, Eddie! I think you're right." Eddie didn't muck about. "I'm going to get Nan and Granddad. You get Michael and Terry. Quick!!" (Davey was standing beside me). That fucker was closer!! Nan and Granddad flew out of the pub, closely flowed by others. He took one look, "Come on, lively, over there to the ditch." We were only halfway there when, SILENCE. The flames died out.

Granddad pushed us, very roughly, into the grass ditch. Face down. "Keep your heads down, don't look up!" He screamed. I couldn't do that!! I looked up!! This thing was headed our way. Silent. It was now only about a couple of football pitches away. Drifting. It seemed to pitch and turn. It landed the other side of the big railway arch that spanned the main road. There was this enormous explosion, followed by a massive ball of yellow flames. We were all looking now, then the rush of hot air followed by dust. Luckily, we were far enough away to avoid any debris. It was strange how quiet it went for a while. Then turmoil. We were told to stay with Nan but Eddie and Granddad, alongside other men and ladies, dashed under the arch. Very shortly, fire engines and police arrived. They cordoned off the area, which meant we couldn't get any closer. After a while, Granddad and Eddie came back. Now, here's a bit of good fortune. The rocket had landed on an empty school which took the brunt of the explosion, alongside some small workshops which, being Sunday, were empty. There were some houses opposite but they took light damage. Doors, windows and the odd roof. I don't think anybody was killed, thankfully.

It must be hard, in present days, to understand what followed. Nan, Granddad and others returned to the pub and carried on enjoying themselves. We played outside, talking excitedly about what had gone on. The publican and a few helpers carried a few jugs of beer over to the firemen and police!! They didn't waste much time polishing that lot off. That probably wasn't the closest I'd come to being killed but it was the closest I'd seen!!

The doodlebugs weren't coming over in such great numbers now and August was upon us. The weather was still horrible but we enjoyed ourselves. Aunt Sarah hadn't heard from Uncle Dave but, by now, we all assumed that he'd be in France somewhere. We knew that our troops were now advancing and pushing the Germans back.

"Time to go back home, boys. The Germans must be running out of rockets. We've got to start thinking about school, again. They will probably reopen in September."

Granddad had bought down a letter. Eddie was going to a secondary modern school over Shoreditch, in the East End. It would seem funny without Eddie in school.

We had said our goodbyes and were soon on the train, and very shortly we arrived at the Elephant and Castle. After a couple of months in the country, it seemed very strange. We struggled down the stairs with our luggage and there he was with his van, Uncle Nathan. We were glad to see him and he us. Nan, Eileen and Nathan exchanged stories. Nan was interested in daughter, Annie, and her two boys. "She'll be over to see you tomorrow, Mum. Happily, we're all well."

We were home and soon settled in. Johnny was genuinely pleased to see us and was soon relating stories about he damage the doodlebugs had done. They were still coming but not so many of them now.

However, in the next few short weeks, our lives were to take yet another dramatic turn!!

In Spite of Everything . . . .

We soon settled back into our old routines. Eddie got his Saturday job back; Kit and Michael were only too pleased for Eddie to return. He was a crowd pleaser. I was now very busy helping Uncle Nathan and Granddad. Michael was now able to take over my messenger job for Kit, running stock up to the stall in the Blue. Whilst we'd been away, that area had taken a few hits. It was not much more than a bomb-ruined market. Most of the rubble had been cleared into great piles, thus leaving a nice open space for the market.

Apart from the odd doodlebug, not to be too blasé about it, life was fairly good. Nan was getting us prepared for our new term at school. Eddie had special treatment—a new blue jacket and long, yes long, trousers. He looked smart and very grown up.

It was strange, just Michael and I, walking down Bermondsey Street without Eddie bossing us about. I did, however, miss him. This was the first time we had ever been separated. Eddie had gone off earlier to catch a bus over the water.

Our school was still only operating two classrooms because none of the damage had been repaired. We were still in the same classrooms as before. Me in 10-14, Michael in 5-10 years. A few old faces had appeared. Sadly, others had gone. It seemed as though normality was being restored!! Was it hell!!

Then there was a loud bang all over the sky. Everything shook. Then there was this rumble of a large, very large, explosion. What the hell was that?! A new chapter of terror had started. The difference was that there had been no air raid siren, therefore no chance to take cover. Here we go again, I thought. Just as the air force had managed to shoot down or tip over the doodlebugs, a new menace. The news was full of this new terror and, to make matters worse, talk of forced evacuation for all children!! Nan was very worried. We never went back to school. Over the following days, more rockets hit London. They were all over the place. They seemed to be landing all around us. The noise was truly terrifying. Aunt Anne turned up, one day, looking very shaken. A rocket had exploded in her next street. She was very frightened. These things just came out of the sky and it was potluck whether you got blown to pieces or not. It took me years to understand the great booming noise, which made all the windows rattle. It wasn't until we broke the sound barrier years later, that I could understand sonic boom.

We sat round the kitchen table and chatted. Nan had been informed that we three had to report to Webb Street School for evacuation. It was government orders. We had no choice. Nan was concerned that we would be split up and this was something she had vowed would never happen. I don't think I helped matters much by adding that if we were split up, I would run away and get back home, one way or another. Not very helpful, but I was only eleven. Eddie said that there was no way Michael would be left on his own. I looked at Eddie and knew that he meant what he said!! I certainly wouldn't have wanted the job of parting them. No way!! Eileen said that she would come with us, so as to make sure that we were not separated. In the end, Nan said, "I'll go round to the school in the morning and see if I can get an assurance that you will all be together. I would imagine that I will know a few of the organisers." We left it at that.

We laid in bed, wide awake. Michael was very distressed. I was very annoyed (here we go again, people messing my life about). Eddie seemed strangely calm. "Please go to sleep. Mikey, I'll never leave you alone, I promise, and you over there (me), be quiet and go to sleep. Nan will work it out. Goodnight, God bless."

"Night, God bless, both of you. See you in the morning." It still wasn't completely dark outside but, with the heavy curtains, it was certainly dark in our bedroom.

We were woken up by a boom, followed by a large explosion. Everything was rattling so we jumped out of bed and peeked out the windows. We couldn't see anything out of the ordinary until the fire engines made their way down Bermondsey Street, towards the river, in the direction of our school. We heard Nan, Granddad and everyone else getting out of bed, so we dashed downstairs. "Was that a bomb, Nan?" Eddie asked. "No, son, it must have been another one of those rockets and it was pretty close. Come on, John, get dressed. We'll

In Spite of Everything . . . .

have to go down there and see what we can do." With that, Granddad and Johnny got dressed and hurried off down the street. By this time, there were many more men doing exactly the same thing. "Can we get dressed, Nan?" Eddie asked. "Well, I suppose you might as well. You're all wide awake anyway. I'll get you some breakfast ready. Fancy a cup of tea, Eileen?" "Yes, please, Mum. That was close." Even as she spoke, another much more distant boom. Then another explosion. We looked at each other. What next?!

We'd had our breakfast, washed and dressed. Granddad and Johnny hadn't returned. "Can we go and meet Granddad, Nan? We might be able to give a hand." Eddie looked pleadingly at Nan. She looked at us, took a few moment, "Yes, you two can go, but I'm sorry Michael, you're a bit too young. Anyway. I want you to come with me to Webb Street. I've got to get this evacuation sorted out." Evacuation, fucking evacuation. They can all go and fuck themselves. I'm going nowhere. She's a bloody witch, she knows! "Don't worry, Paddy, I'll make it all right for you all. Now, off you go and be careful and do exactly as you are told. Tell Granddad where I'm going. What about you, Eileen? What are you going to do?" "I'll just get ready and go along with the boys." With that, Eileen gave me a cheeky smile, "Don't worry, I won't get in your way or show you up in front of your mates."

We were on our way in half an hour. As we got closer to the arches, we could see hundreds of people milling about. There were barriers up. A small stream of people were coming back towards us, most covered in dust, some crying and some with blood on tattered clothing. What we saw next, wow!! The custard powder company, Monkhouse and Glasscock, was almost obliterated. (The Monkhouse part of it had something to do with the famous comedian of later years). Eileen and Aunt Anne worked there from time to time. "That's my job finished with," she said in a whisper. There were ambulances, fire engines, police, air raid wardens, Red Cross and many others. We could hear all the hollering and shouting. The sight I saw, as we entered Snowsfields, I will never forget. The large block of the Guinness buildings had taken most of the blast. The whole front was in ruins. What was left standing, looked like an open doll's house. The miracle was that there were people still alive, actually in full view, standing, sitting or lying in many of the flats. Some (mostly women) were calling out for help. The rescuers were trying desperately to reach them but first they had to scramble over piles of rubble desperately searching for survivors. There were lots of bodies covered in blankets. Eddie asked the nearest copper if there was anything we could do to help. "Sorry, I don't think so, son. You might wind up getting hurt yourselves." He looked at us, deep in thought. "Tell you what, go over to the Red Cross or Sally Army, they might find something for you to do." A large group of soldiers had turned up. I think they were Yanks, probably from the tower. They very quickly got into the thick of it. Opposite Guinness buildings, the block of 30s-built flats, although damaged, had withstood the blast. There were no windows intact and lots of doors had been blown off their hinges. Below these flats, there had been four or five shops. They were no more!! Amongst these had been a fish and chip shop. "No frying, tonight." That notice would hang around for a few years (hence, the old music hall joke: "I'll never forgive the Germans. They blew up our fish shop.")

Granddad's small yard was behind the fish shop so he used to do a bit of trade with the owner. We'll worry about that later, I thought. Eddie shouted, "Come on daydream, over here." We did find a job to do. We helped carry urns of tea and jugs of water over to the army of rescuers. It was a desperate race against time because, as they were clearing rubble and getting nearer to people, parts of the buildings were falling away. Those people, who were trapped, were screaming and sobbing, begging for help. It was very upsetting and frightening. There weren't many people around who didn't have relatives in those buildings. It was a massive block, some eight floors high and stretching a good hundred yards. It's strange, in a scene like this, how you gradually notice more and more things. Behind the buildings stood the Protestant school. That was also badly damaged. I remember thinking how pleased some of my mates would be about that!! Then it struck me that some of them lived in those buildings. It made me shudder. How many more? How many more?

The Red Cross and Sally Army were real diamonds. Sandwiches, rolls and pies began to appear. We had our share but made sure that the workers got theirs, then a couple of army trucks (Yanks) turned up. You've got to admire them. They didn't fuck about. They had everything: medicine, bandages, stretchers and loads of food and drink. We were all glad that they were on our side!! I began looking around and noticed that part of our school had also been damaged. The main school was about 50 yards away, but part of the wall around our playground had been flattened and the small building, used for the infants, had been split apart (would I ever go back to school?). The rescuers worked in relays, each having rest, now and again. We saw Granddad and Johnny and a few of Johnny's mates (a bit different from Horsmonden Green). Granddad looked exhausted and Eileen, who was issuing tea and cake, said, "Dad, once you've had something to eat and drink, I think you should go home. You'll make yourself ill. There's plenty of help here now and Mum will start to get worried." Johnny chipped in, "I think she's right, Dad. This will all be sorted out in a couple of hours. There's enough of us here now." Granddad sipped his hot tea and nodded. He was like a coalminer: dirty, black, covered in dust and muck. His hands were cut and bleeding. A nurse turned up and washed and cleaned his hands, then wrapped them in bandages. "That will be the end for you today, sir. I think you should go home and have some rest." Eileen gave him a look that said, "I told you so!"

Granddad left for home and I went with him. It looked like they were losing the fight to save many more people. There must have been hundreds killed that day. They didn't even have a warning. They never knew what hit them!!

We walked slowly back up Bermondsey Street. Granddad looked tired and old. He didn't speak. I pretended not to notice but he was crying. That's the second time I've seen him cry. I was now deep in my own private world. A very dark place! I was seriously getting pissed off with this war. The newspapers had said that the war would be over after D-Day. I learned a very early lesson—don't believe all you read about in the newspapers.

When we got home, Michael was visibly shocked at the sight of Granddad and Nan wasn't too pleased, either. Aunt Anne and the boys were indoors. They were larking about with Michael, well, Wally was anyway.

"We are all going to a place called Newcastle," Michael blurted out. I looked at Nan in complete horror (where the fuck's Newcastle?). Nan took one look at my face, "Paddy, don't worry! It's all been sorted and we are all going together and, I mean, all! I'm going with you. I'll tell you more about it after tea, as soon as Eddie gets back. How long do you think he'll be, Pat?" She called out to Granddad who, by now, was having a wash. You could hear him, he made so much noise washing.

"I don't think he'll be much longer, Nan. There's not a lot more they can do. Do you know what's gone on down there?" "Yes, son, Uncle Nathan has been here and told us all about it. Was it very bad?" I thought (Uncle Nathan), I never saw him. "I've never seen anything like it, Nan. It was very bad. What's this Newcastle all about, then?" "You are an impatient little sod at times. Trust me. Have your tea first because I don't want to have to repeat it all again for Eddie's sake. When Granddad's finished, go in and have a good wash. You're filthy." My mind was in a whirl. I've always trusted Nan but this had better not be a trick!!

Eventually, Eddie turned up with Johnny. Johnny was covered in dust and grime and he was visibly upset. I carefully avoided him. I found out later that one of his best mates had been killed by the rocket. This incident left a lasting impression on him. Over the coming years, he often talked about it and still managed to get upset. I can assure you that finding dead bodies is no fun at all, even if they are not very close to you. Finding friends and relatives is awful and scars you for life.

I gobbled my tea down, anxious to find out about evacuation. Eventually, Nan called us into the kitchen. "Now, listen carefully to what I'm about to tell you." We were all ears, as were Eileen and Johnny. "I have no choice. You must all be evacuated out of London. There's no defence against these rockets and we don't know how many will be coming over. But, before you panic!" Giving me her steady look, "I will be going with you." "What? All the way to Newcastle, Mum?" Eileen looked shocked. "Yes, Eileen. They couldn't promise me at the centre, that they could guarantee that the boys wouldn't be separated. I told them that I couldn't allow that possibility." Eddie looked at Michael and me and smiled. "Are you happy now, Paddy?" Well, I wasn't exactly *happy*. It all sounded a bit uncertain to me but I trusted Nan. "I don't know about *happy*, Nan. I'd sooner not be going anywhere but as long as it's with you, Eddie and Michael, I'll do what ever you say!" Eddie and Michael were OK with the idea, so that was that!

"When have we got to go, Nan?" Eddie asked.

"We've got to be at Webb Street School at nine o'clock, the day after tomorrow. We won't be able to take much luggage but you don't have to worry about that. Me and Eileen will sort out your clothes. Now, be off with you and go out to play. Don't go far away, you've only got an hour, anyway."

We nipped out and met a few mates from over the buildings. There was a lot to talk about!! We heard Nan's voice calling out for Michael. Time for bed. I walked home with him. Eddie stayed out a bit longer. That was a big brother thing.

It was a long time before we got to sleep that night. The topic of conversation being Newcastle! We didn't know what to imagine. As usual, Eddie and Michael were looking forward to this new adventure. I wasn't. I was always worried about saying goodbyes because there was no guarantee that they wouldn't be permanent. We were nearly off when Boom! Followed by bang and the rattling of windows. That must have been less than a mile away. London, indeed, was fast becoming a very dangerous place. Eileen opened our bedroom door, "Nothing to worry about, boys. It must have landed up Camberwell way. Try and get to sleep, you've got a busy day tomorrow. Night, night, God bless." With that, she closed the door. I could hear her going down the stairs. My immediate thoughts were, I'll miss her and just pray that nothing happens to her. I wished she could have come with us then it took me hours to get to sleep, as usual!! The next day went by in a blur. Eddie and I popped in to see Kit and Michael. They were sad to learn that we were going but very happy for us, at the same time. Kit said, in that strange accent of hers, that it was a good thing that we were getting out of London. Then she gave both Eddie and me a big hug. She'd never done that before! Michael called Eddie over and I saw him give him something. Eddie very quickly trousered it (slipped it in his pocket). Even Michael gave us a little hug. "Make sure you look after each other and make sure to send young Michael up to see me, before you go." As we got to the bottom of the stairs and just as we were going out, "If you see your Uncle Nathan, please ask him to pop up and see me. Be lucky!!" He sounded panicky. We smiled at each other. He's worried about his business; you've got to laugh. We could all be blown to kingdom come at any minute. He's worried about nylons!! He was a nice bloke, though. "What did he slip you, Ed?" "It's some money, but I could not count it in front of him, could I? You silly sod." He did count it later. I could not believe it. "Three pounds." Now that may not seem like a lot of money now, but then!! Some grownups only earned that for a week's work. "That's a lot of money. I'm going to give it to Nan. She'll look after it for us. Are you happy with that?" I nodded in agreement.

Aunt Anne, the boys and Uncle Nathan turned up and we passed the message on. Then a very big surprise!! Uncle Pat showed up and he wasn't in uniform. He and Nathan went upstairs to the top kitchen, so we didn't see much of them for a while. Nan was out shopping so Aunt Anne and Eileen busied themselves, packing a couple of small cases for us to take with us. We weren't allowed to take much (which was quite handy because we didn't have a lot). Then Aunt Lil showed up. The house was buzzing.

Nan gave us some money, "Eddie, take the boys over to the pie and mash shop for your dinner. We'll all be over the Horseshoes for a farewell drink." That's why they've all turned up, I thought. I didn't mind one bit. I loved pie and mash (still do). "Have we got enough for some jellied eels, Ed?" I asked. "I think so, greedy guts." I also loved jellied eels. It didn't really matter whether Nan had given Eddie enough money because I had money of my own but, in this case, I didn't need to touch any of it. After our dinner, we wandered down the market, saying our goodbyes to the stallholders we knew. They all wished us good luck and by the time we got back home, the house was full. It was very noisy, with a party-like atmosphere. There's the

In Spite of Everything . . . .

Irish influence. Whatever the occasion, drink and be merry. Eventually, they all went their separate ways, including some of Mum and Dad's cousins. They always seemed to be around when drinking was taking place. I could never work out why they were not in the army. Come to that, what about Uncle Pat's not in uniform. I don't think I'd ever seen him without a uniform before. One thing I did notice was that he always seemed to be in deep conversation with Granddad and Uncle Nathan. When he said his goodbyes to Nan, I noticed that she looked rather worried with that deep pensive look of hers.

After tea, we helped to pack our two small suitcases (good old Uncle Nathan had provided them. Who else?!) Eddie and me shared one and Nan and Michael, the other. Eddie gave Nan the money that Kit had given us. She was visibly shocked. "I'll have to go next door and see them before we go." She never said, "Thank them." I thought that, just possibly, she'd give the money back. I knew what a very principled lady she was.

We played cards together and whiled the evening away. Granddad had the wireless on and listened to the news bulletins. There were some large battles going on in Holland but we never knew the outcome. Thankfully, there were no more rockets that night.

Chapter 8

*E*ileen came into our bedroom to wake us up. "Come on, you lazy lot. Nan's got your breakfast ready. Get washed and dressed. Here's your clothes. Hurry up, now! You've got a bus to catch, remember!!"

Remember!! You bet, I did. I was dreading this day. Newcastle—where the fuck's that?! I tried not to show my mood but I don't think I kidded Nan. "Come on, hurry up and eat your porridge. It won't be that bad, Paddy. Cheer up. You look like you've just lost a shilling and only found a penny." That cheered everyone up.

Before leaving our house, Nan made us put on our heavy coats. It wasn't really that cold but Nan said we'd need them, where we were headed. Granddad and Johnny carried our cases. Us three, Nan and Eileen followed behind. Kit and Michael were outside and they waved us off. Kit actually started to cry! That didn't cheer me up (what does she know that I don't?). I hated uncertainty!!

The school was only a couple of hundred yards away. When we rounded the corner, mayhem!! There were hundreds of families and a row of Charabancs, all with large numbers stuck on them. There were people shouting out orders and, first thing I noticed, was children saying tearful goodbyes to their parents. They all had labels attached to them. I shuddered!! Very quickly and quietly, I decided that there would be no way, no way at all, that I would be labelled and stuck on a coach with a load of strangers. Eddie noticed immediately that

I had held back. "What's your problem?" He asked me very quietly. "I'm not going without Nan, she promised." "Hey, Nan," he called out, "this silly sod is worried about you not coming with us. Tell him will you? You know what he's like." Nan looked round. She looked a bit annoyed but soon softened. "Paddy, did you not listen to anything I told you? I am coming with you! Now, behave, don't be a nuisance." Johnny looked back at me, with a slight smile on his face. "You are a miserable fucker! You know that, don't you?"

Granddad eventually appeared with labels, four of them. He waved them in my face. Nan put Michael's (who was sticking to her like glue) through his buttonhole in his collar. Then gave Eddie and me ours. I put mine in my pocket. I didn't fancy being labelled. Granddad showed us down the row of coaches and we finally reached ours. Our luggage was put on board. These had labels on them, as well. It was at this time that I noticed that there were a few ladies getting on the coaches, alongside the children, but not many. It was time to set off. More cuddles and kisses. Eileen got very upset. Nan promised to write a letter as soon as we were settled. Then, with a crump, crump, off we went. There was a lot of crying. Nan, being how she was, soon made herself busy. She helped comfort some of the younger kids. At the time, being so concerned with my own issues, I didn't stop to consider that we were leaving Granddad, Eileen and Johnny in a very, very dangerous place. We were off to safety. They weren't. Nan was thinking all about it, but she hid those worries from us. What a brave and courageous lady she was. To think that she wasn't far off sixty years of age. Luckily, for us, a strong and determined woman.

The coach gradually quietened down and soon we were crossing the Thames. From our high vantage point, I could see the ruined city then we arrived at an enormous railway station, Euston. It was buzzing, loads of Charabancs, children, police and railway officials. It looked very chaotic but it was actually well organised. There was a short wait but in no time at all, we had been placed in long lines. We were led into the vast station and then onto a platform. Nan made sure that we all stuck together. I had to produce my label to a station porter. I told him that it had fallen off in the crush. He was happy.

There was a very long train waiting at our platform. We all stood about four deep in front of it and I could hear the mighty steam engines, hissing and clanging, and the whistles of the train guards. Added to that, the noise of all of us humans. It was a very memorable moment. A little bit frightening. Ladies appeared, pushing trolleys on which were tea and other drinks, pork pies, sandwiches and fruitcake. They worked their way along, issuing us all with this food and drink. It was free! We made sure that we got our share and once Nan had looked after us, she started to help other children nearby.

Eventually, we were ordered to get on the train. Well, guess what? Eddie was first on, carrying his case with him. We were not far behind. We had two window seats (of course). There were eight to a carriage and this train was a corridor. That meant we would have some room to move about. There was one other lady sharing our carriage. The rest were children, like ourselves, but the difference being they were on their own. They looked nervous, so Nan tried to put them at their ease and I think she succeeded.

The whistles went. The flags were waved and with a banging and puffing and rattling, we were off. Another unknown!!

The journey was horrendous, noisy and tedious. We never had any of those games to play with. The ones that, in later years, my own children used, in order to soften the journey time. Although we were able to leave our carriage and explore the corridor, this was packed with lots of children, like ourselves. This made movement very difficult. There were also adults, some in uniform. These being as varied as the four seasons. There were also the train guards, who shouted at us to keep quiet and not disturb other passengers. To achieve this, we were told to go back to our own compartment. There were endless queues to use the lavatory. Children, like (as I've found out) older people, are not able to hold on too well. There were a few unfortunate accidents. After many hours, a trolley appeared and a couple of ladies gave out drinks and fish paste sandwiches. We were, as usual, lucky because Nan had also made some sandwiches filled with spam. We took the food offered and Nan (being Nan) shared some of our food with the others in our carriage. The drinks were welcome all the same. We seemed

In Spite of Everything . . . .

to be forever pulling into sidings to let massive trains go past. Some had guns and tanks and some were crammed full with soldiers, all waving and shouting as they flashed by. Inevitably, we all fell asleep. This helped the time pass. The scenery changed. We could now see big rivers full of cranes and boats and coalmines. There seemed to be lots of smoke in the air, with many large factories.

We shortly arrived at our destination, Newcastle. We pulled into a very large, noisy and busy station. Eventually, coming to a shuddering halt. I was very apprehensive. This didn't look like a very nice place to me. Nan noticed. "We'll be all right here, Paddy. Come on, boys, get your things together. We've got to get off here. Eddie, don't dash off! Wait on the platform for all of us." You see! Eddie was off like a rocket. Once on the platform, we were told to wait until we were instructed. It was organised chaos, but to be brutally honest, it wasn't that bad.

By now, it was evening. We were tired, dirty and hungry. Therefore, hanging about was a real bummer. Our turn arrived and we were told to follow this group of ladies, headed by one of them in a dark uniform. One thing I noticed straight away. It was windy and cold! We were directed to a group of old buses (they weren't red and that seemed strange). Once the bus was full, off we lurched! This part of our new home looked very shabby and dark. It took a while to register but no bombed ruins!! We eventually pulled into a modern built building. It was just a single storey building but looked very welcoming. We were offloaded and, as we entered the building, I could smell cooked food!!

There was a great big open room and there, on the floor, were rows and rows of mattresses with blankets and pillows. We followed Nan as she was shown towards our area. Nan picked a corner spot and once we had dropped our cases off and our big coats, we were led to the dining hall, where we were given plates and followed in line to have these plates filled with food. This was the first time we'd had canteen-served food. It seemed odd. The ladies were very pleasant and piled our plates full of hot food. Mainly vegetables but very, very welcome. I couldn't understand a single word they spoke. They seemed to find it very funny, but they were nice people. After dinner, we again lined up for what they called pudding; it was in fact rice and custard (what we called afters!). Again, very nice and lots of it.

After dinner, we had an assembly. The lady in the dark suit was in charge. She welcomed us all and explained that, in the morning, we would be taken by bus to the places where we would be billeted. She explained that these were all family homes and that we would be made welcome and be well looked after. Where possible, brothers and sisters would not be separated (I took notice of that "where possible"). I could sense trouble and I was ready for it. She continued, should there be any problems whatsoever, she would be available to sort them out. Then informed us that she and the other lady helpers would be going home shortly, but there would be a couple of overnight caretakers available to take care of any problems, should they arise.

I only understood half of what the lady had said. I certainly understood "where possible".

We sat around in small groups for the rest of the evening, but the long day took its toll and we soon tucked up under our blankets and went to sleep. It reminded me a little bit of the arches, but without the bombs.

Morning was strange. All those people milling about. We found the toilets and the washrooms. There was soap and towels aplenty. This place was almost brand new. Once we had washed and dressed, Nan made us tidy our beds up. We were then ready for breakfast. The ladies had returned and I could hear the noise and smells of cooking coming from behind the kitchen doors. I was now starving, as was Eddie and Michael.

Food started to appear. We lined up behind about a couple of dozen other children. This really pissed Eddie off. He liked to be in the front but Nan wouldn't allow us to push our way in. She was very particular about things like that!

There were great steaming containers of porridge. I had a great plateful. There was also some toast or fried bread. I was happy with porridge, rounded off with a big mug of hot tea. We thanked the ladies and they couldn't stop laughing. Apparently, we talked "funny". I took a big spoonful of porridge. It didn't taste much like any I'd eaten before. It took some getting used to but I was hungry. Michael didn't like it one bit. Nan had gone over to the serving area and when she came back, she said, "Can you eat that porridge?" Looking at Eddie and me. "Yes, thanks, Nan, but it's got a funny taste. Why?" "I've just found out that they add salt to their porridge. If you don't like it, leave it." Salt, I thought, now that's a funny thing. It didn't bother me in the least. They had made it with milk and not water after all. It wasn't that bad. "No, thanks, Nan. We're all right, honest". We polished off our breakfast. Odd people, I thought!

We all assembled and the dark-suited lady, plus a couple of helpers, told us that our bus was outside. She asked us to give our names to one of her helpers, who was standing in the doorway. I was glad that Nan had told us to put our big coats on because, as we emerged into the car park, it was cold. The weather was fine and quite sunny and soon, we were all loaded onto the bus. We had our suitcases with us then off we went. We started a tour around the city. At each stop, one, two and sometimes three children got off and were taken into houses and flats. The boss-lady returned alone. Off again. I didn't like the look of any of the places we had stopped off. They were grim and shabby and looked mostly run down. People were in the street gawping at us.

Boss-lady came upstairs and called Nan. I overheard the conversation. She wanted to split us up because she couldn't find anywhere that would or could take four. Good old Nan. I heard her tell the lady that there was no way we would be split up and, if necessary, she would take us back to London. I didn't give it much thought then but how she would have done that, God only knows.

Three quarters of the bus had now been found lodgings. The bus had brought us back to the centre. We had a bite to eat and something to drink. I noticed Nan in deep conversation with Mrs Donald. They were smiling a lot so nothing to worry about.

Off we went again. This place is getting even shabbier. The people looked very poor.

Now, when you think, we lived in a very rundown war-ravaged place but, somehow, these people looked truly wretched.

One by one, our fellow passengers left the bus, never to return. We were now alone, the four of us, Mrs Donald, the driver and the two other women. Except for Mrs Donald, they didn't look too pleased. We pulled up time and time again. Eventually, she returned smiling. She beckoned for Nan to follow her into the big old dark house. There were a couple snotty-nosed kids standing outside. The moment I put my foot inside this place, I decided that there was no way at all that I would live here. It was so dark and dingy. Nan took one look at me (now, I don't know why she always looked in my direction, but she did!). I didn't hold back, "Nan, this place stinks. I'm not going to sleep here." Mrs Donald and the old hag, who's house it was, stared in amazement as I about-turned, walked out of the house and got back on the bus. I was quivering with rage. I knew, *I knew*, this fucking place would be a problem! My mind was in turmoil. I thought my head would explode! Within seconds, Eddie was beside me. "Paddy, will you do yourself a favour and calm down. You've frightened Michael and got Nan worried." He started to grin. "You should have seen the faces on those other women. They were a fucking picture."

They all clamoured back on the bus. Nan gave me a thoughtful, deep look. "You've no need to worry, Paddy. I wouldn't have lodged at that place, either, but you must trust me and not fly into a rage all the time. Come here, you silly young so and so." With that, she claimed me by my shoulders and gave me a big hug. She didn't miss a trick, that old girl. She also gave Eddie and Michael a big hug. We stopped once more. Very shabby! Nan went to have a look on her own, this time. I saw her face as she emerged. I knew that we weren't staying there either! Nan was in deep conversation with Mrs Donald, the other lady and the driver (he had just joined them). Nan smiled a lot; she kept glancing towards us on the bus. She shook her head a couple of times. Eventually, they all returned to the bus. We were on our way again. I could hear bits of Nan and Mrs Donald's conversation. Mrs Donald was trying to reassure Nan that we would be well looked after, if she would agree to us being split up. It was proving very difficult to house us all together. Nan point-blankly refused to consider that idea.

I could see by the way Eddie had his arms around Michael that it would never be an option. We were right to trust Nan. She would never go back on a promise. I did, funnily enough, feel a bit sorry for Mrs Donald. She was a very nice lady but she wasn't as strong as Nan or nearly as tough. She was wasting her time. To my surprise, we eventually arrived at the rest centre. What now, I thought?

Mrs Donald showed us back into the main hall; all the beds had gone. Once again, Nan stood talking with Mrs Donald and another couple of ladies. Nan turned and told Eddie to help fetch four mattresses and blankets. He followed one of the ladies out into a side room, very shortly returning with mattresses and pillows and blankets. Nan noticed my questioning look. "We are going to stay another night here and see if we have any luck tomorrow. Run over and give Eddie a hand. You, as well, Michael, make yourself useful." It didn't take us very long to lay our beds out. We then went over to where Nan was. "Nan, I'm starving. Is there anything to eat?" That's Eddie for you. "Don't be rude, Eddie! That was one of the things we have all been talking about. There is no food left in this place, although, we can make a cup of tea. Just to let you all know, we are staying here tonight." With that, Mrs Donald butted in. "There is a very nice fish and chip shop not far from here."

She looked at Nan. "Would that be all right for you all? If so, I'll pop round in my car and bring some back for you. There are plenty of plates and cutlery." Nan answered for all of us, "Yes, dear, that would be very kind of you. We are all fond of fish and chips." Mrs Donald asked Nan if we had any favourites. "No, no, you've done enough already. Cod will do for all of us. That's if they've got it. Do you need any money?" "No, thank you, the council will take care of it. Thank you for offering though." With that, she was off. As she got to the door, she looked back. "Would one of you boys like to come with me?" Eddie glanced at Nan. She nodded and he was gone.

Nan went into the big kitchen, where she helped get crockery and knives and forks. At the same time, the canteen lady was boiling up a large urn for tea. Mike and me had a good look around and found a room full of games and gadgets. This wouldn't be too bad, after all! (But it did seem eerily quiet) All we could hear were our own footsteps and the clinking and clanking coming from the big kitchen.

Before we knew it, Eddie and Mrs Donald returned, carrying two enormous bundles. She laid them down on one of the tables. The women shared out the food, which was steaming hot and smelt beautiful. We had fish and chips, bread rolls and something called "mooshy peas". I don't know whether it was because I was extra hungry but, to be honest, it was the best I'd tasted. There was lots of it, as well. All six of us sat down and ate together (I still like mushy peas).

We played around whilst the ladies cleared up. Then Mrs Donald and helper said their goodbyes. She told Nan that a caretaker would be on duty through the night, explaining how to get hold of him, should it be necessary, and that she would be back in the morning at about eight o'clock. Then we were on our own. Just the four of us in this great big hall and in a strange city. Good job we had each other for company. It must have been extra boring and worrisome for Nan. Not only did she have us lot, but her other family were facing unknown dangers. We all got to bed very early; Michael tucked up close to Nan and Eddie and me close by. Eddie had the job of putting the lights out, taking care to leave on the light where the toilets were. I lay in the dark, unable to go to sleep, as usual! My mind playing tricks with me. What would become of us tomorrow?

We were up, washed and dressed, well before eight o'clock. Nan made some tea but I could have done with that fish and chips because we had no food. Good old Mrs Donald. She turned up, cheerfully carrying a large shopping bag.

"Good morning. I hope you slept well. I see you've made some tea. I've brought you some toast." There was loads of toast and some small homemade cakes. We didn't take long to eat the lot. Nan had been deep in talk with Mrs Donald. I wondered what that was all about. We soon found out!

"Get yourselves ready, boys. We'll be leaving shortly. Don't leave anything behind because we'll not be coming back." There was short pause. Nan continued, "Mrs Donald has offered to put us up in her own house. She's got her own car, which we can all squeeze into. I've thanked her for her kindness, so remember to be polite and be on your best behaviour. She's a very kind and caring lady. Now, chop-chop, she wants to get going." We were soon on our way; Nan in front with Mrs Donald and us three in the back. Our couple of cases easily fitted into the car boot, so we weren't that squashed. Michael was very excited because he'd never been in a car before. Eddie and me hadn't either but we'd been in Uncle Nathan's van, so there wasn't much difference.

Newcastle was a big city but we very soon left the really built up area behind. There were now fewer buildings and more houses and green fields. Mrs Donald had been giving a running commentary all the way. She was the head of the local welfare (now described as social services) and she worked fulltime. Her husband was a miner. He, therefore, wasn't called up into the army. She had one son, who was sixteen, and he also was a miner and one daughter, who was nine. She was, obviously, at school. Mrs Donald promised Nan that she would do her best to get us into the local school. I thought, don't try too hard, lady. Her son was vacating his bedroom and going to stay with a relation, who lived opposite. This meant, that us boys could have our own bedroom and Nan could share with the daughter. It all sounded very nice. Nan didn't stop thanking Mrs Donald. I could tell that Nan was very relieved and comfortable with all of these arrangements.

We arrived at an estate of nearly new houses. The place reminded me a little bit of Davey's area at St Mary Cray. Eventually, we turned into a side road and drove up to the end. Her house was the last one on the right. Green fields were beyond that. I noticed a fair few goalposts (good, they play football up here).

"Here we are, this is home. I'll open up the front door, bring your things and follow me." Out we scrambled. That cold wind was still blowing. I wondered if it ever stopped!! She showed us to our room, explaining that there would be another bed brought over some time during the day. The same went for Nan. Once we'd got ourselves settled, I could hear Mrs Donald explaining to Nan that she would have to go off to work, therefore, leaving us on our own. She showed Nan around the kitchen and told her to make herself at home and to make sure that we had something to eat at dinnertime. She promised that she would be back at about three o'clock, well before her daughter came home from school and before her husband got in from work. In no time at all, she was gone. Now, how weird was that? Leaving complete strangers in your house. People she'd only known for a couple of days. It felt very strange. Here we are, God knows where, all alone in a stranger's house. Remember, it was still wartime!

It was very nice clean and modern house. There was a nice bathroom and separate toilet upstairs with three big bedrooms. Downstairs, a nice size hallway, a big well-furnished front room and a dining room with the kitchen off of it. They had a nice big back garden, (about the size of Aunt Sarah's), with a couple of big sheds at the back. We went out into the garden for a look round. There was this great big rabbit sitting in a cage next to the kitchen and, in and around one of the sheds, were a couple of dozen chickens. They were kept in by wire netting. The lady from next door appeared and said something to us but we couldn't understand her. She sounded foreign! Eddie went in and called Nan. She came out and started chatting to the neighbour who seemed very friendly. I don't know how much they understood each other. A Cockney lady from Bermondsey and a Geordie lady from Newcastle, but they smiled and laughed quite a lot.

"Can we go for a look around, Nan?" Eddie asked. Nan stopped talking for a moment. "Yes, of course, you can. Don't go too far though. I don't want you getting lost. I don't even know where we are and we're certainly a long way from home. Take care of Michael, you know what he's like. Don't let him out of your sight, both of you! And don't be too long." "We'll keep sight of this house at all times, Nan. Don't you worry." Nan went back to her chatter and we were off.

The garden had a side gate and once we'd walked round some tubular railings (Michael climbed over them), we were in green fields. They seemed to stretch for miles with ditches full of water criss-crossing them. Every now and again, there were small wooden bridges. There must have been ten football pitches marked out. It reminded me of Southwark Park, not so many trees and a lot bigger. I had to test the water and it was freezing, not very deep but it was still windy. After a while, we went back to our new house. As promised, we'd kept it in sight. There were quite a few houses all around and they all looked very much alike.

"Had a nice time, boys?" "Yes, thanks, Nan," we all answered. "Did you see anybody on your travels?" "No, Nan, not a soul," Eddie answered. "Well, that's not surprising. All the children are at school and most people seem to be at work. There's a lot of support work for the war going on up here. The lady next door told me that they make lots of things round and about. Ships, guns and tanks and a lot of coalmining." "However, did you mange to understand what that lady was saying to you, Nan? She's foreign, ain't she?" She smiled at me. "No, no, Paddy. She's not foreign. She's a local. They talk a lot different up here. Luckily, your granddad had a drinking mate who came from these parts and I met him on a couple of occasions. I learned a lot from him so I was able to understand most of what she was saying. However, she had a great deal of difficulty understanding me. She'd never met a Cockney before." We all laughed at that. "They seem to be nice and friendly people. She insisted that she would make us something to eat and she's bringing it round in about half an hour." And she did!! Nan let her in from the back door and she had a great pile of meat pasties. She was indeed a very pleasant woman. There wasn't a great deal of meat in the pasties but they were big and delicious. She placed half a dozen of these pies on the side and explained to Nan that they were for Mrs Donald and family. She apparently did a lot of the cooking for Kirstie because as she was at work most of the time, it was difficult for her to prepare meals.

We were out in the fields again when we heard the sound of children. The schools were turning out. I didn't realise how close the local school must have been. In no time at all some boys appeared. They didn't take much notice of us. Some started kicking a ball about. The noise was very familiar but every now and again, something was shouted out and I couldn't understand what was said. It was very strange. I would have loved to join in but didn't. Maybe another day!

We had made our way back to the house and it seemed like the whole area had come to life. Mrs Donald was home as was her daughter, Margaret. She seemed a bit shy and nervous (well, she would be, wouldn't she?!).

The back door opened and in came two very dirty men. One young man of about Johnny's age and an older man. Mrs Donald went to them immediately and introduced Nan. They said hello. The older man didn't seem that friendly. The younger was loud and excited. Mrs Donald soon had big mugs of tea for both of them. Ron, the dad, took his boots off and went upstairs for a bath. Ben was happy to sit at the table and drink his tea, talking for most of the time. I was slowly beginning to pick up more of what he was saying. He joked about being chucked out of his home by Southerners but on the whole, a friendly sort of bloke. A bit like Johnny, I supposed, but not as big. Eventually, he went up to have a bath. Ron disappeared into their front room, clutching the local paper. We stayed in the kitchen.

This seemed to please Mrs Donald. Then all hell broke loose. There was a bang on the front door and I could hear excited voices outside. Once the door was open, I could see half a dozen people carrying a couple of beds. They obviously knew each other and very quickly, not without a lot of shouting and calling, manhandled the beds upstairs. I could hear Ben chatting away. He then appeared in their hall with a big suitcase in one hand and some loose clothes in the other. He and his mates were finding it very amusing. They were a cheery lot. Before they departed, Mrs Donald introduced them to Nan. They all smiled and said their hellos, although it sounded like "Aye, ye" (strange language). They mainly just nodded at us three.

After they had all gone, Mrs Donald got on with cooking the evening supper for her husband and son. Nan helped and made us our tea. Bread and jam and lots of it.

Ben returned and he and his dad sat down to eat. We left them on their own so we were now able to listen to the wireless in the front room. Everyone was a bit wary of each other, at first, but things in that direction were to improve, although with a few hiccups on the way!

We woke up in our new comfortable surroundings. As usual, Eddie and Michael in one bed. Me on my own. Just as I liked it. Even though it was now Saturday morning, I had heard Ron go out to work very early. He was a noisy bugger. Mrs Donald was off work and after breakfast, she volunteered to show us around the local area.

Before we left home, she advised us to wear our overcoats. I'm glad she did, that chilly wind was still blowing and it sent a chill right through me. As we passed the nearby houses, any adults that were around called out and waved. Most were staring at us in an inquisitive way. There were a few youngsters about and they also looked curiously in our direction. She showed us the local shops; there was a parade of them, the local school, which she was very enthusiastic about, and the local playground. She pointed out the small bus depot. The buses were single deckers and I could hear her telling Nan that in less than half an hour, she could be in the city. That sounded interesting. Eventually, we returned home. Ben and Kirstie were both in. Ben said that if we wanted to, he'd take us over the rec after dinner, so that we could meet with some of the local boys. "Yah pley foota, do's yees?" Eddie looked at me, shrugged, "I don't very much but Paddy here does. You was talking about football, wasn't you?" Ben roared with laughter, he nearly fell off his chair. "Aye, aye, yoos tak soo foony." Now, I know that we didn't talk that well, not like those blokes on the wireless but talk about calling the kettle black. He did seem a nice bloke, though.

He was as good as his word. He showed us off to various group of lads. Michael hadn't come with us. He'd stayed behind with Kirstie and a couple of other youngsters. She had promised to show him how to feed the chickens and promised that he would be able to play with the pet rabbit. There would be drama to come with that one.

The locals were no different from us mob at home. Some were indifferent, some curious, some friendly and some hostile! Fuck them, I thought. I would have loved to join in with the footie but I had not boots with me and Nan would have killed me if I'd ruined my shoes. To my surprise, Ben said that he thought that he may have an old pair that might fit me. Ben eventually sloped off so Eddie and I just wandered around, gradually getting our bearings.

"Can you understand anything they say, Paddy?" "Not much, there's a lot of guess work going on." "Oh, well. We'll probably get used to it."

When we got back, we'd been away hours. Ron was home sitting in his armchair reading. He gave us a cursory nod.

I did feel a bit sorry for the bloke. Here he was, minding his own business, when all of a sudden, a bunch of strangers were forced upon him. No doubt, upsetting his whole routine.

I did, however, have mixed feelings. It wasn't my fault that our dad was fighting miles away in the army and getting fucking wounded. While this bloke sat smoking and reading his newspaper (calm down, Paddy, calm down).

"Can I go into the front room and listen to the wireless, Mrs Donald?" "Just wait a minute, Paddy." She turned and walked into the parlour. "Ron said that would be fine but please listen quietly and don't disturb him. He's been working very hard." "Thanks very much." When I got in the parlour, the wireless was already on very quietly. Ron grunted and just like Granddad, buried his face in the paper. He smoked and coughed a lot.

I couldn't wait much longer, when curiosity got the better of me. "Excuse me, Mr Donald, do you work in a coalmine?" Now, you must remember. Although I knew what coal was, I didn't know exactly where it came from. He dropped his paper, took a long drag from the cigarette in his mouth. "Aye, why dis thee ask?" "Well, I don't know much about coalmines. To be honest, nothing." He stared at me, an odd look on his face. My immediate thought was, fuck, even if he tells me, I won't be able to understand a fucking word he says).

He did talk to me. I probably understood about half of what he said. I could have done with Mrs Donald being there. She could be the interpreter. I did learn that they went deep underground to dig up the coal and that great lifts took them down into the deep, some of the mines went out under the sea. I didn't fancy that very much. He told me that his son, Ben, worked at the surface for the time being but he would go underground soon. It was all very interesting but I was to find out, at a later time, when Mrs Donald and his family were present and, especially when Nan was among us, that he was a bit of a loud-mouthed braggard!

Mr Donald was initially a bit hostile towards Nan but this all gradually changed. Nan was a very good cook and what with Mrs Donald being busy at work and Nan feeling her way about the house, she took up responsibility for cooking the main evening meal. Mr Donald, son and family hadn't eaten like this before. Nan would take all the ration books to the shops and buy the provisions. She could make a feast out of virtually nothing but bare bones. It turned out that Mrs Donald wasn't a very good cook anyway. The upshot of all this was that Nan was adored by dad and son. They had never eaten food so good. Ron wanted Nan to stay forever. They say that good food is a way to a man's heart. I saw it work with my own eyes!! The atmosphere in the house completely changed for the better, I might add. Sadly, nothing lasts forever.

Mrs Donald returned one afternoon with the good news. She had arranged a place in the local school for Michael and me. Eddie was too old for this particular school and the nearest secondary was too far away.

To say I wasn't happy would be an understatement. I wasn't looking forward to going to this strange school, where I would be mixing with people who I could hardly understand. When you add to this the fact that Michael would also have to face the same problem. I began to worry. Now the problem with me and worry is that it only produces aggression. I couldn't help that feeling it just occurred naturally.

Many years later, after I had badly beaten a bloke outside of a pub, Michael, who was visibly shocked, asked me why I was so merciless and cruel. I pondered that question for a while. "I think it's because I'm terrified of losing." It is something that I am not proud of, or ever thought of as clever or worthy, but it's in my nature. I really can't help myself. In my own defence, I have never bullied anybody or sought to gain any advantage through aggression. I have only reacted to threats and defended those I love.

The morning arrived (as they always do). Mrs Donald and Nan went with us to our new school. Mrs Donald explained to Nan that this was a Church of England school but the morning assembly was not religious, in any way. There would normally be just one hymn sung but no church officials would be present. She didn't think it a good idea for us not to take part because we were be a bit of a curiosity as it was; she didn't think it wise to add to that. Nan agreed. Michael and I didn't care, either way. We were met by a lady teacher, who introduced herself as assistant head, then after a small chat, Nan and Mrs Donald left. Nan didn't look back.

We were ushered into a big assembly hall and told to stand at the back. A few heads were turned in our direction, mainly from those at the rear who were the older pupils, some of whom would be coming up fourteen. Finally a hymn was sung. We didn't join in, simply because we'd never heard it before.

The assembly broke up, not before the head teacher had informed the entire school, that there was a couple of evacuees from London at the school and that we should be given a warm welcome. That was a stupid thing to do (or so I thought). An older girl, with a prefect badge on her blouse, introduced herself and proceeded to show us to our classrooms. Before we separated, I told Michael that I'd see him at break time. As I entered the classroom, it all went quiet and all 25/30 pairs of eyes stared at me. Girls and boys. The teacher welcomed me

In Spite of Everything . . . .

and quickly ushered me to a vacant desk at the back of the class. A couple of lads turned and tapped me on the shoulder, friendly like.

A pencil, pen, ruler and paper had been placed on my desk. The teacher asked me to introduce myself and tell the class where I came from. Luckily, I've never been shy (over the years, people have said I'm the complete opposite). The funny thing is that I would prefer to be left alone but, where necessary, I am able to go any way that was needed!! I stood up. "Good morning. My name is Patrick but I'm always called Paddy. I live in London and have two brothers. The younger one, Michael, is here in school, as well. We were forced to leave London because of these new rocket bombs that the Germans are using. We are living with Mrs Donald and her family not too far from here." The classroom was buzzing; every head turned in my direction. There was some giggling. I think because they only understood half of what I had said. The accent thing was a double-edged sword. We couldn't understand each other. This was gonna be fun!

The teacher thanked me and brought the class to order. Lessons commenced.

It didn't take me long to realise that I was miles in front of this class. Now, I'm not being flash or trying to make more of myself, it was simply that I had been sharing the same class as Eddie and the older pupils so, therefore, I was ahead in my learning. I decided that the smart move was to keep "stumm" and just go along with the flow. At morning break, I was surrounded by my new classmates who wanted to know about the bombings and the rockets. There had been some air raids on the Newcastle area. Not that much and by now certainly finished. They wanted to know if I had ever seen the King and Queen or Mr Churchill. They were unlucky there!

I spied Michael, who was also surrounded by schoolmates. I dashed over to him. "Are you all right, Mike?" I was concerned but I need not have worried. He was a very outgoing person, sometimes, I thought, too much and he seemed to have made friends already. Back to class. The lessons were boring because I had done most of it before. Oh, well. Keep your head down. Remember Uncle Nathan (never let anybody know what you know. Education has to be paid for). They were very wise words.

Dinnertime came and we, like most of the others, had a school dinner. It wasn't that bad. I made sure that I ate with Michael. He was a bit fussy so I didn't want anybody putting any pressure on him. He filled himself up on my afters (dessert). I kicked football with some of the lads, after dinner. Some of them thought they were a bit "rufti-tufti" but I didn't mind a bit. I always played it pretty rough myself. Sport does bring lads together and I already made some pals. The nice thing is that there are no language barriers with football. Kick, move into space, pass or tackle. There is always a downside, however. Some lads don't like losing or being tackled too hard. I had already pinpointed possible trouble. The older boys gave me plenty of verbal[29]. That was when I missed having Eddie around. I had enough on my plate worrying about Michael. It didn't matter what I was up to, half an eye was always on him. We got through our first day, and there, waiting at the school gates, was Eddie. He was visibly pleased to see us and asked a million and one questions on our way home.

These were repeated by Nan as soon as we put our feet through the door. Eddie had spent the day out with Mrs Donald in her car. He'd definitely fallen on his feet.

We now settled into a fresh routine. School wasn't that bad but as always (it seemed), there were a few arseholes who were about to muck things up!!

I had noticed that there was this small group of boys and a couple of girls who hung around together. They were a bit mouthy and more and more of their comments came in my direction. I had promised Nan that I would behave myself and I had. Once again, however, something that was to repeat itself over and over again, in years to come, happened. Never confuse politeness with weakness. It's quite amazing how many dopey fuckers have gone down that road! I promised myself not to take any notice of these morons. Then came the big mistake. I was playing football when I heard this commotion. A small group were pushing Michael about. I rushed over and smashed them apart. It was that group of arseholes! I tore into the lot of them but before anything nasty could happen, a teacher arrived and broke it all up. They said that Michael had sworn at them. Michael didn't deny it but I was raving mad. "I'll fight all four of you cowardly bastards," I screamed. The teacher led Michael and me away and told me to calm down. That was impossible. I don't know how I managed to get through that afternoon. This was not finished!! The bell went, and it was time to go home. Eddie was at the gate and not far away from him, the arseholes. Eddie was totally unaware of what had gone on. I walked straight pass him and smashed one of the boys in the face. He went down. The others jumped on me and I was on the floor, kicking, punching, and biting (yes, biting). Eddie was amongst us in seconds, as were some of the parents and a teacher. We were pulled apart and I scrambled to my feet, like a wild animal. Luckily, Eddie was on hand to calm me down. One of the other lads was doing his best to get at me but, like me, was being held back. I screamed at him and challenged him to a straightener. He obviously couldn't understand what I meant. Eddie called out and told them I wanted a one-on-one fight with no interference, whatever the outcome!

I challenged all four of them, one by one. They all jeered at us. The ringleader just smiled and said he'd "Jus goo an get buts in." Well, it sounded like that. I didn't know what he meant! Half an hour on the rec. That was the meet.

Eddie led us home, telling us not say anything to Nan. "We'd better go home first because Nan will wonder why you two are late from school. Michael, don't you dare mention a word to Nan or anybody. You'll have to come with us, anyway." Michael said, "You've got to be joking. I wouldn't miss this for the world. You'll be all right, won't you, Paddy? That bloke looks tough." I just nodded. I was so mad that it hurt. I didn't go into the house because I knew that Nan would tumble that something was up. I just kicked a ball around in the garden.

Eddie and Michael appeared so I gave Nan a nice wave. She stared at me. She knew something was up. We headed towards the rec and Eddie said, "Calm down, Paddy. I think this lad is a bit tasty, so be careful, please!"

There was a large crowd, all milling around on the rec. Boys and girls of all ages. I could hear the chatter going on.

The crowd parted and there he was, surrounded by his mates. They all jeered at us. Eddie was amongst them. "Remember, no interference from anybody." He spoke very slowly to make sure there was no misunderstanding with that. An older boy came forward and promised that, "Na en wood interfere." I hadn't taken my eyes off my opponent. He had a fucking great pair of boots on. We squared up to each other and I got a very slight push in the back and, as if that was some kind of signal, he rushed toward me. He took me by surprise!! He gave me a hefty kick in my shin. The pain shot straight up my leg. It was more painful than that slate all those years ago.

It was probably the biggest mistake he made in his whole life. For whatever reason and I'll go to my grave not knowing, pain just makes me really mad and more focused! I hit him straight in the face. Left, right, left. Every punch landed on target and, with him coming at me, the result was a forgone conclusion. He fell backwards, covered in blood, right on his arse. He was tougher than most, however, and not afraid of blood. He jumped up and came at me screaming. Arms and those fucking legs flying everywhere. He landed a few but he was too eager to get to me and therefore unguarded. I never took my eye off him. I hit him with a right-hander and it made my shoulder shudder. His left eye just burst, blood everywhere. He went down again, then somebody shouted for me to leave him alone. I shouted back, "If he stops getting up, I'll leave him alone." Luckily, he had finished fighting. It was then that another boy came dashing towards me! That was an even bigger mistake. Eddie grabbed him by the throat and shook him like a rag doll. When Eddie let him go, he thought, that was that. Mistake! Eddie clipped him with his famous left hook. He went down and out. Eddie had a knockout punch. I didn't but I had very, very quick hands.

It now started to get a bit ugly but, fortunately, a man's booming voice called out, "Enough! It was a fair fight. Now, all go home. There'll be no more scrapping here!" There were a couple of tough looking men, obviously miners, on their way home from work. Everybody slowly dispersed. We weren't the flavour of the month but I never started it. I only wished everyone would just leave us alone.

Nan squealed as I went into the kitchen. "I knew you were up to something, you've been fighting. You've got blood on your face and there's blood soaking your socks. It's your fault, Eddie, you should have stopped him."

"They had a go at Michael, Nan. We can't stand for that, can we? It was a fair fight anyway." She just grunted. Mrs Donald looked on in horror. "Sit down on that chair, I want to have a look at that leg." I did as I was told. The amazing thing was that I hadn't even been aware I was hurt, let alone bleeding. Nan rolled my sock down. There was a nasty cut and a great big bump was beginning to form. "How on earth did you get that?" Mrs Donald asked. "The fucking coward kicked me." Nan gave me a clip round the ear. With that, the kitchen door sprung open and Mr Donald appeared. He had heard part of the conversation. "One of these days, I'll give you a smack on the head, if you swear in front of my wife."

"Don't ever try," I answered. Nan gave me another clip. "You're lucky you never went down, young lad. I know that family and that boy would have kicked your head in. Some people fight like that hereabouts."

"Well, he's got a lot more to worry about," Nan brought over a basin and wiped my face first. I had a small cut and some bruises. I'd never felt a thing. It did make me wince as she cleaned up my shin. She put some ointment (Yellow Basilicon, I think) over the cut then tightly bandaged it.

Eddie went into the parlour with Mr and Mrs Donald. He gave my side of the story. In burst Ben, as excited as ever, "You've been fighting, you bugger. You've made a right state out of that Jim Newlands. They are a nasty family. He probably deserved it anyway. Was that a kick?" He was pointing at my now bandaged leg. "Yeah, but I made him pay for it." "Good, good. Where's Mum?" Nan pointed to the parlour.

There was very loud banging at the front door and once Mrs Donald had opened it, I could hear very loud women's voices and the sound of a crowd of children. The women were screeching about what I had done to their boy. He had been taken to hospital. Nan tore out to the front door, not before telling me to stay put (an order, not a request), with Eddie was by her side. They were calling me all the names under the sun. Nan was having none of it. I heard her say that their boy had picked on my younger brother and that it had been a fair fight, except for their boy using his feet. I don't know how much they understood of each other but it could have all been acted out as a silent film. The messages were clear and with the help of the Donalds, calm was restored. We were kept indoors for the rest of the evening.

My leg started to throb. I was scarred in that incident. It's still visible today after almost 70 years. Amongst many, I hasten to add.

The Donalds were visibly shocked by all of this. They were a very respectable family. Mrs Donald had an important job.

There was an atmosphere in that house from then on, sadly to get even worse.

That evening, a policeman called round and questioned me about the incident. He wanted to know what I'd hit the other boy with. He was surprised when I told him, "Just these," holding up my fists. I got a lecture about fighting and he told me to confine my talents to the boxing ring and not in the public park. In my defence, I showed him my leg and explained how I'd got the injury. He made some notes and left. Mrs Donald was not at all pleased over a copper coming to her door because it had never happened before.

Nan and Eddie walked to school with us that morning. There were hundreds of eyes on us. A teacher was standing at the front gate and Nan had a long chat with her. There was lots of pointing in our direction.

When it was time to go into school, Nan called me to one side. "Paddy, now listen to me. I don't want you getting into any more trouble. Do you follow?" "I know, Nan, but they had better leave Michael alone." "You saw me talking to that teacher. She is going to make sure that Michael is not bothered. So, calm down!" I went away mumbling, "They fucking better." Eddie gave me a wave and a smile. "See you later," he mouthed.

We were lining up to go into assembly when I spied some of that gang. They were looking at me. I couldn't help it! I was in their faces in a shot, my eyes staring into theirs. "If any of you bastards harm my brother," I took a deep breath, "I'll kill you!" One of them answered, "We'll fook yas!" I stared at them again. "I'll kill you!" And, I meant it! I think they got the message. Michael was never bothered again.

School was a very uneasy and now a somewhat unfriendly place. No one threatened Michael, and I was left alone!! Just as I liked it. Nan was very aware of what was going on around us. She often asked me how I was getting on. My usual reply, "It's a dump, Nan."

One morning, Nan gave us some good news. "Day off school today, boys. I'm taking you for a bus ride into Newcastle. Mrs Donald has arranged a get-together of us evacuees and it's at the rest centre we stayed at for those couple of nights." I could hardly think of anything more boring. Well, maybe school.

We all went together, including Eddie. Mrs Donald had gone earlier. I enjoyed the bus ride. Newcastle was a big busy place although, in truth, not a lot different to London. Apart from the language and much less war damage.

The centre was busy. Besides the few faces I recognised, there were loads of complete strangers. The oddest thing was the ability to understand what was being said. I did get the impression that some of the other children looked dull-eyed and unhappy. We, luckily, had been unaffected by being away from home. Thanks to our nan! It would be a bit unfair, however, not to mention Mrs Donald's part in all this. She was a good woman who had quickly recognised another good woman. Nan!!

The day had been a success, mainly for Nan. Giving her a chance to have a good old chat with a few of the other ladies. I enjoyed the change and the happier and relaxed atmosphere. The cakes and sandwiches weren't bad, either. There was quite a buzz of chat amongst us all on the way back. The news was good, as well. Our army was pushing the Germans back and the rocket attacks on London had almost ceased.

Teatime at the Donalds was lively and got even better when Mrs Donald promised to take us all to the seaside on Saturday, as long as the weather wasn't too bad. So far, although it had mostly been cloudy and overcast, it hadn't rained much but it always felt very breezy!

Saturday came. The weather was quite good. Eddie said, "We haven't got any swimming costumes with us. What can we do?" Mrs Donald burst out laughing. "It'll be much too cold in the water for any swimming. We'll just have a run about and get in some good clean sea air. There is a funfair there." We looked at each other. "Still got some dosh, Paddy?" "Yeah, lots. Haven't spent anything since we've been up here." "Let's get going then." He looked pleased with himself.

We all squeezed into the back of the car, including Mrs Donald's daughter, Margaret. She and Michael got on very well but I didn't take much notice of her.

I saw the sign "Whitley Bay 3 miles". My first sight of the sea reminded me of Devon. The sea was very rough. Great big white waves crashing into the shore. We got out of the car and I was hit by a cold piercing wind. Never mind, we were at the seaside. Nan sat down and took shelter. "Don't go too far and stay away from that sea. Eddie, make sure you keep an eye on Michael and Margaret."

We were soon scrambling across the beach. Shoes and socks off then tiptoeing in the incoming waves. The water was cold but, to me, very impressive. Remember, I love rough seas (and still do!). We eventually made our way to the funfair and had some rides on the bumper cars (nearly got chucked off for crashing). I thought that's what you were supposed to do!! There were a lot of the usual attractions and we had

In Spite of Everything . . . .

a great time. Candy floss. I didn't like it! Much too sweet for my taste. There certainly weren't any signs of wartime here. The day went by in a blur and before we knew it, we were on our way back. It was a happy journey, I didn't know it then, but there wouldn't be many more happy days whilst we were living up here!

Sunday! It all started so nice and peaceful. The weather was bright and quite warm. We'd had a truly adventurous day on Saturday and the evening news on the wireless had confirmed what had come out of the rest centre. Heavy fighting in Germany and the Germans in retreat. There was talk of the war being over by Christmas and London hadn't had any rocket attacks for many days. Happy days!!

Margaret and Michael were playing with her big pet rabbit. I still don't quite remember to this day the full details, but Margaret asked me if I would like to hold her pet. She told me to be careful that I didn't do it any harm. I wasn't at all interested in the rabbit. "How could I harm that great fat thing? It looks very strong and healthy to me but thanks, no, I don't want to hold it." She looked very disappointed. "It is strong but you can kill it if you were to hit it behind the head." She made a chopping action with her hand, by way of explanation. I, to this day, don't know why she did that because although I wasn't in the least bit interested in animals, I certainly wouldn't harm them. Sadly, what she did fascinated me. I thought, that can't be right. A small chop with an open hand. How could that hurt that great furry thing?!

"You're talking rubbish, as usual." With that, I smacked the rabbit behind the head. It shuddered and was dead. I'd killed the poor thing. I couldn't believe it. I tried my best to wake it up but didn't manage to do that. I must admit, I panicked a bit.

Margaret gave out the loudest scream I'd ever heard. Nan and Mrs Donald dashed out into the garden, looking very alarmed. I just stood there. "I'm sorry, really very sorry. I didn't mean to hurt the rabbit. I only just touched it, honest, Nan, honest." Mrs Donald was comforting her daughter. The rabbit was now on the floor, motionless. I was willing it to wake up! "Calm down, Paddy. Come into the kitchen and tell me what happened." Michael was sitting on the grass. His eyes were nearly popping out of their sockets.

Over the years, we talked about this incident. Not trying to be horrible but we had many a laugh. We weren't laughing now! Mrs Donald managed to calm her daughter down with some success. I apologised and protested my innocence but neither of them spoke to me again. Their hostility actually helped me get over it because the more I'm pushed, the more I push back and it somehow seems to give me strength. So, unfortunately, fuck 'em!

Mr Donald was very angry. He wanted to chuck me out but, give her credit, Mrs Donald was unwilling to do that. I don't know how that would have worked anyway.

Surprisingly, their son, Ben, saw the funny side of it. We were now on the rec. All three of us and Ben approached with a few of his mates. He asked me to tell them what had occurred and because they couldn't pick up every word I said, it took quite a time to get the story out. They all fell about laughing with jokes about rabbit stew for supper. It did help to relieve the tense atmosphere out here on the playing field, at least!

Sadly, matters were to get even worse! The situation at school was very tense. Let's not beat about the bush. I wasn't that popular with the vast majority of the other pupils (boys). There weren't any more fights and Michael was being left well alone. I suppose best described as a standoff. I also detected a bit more than usual aggression on the football field. This, I didn't mind. I gave as good as I got. I enjoyed the rough and tumble anyway. The one positive outcome was that I seemed to be well supported by the team I was playing for. That's sport for you. If you are successful, everything else is soon forgotten.

Just to add a bit of spice to things, where I had been reluctant to raise my hand and offer up answers, I now wasted no time in showing off, letting the class know that I was a clever dicky. This really got under their noses but they couldn't do a fucking thing about it! Not very nice, I know, but I'm not pretending to be a saint.

In Spite of Everything . . . .

Things in the Donald household were not much better, that is, as far as I was concerned. Mr Donald's attitude towards me was very aggressive. However, I did notice that he was very careful not to act up in front of Nan. He was that stupid, he never realised the advantage I took over that one!

We used to sit in the parlour and listen to the war news. Our forces seemed to be winning on all fronts. London hadn't been bombed or rocketed for a few weeks. That fact alone made Nan happy even though she still had sons fighting in the front line.

I seized my opportunity by asking Ron (that annoyed him), why it was that he kept telling us that he and his mates were really tough and the backbone of the country, and yet it was our dad and uncles from down south that were doing all the fighting. They were saving his skin and risking their lives, while he and loads of men from this area were working steady jobs and were off to the pub most nights for a drink. I continued, if you were as tough as you think, you should join the army!

Nan told me I was being rude and that I didn't understand how things worked. "Be quiet, now, you're upsetting Mr Donald." I kept my mouth shut. It was a good job Nan couldn't actually read my mind (that's the fucking idea, the stupid idiot).

He was as mad as hell. He started to blubber about his work being vital for the war effort and that many men from this area were in the army, as well. I drove him mad (intentionally) by making out that I couldn't understand what he was saying, and time after time made him repeat himself, very slowly! Nan and Eddie knew that I was winding him up but he was so full of his own importance that he didn't tumble it[30]. A typical bully!

As I've told you before, the Donalds had loads of chickens. We children used to collect the eggs but ever since the rabbit incident, I was barred. I was ordered never to go near those chickens. Another reprisal for something that had been an accident. This amused me because I hated the chickens anyway and, if they had bothered to find

| 231

out, I had never been involved in egg collection. Michael loved that job so he didn't want me getting involved.

Eddie continued to go out most mornings with Mrs Donald. Nan, by now, virtually ran the house and did all the cooking. Mr Donald had never had it so good (his words). I mostly played around on the rec. There was always a football match going on, even in the bad weather (of which there was a lot). There were amusing moments because the jokes never stopped coming about the rabbit incident. Some of the older boys used to call me "Boona" (bunny, in our talk). It was very light-hearted. Unfortunately, these moments were rare. Most times, the atmosphere was sullen and suspicious.

"Paddy, come here. I want to talk to you for a minute." I had just come into the kitchen after cleaning the mud from my boots. "What do you want, Nan?" My immediate thought being, what had I done wrong now?! She stared into my face. "Tell me the truth. Are you happy here?" It didn't take me long. "No, Nan. I hate it here. Sorry."

She gave me a soft cuddle. "Don't be sorry, you silly sod. I don't much like it neither. Shall we go home?" I jumped for joy. "Can we really, Nan? Can we?" "Now, don't go saying anything to Michael just yet. I've got to make the arrangements but I'll be going into Newcastle tomorrow with Mrs Donald and Eddie and I should be able to get things sorted out. Remember, keep quiet and for God's sake, keep out of trouble." To say I was happy was an understatement. "Trouble, trouble, what me, Nan?" With that, she gave me a friendly clip round the head.

Michael and I went off to school the next day. Eddie gave me a knowing look and put his finger up to his mouth. Meaning keep quiet! I did! I was a real happy soul that day. Even Michael asked why I seemed so pleased with myself. Johnny might have been right when he said I was a miserable bastard.

That dinnertime, I made a special note of where Jim Newlands (who had a nice scar over his eye) and his mates were hanging about. I made sure that I played close to them because if I was about to go home, I wouldn't have minded having another pop at them. Very mindful of what Nan had said, I didn't however cause any trouble. They, for their part, kept clear of me. They weren't sure!

When we got home that afternoon, you could feel the buzz in the air. The kitchen was full: Nan, Eddie, Mrs Donald, Ben and Margaret. Eddie blurted out, very excitedly, "Guess what? We are going home in a couple of days' time." I looked at Mrs Donald. "Good." That's all I said (if looks could kill!).

That evening was very excitable; all the talk, obviously, about us returning to London. Mr Donald certainly didn't want Nan to go. He'd miss the great food but he didn't mention us three!

Next morning, it was my joyous duty to tell the headmistress that this would be our last day at school. She was very interested to know about our return to London, being aware that London was now a much safer place. She asked about our dad and seemed to be honestly concerned when I told her he had been wounded. "Give your grandma my blessing and have a safe journey home." I thanked her and went off to my classroom. I was closely followed by the headmistress, who had a short chat with our teacher. Once we had all settled down, our teacher let all the class know that I was leaving to go home. To my surprise, there were a few "oohs" and "ahs".

At playtime, I had to answer a million and one questions. I noticed Michael was also surrounded by crowds of children. I suppose we were a rare breed to these people.

After dinner, as usual, I was kicking a ball about with a few lads when I noticed Jim Newlands and about five of his mates making their way towards me. This is it then! I knew that I wouldn't be able to handle all of them but a couple would definitely get hurt. I prepared myself for a good kicking. Surprisingly I wasn't a bit scared.

They came towards me, Jim Coyne in the lead. Surprise, surprise. A hand was held out to me. We shook hands. In their rough Geordie accents, they wished us all the luck with no hard feelings. That was one of the biggest surprises of my life, so far!! They didn't overdo the friendliness, just turned around and strolled away. The football kick-about had come to a grinding halt and the silence was deafening. Then, it all started up again and returned to normal. Just like that!

At the end of class, I said goodbye to the teacher and to a few of the boys and girls. Eddie was already outside the gates; with him was Michael. Again, lots of children saying their goodbyes. A great many of the boys gave me friendly taps on the shoulder as they dashed by. The heavy mob were nowhere to be seen.

"No trouble, today, then?"

"No. Although I was expecting something to happen and it did!" Eddie looked a bit puzzled. "That little mob, I've had a problem with, came over and shook hands."

"Blimey," Eddie whispered.

"Yeah, I wasn't expecting that. I suppose they weren't that bad really."

"Let's go." We followed Eddie home for the last time. It's always funny when you do something for the last time.

I never looked back at the school. The house had an excited feel to it, since I should imagine that the Donald family had found our stay an unforgettable experience. I never forgot my time in Newcastle nor did that family, I should imagine. Nan kept in touch by letter for many years after but I was never that way inclined.

Before we went to bed, we said our goodbyes to Mr Donald and his son, Ben, because as usual, they were off to work in the early hours. Ben was almost in tears when saying goodbye to Nan. He had become very fond of her.

Nan made us all shake Ron's hand and thank him for his hospitality.

"Goodbye, Ron, and thanks for everything."

"Aye, goodbye to yees, you cheeky little scamp." He did give me a wink!!

Eddie and Michael were much more polite and he shook Eddie's hand vigorously, saving a big cuddle for Michael. There, again, everybody loved Mikey. He got quite upset when it came to Nan because he had got very, very fond of her, possibly because of the fact that she cooked them all a tasty hot meal every evening, plus Sunday dinner. She also washed and ironed, making sure they all had clean clothes to wear. It was her way of paying something back, I should imagine.

Ben eventually went over the road, probably for the last time, and Mr Donald went off to bed at the same time as us.

We would see them no more.

Breakfast was a subdued affair. It has always amazed me, why on these occasions, everyone is a bit quieter and more polite.

Mrs Donald walked Margaret to school. They all said their goodbyes, except me of course, remember the rabbit, she never talked to me again. Silly cow, I didn't give a tinker's cuss, she was a bit of a whinger anyway.

We were packed and ready to go, couldn't wait!! "You look pleased with yourself, don't you!" "Ed, honestly, I hate this fucking place!" I got a clip round the ear from Nan, a pretty heavy handed one, at that.

"Paddy, behave yourself, I mean it! And, don't forget to put those boots outside."

I had made sure to give the football boots, that Ben had loaned me, a very good clean. I even dubbined them. They were now in better condition than when I first got them. It's amazing that after all this time, I can so vividly remember placing those boots on the back doorstep.

Mrs Donald returned and since she had offered to take us to the train station, I think it was Newcastle Central, we loaded our couple of cases and big coats into her boot. There were a couple of neighbours standing around and Nan gave them all a cuddle, the same time wishing each other the best of luck. Hurry up Nan, let's get out of this fucking place. I kept that to myself, wisely, then we were off.

We were soon in the city and in no time at the station. She found a place to pull up with some difficulty because the place was very busy. There were quite a lot of soldiers milling about so we waited in the car whilst Nan and Mrs Donald disappeared into the station proper. Nan had checked that she had our return tickets, I know because I had examined them for her, that morning.

"Stay in the car, don't get out. Eddie, are you listening? We're sorting out our platform. Won't be too long."

"Ok, Nan," Eddie answered.

They were gone about ten minutes.

"Come on, lively now, Michael hold Paddy's hand. You take that case, Eddie, and put your coats on." I had to hold Mike's hand, something I hated (another thing). I also carried an enormous bag of sandwiches and cakes. Mrs Donald helped us all the way to our platform. The goodbyes started there. Here were people whose lives had crossed, due solely to the war, and would never see each other again. Or, so we thought at the time!

It got quite emotional, that is, except for me. Mrs Donald hadn't spoken to me ever since that stupid rabbit.

I just hung around but then, to my surprise, she turned to me. "Come here, you silly arse, give us a cuddle." She grabbed me. Eventually, once she'd let go, I looked her straight in the eyes. "It was an accident,

I didn't know that I'd kill Margaret's rabbit. I'm sorry." "I know you didn't, I can see that in those great blue eyes of yours. Goodbye and God bless, and remember always look after that nan of yours. She's a very special lady."

I didn't have to be told that. Whistles were blowing and the great engines were starting to get up steam. She reluctantly let us all go and on the train we all scrambled. The train was again a corridor type and, although it was pretty full, we soon found a carriage to pile into.

We were soon away. Eddie had his head stuck out of the window, waving frantically at a fast disappearing Mrs Donald.

We were soon rattling along over great iron bridges and busy rivers.

I didn't know it then but more than likely over one of the iconic bridges in the world.

And that, as they say, was Newcastle.

Chapter 9

*I*t was another long tedious journey. Thank God for the corridors. If anything, the railway was busier than ever. Usual stuff, us pulling into sidings whilst the goods trains trundled by, all going south.

Eventually, the houses and chimneys increased in number. Then, at least a couple of hours wait before we steamed into Euston. No welcoming party, we were on our own. Once off the train and into the vast station, Nan popped over to the enquiry desk. She returned armed with the bus numbers we needed to get back to South London. Nan was terrified of the tube; she didn't like going underground. In actual fact, she never ever went into the Rotherhithe Tunnel. She couldn't understand what kept the water out.

We changed three times, eventually getting the no.1 from Waterloo. This bus stopped exactly opposite our house in Tower Bridge Road.

Seeing the familiar sights of market stalls in Flat Iron Square, brought a sense of calm and relief to me. Although this was a shabby war-torn area, it was my manor. Before the bus had actually come to a stop, much to the annoyance of the bus conductress, Eddie and I jumped off. Jumping off a moving bus had become the thing to do, the faster the better!

We knew the drill. Wait for Nan, don't dash across the road. I don't know for how long she had been sitting by the window but there was Eileen! I thought her face would split apart from the smile she gave

In Spite of Everything . . . .

and I don't know how her arms stayed stuck to her shoulders, she was waving so widely. I think she was pleased to see us all!!

By the time we had entered our back alley, she was rushing toward us, tears streaming down her face (girls do cry a lot, don't they?). There was a great turmoil, all of us grabbing, kissing and cuddling.

"Let's get indoors, Eileen. I'm dying for a nice cup of tea. Are you in on your own?"

"No, Mum. Annie and the boys are upstairs. We've been waiting all afternoon. Dad went out. I think the boys were driving him mad, and Johnny's not in from work yet. Lovely to see you, boys, lovely."

Aunt Annie had already put the kettle on and the excited greetings carried on. The boys, Walter and Seamus, well mainly Walter, were manic. No wonder Granddad had scarpered!

We took our case up to our bedroom, the nice old familiar room. The view from the windows didn't look on to green fields, just drab shops and the bustle of the market, but I was happy. This was my territory!

Nan called us from the kitchen. "Come down, boys, quickly. There's a letter from your dad." We galloped down the stairs. "Here, Eddie, read it out to us."

There was good news. Dad's leg was getting better and he was now out of the hospital. He was convalescing (I didn't fully understand what that meant, at the time but knew that it was good news). He was now a sergeant and was going to receive a medal. That medal turned out to be: "Mentioned in Dispatches".

[Nephew Terry has all of Dad's medals, the reason for that will be made clear further on in the tale.]

I noticed that Eileen had all of Nan's letters that had come from Newcastle, so all the family knew how we had been getting on.

Many years later, after Nan's death, I was to read most of them and it was indeed humbling how concerned Nan had been about my well-being. She was also concerned about Eddie and Michael, but she seemed most worried about me, (her blue-eyed boy). This was a friendly comment made by many of the family, about me.

We heard Granddad coming up the stairs with Uncle Nathan right behind him. Again, there was the usual family kissing and cuddling. Johnny showed up shortly after. He gave me a wink and ruffled my hair. "Enjoyed yourself up there, then?"

It was now getting dark and just as Nathan was leaving, he whispered in my ear, "Have a couple of days to settle in, then it's back to work, lad. You happy with that?" Not arf, I thought, I'm brassic[31]. I just smiled and nodded.

There wasn't much food in the house, so Eileen and Eddie went over to the fish and chip shop and brought back a great pile of grub. One thing I must give those northerners, their fish and chips was much better than ours. Having a big mouth, like I do, I got myself chucked out of the chip shop for telling them just that.

There was loads of talk about, not least, the fact that there had been no bombs or rockets falling on London for the past month. The blackout was still in force, however.

Nan suggested to Eddie that it would be a nice idea to call on Kit and Michael, before we went to bed. He did and they were over the moon to see him and to learn that we were all now home.

"Eileen, me and Dad are going to pop over the Horseshoes for a couple. Are you going out?" "No, Mum, honestly, I'll stay in with the boys. Don't you worry. Pattie Bygraves is coming round, anyway." (Yes, the sister of that great entertainer. Not at the time though! He was in the air force!)

Johnny went out with his mates, to hang around the Brick (The Bricklayers Arms pub), a notorious area at the time.

In Spite of Everything . . . .

Pattie and another mate, Sheila, turned up and they listened intently as Eddie and I told them all about our adventure. Eileen in her clever, sarcastic way, said, "I bet you shook them up a bit, Paddy. I hear you left your mark on them!" Her mates weren't in on the joke. They just smiled.

Nan had written it all down. I buried those letters with Nan. I now wish I hadn't but, at the time, I reasoned that they were her private business. I do things like that!

The cards came out, I stoked up the coke fire and we enjoyed a nice game of pontoon (guess who won?).

We were now in our familiar bedroom. Lying there in the pitch black, I could hear the sounds of people and the odd bus and the clanking trams going by. What next? I thought, when will the war be over? What will it be like, peace time?! I had only memories of this war, I didn't want to go back any further. That would be painful. Erase, erase!!

We didn't wake up very early the next day. Well, it had been a long day, yesterday. It felt strange, at first, to be home but normal service was soon resumed. Nan made us a nice breakfast and once we had finished, Nan asked me to fetch a pencil and paper so as to write down her shopping list. There wasn't much in the house. I was to learn, at a later date, that Granddad had made Nan take his ration book with us to Newcastle. We used to joke that they must have survived on fish, whelks, shrimps and cockles.

Once I'd finished that, and with a sly wink and a nudge, I slipped out and bought Nan a quarter of blind man's[32]. She kept that a secret from Granddad (I don't think he approved) and, remember, Nan was the only person I would run an errand for. I took years of, fairly friendly, abuse over that. Honestly, even bribery didn't work.

It's very difficult to explain but, for some reason, I was not comfortable at running errands. I didn't think that I should and couldn't think why they didn't go themselves. I wasn't anybody's fucking slave!

Johnny: "You've always been a real awkward bastard!" Bless him!!

"Paddy, I want you to go down to your school and see if they are open."

"I've got nothing to do, Nan, I'll go with him." Eddie gave me a crooked smile at that one. He's a fucker sometimes. He knew what I was like, would I tell the truth?!

Our school was open. Just!! The couple of teachers seemed pleased to see us (well, Eddie, mostly). There were only a sprinkling of pupils, probably no more than a dozen, but more children were expected now that the bombing seemed to have stopped.

Sadly, I was instructed to bring Michael and myself into school next day. What annoyed me was 'instructed' not 'asked'. There again it was the law of the land and Nan wouldn't want us hanging around.

We strolled back past Guinness buildings in Snowsfields (what was left of them anyway). The place had been tidied up quite a bit. The roads had been cleared with great piles of debris on the sides. The old custard powder factory was a burnt out skeleton and our old favourite, Vinegar Yard, had all but vanished. No more horses!! That was sad. I did wonder where the ones that had survived had gone to. Eddie wasn't any the wiser either. As we strolled along Bermondsey Street, we came across the old Italian's sweet shop. In we went and, with a wink and a nudge, old Nicki produced a selection of boiled and chewy sweets. He took no money but took great delight in asking how the family was, especially Uncle Nathan! I wonder why?

Nan was pleased to find out about school. That got Michael and me out of the way. Eddie didn't go back for a couple of weeks, which pleased Kit and Michael. They loved it when Eddie worked for them and he wasn't too sad either. They were very fond of Eddie (but then again, he was a bit of a charmer, that brother of mine).

School was quite interesting because there was only about a dozen of us, for a time. At that time, the school was divided into the halfs, juniors and seniors; one class each. Michael was in the juniors, me in the seniors. We had virtually one-on-one teaching for a while. I think it must have helped me because I was learning things ahead of my natural time. I quite enjoyed it and, to my surprise, found no problem keeping up. We carried on in this way for a while but gradually the numbers were increasing, as more pupils returned. There were many varied stories floating about concerning the evacuation, some funny, some horrendous.

Our lives settled into the old routine and, before we knew it, Christmas was upon us. We all thought that the war would have been over by now but, instead, we were hearing of big German attacks and we were on the retreat once more. Although we all enjoyed Christmas as much as possible, the fear of more bombings and of possible family casualties, was always in the background. Another worry for Nan was that Johnny would be called up in 1945.

Another New Year. What would this one bring? We were all uncertain.

There were certainly a few plusses. London was running with petrols[33] which meant business, for Uncle Nathan and mates, was very brisk. Also the cinemas were opening again, which meant we were able to go to the pictures. We used to go nearly every Sunday afternoon with Nan and her older sister, Mary. They liked to sit in the same seats every time and they got very annoyed if they couldn't. Michael, who was a fidget arse, didn't come with us.

There was an elaborate plan to get rid of him. Either Eileen or Granddad would take him out for a walk with the promise of sweets or broken biscuits. It never failed.

I enjoyed most of the pictures we saw but the added bonus was the quarter of an hour news. We were shown up-to-the-minute and graphic pictures of the war. Luckily, we now seemed to be winning both here in Europe and in the Far East. Our eyes were glued to the big screen hoping to see Dad or one of our uncles but we never did.

It seemed as though all the church bells in the world were ringing. People were dancing around in the streets, many waving flags. The war was over.

The problem was that peace had come to Europe but not in the Far East. Nan and Granddad were very, very happy but still had this lingering worry over Uncle George.

London was a happy place to be in. The pubs were doing a brisk trade with many of them running out of beer and spirits.

No worries! In stepped Uncle Nathan and, by now, Uncle Pat. Eddie and I were running about like blue-arsed flies. The west end of London was just a mass of people, all enjoying themselves. People today think that London is full of foreigners; well, it certainly was in the summer of 1945. It was such a joyous time; people were happy and, for the first time in years, hopeful. Sadly, and there seems always to be a flipside, many families, our included, would never completely recover from the dreadful war.

More good news. The Japanese had, at last, surrendered. This brought renewed celebrations. People were emptying out the shelters and making large bonfires of the wooden and canvas beds. There was also a plentiful supply of wood, from the rows of bombed-out houses (we were to regret that in the not too distant future).

We were in for a couple of disturbing surprises, however. The pictures we saw on the newsreels in the cinema showed the devastation caused by the atom bombs. They were terrifying but worst was to come. I will never forget, to my dying day, those scenes showing those poor wretched people in the concentration camps. I don't think I've heard a cinema full of people so quiet, as those scenes unfolded before us. You could have heard a pin drop. It's crazy to hear that there are utterly stupid people around today, who actually deny the holocaust. I can assure you that it happened, and what I witnessed was truly horrifying.

As I sit and write this down, the pictures of awful scenes are bright in my mind. The even sadder thing was that Belsen was repeated many times over.

We received a long letter from Dad. He was in Egypt and his letter hadn't been censored. He was now a staff-sergeant and had recovered from his wounds. He wouldn't be coming home any time soon because he was involved in the formation and training of the Arab armies. He was going to Iraq for a few months and he promised to write again soon. Eddie was a bit unhappy about that piece of news, as was Granddad. Nan, as usual, showed no emotion, stressing the fact of his recovery and his promotion.

I was happy just as I was and my honest feelings were that he could stay there forever. I didn't want any more changes. My wish was not granted.

There was a special mass taking place on Sunday morning and, amongst other things, there would be a dedication for the victims of the bombings, as well as a thanksgiving for the peace. Nan called me to one side and asked me to please go to this mass and stay there to the finish. Eddie and Mikey would be singing in the choir with Michael singing solo. I promised her that I would but refused to take Holy Communion (this is when you go up to the altar and the priest says a prayer over you, then sticks a piece of *very* dry bread in your mouth). I didn't believe in it, so I figured that I would be dishonest, a hypocrite.

Eddie and Michael went off early and Eileen and I followed. I wasn't exactly over the moon but Eileen was able to make me relax.

"I'm not having Communion, Eileen, so can I sit at the back?" "Now, please, Paddy, you're not going to slip out halfway through, are you? Remember, you promised Nan! Anyway, don't you want to hear Michael?"

"I promise I'll stay! Promise."

"You are such a lovable rogue, you know that, don't you? Just this once won't hurt you, will it?"

There were crowds of people making their way into the church. That many, that it was necessary for a couple of ushers to keep people moving. We knew almost all of the people, quite a few being relatives. Eileen went in first, giving me a backwards glance as she blessed herself with holy water.

I eventually did the same and, as I was about to take my seat, an older cousin of mine turned her head towards me. She didn't look too pleased to see me. To be honest, I didn't much like her anyway.

"What do you think you're doing here?" It was said in a spiteful hissing way. "Your mum wasn't killed by the bombs. You've got no right to be here!"

For a moment, I was dumbstruck. A few faces were now staring in amazement at me. The red mist descended!!

"What are you talking about, you fucking fat bitch?" I made a lunge at her but felt a couple of strong hands grabbing me from behind. Two of the ushers had grabbed me. I'll never forget the smirk on that horrible girl's face.

"Shut that blasphemous mouth, you disgusting boy. For God's sake, remember where you are." Gasped one of the men, at the same time dragging me from the church. In seconds, I was outside but I was still being pulled about by those two men. I was both confused and wildly angry and they weren't quite ready for someone like me. I suddenly remembered that move that Peter, from down hopping, had played on me. Their mistake was to let go of me. My chance! I went low and fast, hitting one of them below his waist. He flew over my back and was sprawled on the ground before he knew it. I went after him like a wild thing, punching and kicking. I would imagine that a man such as he had never had a fight before. I was grabbed by his mate and lifted off the floor, still lashing out at anything.

A deep loud voice called out, "Put that boy down, now!" I recognised the voice. It was one of Uncle Nathan's friends, Big Joe, an ex-boxer. He did as he was told which was just as well because he wouldn't have been told twice!

I squirmed free, snarling at the two men who had thrown me out. I tried to go back into the church. I badly wanted to see that fat bitch again and find out what the fuck she was talking about.

Joe caught hold of me. "Belay, there, Paddy. Calm down, will ya? You'd better not go back in there. Remember, there's a church service going on. I don't know what set you off, but the best thing is for you to piss off and let Eileen sort it out, don't you?" As mad as I was, I could still understand the difference in a request or a command. It's something to do with tone.

I looked at Big Joe, who I knew was a devout Catholic. "It's all those two fucking bastards' fault." I turned towards them, "Fuck you!!" I then gave the church a kick and was gone.

My mind was in turmoil. That terrible feeling like my head would burst. What the hell was she talking about? I knew that she didn't much like me but why did she say that cruel and stupid thing?

I wandered around for some time, not really knowing what to do. The rage within me is hard to describe. One thing I do know, that rage made me stronger and more determined. Nothing will get me down for too long! I know what I'll do. Go and see Granddad. He'll have some answers!

It was Sunday morning after all and Granddad will be getting his fish ready. I headed straight for his small yard.

"What you doing round here, Paddy? What you been up to, son, you don't look too happy to me. Anyhow, ain't you s'pose to be in church?"

"I was, Granddad, but that cow, Sheila, told me that I shouldn't be there."

"Mind your language, Paddy. Remember, she's my granddaughter."

"She said that Mum (how I hated saying that word) wasn't killed by the bombs. What did she mean?"

I don't think Granddad could have stiffened more if I had kicked him. All the colour drained from his face.

"Paddy! Listen to me. Now, listen well." He held me tight. "Your poor mum is dead and buried and the bombings and the war caused it. Don't take any notice of Sheila or anyone else. She's still a child, like you, and children can be cruel, most times without realising it. Please forget what she said. Remember, she's a girl, after all! Can you do that, son?"

I had this odd feeling that there was a bit more to this than the stupid rantings of a girl but I tried to put it out of my mind. I could see that Granddad was becoming upset, worrying about me, no doubt! I also remembered that Sheila's mum's sister and two of her children had been killed by the bombing. Perhaps she was overcome by the stupid church service. I would never forgive, never! But I could forget.

Granddad must have sensed that I had relaxed a bit, so he loosened the bear hug he had me in (more like a fish hug by the smell!).

"I understand, Granddad, thanks for clearing that up for me. Promise I won't say another word about it. Can I help you get your fish ready?"

"Not in your Sunday best, you can't, your nan would kill me. By the way, son, don't say anything to Nan about what's gone on today, it'll only upset her."

"I won't, promise! I won't go anywhere near Sheila, either. I'll come back and give you a break later on, so that you can have a pint or two." "Ger-cha, you rascal!! Remember, stumm." He placed his finger over his closed lips.

I was still a bit disturbed and unsettled and didn't fancy talking to anybody. I wandered up to Tower Bridge and gazed over the bombed city. Being Sunday, the river was quiet. It was peaceful and, as at many times in the future, this quietness and the feeling of being totally left alone relaxed me. Why do people seem to wind me up?

Toot! Toot! I was miles away! I turned and there was Uncle Nathan waving to me from his van. "Over here, Paddy, lively now." He looked relieved to see me. I walked over to the van and, as I did, he leaned across and pushed the passenger door open. "Jump in, boy, we've all been worried about you. What ya been up to, now?" I jumped in. Once again, I could recognise a command from a request. "Oh, nuffin really, just a bit of trouble at the church. Nuffin to write home about." "Yeah, so I heard. Granddad told me." He was having difficulty in keeping a straight face. "We'll just pop home to see Nan, all right?" "Yeah, thanks."

I'll have to take a bollocking. I wasn't going to tell Nan the truth!

When we got home, I was surprised by the fact that Nan and Eileen didn't seem to want to talk much about what had gone on. Nan actually gave me a cuddle (I was expecting a clump round the head).

"You all right, darling? Sheila has been here in tears. She's so sorry. She didn't mean to upset you." That lying cow, I thought. "I'm not bothered one bit. Can I go and help Granddad?" I turned to Eileen, "Sorry I didn't manage to make it to the end. Did Michael sing OK?"

"It wasn't your fault. I was told all about what went on and, yes, he sang beautifully. By the way, Joe sends his regards." She flashed me that lovely smile of hers.

"Nan, I'm off to give Granddad a hand. Where's Eddie?" Eileen quickly chimed in, "I think he's with Granddad. He was looking for you. You must have just missed each other." Nan was surprisingly quiet and hesitant.

I was bursting to ask Nan why Sheila had said what she did, but I had a strong feeling that she didn't want to talk about it. As I left the house, Nan called, "Don't be late for dinner."

I crossed the road and something made me look back. Believe it or not, I very rarely look back. There was Nan at the kitchen window, watching me!

What's going on? Is there something I don't know? I never, in all the years that Nan lived, brought that subject up. I never asked a question of anybody. I put it in that vacant part of my mind and I forgot it!

What a shock was in store for me many, many years later. I was told the truth by Rosie, yes, my Rosie. She had been sworn to secrecy by Aunt Anne. It was after Annie's death that Rosie told me the awful truth. The family had been in fear of my reaction as a young man. Nan died in the comfort that I was unaware of the true story.

I'll keep my life story in the order that it evolved. The truth will be revealed at the time of my life when it was finally uncovered. They were correct in not telling me!!

It was quite a sight there, running down the centre of Weston Street. A long line of trestle tables, must have been fifty yards long, with coloured balloons and flags, all filled with food. Sandwiches, cakes, jelly and custard. This was just one of the many victory parties going on all over the country. We all had a seat to sit on and the ladies were looking after us, making sure that we all got our fair share. It must have taken a lot of ration cards to get this lot, although I would imagine that a few corners had been cut! Some men had even managed to pull a piano into the middle of the street. Then the beer turned up. This wasn't just a children's party anymore. There was singing and dancing in the street. It certainly was a sight, men and women, some with silly hats, some with flags draped around them. There were men and women in uniform, air raid wardens and even a few coppers! A couple of women even nicked the coppers' helmets and were dancing around with them on their heads. It was indeed a very happy time. What made it more surreal was the bombed out houses on the side, although most of these had flags flying from them. Nothing was going to spoil these celebrations.

The partying (by the adults) seemed to carry on for weeks and my trips over to the West End increased. The West End and Soho were manic. People certainly made sure that they enjoyed the end of the war, it had gone on for a long while and the people of London had taken a right pounding. So it was their right!

Our lives, i.e. Eddie, Michael and me, had now settled into a more relaxed way. It was approaching the end of the summer term, which meant end of school. I knew that next year I would be able to take my scholarship exams. Nan was really keen for me to do that because our headmistress had told her that I should pass that exam with ease. She stressed on me, time and time again, to do my very best. "You have a duty to be the best you are capable of and don't ever forget that, young man!" I heard that many times so I decided that I wouldn't let her down. And I never did!

Our summer holidays were great fun. Cousin Jim stayed with us all through because, sadly, Aunt Emma was very ill. She had TB. A couple of the girls had to be looked after by Catholic nuns. They lived for a while in a convent. Years later, they told me of the torrid time they had experienced. The nuns apparently were very cruel. Uncle Pat did his best but he found it very difficult looking after Aunt Emma and all of his children.

It was at this time that I had found out that Uncle Pat had actually deserted. Now, he had been a professional soldier and had fought at Dunkirk. He had risen in the ranks to become a sergeant major! There was a funny story, told mostly in the pub by Johnny, that on the day before D-Day, Uncle Pat stood in front of his battalion on the parade ground and informed them that the time had come for revenge; payback time. They were instructed to fall out and go and enjoy themselves, but he expected every one of them to be on parade tomorrow because they were off to France.

"Faall out!" came the command.

They were all there, bright and eager that next morning, except for one man—the regimental sergeant major. He had scarpered. I think the story had been ever so slightly exaggerated but it was a good story nevertheless! Uncle Pat never talked about it but I know he did it in order to look after his dying wife. He figured he'd done his fair share; also he had four brothers fighting for our country. Unfortunately, he spent a short spell in prison for his desertion.

There is always a flipside and the *flip*, at this moment in time, came and bit Uncle Nathan on the arse. Unbeknown to all of us, he had actually had his call up papers in late 1944. I think they were getting desperate for men and the minor problem that had kept him out earlier was now overlooked. He had decided that army life wasn't to his liking and that he had a more pressing duty to look after our family. By that, I mean, his own, his parents and his brothers. He certainly did that! His problem was that now the war was over, there were more police and specials with time on their hands. Time to round up all the scoundrels, which, of course, included Nathan. He also had to do a bit of porridge[34]. That meant that I had a lean time as well.

Johnny went into the army and was posted to Germany as part of the British army of occupation on the Rhine (BAOR) and, at the same time, soldiers were returning home and getting demobbed.

We used to make up signs. The first one being "Welcome Home, Dave." These signs, alongside the Union Jacks, were hung out of the window. There were literally thousands of them. The shock on the men's faces when they saw the bomb ruins was of true amazement. More good news came our way when Aunt Lil came dashing round to tell Nan that Uncle George was alive and well. Not even a scratch. It would be well into 1946 before he got home, however. It's a shame to say but, unfortunately, by the time the men from the Far East did get back, the flags and banners had started to fade and the parties and celebrations had become a bit muted. We all had worse problems. Starvation!

We had all thought that once we'd won the war everything would be nice and cosy. How wrong we were! The shortages got much worse, even bread and vegetables were rationed. We hardly had enough to survive on. That was a nice welcome home for our conquering heroes. We were sorely missing Uncle Nathan and pals. Luckily, Granddad had a few contacts so we were better off than most. Nan was also getting money from Dad and that had increased.

The next home was Uncle Jim, the sailor. He was still a very young man and unmarried, therefore, he lived with us. The war had taken its toll on Jimmy. He had a bit of a nervous twitch although not too pronounced. I think that living in the same house as he did meant that I noticed those things. With the going of Johnny, our house had quietened a bit but now we had Jim instead. He was able to play the piano and he loved music. He bought a windup record player and the house was soon full of the sounds of Frank Sinatra, Dick Haymes, Ella Fitzgerald, Billie Holliday and the big bands like Tommy Dorsey. I loved that type of music (and still do). Eileen was another music lover so the house was very rarely quiet. Their friends were always in our house, which was a very happy house at that time. What could possibly go wrong?!

The rest of the year soon passed and before we knew it, Christmas was upon us. Surprisingly, it was a happy Christmas. Nan had struggled to get some decent food; we even had a chicken for our Christmas dinner (yes, chicken! I suppose it's hard for the modern generation to imagine that the humble chicken was a luxury item at that time). Eddie and Michael sung in the choir on Christmas Day and Eileen said that it was a wonderful service. I refused to go anywhere near the church. I just wandered around, happy with my own company and those deep and worrying thoughts of mine. Because it was Christmas, Granddad didn't open his stall, therefore, I wasn't able to help him either. We all met up after the service and then spent a nice day together. Aunt Anne and her boys, as well as Aunt Lil and her young boy, George, all came round for dinner. It wasn't just a family get-together, the brutal fact was that by combining all our ration books, Nan was able to buy a great deal of food. There were no toys whatsoever but we managed to enjoy ourselves.

Then in 1946 came the first bombshell! Nan received a letter from Dad. I knew that there was a problem because she didn't give it to me to read out for her. Uncle Jim was given the job! A couple of days went by with the odd whispered conversation between Nan and Granddad. By now, I could wait no longer. "Nan, was that a letter from Dad? He's all right, ain't he?" "Yes, don't be silly, of course he is but there's something I want to talk about with you and Eddie and Mikey. Once you've finished your tea, we'll all have a chat. Now be off with you. Go out and play." I noticed that Nan was a bit tense and that bothered me. I wasn't exactly happy!

We were sitting round the big kitchen table: Nan, Granddad, Eileen and us three. Jimmy had gone out.

"Eddie, I want you to read your dad's letter out. There's some serious things in it and we will all have to come to a decision." My immediate thoughts were, here we go again, something else to fuck things up.

Even I was agog as Eddie read out aloud the contents of the letter.

Our dad had been offered the chance to stay in Iraq to help train an Arab army with the promise of a commission, which meant he would become an officer. He had been offered a massive house with a swimming pool and a string of horses. There were a couple of pictures attached. He wanted us three to come out and live with him. There were good English schools apparently.

Eddie was so excited, as was Mikey (have a good guess!!). I thought he must be fucking mad!! I made my mind up right there and then that I was going nowhere!

Eddie finished reading the letter and, for a short while, our kitchen was a mad house. It suddenly went quiet. Then, I broke the silence. I looked at Eddie and Mikey (who were both wide-eyed), then straight into Nan's blue eyes, "Nan, I don't want to go away. Do I have to?" "Now, Paddy, don't get yourself all wound up. We all need to think this over." I jumped up. "I wish he'd been killed. I'm not going away, Nan! Never!" With that, I dashed out of the kitchen, down the stairs and out into the street. The paper seller said something to me, as I pushed past but it didn't sink in.

It's difficult to explain the rage within me. It seemed that every one was determined to destroy me and I was never going to let that happen. Then I heard Eileen calling out for me to stop. I turned and she was only a few yards behind me. There were tears in her eyes and that annoyed me even more because it wasn't my fault! She coaxed me back home, where Nan was waiting.

"Oh, Paddy, oh, Paddy, you silly boy. You'll be the death of me. I worry so much about you. How many more times have I got to tell you! Listen! Look at me! I'll always look after you and never let you come to any harm! Now come upstairs. Michael is getting very upset, worrying where you've gone!" We all went upstairs into the kitchen, where Granddad wasn't looking that happy.

Michael was overjoyed to see me. "I thought you'd run away and I'd never see you again." "Don't be silly, Mikey, I'll never leave you or, you, Eddie." Michael smiled and Eddie just nodded (he didn't look that happy).

Granddad eventually chipped in. "Your dad loves you and it's only right that he wants to do his best for you. He's got a wonderful opportunity and although we love you being here with us, your dad must decide what's best for you. Sadly, it's not really our decision to make." He then turned to me, "However, we will write to your dad and tell him our opinion. I also want you boys to have a long talk with each other and give us your thoughts on the subject. Remember, Paddy, he is your dad and that was a bad thing you just said, but I don't suppose you really meant it, did you?" "No, sorry, Granddad" (in truth, I was far from sorry).

The meeting broke up. Eddie said, "Let's go upstairs and have a chat."

We sat around on our beds and Eddie started, "I don't know what you're so worried about Paddy. It looks like a beautiful place where Dad is. Did you see that house and those horses? He's even got servants. You fancy it, don't you, Mikey?" Michael just mumbled, "I suppose it would be nice but I'd miss Nan and Granddad."

I really felt sorry for Eddie because knowing what he was like, he loved something different, unlike me. There was no way, other than in chains, that I would ever go to fucking Iraq.

"Ed, remember, in a couple of years, you'll be leaving school. Where you going to work? Surely you're not gonna join the army? I think that if we left Nan, it would break her heart (no matter what she says). What about you, Mikey? Do you really want to leave Nan and everybody around us? I don't think you do, somehow."

Eddie chipped in, "Let him make his own mind up." "I'm only pointing things out to him and, yes, you're right, he can make his own mind up." I paused for a moment and gave my mind a chance to work before my mouth. "Look, I love you two about as much as it's possible but here it is. There is no way that I'm going to live abroad. I don't care what Dad says. No way! Now, if you two really want to go, I don't mind. You won't be gone forever, so we'll see each other again. I'll stay here with Nan." I turned to Eddie. "Honest, Ed, I'll be alright and I'll never hold it against you." My mind was quite clear, if they went, I would never forgive our dad and would certainly never talk to him again (he'd be as dead as our mum!!).

More and more children were showing up for school and, despite the hard work being put in by the builders, the damaged classrooms were very slow to be ready for us to use. We even had desks in the passageways. In truth, it made school exciting.

It was springtime once again and we received a couple of good bits of news. Uncle Nathan was being released (Uncle Pat had already been pardoned) and Aunt Lil had given Nan the news that Uncle George was home in England and would be home in a couple of days (get the flags and bunting out, "Welcome Home George!!").

After weeks of discussion between us boys, Nan, Granddad, Annie and Eileen, we had agreed (although reluctantly by Eddie), that Nan would write to Dad and tell him that we were not happy with his idea. Nan would explain that although he was, of course, our father, any further major disruptions to our (by now) settled life, was surely not a good idea. It was, yet again, a very nervy and unsettling time for Nan. I was annoyed with the whole matter, seeing it as yet another intrusion into my life.

We and the rest of the country were confused by the continuing shortages and rationing. If anything, much worse than when the war was on. Thank God Uncle Nathan and, to some extent, Uncle Pat, were once again on the scene. The old still in the top kitchen was slowly put back to work. Nylons, Spam and dried egg were making a comeback, which meant fuller bellies and some extra cash.

More and more boats were being unloaded, all along Tooley Street, which was more like Granddad's and Uncle Pat's territory, so a fair bit of black market started to appear.

We were receiving regular letters from Johnny, in which he often put pictures that he'd taken of Germany. Them poor bastards were in a worse state than us. I didn't ever think I'd feel sorry for the Germans!!

We got home from school, one day, and as I opened our front door, I could hear the excited buzz from upstairs! Uncle George was in the kitchen. He gave Michael and me a great hug, at the same time saying how much we had grown. He looked a bit slimmer than the last time I'd seen him, but he was probably the first man I'd see with a suntan. I did ask him why he was that funny colour. He answered, "It's very, very hot where I've just been!" He looked so smart in his brand new demob suit, the complete monty. So called because all returning soldiers were kitted out with shoes, socks, underwear, shirts, tie, suit (two pairs of trousers), overcoat and hat. All supplied by the tailor, Montague Burton—the full monty.

Very soon, the party would start because they were all turning up: Uncle Pat, Davey, Nathan, Aunt Anne and, of course, Lil, plus many friends and various cousins.

Nan gave us some money for fish and chips and, as soon as Eddie got home, off we went. "Can we eat in the fish shop, Nan?" "Yes, of course you can, Eddie. That'll be a good idea. You've got enough money to buy some doughnuts, if they're cooking anything today." These were freshly cooked doughnuts, all covered in sugar—if any supplies had arrived. They relied a great deal on the likes of Uncle Nathan for the sugar.

The fish and chips were lovely, still not as good as Newcastle though, but I kept my mouth shut. Sadly, no baking today! We wandered over to the pub. They were having a rare old time. The bar was packed, mostly by our family. Pubs were always a mystery to me. Everyone looked so happy and, by now, the old Joanna[35] was being played. They were certainly enjoying themselves. It must have been such a relief to Nan and Granddad, seeing their sons again and, thank God, all in one piece. Suddenly, it came to me that, in fact, Eddie, Mikey and I were the unlucky fuckers! That feeling quickly went away amongst all the merriment.

We knew that our family certainly knew how to party, so there wasn't much point in hanging about outside the pub. It was fast becoming silly talk time anyway!! We all went our own way to play around with our mates, "Keep an eye on Michael for me, Paddy. I'm just popping up to the Brick." "Yeah, I will."

We hadn't got far when Eileen appeared. "Paddy, as soon as it gets dark, Nan wants you home indoors." "Yeah, OK!"

We were home well before they all got back from the pub and, as usual, they had brought a lot of booze back with them. George didn't look so dapper anymore!

We quickly got ourselves off to bed before we were cuddled and kissed by the [now] half-pissed relatives. We knew the drill by now! I hated it!

Very soon, the piano started playing out a sort of tune then the singing started. A few obligatory rebel songs and then with complete order (silence), Nan would belt out a song or two. She had a beautiful voice, as did Eileen. I used to get out of bed and sit on the upper stairs, listening to all the merriment. It was a magical time. That scene would be repeated time after time over the coming year. Would the partying ever end?

Uncle Jim had written the letter to our dad, on behalf of Nan, of course. I don't think she wanted me to know what she had to say. I couldn't blame her for that, could I? Whatever she wrote certainly did the trick (for me anyway). We received a letter in which the main point was that Dad was coming home to be demobbed from the army. He would be back sometime in the summer.

I felt that Nan was pleased with the outcome. Sadly, Eddie never was. Me? Now, I had really mixed emotions. I didn't know why but I was not looking forward to Dad returning home. I realised that things must change with the arrival of my dad. What would Nan's place be in my future life? Where will we all live? How will I get on with him? He felt like a stranger. Eddie was very excited and Michael was a bit confused by it all, which made me feel a little bit guilty, but I couldn't hide from the way I felt and it certainly never bothered me (whatever will be, will be).

Our lives carried on as usual. By now, I was taking my scholarship exam and (certainly not being bigheaded) found the exam a piece of cake. I have been blessed with an almost photographic memory. This made exam papers easy to do because I could actually see the textbook in my head. It felt almost like cheating. I hasten to add that it doesn't necessarily make you intelligent (it doesn't make you a dope, either!). I always felt a bit sorry for most of my mates because they were unable to cope with this education lark. I had the piss taken out of me over my keenness to learn.

I was playing cricket for the school team in Southwark Park, when I noticed a man approach our sports master (yes, master, the only man in our school). I remembered that man from last summer when I was playing with Cousin Jim. They were having a long chat; both of them seemed to point in my direction from time to time.

Once the game had finished, our master called me to one side. "How would you like to have a trial for the Borough?" "Yes, sir, I would. Was the man you were talking to anything to do with the cricket team because I've met him before?" "Yes, he's the head coach and he was certainly impressed by you."

"How will I go about it, sir?" "I'll let you know, don't worry yourself. Now, get in line with the rest of the boys."

I went to my trials and was picked for the team straight away. That started my love of cricket, which I still have to this day.

Most of the evening coaching took place at the Oxford and Bermondsey Club, which was a Church of England run club. They didn't have a problem with my being a Catholic (now that's a laugh in itself!). There was a very nice flipside to this however. I didn't have to attend the small service taken by the vicar at the beginning of each evening. The fact that I wouldn't have done, never reared its ugly head. It's what you call a win-win.

I fell in love with that club. There was a good bunch of boys around me and besides cricket, there was athletics, a gym and even a billiard table. I was in heaven; it felt like the place I should have always been in and I soon settled. Nan seemed pleased that I had found something I was happy with and, another bonus, it was only a ten minute walk away (or a four minute run).

That was a good summer. Nan had received a letter from the school board and I can remember Eileen reading it out loud. I had won a scholarship and there was a place in a grammar school for me. You cannot imagine how proud Nan was. Nobody ever before in our family or, for that fact, anybody that we knew, had ever gone to a grammar school. I knew that Nan wasn't really aware what a grammar school actually was, but she was as proud as punch. She spent the next month telling everybody she met that her Paddy had won a scholarship. It was a great embarrassment to me but she didn't care. She was very proud.

Now, it's a funny thing, humans are a really strange bunch (well, Bermondsey people anyway). Why is it that a lot of the local lads, who knew me very well, somehow got into their silly heads that because you've got a brain, you suddenly become soft?! There would be a fair deal of pain dished out to dispel that idea!

We got a message, through one of Dad's brothers-in-law, Bill, that Dad was home. He had landed in Liverpool but he would be up there for a few weeks getting his papers sorted out. Things were about to change! Bill had a telephone (a rarity in those days). He worked in the print and had worked all through the war, one of the lucky bastards, that's why he had plenty of money. It had never escaped me that he or his wife, our aunt, had never looked in on us throughout the war. I despised the little fucker! Dear Eddie never had the depth of feeling that I seemed to have, that's why both he and Michael got on quite well with him. Dad had arranged to let Bill know the exact day he would be home.

The summer holidays were now upon us but I certainly never guessed what bombshell awaited! Cousin Jim came to stay with us for the summer holidays, as usual. His mum was by now gravely ill. She had contracted TB and was in a bad way. Jim's brother, Patsy, also stayed with us. He was a nice lad of about Michael's age but there the similarity stopped. Michael was a boisterous fidget arse; Patsy was quiet and timid. He had a very bad stutter, which didn't help matters. It's sad to say but I wouldn't mind betting he suffered abuse at that Catholic convent. He thankfully is still alive today and he has a truly lovely wife. They have three boys (men) and a few grandchildren. His family are a credit to him, proof, if it were ever needed, that you don't have to be aggressive to bring up young boys. His boys love him dearly and at Patsy's 70th, they quizzed me about his childhood. I told them all I knew.

The summer holidays seemed to fly by. It was a nice warm one, as I recall, although young people seem only to remember the good days. Not a bad idea really! There was one incident that I recall but only, in truth, dedicated to the memory of my late Cousin Jim (he never left off about it!)

Jimmy, Eddie and me had decided to have some cricket practice, so we trundled off to my club (O&B) because they had a large net on the roof (actually a steel cage). It was a great facility because you didn't have to run too far to retrieve the ball. I had my own bat; the rest of the equipment was supplied by the club. We had a great afternoon with me making both Eddie and Jimmy duck and dodge some of my quicker balls. A couple of other lads joined us, which made it even better.

I don't know how it started or even what it was about but on the way home, we started arguing. The row got quite heated, mainly between Eddie and Jimmy. I can't remember how I became involved but I did. Whack!! I smashed Jimmy across the head with my cricket bat and he went down. Eddie smacked me in the face. Poor Jimmy was moaning. I think I'd knocked him out!

"Put that bat down immediately!" Came the cry. There, dashing towards us were two coppers. I did as I was told. "Stop this fighting and give me your name and address!" With that, Jimmy scrambled to his feet, rubbing the side of his head. "It's alright, constable, we're cousins. He didn't mean to hit me. It was an accident. Our Nan will murder us when we get home, if she finds out we've been fighting." The second copper examined Jim's head. "You're lucky. No cut but you're gonna have a nasty bump, lad. Accident, you say!! Well, I wouldn't want to be on the receiving end of a real hit. Give me that bat, lad." The first copper took our names and addresses (the same, obviously). "Come along with us, we're taking you home."

He turned to Eddie, "You live with your grandmother, don't you? Where's your mum and dad?" Nosy bastards!! "Mind your own fucking business!" I got a clip round the ear for that. Eddie shoved me away, "Our dad's still in the army. Should be home any minute now and our mum was killed in the bombing." The two coppers looked quite shocked. "More reason for not fighting amongst yourselves!" Said the copper holding my bat.

Nan was shocked to see the two coppers at our front door. "No cause for alarm, madam, the boys were fighting in the street and we thought we'd better bring them home before they killed each other. There won't be any charges brought against them."

Nan took my bat, thank God, I thought I was going to lose it and ordered us upstairs. She gave Eddie a clout behind the ears, followed by another to Jimmy. Now, the reason Jimmy never forgot it (bless him)—I never got a whack. Just a stern, fixed disapproving stare! Jimmy protested about the unfairness but Nan replied, "You two are the eldest, you should have stopped it!"

Over the years, Jimmy never stopped telling that story, always in a funny and amusing way. There was no anger or jealousy. (That bit's for you, Jim).

We received the letter confirming my place at the grammar school and Nan and I went to the school to buy my uniform. It was a bus ride to St George's Circus and then a tram ride to Battersea; took the best part of an hour.

My first impression of the school was a bit negative. Surrounded by a high brick wall, the entrance by a large wooden gate. We were met by the deputy headmaster who was very polite as he showed Nan and I part of the school. It was bigger than I had imagined; big, old and formidable! Poor Nan was out of her depth, but she was as game as a bagel (brave). One positive thing I noted was the very large playground. In one corner were cricket nets and in another part there were tennis courts. The teacher must have noticed my interest because he said, "Do you like sports? Because if you do, you'll get on well here because we are very sports-minded." He paused for a moment, "After lessons, obviously."

We were shown to a large room, which was full of clothing, the uniform shop. Nan had to buy a blazer, tie, trousers (shorts unfortunately) and a cap. I was dreading the cap. I knew this was coming because Eddie had a school cap but he seemed to like wearing it. Sadly, I did not! There would be trouble ahead!

There was another, more sinister, thing that I had noticed. There were a fair few, priests strolling around. They mostly dressed like those vicars did, of the other side.

We bade our farewells, me clutching a massive parcel, Nan as proud as a boxing champion, on the way back. She never stopped talking. She really wanted me to do well, letting me know how proud she was. I don't think she'd ever imagined she would have visited a school like that, let alone one of her grandchildren actually going there. The look on her face told it all and I vowed to myself that I would not let her down. Little did I know, that I was to regret that particular vow!

Eddie and Michael wanted to know all about our visit and were impressed by my uniform, as was Eileen. Uncle Jim had other things on his mind and Granddad was mildly interested (no surprise there).

We came home covered in dust because we'd been larking about in the ruins. We'd spent the last fifteen minutes trying to get the dust off our clothes and shoes, mainly because Nan didn't like us playing in the bombed ruins. "They're dangerous," she'd say.

There were acres of bombed out buildings. The biggest local ones being where the modern day Guy's Hospital now stands. That whole area between Maize Pond, St Thomas Street and Fenning Street had been flattened. From the point of view of us youngsters, this was a wonderland. Boys and girls had made camps and the old rivalry between us Catholics and the Proddies (Protestants), reared its ugly head. We used to have vicious stone fights, hurling stones, bricks and anything else we could lay our hands on, at each other. The point being to take over the other's camp, some of which were actually quite elaborate. There was lots of timber lying about and that, combined with old cellars, made for wonderful camp opportunities.

We were often chased away by the local police, who seemed to be everywhere these days. I supposed now the war was over, there was more of them with less to do. Remember, there wasn't much traffic to worry about at that time.

There was one particular thing we, or to be more precise, Michael, were famous for—climbing. As I look back, it makes me shudder. Michael, as I've said before, was a fidget arse. He never stood still but, boy, could he climb. He could hang on to anything. He was like one of those monkeys in the Tarzan films that were just coming out. He could hang on one-handed, just like them.

Amid the ruins, there would often be single walls still standing and I mean, very high walls. This was a particular case amongst the factories in Leather Market Street. Try to imagine it. Single brick walls, some with smashed and burnt out window frames. The challenge: to climb as high as possible. Well, Michael was the 'guv'nor'. He would climb just like a cat. I know it's hard to believe but sometimes bricks would be breaking away as he made his way up. He was the only one who ever reached the top. He'd even start throwing bricks down at us. We never told Nan, of course, she'd have gone mad!! I don't think I would have blamed her but, remember, this is in hindsight and I am now much, much older!

We came in one day, thirsty and hungry, as usual, and Nan was holding a letter in her hand. It had come from Larkins in Horsmonden. It was her invitation and offer of a bin for this coming hop picking season. She was very excited. She loved the time spent in the country, getting away from the drabness of Central London, she also knew that she would be able to make herself a little of bit of pocket money. As I read the letter out, and seeing the starting date of 1st September, it dawned on me that my start date for school was 11th September. There could be no hopping for me or Eddie! I pointed this out to Nan and this brought her down to earth with a bump. She had the look of someone who'd lost a pound and only found a shilling. Then, as quick as a flash, in stepped Eddie, "That won't be a problem, Nan. We can all go down together and get you set up and spend the first week with you, then Paddy and me can come home and go to school. Eileen will cook us some food. Remember, we both have school dinners. We're not exactly babies anymore, are we?"

Michael piped in, "I don't mind being on my own with you, Nan. Please let's go." He could tell that Nan was having second thoughts. "Yes, Eddie, I'm fully aware that you're not babies anymore, but I don't know how I'll feel about you and Paddy being out of my sight, for a couple of weeks." She stopped talking and went into a thoughtful silence. I could almost see her brain ticking over. She looked at me and gave a sly wink, at the same time nodding her head in the general direction of the little corner shop. I didn't need much more than that (a quarter of blind mans). I took a few coppers out of her hand and was gone. It was the worst kept secret of all time and Nan trusted me.

"I'll have a word with Eileen, when she gets in from work, and see what she thinks about it."

"Please, Nan, we'll be alright, you know how much you love hoppin'."

"Yes, yes, Eddie, I understand. I'll think about it. No more for the time being, please."

That night, there was non-stop chat about (what else?) hop picking or not. Eileen tried to reassure Nan that she would take care of us, at the same time, reminding her that Annie would also give a hand. Granddad and Uncle Jim stayed out of it (I didn't blame them really).

A couple of days had gone by when Nan got us together. "I've taken up my offer of a bin." "Hoorah, that's lovely, Nan." "Be quiet a minute will you, please, Eddie? There are a lot of arrangements to get through. We've only got a week."

Michael gave me a nudge, "Yippee!" He was definitely pleased. Nan tut-tutted. "Aunt Anne is going to make sure that all your school clothes are washed and ironed and she will be here, when you get home from school, to get some tea ready for you. Eileen will take care of everything else. She'll have your school dinner money and anything else you might need. You'll have to be on your best behaviour (a special little glance in my direction) and try to keep yourselves tidy (again, eyeing me)."

There was no need to remind Eddie about keeping tidy, he was always immaculate. He used to spend half an hour combing his hair. I'm sure he came home tidier than when he first went out. Unlike me, he wasn't bothered about sports; he preferred to stand about chatting (especially if any girls were around).

That was that, then! Nan laid my school clothes out and went through her instructions, time and time again, at the same time, packing clothing for "hoppin". The arrangements were made, Granddad would be taking us to Horsmonden by train, as soon as we got home from school on Friday afternoon and, if Uncle Nathan wasn't about, then back by train Sunday evening.

Nan appeared comfortable with these arrangements and that made me very happy. Eddie felt the same way, as well.

What could possibly go wrong?!

The summer holidays were coming to an end, and hoppin' and a new school term were fast approaching. Then, just a couple of days before we left for Kent, another letter arrived from Dad. He would be leaving Liverpool in the next couple of weeks and would be going to Hartney Whitney, the home depot of this regiment, The Royal Berkshire Fusiliers. He reckoned to be there for a couple of weeks and then be demobbed. That would get him home in mid-October.

He sent us all his love and was looking forward to seeing us again. There was a P.S. at the bottom of the page (he had some exciting news to tell us!).

That bit, on the end, certainly had Eddie in a spin. I was just intrigued and, sad to say, not that interested. There were going to be changes and I was not looking forward to that, one little bit! However, I would be glad to see my dad again and to hear all about the war. There was no mention of his injury, so I guessed it must have healed up.

Friday morning, just getting light and once again trundling along towards London Bridge Station, Granddad, Nan and us three, pushing that great chest. We had said our goodbyes to Eileen, with Eddie and me reminding her that we'd see her in just over a week. "Enjoy yourselves. I'll be ready for you. Bye Mum, bye Michael, give us a kiss." The station was as crowded as normal, mainly with hop-pickers. The morning rush hour had yet to start. Once Granddad had got our chest put in the guards van, we were off.

Although we'd done all this before, the excitement was still there. Nan was happy and relaxed, which had a settling effect on me and, to be honest, on Eddie and Mikey, as well.

There were not as many men in uniform nowadays and, certainly, no heavily loaded goods trains thundering by. This, combined with the fact that my days of hop picking were coming to an end, made me think and go deep within myself.

"Are you alright, Paddy? You're a bit quiet, ain't you?" "Sorry, Nan, I was miles away. Just thinking! I'm alright, honest." I made sure that I didn't daydream anymore. We changed at Paddock Wood, as usual, and were soon on our way to Horsmonden. Once there, we were helped onto an awaiting horse-drawn cart and, in no time at all, onto the Common.

I suppose because we were a couple of years older now, the setting up seemed very easy. I had Nan's fire and cooking area all completed in no time. Eddie helped Nan prepare her hut and Michael fetched faggots and water. We were well organised! I recognised many of the families and they remembered us. There were a few more men around now, but no Peter and family. I was a bit sad about that because I bore no grudges. It was only a fight, after all, and I was fond of Peter.

In Spite of Everything . . . .

I really enjoyed that time down hoppin, maybe it was because I realised that my life was about to change, and that I would no longer be able to spend the whole month down here, anymore.

We worked very hard for Nan and gave her a good start, by picking her as many hops as possible. Eddie renewed his acquaintance with the village butcher. He apparently was really pleased to see Eddie, especially when he told him that Nathan had sent his regards and would be down to see him at the next weekend.

There weren't many lads of mine and Eddie's age, I suppose for the same reasons as us, secondary schools. Luckily, quite a few in Michael's age bracket and he had already made some friends. I just couldn't help reminding people to take no liberties with Michael, once we'd gone home.

"I don't know why you're so worried, Paddy. He'll be alright. There's no nuisances around here, well, no one to bother him, anyway!"

"Yeah, I know that but it's worth reminding everyone that we haven't gone forever. It'll really piss me off, Ed, if anyone took liberties." "Calm down, look at yourself, you're getting all worked up. Don't let Nan see you like that." "Sorry, Ed, you're right."

The week had flashed by and Sunday had arrived. It was mid-morning when I heard that familiar toot-toot. Granddad jumped out, quickly followed by Uncle Jim. They were really pleased to see that we had managed to get Nan well settled. Uncle Nathan explained to Nan that Aunt Anne and the boys were keeping Eileen company, and that he would be taking Eddie and me back with them. I must admit, that up to that time, I hadn't given that much thought about my new school. I did now! There was a certain amount of fear and apprehension running through my mind, but I dismissed those thoughts in a flash. "Yeah, that's great, Uncle Nathan. I'm really looking forward to my new school." (You liar). He looked over to me, "Son, you should be really proud of what you've done. We all are! I could do with you back home, there's a few things you can do for me, next week." (Wink, wink).

| 269

It was a lovely Sunday but now we were in Horsmonden village, waiting for the grown ups to finish their beer. We would soon be on our way. It was while I was saying goodbye to Michael, it suddenly dawned on me that I had never been apart from him. Never! I had a very uneasy feeling and nearly changed my mind about leaving for school or, for that matter, ever going back to school. I said goodbye, my life would never be the same again!

Nan was a bit tearful when she said goodbye to us, what with the combination of a few Guinnesses, and the fact that we had never been apart before (she repeated that a few times). It was a difficult time for her. "Nan, please, we'll be alright, won't we, Paddy?" "Yeah, honest, Nan, don't worry yourself over us. We'll be fine, we're big boys now and, anyway, we'll see you on Friday, won't we?" She still wasn't too happy but she let us go. Luckily, she wasn't able to see what was to come in the future!

We scrambled into the back of the van and sat on some old fruit boxes (you couldn't do that now, could you?!"). It was a bumpy old ride but very enjoyable. The chat amongst the adults was eye opening. We were growing up fast, so the men didn't hold back (it was an education).

It was nice to see Eileen and Annie, of course. The two boys, well, Walter, really, were excited to see us. We all had a very excited chat and, eventually, Nathan and Aunt Anne went home. Annie surprised me by coming over and giving me an enormous hug. "I know you don't like me doing this but tough! Enjoy your first day at your new school, we're all proud of you. I'll be here when you get in tomorrow afternoon." She even had the nerve to give me a peck on the cheek.

In all the excitement, I hadn't realised that Uncle Jim hadn't come back with us. He had decided to stay with Nan and Michael for a few days. Now, if anybody was out of place down hoppin', it was Uncle Jim. He was a very smart and fussy person and did not like the very basic life, that was to be had in the hop country. He was a very private man and I smiled to myself, when I thought of him washing in public! I tried to recall whether I had ever seen him dressed in anything other than a

In Spite of Everything . . . .

smart suit but I couldn't. He'd certainly cut a comical figure picking hops around Nan's bin. There was an old photograph of him sitting on the bin, minus his jacket and tie. He still looked out of place!

"Come on then, you two, I'll just make you a cup of cocoa each then you'd better be getting off to bed. You've both got big days tomorrow. Granddad will give you a call in the morning, so get up straightaway. No turning over! I'll be up to make you breakfast. Porridge oats okay?" She said that last remark with a cheeky grin on her face.

Granddad usually got up very early, normally about five o'clock, even when he wasn't off to the fish market. He was in the habit of waking up his little favourite, our Mikey. They used to have cups of tea and Granddad would fuss over him (he was the baby of the family, after all).

I was always a bit miserable first thing and preferred to be left alone. This was something Granddad could never come to terms with, so we usually tried to avoid each other (politely, of course).

We got our morning call, with Granddad standing over us, holding two mugs of tea. "Up you get, me boyos, a nice cup of Rosie for you. Don't dawdle, Eileen is getting your breakfast ready." Eddie jumped out of bed, "Aw, thanks, Granddad. Be down in a minute. Come on, Paddy, rise and shine."

I could have easily rolled over but not with Granddad holding a mug of tea, in my face. I liked to take my time getting out of bed (no change), "Ta, Granddad, will you put it down on the floor for me?" "Nooooo, no way! Out you get! I know what you're up to."

Reluctantly, I pushed the sheets back and took my tea from him. I drank it in silence (Eddie had already gone to the toilet). My mind was now solely occupied with my new school. Images were flashing about in my brain, not all of them negatives (although there were many of them); there were some positives.

I was soon washed and dressed and down for breakfast in the kitchen, where Eileen had a nice plate of porridge for me. Granddad popped his head round the door, "I'm off now, Eileen, see you when you get back from work. Have a nice day at school, boys. Happy now, misery guts?" That remark was aimed at me. I just grinned back (probably the falsest grin of all time).

Eileen was well prepared, making sure that I knew what bus and tram I had to get. She had my dinner money and bus fare all at the ready. I had further to go than Eddie, so I was leaving earlier.

"Come on then, let's look at yer with your full uniform on." I think Eileen was as proud as anybody. There I stood, full brand new uniform with a jacket, tie and cap! "I've never seen you so smart before. Honestly, you look lovely! One thing before you go, Paddy. I don't think you need to wear your cap, not until you get to school. People round here are not used to seeing people in school caps." I hadn't given it much thought, but Eileen was a bit shrewd and I trusted her judgement. Off came the cap, straight into the bag. That was a stroke of genius on Eileen's part, as events would illustrate.

"See ya, Eileen, and thanks. See ya, Ed!" Eddie looked up at me; I could see the pride in his face. "Good luck, Paddy, you'll be alright. See ya later this afternoon."

He got up from the kitchen table and gave me a friendly pat on the shoulder. Off to college I went.

Chapter 10

The bus stop was just outside our house and, as usual, there were a few people waiting in the queue. The no.1 bus turned up within five minutes and, as I was about to get on, I glanced up towards one of our windows; Eddie and Eileen were there, waving and smiling at me. I thought, leave off, I'm not a baby, but I gave them a friendly wave.

It was still quite early, so most of the people on the bus were grown-ups. There were a few who knew me and had taken a while to recognise me, dressed as I was, like a posh kid. I received some smiles and even a thumbs up! We passed the Elephant and Castle and were soon at St George's Circus. This is where I get off. Just around the corner was the tram stopping point. There were a few people waiting about, amongst them, children of my age and older ones, most of them dressed in the same uniform as me. What stuck out a mile was the fact that they all had their caps on. A few of the older kids stared at me but said nothing. The tram arrived and I clambered on making my way up the stairs. It was nearly empty but most of the passengers were dressed like me.

We made our way up Lambeth Bridge Road then along the Embankment, past Nine Elms then the Battersea Dogs Home until finally arriving at The Latchmere Arms. By the time we'd arrived here, the tram was nearly full. Most of the people on board were obviously going to the same college as me. There were a few kids from other schools and there was a great deal of leg-pulling and general shouting between the rival groups. The lady conductor came upstairs and brought a bit of order and calm to the situation. I'm glad that I hadn't put my cap on because they seemed to be a bit of a trophy for the lads who weren't going to my school.

We all piled off the tram, there being lots of pushing and shoving. That didn't bother me one bit. "Oi, mind who you're pushing mate," came a cry from behind me. I turned slightly. "Fuck off," I said in a very loud voice. The conductress gave me a stern warning about using such bad language. She would have chucked me off the tram, if I weren't getting off anyway.

There were literally hundreds, of all ages, making their way towards my college. So I just followed the tide.

There was a call from behind me, and as I turned, I saw a small group of lads of about my age. One of them called out, "Oi, you, I'll 'ave you tomorrow." I just shrugged and carried on walking.

We were getting quite close to the school gates, when a much older boy came up beside me. "I'd put my cap on if I were you. The Head waits at the gate and you'll get a detention if he sees you not wearing it. Are you a new boy?" "Yes, this is my first day." I fished out my cap and put it on, "Thanks."

He was right. There was a teacher at the gate. I didn't know if it was the Head or not. He said, "Good morning," to all the pupils, including me. No one had ever done that before.

I followed the stream through the gate, under a small arch, emerging into the main body of the school. Most were making for the massive playground but the noise coming from that direction gave me a clue.

There were at least a dozen footballs being kicked about. The nearest group were roughly my age with ascending ages stretching the width of the playground, ending with the seniors, virtually grown men, in the distance. The time approached nine o'clock and I noticed the arrival of dozens of teachers, at least half of them were monks.

In Spite of Everything . . . .

The whistle blew and all games stopped almost immediately and lines began to form in front of the various teachers. I, like many other newcomers, didn't know where to go. There was a clue, however. The teacher standing alone. He called out, instructing all new pupils to line up in front of him, "No pushing!!" He barked out. Once we had settled, we were instructed to follow him to assembly. We did this, followed by the rest of the school.

The assembly consisted of the usual old thing. The Deputy Head welcoming us all, with a special mention to the newcomers, a run down of the main points of interest for the coming year and then a priest saying morning prayers (yuck!).

We, in the front rows, were told to stay in our seats, to let the older classes get away. Two teachers stayed with us, then we were split into two groups of 28 and led to our classroom. Surprisingly, we chose our own place to sit, so I quickly made my mind up and took over a desk by the wall, about halfway down. There was a lot of scrambling going on behind me. No one fancied the front row.

Our form teacher introduced himself and gave out various textbooks. He explained that he would teach English and that there would be five periods of learning. There were to be two periods, followed by a ten-minute break. That's when you may use the toilets. "You are not babies, anymore, so I don't want any hands up asking to go to the toilet, please." There would be another period before the one-hour dinner break, after which, there would be two afternoon periods. We were all given timetables. Other than woodwork, metalwork and music, the relevant tutors would come to us. It struck me, immediately, that these people were organised!

Eventually, we got out our English book and lessons started. It was a very hesitant and self-conscious start. Everyone was wary of each other with plenty of false laughter. Time whizzed by, another teacher appeared, different approach from the form teacher. Then a break, at which time, I made sure I had a piss, as did most of the school, it seemed! A few of the lads from my class were chatting together and I tumbled that they were schoolmates from a previous school.

Everyone smiled a lot. Back in class, another subject, another teacher. It was becoming a bit bewildering, then dinner.

"Where do we go for the dining room, please, sir?" One of the lads asked (one of those sitting in the front).

"All of you, having school dinner, follow me. You may leave your outside coats here in class. The classrooms are not locked. Remember, you are not allowed food or drink in the classroom." Most of the class and I followed across to another part of the school. It was then I realised the college was made up of four separate buildings.

Two things told me where the dining room was, the smell and the din!! As I entered, the noise of the plates clattering and knives and forks banging against each other was deafening (this was a *big* school). A bit different to what I'd been used to!

A lady was at a big till, "Do you want to buy dinner for today or for the week, darling?" "I'll pay for the week, please." I paid my money over, "What do I do now?" "Just take a plate, luv, and those ladies over there will serve your dinner for you. There's a couple of choices. Now, off you go, I've got a lot to get through."

The food wasn't bad, mainly potatoes and vegetables, with a small portion of meat or fish and a selection of sweets (afters).

I picked a table to sit at, choosing to sit with my own age group again, all smiles and nervous hellos. It was a bit daunting. This place was enormous.

After dinner, things got much better. I joined in a football game, which was being played amongst my own age group. It was apparent that each age group was strictly partitioned. Eventually, a sports teacher joined us and very quickly singled out certain players, me included. He pulled about 20 of us to one side, telling us that, if we were interested, we could come along to football practice on Wednesday afternoon. I had noticed on the timetable that Wednesday afternoon had two periods of sport. I jumped at the chance.

"Don't forget boots and shorts with you on Wednesday. Meet me here. Now, I think it's time to get back to class."

The two periods went by in a whirl. I couldn't believe it, I was learning French. Wait until I tell Nan.

The journey home went without incident and, as arranged, there to greet me was Aunt Anne and the boys. She fired question after question at me. I explained as best I could, but she had never been to school like mine and didn't really understand the working practices. "Wait til you tell your nan. She will be pleased. Is there anything special that you'd like for your tea? I bet you're starving, ain't you? Oh, I nearly forgot, how did you get on with school dinner? Was it alright?" "Yes, thanks, Auntie. Not too bad really! Not as good as Nan's cooking though! Have we got any of that American powdered egg because, if we have, I'd love a nice big sandwich, please."

We had and she made me a thick crusty egg sandwich. It was lovely and, halfway through, Eddie showed up. Anne joked with him, "You must have smelt me cooking. Do you want the same?" "Yes, please, not 'arf. Hey, Paddy. How did you get on at school? Everything alright?" I had a mouthful of sandwich so I gave him a thumbs up, eventually saying, "Yes, thanks, Ed. It's okay. A bit different from what I'm used to but I'll manage it." I did wonder how I would get on in the long run. My deep down worry was the strong emphasis on the Catholic religion. I hoped it was only just my imagination but I decided to keep those thoughts to myself.

Eileen and Granddad came home soon after Eddie, therefore, I had to repeat all over again my first day experience. Eileen listened to every word, but Granddad seemed only half interested but, in truth, I don't think he fully understood. He was pleased, however!

Aunt Anne was picked up by Uncle Nathan, who also wanted to know all about the day's goings on. I was, by now, getting bored with the whole thing.

We spent the evening chatting and playing cards with Eileen and a couple of her mates, who had shown up. Eileen kept stumm so I didn't have to repeat myself. I felt a bit tired which was unusual for me and decided to go to bed early, not before telling Eileen about Wednesday's football. "I'll make sure everything will be ready for you. Goodnight, Paddy, God bless." "Thanks, Eye. Goodnight everyone." They all called out as I left the kitchen. I didn't need any rocking; I was asleep as soon as my head hit the pillow!

The same routine was repeated next day, minus the incidents with the other lads. Slowly, but surely, I met all the various tutors, teaching subjects like English, Maths, Physics, Chemistry (we went to a separate laboratory for that), History, Geography, Technical Drawing, French, Latin (yes, Latin! A teaching monk took over for that) and Religious Studies (that one was taken by a priest). We hadn't yet done woodwork; that was two periods on Wednesday morning.

Boys were gradually coming out of their shells and friendships were starting to form. I was friendly but took my time making friends too quickly (that was my natural way). I was looking forward to Wednesday.

Eileen was as good as her word. She had my football kit all laid out for me and off to school I went.

I had a good feeling about today and wasn't disappointed. The woodwork classroom was situated in the far corner of the vast playground, well away from the rest of the school. It was superbly kitted out with numerous large workbenches with vices and all the tools that would be needed. We were given overalls to wear and shown all the tools and what they were used for. There was also a metalwork area. I liked this place!

I didn't hang about eating dinner, very quickly dashing back to my classroom to pick up my coat and football boots. There were already a few boys at the meeting place. At the corner of the playground, which was eerily empty because most of the school (well, those not playing sport) had gone home.

In Spite of Everything . . . .

Our numbers increased by quite a lot because boys from the year above us were also gathering. They knew each other very well so there was plenty of friendly banter with some friendly pushing and jostling. Our group were shyly getting to know each other. A couple of tracksuited teachers arrived, soon having us lined up into two groups and then leading us off to the Battersea Park).

We gathered round our teacher and I was surprised when he told us what positions he wanted us to play. He must have taken a lot of interest in how we had naturally positioned ourselves, when kicking about in the playground. There was a natural goalkeeper (as there always seems to be); I was told to play at halfback (which today would be defensive midfield). I was a round peg in a round hole!

I had a lovely couple of hours and, as sport normally does, started to make friends and get to know other boys from my class. I was in for another surprise when we finished. We had to line up again and were led back to school (ten-minute walk). The journey back was a noisy chatty affair and we were told to quieten down a couple of times. Us boys were feeling more relaxed with each other already.

We were shown to the washrooms and told to clean ourselves up, get dressed and report to the dining room. (Dining room? I've had my dinner).

What a nice surprise! There was tea, lemonade and cakes, plenty to go round. The room was crowded with boys from every year but, now that our year was getting to know each other, it wasn't half as daunting. Our sports master told us to help ourselves and, once finished, make sure we reported to him before leaving for home.

I could smell cooking going on from the kitchens at the back of the hall and asked what that was all about. That was when I found out that about a quarter of the boys actually boarded at this school. That's why there was always food about and ladies to cook and serve it.

Aunt Anne was getting a bit anxious because of my lateness but Eddie (who was home already) kept telling her that I was playing football.

Nevertheless, she was pleased to see me. I told them all about what had gone on today. They could tell that I was more at ease.

After another nice tea, by which time Eileen was home, I asked if I could go to my club and play table tennis. Eddie said that he'd come along with me. "Yes, of course, you can. Don't be too late back though! Remember, you're up early for school."

"Yeah, don't worry, Eye. We won't be late. I'll take care of him." I gave Eddie a playful shove, "Piss off, I don't need taking care of!" We had a good night and I was pleased to make contact with some of my old schoolmates. Even at that early date, I had a feeling that I wouldn't be making lifelong friends at college.

As I got off the tram, there was that little group of herberts (my name for tough guys who weren't). They were obviously hoping to bump into me. I thought, here we go again, will people never leave me alone? This was really beginning to wind me up.

"Oi, you, that posh kid without a cap, come 'ere and say sorry for swearing at me the other day." I carefully made sure that I kept my eyes levelled at them, noticing at the same time, that some of my new schoolmates were trying to do a disappearing act and skulk away. I didn't blame them!

"I'm in a rush to get to school and I'm not looking for a fight." I hesitated to make sure they were paying attention. "Now, fuuuck off and leave me alone." I turned and slowly walked away. No footsteps came rushing toward me!

"We'll get you tonight, you bastard!" The rest of the day went by as usual. The general feeling in class was getting much more relaxed. That afternoon of sport had helped.

I was having a kickabout after dinner when a couple of year two boys sidled up to me. "I'd be careful if I were you. Those boys from this morning are a bit spiteful and the Head doesn't like us fighting. He says that it brings a bad name for the school. I'd try to avoid them if

I were you. You would be better off getting on the tram at the earlier stop."

"Thanks, lads, but I can take care of myself. Thanks, anyway."

They walked away and I got on with the game. My mind was made up. The Head doesn't like fighting. Well, nor do I, but unfortunately sometimes it can't be avoided. He can go fuck himself. I don't like running away!

There they were, a big group of boys and girls, all hanging around the tram stop. They looked very confident. I got within fifty yards then all the shouting and catcalling started. I've always found the mob culture very hard to understand. Most of the kids that were shouting out wouldn't harm a fly on their own and there they all were, acting tough!

Boys from my school were (well, most of them, anyway) making themselves scarce. Stick to the plan, Paddy, my boy.

I took my coat off and hung it over my shoulder. "Oi, yes, you, big mouth! Come over here, you prick!" He made a big mistake. He came dashing towards me, full of confidence (he was going to bash the posh kid up). He was that stupid, he hadn't even put his guard up.

I dropped my coat onto my bag and hit him, once, twice, three times. Every punch on target! His nose seemed to explode. There was blood everywhere (some of it, unfortunately, over my new white shirt). He went down on his knees moaning and clutching his face. I smacked him hard to the side of head (it made my hand sting). He started to sob (yes, cry) and said he'd had enough. Luckily for him, the driver of the tram yanked hold of me and pulled me away. "He's had enough, son. Now, put your jacket on and get on the tram." He turned to the crowd of kids. "See what you've caused, you bunch of animals! Get off home before I call the police." He then helped the other boy up. "Here, son, stick this piece of towel over our nose and get off home, as quick as you can."

Just before the tram pulled away, he came up to see me. "I don't know what that was all about, but I won't stand for any trouble on this tram. Do you understand?" I stared at him, "It wasn't my fault." "You've got blood on you. Are you hurt?" "No, it's his." I nodded towards the street. He stared at me for a while, "Are you related to Nathan Stewart?" I was gobsmacked (how did he know Uncle Nathan?). That's when I remembered that the trams terminated at the Borough, now! Everyone knows Uncle Nathan.

"Yeah, what's it to you?" "Whoa, whoa, I don't want any trouble. It's just that I know your uncle and he'd certainly want me to look out for you. Not that you need much help from what I just witnessed! I thought I recognised you the other day. It was the uniform that put me off. I've seen you hanging around the Borough Market, haven't I?"

"Yeah, probably, thanks anyway."

"Last thing, son. Watch out for that crowd. There's some nasty bastards amongst them, although, as I've just said, you can look after yourself." With that, he rushed up to his cabin, where the conductress was getting very agitated. Off we went.

Aunt Anne's face was a picture. "What have you been up to? Are you hurt? There's blood all over your shirt. Please tell me you haven't been fighting, you've only been at school for four days."

Granddad had been reading his paper. He dropped it down in front of him. "You can't keep out of trouble, can you, Paddy? Come on, what's the story?"

I told both of them the full story. "Sounds like that bastard was asking for it, if you ask me. You won't get into any trouble at school, will you?" Annie was more worried about that than anything to do with fighting. She was a tough and fiery woman (she had to be to be married to Nathan). "It's no business of the school. I was well away." Granddad just gazed at me, "Be careful, son, be careful." He then carried on reading his paper. I thought I heard a couple of low tut tuts). "Get that shirt off. I'll give it a rinse before I get your teas ready. Eddie will be home soon, so I don't think it'll be a wise move for him to see you with blood all over your clothes. You know what he's like!"

Yes, I do! He'll be as mad as hell (a very dangerous state of affairs). You see, he's my elder brother and he's very, very protective (I don't think I need any of that but he does!).

Eddie came bounding up the stairs and I immediately put him in the picture. He was slowly shaking his head, looking very concerned. "I'm going over to the club after tea. I'd like you to come with me. That'll give us a chance to have a good chat about how we're going to handle things. That's all right with you, ain't it?"

"Yeah, sure, Ed, I'd like that. I was going down there anyway. Remember, we're off to see Nan and Michael straight after school tomorrow."

Eileen came cheerily up the stairs and into the kitchen, where Annie buttonholed her straightaway and, in a whisper, told her the hot news. Eileen kept glancing over at me. She mouthed the words, "Are you alright?" I smiled back and gave her the thumbs up.

We had herrings for tea and, as usual, they were delicious (well, they would be, wouldn't they? Thanks to Granddad). "Oi, oi, anybody in?" Uncle Nathan was coming up the stairs. "What you been up to, m'lad? I've had every tram driver at the Borough looking for me." He was laughing as he spoke. "It's nothing to laugh about, Nathan. You'll just encourage him," was Annie's outburst. "Shuddup, you silly cow! He's got to look after himself. He's not a fucking nancy boy," giving me a big wink.

"You still shouldn't egg him on, he could do without any of that! Eileen, I've managed to get the blood out of his shirt. Has he got a clean one for tomorrow?"

"Yeah, don't worry, Anne. He's got a spare. I'll make sure he goes to school looking smart." With that, Annie came over to me, with a mischievous grin on her face. "Come here, you handsome devil, give us a kiss." She knew I hated being kissed but grabbed me playfully (in spite of everything, I've always considered myself to be very lucky because these two aunts loved me dearly and were to feature in my life for many years to come).

Just as they were leaving, Nathan turned to Eddie and me. "I'll bring you home in my van on Sunday evening. I'll be coming down for the day to take care of some business." He hesitated, "Be careful, Paddy, you're not in your own manor." Then turning to Eddie, "Watch out for him, son." Eddie nodded.

On our way to the club, Eddie and I chatted about how we should handle things. "Listen to me, Paddy. I've gotta tell ya, I'm having a day off school and I'm coming with you. Now, there's no point arguing. What do you think Nan would say if a gang of lads beat you up? Don't let's kid ourselves. I'd bet on you against three but they could come stronger. We've got to let them know that we're firm handed[36].

I didn't bother arguing; I know when I'm beat! As soon as we got to the club (without even discussing it), we both made our way to the gym! Both of us doing plenty of bag work and sparring (not against each other! Nan had absolutely forbidden that).

When we got back home, Eddie told Eileen that I had agreed to his idea of going to school with me, and she looked very relieved and pleased. "Granddad, can you get us up a bit earlier tomorrow morning?" "Yes, of course, I can. Half past six early enough?" "Yeah, that will be great, thanks, Granddad. Come on, Paddy, let's get some shuteye."

Eddie was asleep as soon as his head hit the pillow. Me? As usual, lying awake for hours, listening to the nighttime sounds of the buses and trams and people spilling out of the corner pub, laughing and joking, then it was morning!

We caught an earlier bus so there were no school children at all then changed to the tram. Again, only men and women going to work. We reached our stop and besides us, there was sprinkling of older pupils

In Spite of Everything . . . .

with their dark blue blazers, much smarter than the maroon I was forced to wear.

There was a teacher at the school gates, as usual. He eyed me curiously before saying, "Good morning. Are you this early for any special reason?" "No, sir, couldn't sleep." Eddie was a puzzle to him. He wasn't wearing a uniform and he didn't recognise him. Eddie completely ignored him. "What time are you getting out this afternoon, Paddy?" "Three o'clock on Friday. That's right, isn't it, sir?" "Yes, yes, what's the rush?" Eddie smiled at me, "See you at three then!" He went on his way and I made my way to my classroom. Luckily, it was open so I was able to drop my bag off beside my desk.

At the end of morning assembly, just as we began to file out, I heard, "O'Donovan!" Our form teacher was beckoning me. "The Head wants to talk to you, so make your way over to his office and wait outside. Off you go, you can't keep the Head waiting. You know where it is, don't you?" "Yes, sir." What have I done wrong now?! I thought to myself. I could feel dozens of eyes on my back.

I had only been standing outside for a few moments, when the door opened. "In you come. Stand up straight and answer the Head clearly and honestly." I'd never laid eyes on this particular person but he seemed a bit full of himself.

I stood in front of the Head's desk and looked him full in the face. If he thought that he scared me then he was mistaken.

"It's been reported to me that you were seen fighting in the street. Is that true?" "Yes, sir." I never liked explaining my actions to anybody. He seemed slightly irritated. "Well, explain yourself, you wretched boy. We simply can't allow this sort of behaviour. It imparts a bad impression. Fighting is strictly forbidden." He paused, looking first at his assistant and then at me. "Well?!"

"I was simply defending myself, sir. There was a gang of them and they would have given me a beating." I let that sink in for a moment. "I will not take a beating from anybody! That crowd of boys and girls

|285

are going after boys from this school and some of them are terrified. They snatch caps and chuck them all over the place. They won't terrify me, sir!"

The Head leaned back in his chair and stared at the ceiling. You could hear a pin drop. "I see, I see!" More thoughts. "This is a very unfortunate state of affairs and something, sadly, we are unable to control. But you are more intelligent than them, therefore, you will have to resolve these issues," a pause, "without resorting to violent behaviour. Have I made myself clear?" "Yes, sir!"

"This interview is over. Get back to your class, immediately." He seemed just a little upset! I about-turned and left the room. As I stepped into the corridor, there was a lady waiting for me.

"Can I have a word with you, young man? I am the college secretary, by the way. I caught most of the conversation between you and Head. Tell me, where do you have to go to, in order to get home?"

"I catch a tram at Latchmere, which takes me to St George's Circus, very close to the Cathedral." "Does it pass through Vauxhall?" "Yes, miss." "Good! May I suggest an alternative way of getting backwards and forwards? It's only a short walk to Battersea Park, where you can catch a bus all the way to Vauxhall and then back onto your tram. It shouldn't take you much longer and it will keep you away from those horrible people and, therefore, out of trouble."

"Thank you, miss. I'll try that on Monday. I know where the park is because I've played football there." She seemed pleased with herself!

All eyes were on me, as I entered my classroom. "Next time you enter my class late, kindly knock on the door before entering! Now, quickly get to your desk and get your books out. Stop gaping, the rest of you! You all know who he is!"

In Spite of Everything . . . .

I was the centre of attraction all through the dinner break, with a hundred and one questions being fire at me. I hated it and couldn't wait for classes to end.

Through the tunnel, through the gates and there stood Eddie. "Hi, Paddy. How did it go today?" "Oh, just a little bit of earache from the Headmaster. You ain't been waiting here all day, have you?" "No, don't be silly. I've been home and back." I explained to Eddie about the new route home but he wouldn't have any of that, today! I think (know) that he would welcome a bit of trouble!

There was the usual buzzing crowd milling about the tram stop. I recognised a few faces but not Big Mouth. There was a little bit of very muted jeering in our direction, and as usual, some of my new schoolmates were having a terrible time. I even felt sorry for them but it wasn't my business.

Eddie pushed his way to the front of the crowd (there wasn't an orderly queue) with me right beside him. We were on the tram first and made our way upstairs and commandeered the "coach type" seats at the rear. For those of you who have never seen or been on a London tram, there really wasn't a front or a rear. The tram never turned round. The driver would simply go to the other end, which was a carbon copy, and the rear became the front.

The tram was almost completely full. The noise was deafening. It was funny seeing the conductress trying to maintain order (surprisingly, she did succeed to some extent). The tram came to a stop just past the dogs' home. There was a big estate of buildings opposite and that's where most of the hooligans got off.

They couldn't help themselves! Just as the main group started going down the stairs, a couple of the boys called out, "We're going to get you, you wanker!" I flew at them but, luckily for them, Eddie had a firm grip on me. "If I ever see your ugly mugs ever again, I'll give you what your mate got, you bunch of cowardly bastards." I was in an uncontrollable rage. It was lucky that Eddie had hold of me.

"Calm down, for fuck's sake. They're only a bunch of mugs. They're not worth it. Forget them."

Eddie managed to calm me down and I told him about the chat with the school secretary. "I think that will be a very good idea. I can see serious trouble ahead and that would be a sensible answer to all our problems." "Ed, I'm not scared of that crowd. They're gonna find themselves in a whole lot of trouble, if they don't leave me alone." "Listen, will ya? I know what a dangerous bastard you are but say, for instance, you got badly beaten up by a gang of them? What do you think I'll do? I can assure you, my son, it wouldn't be nice and we could both wind up being nicked! Let's use our brains! Take the other way in. Nan would be happier!"

"Ed, you're right. I'll go that way on Monday." I didn't know it then but I would run into a few of that crowd. It would be much later and in slightly different surroundings.

Aunt Anne had our tea ready and waiting for us, the moment we put our feet into the kitchen. I noticed that she silently mouthed to Eddie, "Alright?" He nodded back and that made her relax. I was surprised to see Uncle Jim sitting, having a cup of tea. Eddie asked if Nan and Michael were all right?

"Yes, of course, they are. I've only come back because there would be no room for me once you two are down there."

"Sorry to chuck you out."

"Don't be silly. I've had enough of it anyway. In truth, hoppin' is not my cup of tea. Too many insects, reminds me of Calcutta!! Once you've had your tea, I'll walk you to London Bridge. Is their gear ready, Anne?"

"Yeah, all ready! Leave them alone to finish their tea in peace and quiet."

I could see that Eddie was a bit put out. "You don't have to, Jim. We'll be alright on our own. We know the way."

"Your nan gave me the order! I'll walk with you to the station, get it?!"

Eddie nodded to Jim then turned to me and just shrugged.

It was quite funny catching the train in late afternoon. There were crowds of well-dressed men, most of them wearing bowler hats and carrying folded umbrellas, all jostling for seats. We were eyed with suspicion.

We changed trains at Paddock Wood. This one was nearly empty. There was only one carriage being pulled by a massive steam engine, whose noise still made me wince.

In no time at all, we arrived at Horsmonden. It was still light because even though it was now nearly seven o'clock, double British summertime (a wartime measure) meant it didn't get properly dark until close on nine. I can still recall the distinct smell of the countryside at this time of year. The smell of hops was everywhere. Even less surprising when there, in a corner of the station yard, were dozens of large sacks of dried and compressed hops, ready for their journey to the big London breweries.

Smell is a funny thing because, although there are very few hop gardens left in the Kent area, whenever I happen to come across one, the smell takes me back to those happy days, more than sixty years ago. It's instantaneous!

We were soon within a couple of hundred yards of our farm, when I spied Michael sitting astride the big five-bar gate. There were a few others hanging on as well. He suddenly started waving and shouting. He'd seen us. Eddie yelled out for him not to run into the road. He was jumping up and down like a maniac (nothing different there, then!) but he stayed put. I think Nan had probably warned him, anyway.

Eddie pushed the gate open and Mikey jumped all over him then dashed off, yelling and screaming, to let Nan know we had arrived.

Nan was standing outside her hut with a smile as wide as the Thames.

"Let's have a look at you both! I've really missed you." There followed a million questions (well, it seemed like a million). She eventually brought out plates of sandwiches, as usual. "We've had some tea, Nan." "Is that a fact? Bet you can eat some more." We made her right!

A few of Mike's mates were hanging around, studying Eddie and me. "That's some of my friends. They're alright."

I ignored them. "Your fire looks a bit scabby, Nan. Want me to tidy it up for you?" "Oh, you're a good boy, Paddy, but not tonight, darlin'. Take care of it for me in the morning."

"Do you want us to get up the field early tomorrow and pick you a few hops, Nan?"

"Yes, please, luv. You don't mind, do you? It will give me a chance to have a tidy up and do some washing." Michael chirped up, "I'll come with you, as well." I gave him a wink and a thumbs up.

"What the fuck's that?" Was my first reaction on being woken up by that rattling and banging going on outside. Yes, I was down hoppin', again. Thankfully, I'd remembered to bring some twigs in before going to bed. Consequently, I had a nice fire on the go very rapidly. I glanced over to the cookhouse. Bollocks, there was smoke curling up into the damp morning air. He'd beaten me.

Nan soon had our breakfast ready, which we demolished, then, off we trooped, all three of us, to pick some hops for her. She must have been telling all and sundry about my new school because, time after time, I was asked how I was getting on (very irritating). We concentrated on giving Nan a good three hours of picking. Even Mikey managed to stand still long enough to be of some help. Nan eventually turned up with a big pot of tea and some cheese and pickle sandwiches. Her eyes nearly popped out when she saw the amount of hops we'd picked for her.

After another hour, the old measurer came by, telling all the pickers that he would be measuring soon and that would be the finish for the day. He eyed me with a very distrustful look. I bet he thought that he'd seen the last of me. Nan was measured out and it was nice to see the smile on her face and, as I took note of the amount of hops she'd picked over the week, I could see why. She wasn't going to earn anywhere near as much money as she did, when Eddie and me were around. Fuckin' school, I thought!

We packed up and made our way back to the huts. Michael had run off with his mates but Nan wasn't unduly bothered. "I've got to go to the village, this afternoon. There's things I need to buy. Do you boys want to come with me?"

"I'll come with you, Nan. I've got to give the butcher a message from Uncle Nathan." Nan gave Eddie a knowing look. "What about you, Paddy?" "Not really, Nan, not if you can do without me. The wooden props beside your fire could do with changing. I'd rather do that and I can keep an eye out for Michael." She smiled and stroked me on the head. "You don't change, do you, son? Yes, that will be fine."

We spied Michael, then Eddie called him and went over to explain what was happening. He did a lot of pointing in my direction.

Off they went and I headed for the woods, armed with my knife. In no time at all, I'd managed to cut some nice thick sticks. It didn't take me long to pull the old, charred supports from the ground and get nice new fresh ones in their place. I bound them nice and tight with wire, put the iron cross member in place and then set about tidying the actual fire area. I stood back and admired my handiwork. That will last to the end of the picking season, which only had about ten days to go anyway.

Whilst I'd been busying myself, Mikey and his mates had been mucking about around me and I wasn't happy with the way a couple of bigger boys were bossing Michael about. I decided to give them a pull[37].

"Oi, you two. Yeah, you two with all the mouth! Who the fuck do you think you're talking to? That's my younger brother. He's not your fucking slave! Now, behave yourselves. Treat him with respect!" They looked shit scared! I hadn't realised that I was still holding my knife. I smiled at them, "Please be more friendly." That managed to lighten the atmosphere. "Sorry, Mike. We didn't mean any harm. Sorry." Mikey seemed just a little confused but they all carried on playing together. No harm done then.

"Mikey! Nan asked me to pop over to the main farmhouse and pick up some eggs and milk. Do you want to come with me?"

"Do I have to? I'd sooner stay here with my mates." "No, don't be silly. I'll be alright on my own. I'll only be about half an hour." I thought for a moment. "I tell you what you can do. Go and bring over a few fresh faggots. You'll give a hand, won't you, boys?" "Yeah, of course, we will. Come on, Mike." They stared nervously at me as they gave that order.

I just looked at them and shrugged. I had two empty milk jugs with me and, as I got to the side door of the farmhouse, having first made the chickens scatter in all directions, the old black Labrador appeared, closely followed by Elsie. She smiled broadly at me. "Good afternoon. How nice to see you, again. Your grandmother has been telling me all about you. She is so proud of you! You are going to grammar school, aren't you" "Yes, miss, it's a college."

"What a clever boy. I could see you helping your grandmother add up her tally. I realised you were a bright boy, even then. Are you down for the weekend?" "Yes, miss. My brother, Eddie, and me go back to London Sunday night."

"Ah, yes, I remember your older brother. Please give him my best wishes. Now, what can I do for you?" She glanced at the milk jugs.

"Some milk and a few eggs, I would imagine." She gave a soft laugh (very refined). I smiled back, "Yes, please. I've brought Nan's tally card with me," which I quickly produced from my back pocket. She took the jugs from me and disappeared. Her dog just stood looking at me, it's tongue hanging out and tail wagging. I think it was expecting a pat on the head. It didn't know it but that would have been a very, very long wait. I didn't much care for animals.

She returned with two full jugs and a carefully wrapped parcel. "Here you are. Tell Granny that I could only spare half dozen eggs. Rationing, you know!" I took Nan's card and my rations. "Thanks very much. I might see you again next weekend. It's been nice to talk to you." "Do well at school, er, sorry, college! Make your grandma proud." I about-turned (couldn't wave) and off I went, trying hard not to spill too much of the precious liquid. As I approached the common, I automatically looked over to Nan's hut and, to my surprise, there seemed to be a crowd of people gathered around it. I quickened my pace but soon relaxed when I recognised Uncle George, Lil and Young George, as well as, Michael and pals.

I entered through the five-bar gate and it wasn't long before Uncle George spied me and gave me a wave. He had lost most of his colour but looked very fit. He'd returned to his job as a docker and, besides working hard, he played football for the National Dock Labour Board (in truth, I don't think it was called that, yet!) but it was the same team, nevertheless.

"Hi, there, Paddy. I see that Nan's been getting you working. Where is she, anyway?" "Allo, uncle, she's in Horsmonden shopping. Eddie's with her. I didn't know you were coming down."

"We decided to give Nan a hand and, if she can get the farmer to find a hut for us, we'll stay to the end of picking," chipped in Aunt Lil, as she busied herself boiling a pot of water over the fire.

Uncle George cast his eyes over the fire and my handiwork. "Did you build all this, Paddy?" I think my chest must have swelled a bit with pride! "Yeah, I did it all myself. Cut the wooden stakes and scrounged the wire. It's alright, ain't it?" "Yeah, son, you've done a good job. That's yours as well, ain't it?" Pointing towards Aunt Dol next door. "Yeah, Nan asked me to help her and her girls. You know what Nan's like!"

I was to find out a few years later that Dol's husband had been killed in the war. That's why Nan gave her a helping hand.

Eddie and Nan suddenly appeared carrying loads of shopping. She was delighted to see George and Lil. We all had a cup of tea whilst Nan was unpacking her bags. She sent Eddie next door with a packet of meat. Within seconds, Dol came over and gave Nan a big hug. She was so pleased.

"C'mon, Lil, let's go over to the farmhouse and sort you out a hut. Luckily, there are a few empty just behind me."

"Paddy, what knife did you cut your poles down with?" I showed him my jack-knife. He smiled, "How would you like this?" My eyes nearly popped out. He was holding a machete. Yes, his army-issue jungle knife. He handed it over to me. "Go on, take it! It's yours." I was flabbergasted. This is what you call a knife!

"Cor, thanks, are you sure? Will Nan let me keep it?"

"When she gets back, you'd better ask her. Don't be silly with it! It's not a toy, remember."

I did ask Nan and she let me keep it, with strict rules about its use. I have still got it to this day. His army number is engraved on the handle and I use it in my garden. From Burma to Kent.

They got their hut and, in no time at all, a tractor brought down some fresh straw for bedding. This meant that Nan had both company and help for the rest of the picking season. Young Georgie was only a year younger than Michael, so that worked out nice.

The weekend flew by and before we knew it, there was Eddie and I sitting in the back of Uncle Nathan's van, on our way home. Nan let me take the machete home with strict orders not to take it out, under any circumstances. Nan was very firm with that order!

Eileen and Granddad were pleased to see us and threw question after question at us. Granddad was happy to learn that they were doing okay and even more relieved, when he heard the news that George and Lil were staying with her.

We had cocoa and some broken biscuits and went upstairs to bed.

"I've got all your school things ready, boys. Have a good night's sleep and I'll see you in the morning. Goodnight, God bless." Eddie gave her a kiss on the cheek. I didn't! I suddenly remembered! "Granddad, will you get me up a little bit earlier because I'm going on a different bus." He gave me a curious look before saying that he'd call me at half past six. "Thanks, Granddad. Night! See you in the morning."

"Eddie, Paddy, up you get. I've made you a cup of tea each. Now, get up, the tea's hot."

He really was an old fusspot, was our granddad, but very reliable. If he said half past six, then he meant it. I was washed, dressed and finishing my breakfast, in no time. Eileen gave me my bus and tram fares and the week's dinner money (it would be a few years yet before it all became free).

My new route was a doddle. The change at Vauxhall was as sweet as a nut. The bus was half empty with no crowds of hooligans. I smiled to myself, thinking Eddie will be pleased.

School was slowly settling in to an easy routine. Some of the teachers were easy to get on with, some were a bit awkward and aggressive but I didn't let it get to me.

I had another good training session on Wednesday afternoon and I was now getting into my natural ways, i.e. being loud and bossy. The other boys didn't seem to be annoyed at all. After all, I did do a lot of running about.

Friday arrived in a flash. This was another day I looked forward to. Metalwork! And the weekend, of course.

By now, I'd gotten used to my new route, which actually turned out just as quick. I couldn't help wondering where those lads on the tram thought I'd gone to. I bet they thought I was scared. That didn't bother me in the least. Anyhow, they would get a shock, one day!

"No need to rush about too much today, boys. I'm coming down with you and a mate of mine has offered to drive us down there. You're in for a treat. He's got a car." That would definitely be a treat, not many people had a car. We had never ridden in a car.

Eileen and Annie fussed over us and before long, there was a toot-toot. A big black car was waiting for us in the alley.

Down the stairs we clambered. I'd never seen this man before but Annie and Eileen certainly had. They all kissed and cuddled. We found out, as Granddad introduced us, that he was a cousin. His name was Terry and he was a bookmaker (illegal, of course). He seemed very interested in Eddie and me, asking question after question of Granddad, or Uncle Pat, as he called him. He said that he couldn't wait to see our dad again. When Granddad told him that he should be home soon, he got very excited.

Once again, the future would be very interesting for me because I would be spending plenty of time with second cousin Terry.

It was the best trip I'd ever made. The car was very comfortable and fast. It did over sixty miles an hour at one time. We were flying!

When we arrived at the farm, I think people thought we were royalty or something. The children scrambled all around us including Michael and George. Their mouths dropped open when they saw us get out.

In Spite of Everything . . . .

Nan, as usual, was pleased to see us and Granddad. Terry made straight for her, giving her a huge hug. It sounded strange, him calling her Aunt Anne.

We soon settled in and, within an hour, all the adults took off to Horsmonden for a drink in The Gun. That is, with the exception of Nan. She busied herself for a while, making sure that Eddie and I were fed and watered. Once she was satisfied all was as should be, she tidied herself up and then gave her orders.

"Boys, we're going up to the village to join the menfolk. I want to leave in five minutes." "I'll just sort out the wood for the fire, Nan." "I'll go down and fetch up some water. You can give me a hand, Mikey, c'mon lively."

"Oh, don't be too rough on him, Eddie! He's been a good boy, all week."

Off we strolled, the mile and a bit to the village. I could hear the piano being played and the noisy chatter. It sounded like they were enjoying themselves, as usual. There was a big cheer when Nan appeared.

We played around, only hanging round the pub for a drink and a snack. Nan called Eddie and told him to go back to the huts, reminding him that we have had a long day and that we would be getting up early.

Granddad and Terry said their goodbyes because they were going straight back to London. They weren't staying.

The weekend went by in a blur, also with a tinge of sadness. The picking would be finished by the end of the week and Nan would be coming home. I had mixed feelings on that one. It would be nice to have Nan back but I'd miss the countryside. I'd have been even sadder if I'd have been able to see into the future!

We were on our way home in the back of Nathan's van. He had been down here on Sunday taking care of urgent business, but unfortunately we wouldn't be doing this again! Before I'd left, Nan had asked me to tally up her card for her. She was pleased!

I was approached by the sports master during Monday's dinner break. There would be a football match against our school's arch enemy (news to me), Archbishop Tennysons. The team sheet had been pinned on the notice board and he wanted me to be captain. "Remember, O'Donovan, this is a great honour and one that I want you to uphold. I have already marked you down as captain, so all your team mates will be aware of it. Play well!"

I had mixed feelings about that piece of news. Yes, I was proud but I never aimed to be too deeply involved with the school authorities and by the time boy after boy had patted me on the back, I was quite alarmed.

We met, as usual, after dinner but now we had to go to Dulwich to play our match. There were a few pitches, all in prime condition, with a big and luxurious clubhouse. There were too many teachers, officials and priests hanging around for my liking, so I was glad when the game got started. Although I can remember the first match I played, I cannot truthfully remember the result. The thing that has always stuck in my mind was that, although some of these boys looked soft and were undoubtedly less worldly-wise than me, they played their games rough. I was like a pig in shit. We all shook hands after the match and I, as captain, had to lead the three cheers for our opponents. All of this was completely new to me but would be repeated time and again, over the coming years.

Once we'd showered (freezing) and had something to eat and drink, we were instructed to hand all our school kit in to an assistant teacher. Eileen will be pleased because she thought that she'd have to wash my muddy kit.

I had no idea how I would get home from Dulwich but a teacher had already thought that one out. "Any pupil with difficulty finding their way home, report to me." I was given precise details for my journey to the Bricklayers Arms, bus numbers and directions to the relevant bus

In Spite of Everything . . . .

stop. It didn't take as long as I thought. I was soon at the top of Rye Lane, Peckham. There, I changed buses and was soon at the Brick, just a five-minute walk home.

Aunt Anne was really interested in my explanation of my day's adventure and, once I'd finished, she confirmed that Nan be home this coming Saturday. Uncle Nathan was borrowing a much bigger van from a friend of his and he was going to bring them all back. He also wanted to pick up a load of apples. He didn't miss a trick.

There was even more startling news. Bill had called round and our dad was coming home tomorrow week, Thursday! Annie and Eileen, with the help of Uncle Jim, were getting the flags ready and the "Welcome Home Ted" banner.

Eddie was getting himself very excited and even I was definitely pleased, even though I couldn't rid myself of a feeling of dread! I was concerned as to what changes would happen and I was getting fed up with changes! Little did any of us know of the bombshell about to descend on us!

Saturday morning dragged by, even though Eddie and I were picking up the pieces and getting back to our old routines. Kit and Michael were delighted to have Eddie back and, to some extent, also pleased that I was around. Remember, I didn't do as much work as Eddie. Quite surprisingly, Kit and Michael were more interested in my college. You'd have thought we were related!

I'd just cycled back from the Blue after dropping off some bits and pieces, when as I approached our house, I saw this big lorry reversing down our alleyway. It was obviously an army surplus lorry because it was still painted in a dull basecoat of green. I pedalled furiously. Yeah, they were back. Nan had been sitting in the front seat next to Nathan. There was another higher one between them. If you stood on that, you would be able to stick your head out of a hatch. He jumped out and let the back down. They were all in there: Michael, Uncle George, Lil, Young Georgie and one of Nathan's mates, Jim.

The lorry was half full with boxes of apples (eaters and cooking). Nathan looked pleased with himself.

Nan gave me a cuddle and I helped unload her booty. She had bags of apples, as well as, a nice big chicken (dead), an enormous pack of sausages, eggs and a shoulder of bacon. We could have supplied half of Bermondsey.

It was a very merry house that particular Saturday night. Uncle Nathan had returned in his small van and was amusing everyone with the story of how he nearly didn't make it up River Hill (a very steep hill outside Sevenoaks). The lorry was overloaded and the brakes were a bit dodgy. That was the way of things in those days.

Nan was thrilled with news about Dad and Michael was jumping for joy (even more than usual, that is). She said that I could stay home from school that day and that she'd write me a note! Now that was a bit of a laugh! She would normally get me to write it, but I said that the school might not be too happy with a note that was written in my own handwriting. Added to that, Nan's signature was a joy to behold (my youngest grand-daughter, Laura, who is only just six, would do a better job). We decided that Eileen should write it and Nan would sign.

When I handed in my note that Monday morning, the house teacher was a little bit suspicious. Most of our soldiers, even those from the Far East, were all safely home. I explained the reasons, and with some hesitation, he gave me permission. I couldn't help thinking what a fool he was. It would have made no difference anyway. I was having the fucking day off. My dad was returning from the war. I realised then that although these people were undoubtedly clever, they didn't have much common sense.

I played football, as usual, but my mind was elsewhere. I jumped off the bus and what a sight! Flags and banners hanging from most of the windows. This was a sight that had, by now, become very rare.

There was excitement in the air that night and everybody was in a happy party-like mood, all except one! You've guessed it! Me! I think it must have been the pending uncertainty and, so far in my young life, not much had been a benefit. I kept my inner thoughts deeply hidden away, although there was at least one person who was able to sense my unease (Nan). If she said it once, she said it a dozen times. "It's lovely that Daddy's coming home tomorrow. I bet you can't wait, can you?"

"Yeah, I'm really looking forward to tomorrow." I was as sincere as I possibly could.

Up we all got that morning (I could feel the excited tension). Eddie and Michael couldn't stand still. They kept running to the window that overlooked the bus stop, even though Nan had told them that he wouldn't be home until about midday.

Aunt Anne showed up with the boys and Uncle Nathan. Eileen hadn't gone to work and Granddad sat quietly reading his paper, trying to pick out the winners in today's race meetings; every now and again, softly tut-tutting. Nan gave me the signal, pressed a few coppers in my hand and off I dashed to get her blind man's. I didn't take long.

I heard the banging on the window then the sound of it being roughly yanked open, "Da-ad! Da-ad!" Eddie and Michael were yelling at the top of their voices. They then made a dash for the stairs. Eddie made them three at a time with Michael close behind. I wasn't far behind, either. "Nan! Nan! Dad's home! Quick!" Eddie was yelling as he went through the front door.

I was in the doorway as he appeared round the corner. He was in uniform (exactly as I'd last seen him). He had a tanned face now. He was carrying an enormous kit bag and seemed even bigger to me, even though I had doubled my size, since we last saw each other. He dropped his kit bag and Eddie leapt into his arms. Even though he was not that much shorter, Dad lifted Eddie off the ground with ease. Michael was clambering all over him and he scooped him up, as well. I gazed at him and smiled. He looked at me and after gently putting the other two on the ground, he grabbed me and nearly crushed me to death. "Hello, son! You didn't think I would be coming back, did you?" "Yes, I did, Dad. I knew those Germans would never be able to kill you!" It all turned into a mad melee. There were even people waving and cheering from the top of our alley, on the pavement.

They all piled upstairs, Eddie shouting out that we'd take his kit bag upstairs. That proved harder than we thought, it was very heavy! I remember thinking that Dad must be very strong. We did it although with a lot of pushing and pulling. It was chaos in the kitchen so we weren't missed.

I find it hard to write down but that was the last time that my dad ever gave me a hug. I gave him one on his deathbed. I nearly didn't but fortunately saw sense, but that's another story!

It wasn't long before they all trooped off to the pub where their numbers increased. My family certainly knew how to celebrate.

We were given some money for pie and mash so we were happy.

In those days, pubs closed at two o'clock, therefore, they were heading back home carrying large quantities of crated beer with some spirits (although there was no shortage of that in the upstairs kitchen). The partying went on all afternoon and with the arrival of Uncle Jim, George and Patsy, the numbers swelled. We had our tea in one of our distant relatives' house (we wouldn't get much joy at home).

Dad was going to sleep in Johnny's old room, so once we had got ourselves to bed and, in spite of the continuing celebrations, got to sleep, we would not be disturbed until morning. Luckily, Eileen didn't drink too much so she was able to make us breakfast.

The house was a mess. There were people asleep on the armchairs and settee, with half empty glasses everywhere. It didn't smell that pleasant, either.

You might feel that all this was a bit excessive but you must remember that with the safe homecoming of our dad, it meant that all the menfolk had survived the war. Our dad was the only one who had been physically wounded.

When I returned home that afternoon, the house was much cleaner and tidier. Nan was busy in the kitchen with Aunt Anne helping. The front room was full of men and when I poked my head round the door, a great cheer went up. They were all still drinking and enjoying themselves. Mind you, this was the first time they had been able to do this for five cruel years.

The partying went on, more or less non-stop, through until Sunday. I can only imagine how they must have felt on Monday morning, returning to work.

That was a crazy and happy few days at our old house but, as seemed usual, there were dark clouds looming very close. A real party pooper.

Dad was up early on Monday morning and ate his breakfast with the three of us. He looked a bit uneasy.

He was full of questions regarding Eddie's and my schools, promising me that he would make a point of visiting my Headmaster in the next couple of days. It would be a couple of weeks before he would be starting work again, returning to the brewers, Barclay Perkins.

"Before you all go out this evening, I want to have a chat with you. I've got some important news to tell you. I won't explain yet because I want to tell Nan and Granddad, first."

I sat on my bus, my mind was in a whirl. What the hell was going on? I couldn't concentrate on anything all day and was repeatedly being shouted at. I'd had enough by dinnertime and, once I'd eaten, off I went.

As I walked up the stairs, I could hear muffled noises coming through the closed kitchen door. It was Granddad's raised voice, "She must have been the first fucking English woman you clapped eyes on. You didn't give yourself much time, did you? What about your fucking boys? How do ya think they're gonna feel?"

"Calm down, Pat, please." That was Nan! I purposely called out, "Anybody in?" I don't know if there is such a thing as a 'hurried quiet', but it went deathly so! Nan's voice, a bit cracked, I thought, "Is that you, Paddy? What you doing home so early?"

A little white lie, "They gave us the afternoon off."

The kitchen door opened and, as I entered, Dad and Granddad were sitting at opposite ends of the table, both looking a bit grim. Dad gave me a weak grin, "Hello, son, afternoon off?" Granddad looked very solemn. What alarmed was the hint of a tear in Nan's eyes. I ignored Dad. "Something wrong, Nan? You alright?" She gave me a quick cuddle. "You are a silly sod. Of course there's nothing wrong." She could always read and understand my state of mind but that was a two-way street. I knew something was up and that she was trying to kid me. I also knew that it was bad news but I couldn't imagine how bad or how it would affect me.

I turned to Dad. "Hi, Dad. What was it you wanted to tell me, you know, what you said at breakfast?"

"I want you all together, son. Eddie, Michael and you. You'll have to wait until they get home from school."

Nan butted in, "Paddy, please! Your dad and us have some important things to talk about. We really need to be on our own. Can you go out and play for a while? I'll talk to you later. Promise! Have you had any dinner?" "Yes, thanks, Nan." I turned and went upstairs and got changed and, as I passed the kitchen landing on my way out, I thought I heard Granddad's slightly raised voice, "See what I was saying? You'll have trouble with that one, for sure!" The last thing I heard was Nan's voice, "Shush! Shush! He'll hear you."

I wandered as I'd done before, through the streets, making my way towards the docks. What's going on? That thought would not leave

In Spite of Everything . . . .

me. I was getting myself pretty wound up! A horse-drawn cart came dangerously close to me and the driver shouted at me. I think he was surprised by the ferocious reply. I strolled down Tooley Street and, every now and again, I passed groups of men, some of them called out to me, probably distant relatives or friends of the family. I waved back. I wanted to be on my own so I didn't stop. Eventually, I arrived at London Bridge and, once there, stared at the frantic work going on at the quayside. The big cranes dipping into the holds of the cargo boats, bringing out great bundles of mysterious goods and the men with their hooks[38], unloading and carting away into the large warehouses. Some cargo for storage and some being loaded onto horse-drawn carts and, increasingly, petrol-driven lorries. It was a fantastic sight (more like a museum piece, now).

When I eventually arrived home, Eddie and Michael were indoors and Eddie looked at me with that concerned look of his. "You alright, Paddy? Not in trouble are you?"

"No, really, Ed. Just the afternoon off." He didn't look convinced.

Eileen and Jim were also home but I could feel a false relaxed atmosphere. I looked at Nan; it looked like she'd been crying. "Where's Dad?"

"He's upstairs in his room. Now that you are back, I'll give him a call. I want you boys to come with me into the front room. There's something we all need to talk about." She turned to me. "Now, Paddy, listen carefully to what your dad has to say. Don't, and I mean don't, get yourself wound up. You are all too young to fully understand but your dad is still a young man." The alarm bells were ringing.

Eddie looked at me nervously and Mikey stayed close to Nan.

Dad came into the room and shut the door behind him. Strange but my first thought was that he looked different, now that he was in his civvies. Dad started (quite formally, I thought, but there again, he had been in the army for the past five years). "I'm sorry that I haven't spent much time with you boys but, as you know, there has been a lot of celebrating going on. Sorry! I know that this has all come as quite a shock to your nan but, whilst I was in Liverpool, I met a very nice lady and she will be coming to London in a few months and we will be getting married." I saw Nan flinch.

"I have applied to the council for a large three-bedroomed flat and, with the army's help, there will be a new one available in the middle of next year." He paused for a moment to let it all sink in.

"You are my boys, my flesh and blood, and I love you all. I also know how much you love your grandparents (that really grated on me) and how much they love you, but I now want to bring you up and get involved in your lives." Again a pause. "I have been talking for most of the day with Nan and Granddad, and they feel that it is right and proper for me to once again take charge of your lives."

"I ain't leaving Nan!" She stared at me. "What did I just tell you? For God's sake, listen to what your dad has to say. Let him finish! It's bad enough as it is without you butting in." She was very angry (so was I).

"We've given it a lot of thought and because of the unusual circumstances, we have decided," nodding towards Nan, "that you boys are now old enough to make your own minds up." Again he paused. "You'll be starting work at the end of next year, won't you, Eddie?" Eddie just nodded back, eyeing me nervously.

"I will not force you to come and live with me, although I'll be heartbroken if you don't. I want you three to get together and make your minds up. You will never know how much this means to me. Sorry to put this on you all."

"How long have we got to make our minds up, Dad?" Said Eddie. "Will we get to meet the lady before you get married?"

"I want you boys to take your time and have a long chat with your nan and, as far as the lady is concerned, and by the way her name is Betty, she will be coming down to meet you in the next couple of months. She's very keen to get to know you and I think honestly you will like her. She's a very kind and thoughtful woman. Please give her a chance." Our eyes met and lingered for a few seconds then he turned away.

That was that then!

We had our tea together, with Nan fussing about, but there was a strange subdued feeling all about us. I think we were all frightened to express our real thoughts. I had plenty of them whirring about in my head.

"Coming down the club, Paddy? That's alright, ain't it, Nan?" "Once you've finished your tea, Ed, of course, it is. You go out and enjoy yourselves." "Can I take Michael with us. He's too young to join yet but it'll only be a few months before he can. Fancy it, Mikey?"

Michael nearly jumped out of the kitchen. "Yes, please, Ed. Yes, please!"

All three of us were making our way along Tower Bridge Road. Michael, as usual, a few yards ahead. "What did Nan whisper in your ear about, Ed?" "She just asked me not to talk about the Dad thing just yet. She wants to talk to all three of us, alone, tomorrow evening. She doesn't want Mikey upset, so keep stumm!"

"Well, Dad can go and get fucked. I wish he'd never come back. He should have stayed in that fucking desert."

"Paddy, please, nit-nit[39]."

Michael was made very welcome and since he showed a lot of interest in the gym equipment, an instructor took care of him. Eddie and I went straight up to the boxing section. We both let off a great deal of steam, sparring (not with each other) and bag work. I was exhausted at the finish. After a nice shower, we met Michael for a cup of tea.

One of the instructors came over to talk to Eddie. "That's your younger brother, isn't it?" "Yes, sir. He'll be old enough to join the club next year. He can't wait." "I can tell you, son, he's really very good. He's a natural. I'll look forward to working with him, next year. You can bring him with you before then but, sadly, only now and again. Cheerio, Michael!"

Dad wasn't in when we got home. The atmosphere was still tense but, luckily, soon livened up by Michael's tale of his exciting evening.

"You've had a good time, then?" "Yeah, not 'arf, Nan. It was brilliant!"

"You'd better calm down or you'll never get to sleep. Stop jumping around. Granddad's trying to listen to the wireless. Anyway, get upstairs and into your pyjamas. I'll make you your cocoa. It's time for your bed."

Granddad looked over, "I've said it before, that boy's got St Vitus Dance. He never sits still." Nan gave him a very old-fashioned look. As I lay awake, I heard Dad go to bed. He'd been out all evening!

"Don't forget, boys, I want to have a long chat with you this evening, so don't go out until we've had it. Got all your school books, Paddy?" "Yes, thanks, Nan. See you this evening. Bye everyone."

The morning assembly had just finished and I was on my way to class when I was summoned by the Head of Year. I'd been captured!

"You missed two afternoon subjects yesterday. Why?" "I felt a bit out of sorts, sir, and couldn't concentrate, so I went home straight after dinner. Something must have upset my stomach." As normal, I stood up straight and looked him in the eyes.

"This is your first term, so let me advise you. It is strictly against school rules for any pupil to make their own mind up, as to whether they can skip lessons. In future, you must seek permission from your form master. Is that understood?" "Yes, sir."

In Spite of Everything . . . .

"For your information, we have a small infirmary here and a nurse is always on duty. Should you feel unwell then you must report to nurse. Your form master will show you where she can be found."

I went to slide away. "Not so fast, young man. I am giving you detention for your actions. This means you must stay behind here after your lessons finish on Friday. Please inform your parents that you will be two hours late arriving home. You are now dismissed. Hurry along to your class and don't let this happen again."

My detention was the main topic of conversation at playtime. Mine being the year's first (there would be plenty more).

I couldn't remember Nan looking so determined before, as she did now, sitting in the front room, opposite us three. Eileen had also sat down amongst us. That gave me the jitters. This just had to be bad news!

Nan started by reminding us how much she loved us and that she would always keep her promise to look after us, and make sure that we were never parted. She then spoke of Dad. He was our father and he also loved us very much and wanted the very best for us. He was our legal guardian and, as our father, expected us to obey him. He was still a very young man and wanted to put past tragedies behind him. He had chosen a woman and wanted to remarry. That was his right and we should not forget that. Once a flat comes available, he wanted to get married and us three come to live together. (I think I must have visibly flinched because Nan looked at me).

"Paddy, let me finish, please. Everything will be all right, I promise!" She continued (it didn't help that Eileen was having difficulty in holding back the tears and her job was to look after Michael).

Our dad had promised that he would bring Betty over to meet her and she would make sure that she was a suitable lady to take care of us. She promised that she would leave her in no doubt as to the difficulties lying ahead for her, in the task of looking after us. At the same time, reminding us that we were growing up. Then came the final promise! She and Dad had agreed that the final decision would be ours and ours alone. She then stressed that it would be all three of us, one way or another. We were never to be parted, not in her lifetime!

What a complete fuck up! That was my first thought. I was angry and, as I write this down, still am!

Nan went on to tell us that we must talk it out amongst ourselves and that there was no immediate hurry. Nothing was going to happen for at least six months.

"What if we don't like this lady, Nan?" She stared at me with moist eyes. "You mustn't make hasty judgements, Paddy. You're a sensible boy. You'll meet her in due course, just keep an open mind and give her a chance, please!"

"If I don't like her, I'm not gonna live with her. It's as simple as that!"

"Paddy, why don't you just shut up. You're gonna upset everyone in a minute." I just stared at Eddie, got up and walked out of the room. I went up to the kitchen where Granddad and Uncle Jim were sitting.

"You ain't gonna let Dad just take us away, are you, Granddad?"

He looked startled. "Hasn't your nan just explained it all to you, Paddy? I'll make sure that you are taken care of, you can bet on that! Now, please, don't worry about it. I can't allow you boys to start getting upset. It's difficult enough as it is. Please try to get on with things and go with the flow. Which reminds me, are you gonna give me a hand on Sunday? I've missed you!"

That night, lying awake in bed, I called over to Eddie. "I'm not gonna leave Nan and Granddad. What about you?"

"For fuck's sake, Paddy, we don't have to make our mind up right now. Let's give Dad a chance. He deserves that, don't he?"

"Fuck him," I mumbled. I didn't want Michael to hear me because he was already getting close to Dad.

I had many a sleepless night over the following weeks and, as usual, crept downstairs to chat and play cards with Eileen and, sometimes, Jimmy. We carefully avoided all talk of moving away. A very taboo subject.

It suddenly dawned on me that apart from hearing Dad go to bed and the odd couple of minutes before going to school, he wasn't around much. He never sat round the table and ate with us and the family. Granddad did not want to have anything to do with him nor did Uncle Jim and, certainly, nor did Aunt Anne.

The honest truth, however, was that there was never a bad word said against Dad, in our presence. Although I did overhear a few . . . well, many, actually. I've got good hearing and voices carry.

Dad certainly had one friend, Uncle Nathan, and to some extent, Uncle Pat. However, in this case, it was purely business because Dad had now returned to work at Barclays, the brewery, which meant that their enterprise upstairs was now really booming. The war was well and truly over but the shortages were becoming worse.

Nathan explained to me, that Dad didn't want me involved in any way, so I was out! That was another little earner finished but, to be fair, Dad gave me decent pocket money.

One door closes, another opens.

Rationing was very severe and there was a serious shortage of sweets. I was able to get a great deal of chocolate, candy and chewing gum from Nathan, via the Yanks, and also a varied amount of boiled sweets and toffees from Dad's Italian friends. I was able to show a very decent profit by selling on to my mates and, now, schoolmates! I soon became very popular at school.

It was soon Christmas and, beside the usual celebrations, Nan had received a letter from Johnny in Germany, which I read out for her. He was in good health and would be demobbed in February. We all looked forward to his homecoming.

This would be the first Christmas where I had a proper present. Dad had given us a choice and mine was a Meccano set. I loved that present and was to build on it over the coming couple of years. There was plenty of fruit and we even had a goose for Christmas dinner. Dad played with us on Christmas morning but left to have dinner with his sister, Kit, and husband, Bill.

To be honest, Dad was good company and it was nice to have him with us again. Eddie said to me, "See, he's nice to have around. He loves us very much. Give him a chance!" "Ed, it's not my fault that he's come back and changed everything. I'm happy as I am and you know better than anyone, I don't like being fucked about. Sorry!"

"Don't let us start falling out. It'll only upset Mikey and Nan. I'm just asking you not to be unreasonable! How you getting on with your Meccano set?" "It's great. I love it."

Christmas Day was always a bit boring because, after dinner, the adults all went to sleep. Remember, there was no TV then. There was an upside, however. Boxing Day!

Dad took us round to see his sisters on Boxing Day morning. They made a fuss of us but I couldn't get it out of my mind that, although they lived within a mile of us, not one of them came to see us during those war years, not even to find out how we were or give a helping hand. Yet, here they were, fawning all over us, in front of their big brother. Eddie always said that I was too sensitive but I cannot and could not stand bullshit. I can't help it. As a consequence, I found it impossible to feel comfortable in their company. Unfortunately, it showed!

On the way back, Dad told us that he would be going up to Liverpool for a few days, and that he would be making arrangements to bring

Betty down to London, in order to meet us, as well as Nan and Granddad. "She's a real nice lady. Please give her a chance. That's all I ask. I know that you boys are a bit concerned but I only have your best interests in mind. Once I've dropped you off home, I've got to go somewhere and I'm staying at Aunt Kit's tonight, they're having a party. I'll see you in a couple of days. Be good!"

It was becoming quite obvious why Dad wasn't hanging around. The family weren't that happy with what was going on and, on Boxing Day, they all came round for the day with most of our cousins, which was great for us.

Dad quickly packed a small suitcase and said goodbye to us, after spending a couple of minutes with Nan. No doubt putting her in the picture.

The first to arrive was Uncle Dave and Aunt Sarah with Davey, Maureen and Terry. It was nice to see them again; it had been a long time. Then Uncle Pat and Aunt Emma with Cousin Jimmy and his five brothers and sisters. The big house was rocking. Then Nathan, Aunt Anne (who looked grimly at me and shook her head) closely followed by Uncle George, Lil and Young George.

The noise was deafening! Luckily, Nan had told us to hide our presents away, out of reach! We had been lucky because our cousins hadn't been given much (the Dad effect!).

It was now approaching pub opening time and Granddad put his best suit on and his best cap and, with that, all the men went over to the pub. This gave all the women a chance to close the kitchen door and have a real good chinwag (guess what they talked about?).

We all just ran wild, soon spilling out into our alleyway. The girls were more than happy to take charge of the younger cousins, which gave the likes of me, Eddie, Dave and Jimmy, a chance to drift away.

Eddie told them about our life-changing news, and I was surprised when they seemed to think that it was quite exciting and something to look forward to.

Not for the last time in my life, I found myself stranded. It didn't bother me, I had my own opinion and I wasn't happy! Exciting, my arse!

Eventually we made our way back to the front of the pub, which was, by now, in full swing. Nan and the aunts had joined the men, as did the usual cousins and friends. They looked and sounded like they were enjoying themselves.

We were soon joined by Michael, Terry and Patsy; all of us skylarking on the wide pavement. Eddie popped into the pub; a great roar greeted his entry. He came out with his hands full of bags of crisps. Following him was Uncle Pat, holding a great tray of drinks for us all. He looked half-pissed.

The pub closed at two o'clock but, in spite of the continuing call, "Time gentlemen, please", it must have taken a good half hour for the pub to empty. The men were all carrying crates of beer (it was Christmas after all).

The men soon set up in the front room, whilst the ladies prepared the food, mostly cold. Uncle Jim was tinkling away at the piano and the party was about to start.

All in all, it had been a lovely day but the fun hadn't started yet! Nobody was going home, therefore, all of us cousins had to find somewhere to sleep. Luckily, Dad's room was empty which made room for a couple of the boys. Bedtime was chaotic but nobody was in that much of a hurry! The party was to go all night, even into the early hours.

Both Eddie and Michael had sung, as well as, Cousin Jim. Nan, as usual, sang beautifully to my ears, but in a slightly sad way (it could have been my imagination).

In Spite of Everything . . . .

Next day (there's always a next day), they all slowly made their way home, the adults being slightly subdued. I did wonder what next Christmas would be like or where we would be!

Dad had returned and had explained to Nan his arrangements for bringing Betty around to meet her and us. Nan suggested that it would be a good idea for them to meet first and give her a chance to talk to us, before our meeting. The next day being ideal.

Dad agreed. Unfortunately, Granddad had already left the kitchen and gone out. He was not a happy man.

Another New Year had begun and, apart for the impending meeting, everything slipped into the normal routine.

Old Father Time waits for no one. The day arrived!

"Finish your tea, boys! I need to talk to you. I've just spent the day with your dad's lady friend, Betty. Come in the front room when you've finished." Eddie glanced nervously towards me. My face, as always, gave the game away. Luckily, it all seemed to go over Michael's head. Granddad quietly read his evening paper.

"Now, boys, listen to what I'm going to tell you. I've had a pleasant afternoon with Betty and, as you know, she's from Liverpool but, apart from her funny accent, she's a fine woman. She's clean and smartly dressed and quite educated. Actually she does remind me of a schoolteacher. She loves your dad and is sorry, really sorry, for any anguish and uncertainty she may have caused. She met Granddad and he got on very well with her. She's a nice lady! She is aware of all the family history and quite understands how you may feel towards her. She is also very aware of the task being taken on and knows that it won't be easy, but she is fully prepared to look after you. She's actually looking forward to it and is dying to meet you.

"What if I don't like her?"

"You know, sometimes, Paddy, Johnny is right. You can be an awkward bugger." (Nan didn't ever swear). "You've heard what I've just said, she's a very nice lady. Now, please, be quiet."

She went on to tell us that she would be happy for Betty to look after us and that, if we all (she stressed *all*) were in agreement, she would give Dad her blessing. She emphasised that we would, after all, only be sleeping and eating away from her and that she'd expect to see us most days. Finally, Betty was coming over tomorrow to meet us. Tomorrow afternoon.

"I want you all to be here. Don't forget." Her eyes never left mine!

I couldn't get out of the house quick enough, straight down to my club. A slight panic was beginning to set in. I felt that I was being quietly ushered into a corner and that made me feel uneasy. I was finding it very hard to hold myself together. My head was buzzing.

It's at these particular moments when you need a friendly helping hand and luckily, I always had!

I came out of the shower, dressed and went down for a cup of tea. "Hi there, Paddy. Had a good session? You look as red as a beetroot. I've already got you a nice sweet cup of tea." There was Eddie, a big smile on his face. He knew that I needed some time on my own to hopefully cool down. Mostly, I had.

We walked slowly back home, chatting away about nothing in particular. Then, "I don't know what you're worried about. You know, you're big enough to look after yourself and, as Nan said, you'll only be sleeping and having your meals there. We'll only be ten minutes away from Nan. When you come to think about it and, I mean really give your brain a chance, Nan would never allow us to go anywhere if she wasn't entirely comfortable and happy. You must realise that surely? Another thing, Paddy, we'll still be all together plus the fact that I'll be starting work at the end of the year, and you'll only be a couple of years behind me." A pause. "Come on, liven up. It'll be a

In Spite of Everything . . . .

piece of piss!" Another pause. "Another thing! You don't think I'd let any harm come to you or Mikey, do you?"

I had a lot to think about!

We were very busy that particular Saturday morning. The two of Kit's stalls were flat out and I was buzzing between both sites. Kit and Michael knew that we would be away for a good part of the afternoon but they understood (having been put in the picture by Nan). As I was pedalling away from the Blue, Eddie called out, "Don't forget! You've got to go home, I'll be with you in a minute. See ya!" I just waved.

I hung around until I saw Eddie walking up the street and the two of us walked home together. "Paddy, whatever you do, please don't be rude. It'll upset Nan."

We let ourselves in and began climbing the stairs. The front room door was closed but I could hear muffled conversation.

"Here they are now. Is that you, boys?" "Yes, Nan," Eddie replied.

The door opened and Nan smiled and called us in.

There was Dad, Michael, Nan and two ladies I'd never seen before, one with dark hair and the other fair.

Everyone seemed hesitant and awkward, which struck me as odd because this household was always so open and relaxed. The dark-haired lady broke the ice and stepped forward smiling. "Elloo, loov, you must be Eddie. I've been dying to meet you." At the same time planting a kiss on his cheek. Then turning to me, I could see anxiety in her face, "And you must be Paddy. What a lovely lad you are. Come on, give us a kiss." Didn't anyone tell her that I hated being kissed by strangers? That kiss, however, certainly did the trick because everybody started laughing and the atmosphere completely changed. The laugh was on me.

The fair-haired lady was introduced as Maureen, Betty's younger sister. I had to reluctantly admit that they seemed very nice ladies. What we would now call small talk went on nervously for what seemed like ages (probably less than half an hour). Nan was quick and proud to tell them all about my grammar school and Eddie's secondary modern placing (it was cringingly embarrassing). "Betty, I'll go and make a nice cup of tea and give you and Ted a few moments to talk to the boys alone. I'm sure there's lots to say to each other and you might find it a little bit more comfortable without me looming over you."

"Don't be daft, Nanna. There are no secrets between us. We all want what's best for the boys, although, I'd luv a brew."

Nan disappeared and Betty spoke to all three of us, going to great pains to stress that she could never, and wouldn't try, to take the place of our "Nanna". She knew that we loved her and the family dearly. She had been made aware of us from the moment that her and Dad had met and she loved our father and, again, stressed that she would be happy to look after us. Nanna would only be a short distance away and she would expect us to keep closely in touch. She seemed very sincere and finished by reminding us that everyone had agreed that the final choice would be ours and that Nanna had insisted that it would be all three or no one. Her and Dad would marry in April or May whatever the outcome. "Your father loves you all very mooch and wants to get involved in your upbringing. For heaven's sake, he's missed so much already."

Michael's big blue eyes were nearly popping out of his head and I'd noticed that he'd edged ever closer to Dad. Eddie seemed happy enough but, forever the party pooper, I wasn't!

Nan came in with tea. I asked if I could go out. "You don't have to be in such a hurry, son! Where're you off to anyway?"

"There's a table tennis competition at our club, Dad, and I want to fill in my entry form. It's alright, ain't it?"

In Spite of Everything . . . .

His shoulders slightly slumped and he did look a bit annoyed. I didn't want to upset anybody but I'd had about as much as I could take.

"Say goodbye to Aunt Betty and Maureen before you dash off and good luck with your competition. I didn't realise you even played table tennis." (I didn't blame him for that).

Eddie spoke out, wary that things might get out of hand, "He get up to so much sport Dad that even I don't know what he's up to!" "I'll see you down there later!"

I said my goodbyes at a distance (no kissing this time). Aunt Bet wished me luck and said that she would be seeing a lot of us over the next few months.

Nan was staring at me and I saw that slightly worried and thoughtful look. I smiled and waved to her, "See ya when I get back, Nan." Then I was out of the there!

The next few months passed by and, yes, we did see a lot of Aunt Bet. For one thing, she and her sister had moved down from Liverpool (I hadn't realised that) and they were living in Uncle Bill and Aunt Kit's house in Nunhead (a short bus ride away). Dad made sure that he took us over to spend a few Sunday afternoons with them and Nan invited Aunt Bet over to our house, and very craftily made herself scarce, which gave Betty the chance to get our tea ready, at the same time, getting acquainted with Granddad and Eileen. Granddad came to like her and they got on very well. She was a very clean and tidy lady and I think he rather liked that. Eileen became quite friendly towards her but, there again, she was as close to a saint as was possible. She would have got on with the devil himself, such was her gentle nature.

We didn't see much of Uncle Jim, nowadays, because he was heavily courting his future wife.

I kept thinking, Johnny will be home soon. I wonder what he'll make of what's been going on. I knew he wasn't aware of developments because, remember, I wrote Nan's letter for her. I can always remember some of his address, Munchen-Gladbach, B.A.O.R. Germany. It sounded so exciting.

Johnny would be home in a few days so there was a lot of rearranging to do. Since Dad was using his bedroom and Jimmy was in the enormous room that sat directly over the big front room, Nan decided there would be a change-around. We three and Dad would share the big room and Jimmy would move into ours. Dad bought himself a new single bed, Eddie and Michael's double and my single fitted easily with tons of room. It made sense but I know that Dad got the impression that he was being sidelined (the gap was getting wider).

Dad used to get up very early to go to work but he finished at around two o'clock in the afternoon, which gave him ample opportunity to carry on with Uncle Nathan with their illicit operations. The fact that Dad had returned to the brewery and the various products he was able to supply, only served to enhance their shenanigans. Usually, by the time I'd got home from school, Dad was already booted and suited and off with Nathan. He came in usually whilst we were having tea, popping his head round the corner and making sure we were all right. He then would go to bed for a couple of hours then washed and dressed, he was off again. The noise he made as he got ready for bed would have woken the dead, but I never spoke a word, very soon dropping off to sleep.

This lifestyle of his continued for many months. Granddad was far from pleased with him but Nan always jumped to his defence, reminding him that Dad was still a very young man, in his mid-thirties to be exact. Dad was only twenty-one when I was born and only nineteen when Eddie was, and he had missed nearly six years of his young life fighting for his country.

Johnny came home and he'd grown even bigger. He was one of the broadest men I'd ever seen. His shoulders were so wide! I was pleased that he didn't seem to have any issues with Dad but they moved in different circles. Johnny idolised our dad and Nathan but he wouldn't get involved in anything illegal. He was one of the most honest men I would ever know. Due to the family ties and connections along the

In Spite of Everything . . . .

river, he managed to get his docker's ticket which meant that he started working down Tooley Street (working is probably far from accurate, as far as he was concerned, but more about that later), and in spite of the fact that he was a face[40] and considering the amount of pilfering and thieving that went on, his refusal to get involved was a testament to his iron will. He was greatly respected by fellow dockers but most of them didn't have the brains to understand a man like that!

Spring was approaching and although we saw a lot of Aunt Bet, the date of the marriage was never mentioned.

My school days were now becoming routine but getting harder by the month. I had been introduced to homework some months previous but the amount was slowly increasing, which meant that some evenings I was unable to go out. I wasn't very happy and nor was Nan. She wasn't entirely comfortable about me staying in, sitting doing lessons at home. We were in agreement that school should have a start and finish and that should be enough. It's worth remembering that never before had homework reared its ugly head amongst our family.

I didn't discuss it with anybody, not ever Eddie, but I figured out that although I had to do homework, I didn't necessarily have to do it that well! I had the best part of any hour to and from school on the bus and tram. I would do most of it then!

Dad popped into the kitchen one evening. "Hi, lads. When you've finished your tea, I need to have a chat with you before you go out. I'll be sitting in the front room."

"Do you want anything to eat, Ted?"

"No, thanks, Mum. I've already had something." He never ate at home anymore. It's not that surprising because the atmosphere was cool. Granddad didn't even look up from his paper.

"Fancy a nice cup of tea, then?" "Oh, yes, please. That'll be nice." "I'll bring it into you. I need to have a couple of words with you, anyway."

Nan took his cuppa in to the front room and I noticed that she took her time returning. What the fuck's going on, now?!

"I've just been chatting with your dad. He's got some good news for you. Don't all rush but off you go." Michael was away like a shot.

"Hello, boys, sorry I've not seen too much of you lately, but I've been busy trying to get the council to allocate me a flat large enough for all of us. They're hard to come by but they are building some new places and with my war record, I'm top of the queue. That's not what I wanted to talk to you about though! It'll be Easter holidays shortly and I've arranged for us to go up to Liverpool and meet Aunt Betty's family. That'll be exciting, won't it?"

Michael jumped for joy and Eddie said, "That will be great!" I was shocked. I felt, once again, that I was being pushed into a corner. I've got a family, one that I'm very happy with. I had no desire to acquire another.

Dad looked at me. "What's wrong with you, now?! Can't I do anything to please you? You really are a miserable sod! You really are!"

There was only one way! "Dad, I'm not miserable. I just don't like being told who I must like or dislike. I prefer to make my own mind up! I think I love you but I don't want to go with you to Liverpool." There, I'd said it. No going back now!

"Paddy, Paddy! Will you please listen to me and get it into your thick head, you are my son and you must obey me. I love you just as much as the others but, sometimes, you make that almost impossible by your attitude. I know that you have all gone through a rough time and, because of that, I'm prepared to compromise. I won't force you to come with us, although it'll be your loss because we'll probably go out to see the sights and go to a place called Blackpool. That's on the seaside." Michael was jumping about. "C'mon, Paddy, we'll have a good time. You'll miss all the fun." Eddie said, "He's right, ya know. We'll have a nice time. Why don't you change your mind? Dad's right, you know. Sometimes, you can be a bit stubborn."

"Sorry, Dad. Sorry, boys. I honestly don't want to go. I just don't feel comfortable." The meeting broke up but not before Dad made a few sarcastic remarks and tried to humiliate me in front of Eddie and Mikey. There would never be any peace between Dad and me from that moment on! It was at that time that we drifted ever wider apart (thank God, settling our differences some 30 years later).

"Where are you off to? I want a word with you before you go out."
"I'm just off to the club, Nan. What ya want?"

"I know what went on in there," nodding towards the front room. "You mustn't be so hard on your dad. He's doing what he thinks is right. Remember, he's been through a very rough time and has probably seen things that would give him nightmares. Please try to be a good boy." She gave me a little squeeze. "Enjoy yourself."

They were all packed and ready to go, "Sure you won't change you mind?" "Not really, Dad. I'm alright here. Have a good time, all of you." Dad just shrugged. There was this toot-toot. "She's here," said Dad. "Come on, boys, don't hang about. We don't want to keep them waiting."

I carried Mikey's bag downstairs and, as I entered our alley, there was Betty and her sister getting out of a taxi. They bore down on me (in a friendly way).

Betty opened, "You are silly. Why don't you want to come with us? We'll have a lovely time. The family are dying to meet you. Please, please, change your mind. It's still not too late." She did look genuinely sad, as did sister Maureen.

Eddie, as usual, got me off the hook. "You're wasting your time. Once his mind is made up, he'll never change it, and I should know. Anyway, you've got an important football match on Saturday, ain't you, Paddy?" "Yeah." I was now in the club football team. "It's the semi-final of the SE clubs." Eddie winked at me, "Hope you win. See you when we get back. Tell you all about it." I gave Mikey a hug. They then all climbed into the taxi and were gone.

Although I missed Eddie and Michael, especially when I was in bed, I actually had a great time. They (Nan, Granddad, Eileen and Johnny) all made a fuss of me (a bit too much maybe).

That Sunday morning (we lost the match, by the way) was nice and relaxing. Uncle Jim was playing records on the windup player. The usual: Frank Sinatra, Dick Haymes, Ella and a new kid on the block, in actual fact, a blind Englishman by the name of George Shearing. He and his quartet played really cool jazz. I loved these sounds and still do. "Coming to give me a hand, Paddy?" You bet I was. "Yeah. When are you going, Granddad?" "In about ten minutes, so get your skates on." (He didn't mean for me to actually put on rollerskates, just hurry up and get ready).

Eileen was helping Nan with the housework, singing away as she went from room to room. She had a very nice voice. The strange thing was, that I hardly gave a passing thought about Eddie and Mikey in Liverpool.

Granddad and I were working away, getting his fish prepared, when a funny thing happened. Granddad's voice became oddly slurred and he had to sit down. He kept rubbing his right arm, which was almost hanging from him. I was quite alarmed!

"Are you alright, Granddad?" He looked at me and his eyes were blank and rolling. "What's the matter? What can I do?" It was frightening because I'd never seen anything like this before. He managed to gasp for a drink of water. By the time I'd got a glass for him, he seemed to perk up. The colour returned to his face and his blue eyes had a sparkle in them again. He sipped his water but I noticed that he used his left hand (he was right-handed).

In Spite of Everything . . . .

"Thanks, boy, ta. There's nothing to worry about. I've just had a funny turn. This can happen as you get older. You'll find out one day. I'll just rest up for a couple of minutes and it'll be alright. Will you carry on with those whelks, please, son? And, by the way, not a word about this to your nan, ya "folla". I did as he said but I was very uneasy. I'd never seen Granddad as weak and vulnerable before.

Within an hour, Granddad had his stall in place and he was back to his chirpy self, but he was still having some problem getting his words out.

Once all the drinkers started to arrive, including Uncle Nathan and a few of his pals, Granddad got very busy so I helped him for a while. A couple of my mates turned up and I knew that Granddad wasn't very keen on boys hanging around. "Alright if I go now, Granddad?" "Of course, boy, you've done a good job. Go and enjoy yourself. Don't be late home for dinner cos your nan will put the blame on me!" Before running off, I put my head in the pub and shouted goodbye to Nathan, who had now been joined by Johnny and Uncle George. The pub was buzzing.

Bank Holiday Monday turned out to be interesting because Uncle Pat and family turned up. Sadly, Aunt Emma looked very thin and pale. It got even better because so did Uncle Dave, Sarah and family. Uncle Pat, as usual, had some light-hearted and friendly jibes at me over my not going to Liverpool, but Nan put a stop to that very smartly! It was obviously a touchy subject for her. I had a great time with cousins Jimmy and Davey and, as usual, when having fun, the day whizzed by.

I'd been out playing and, as I got home for some dinner, I could hear Eddie and Mikey jabbering away. I dashed up the stairs. "Hi ya, Paddy, how are ya?" "Yeah, Ed, alright thanks. Had a good time?"

Eddie went on to explain how they got on and what Liverpool was like (pretty drab by all accounts). Michael kept butting in but I learned that they visited Blackpool and a place called New Brighton. These were both seaside resorts, Blackpool being the biggest. There was a great big tower there. Michael said that it was as high as the sky. I was honestly glad that they had had a good time but, not for an instant, did I ever regret my decision.

The rest of the holiday soon passed then back to school.

The playground had been transformed! There were now half a dozen tennis courts marked out, all with nets, and in the far corner were four cricket nets all with springback stumps. I liked this!

After dinner, I headed straight for the cricket nets. There were a couple of PE teachers hanging around and they made sure we were separated by year. I soon had a hard ball in my hand. It wasn't the normal leather ball but some hard composite material. Remember, we were playing on an asphalt surface.

"O'Donovan! I've been keeping an eye on you. You've got promise. How would you like to help make up the year cricket team?"

"Yes, please, sir. I love cricket."

"I'm gathering a few boys together after class, today. If you're interested, be here once you've finished lessons. It'll only be for half an hour. I don't want your parents worrying about you."

I went to the gathering. There were about twenty of us, most of the boys were ones that I'd played football with. Wednesday afternoon would be our first full practice session but, in truth, the next dinnertime, whilst bowling, the teacher was already handing out advice on action and technique.

I was picked for the school team and we had our first match on our home ground, which was in Ewell. We were told to bring whites.

Talk about being embarrassed! We all got changed in the old wooden pavilion. Yes, I was wearing white just like the rest of them but I had short trousers on. Everybody else was wearing traditional long trousers!

Apart from a couple of fairly close mates, no one took the piss out of me, which was a good job because I wasn't very happy.

Some of the boys had proper studded cricket shoes but, like many of the others, I had stout white plimsolls.

I took four wickets that day and scored twenty-six runs, even though I looked ridiculous! Our teacher pulled me to one side after the match. "Well done, lad. You played very well! Now, about your dress. Long trousers are a must and, if possible, proper shoes because they stop you slipping and, if you get hit on the foot, they offer some protection. I can assure you that it is very painful getting hit on the toes by a cricket ball. Believe me! Once again, however, well played."

I told Nan all about what had gone on and she was distraught at the thought of me being shown up in front of people. "Where can we get hold of the things you need, do you know?"

"Well, Nan, yes, I do. Our teacher told me that there's a sports shop in Borough High Street, not far from the tube station. They specialise in cricket.

"Are you going to play regular because, if you are, I'll get some money from your dad. After all, you missed out on all the fun in Liverpool." She gave me a large wink and a broad smile. Eileen, who had been listening, said, "I've got a few bob put by, Mum. I'll help, if necessary. I'm not gonna see him looking like a proper Charlie!"

"Leave off, Eileen. I didn't look that silly." (I did really!) "Anyway, I've got a few bob of my own money. I don't know what the boots cost but I'm definitely gonna get a pair of them."

That Saturday afternoon, I went with Nan up to the Borough. We easily found Stewart Surridge, the sports shop. Nan bought two pairs of trousers and some socks. I eyed the boots. They were magical to me, at the time. Here I was, holding for the first time, proper solid cricket shoes. I can't remember the exact price, only that they were very expensive, at least double the price of anything I'd had before.

Nan looked at me, "Are they the shoes you need, Paddy?" "Yeah, Nan, but have you seen the price?" "Paddy! Are they the shoes you need?" "I've got some money towards them, Nan. Here!" I fished out a couple of ten bob (shilling) notes and some silver, offering them to Nan.

"Don't be silly! Put your money away. Everybody has chipped in. They're all working, remember. You just try them on and make sure they fit properly."

I made sure that I bought a slightly larger pair, thinking that they'd last longer. I was as happy as a pig in shit.

That evening, I had to show off all my cricket gear to everyone. It felt strange to be in long trousers. All that evening, I kept going to my bedroom and looking at my boots.

Dad was around for a short while on Sunday morning, so he also got a show. I made sure that I thanked him.

"You look very grown up, son, think of it as an early birthday present because you won't be getting anything else." It was said in a playful way. "That's all right, Dad. This is all I want. Thanks, again."

The summer approached. I played a lot of cricket and, although I was handling the academic side of things, I was never entirely comfortable at school. Most of the boys were not my type. Thankfully, the sport side of things somewhat made life bearable.

It was becoming noticeable by the month that we weren't seeing quite as much of Betty. Dad very rarely took Michael over to Aunt Kit's on a Sunday morning. He seemed to be living the life of Riley[41]. There had been no mention of weddings or flats. As you can imagine, I was happy about that. *Status quo*, please. That's a bit flash! So I've been learning Latin. Not very well, I hasten to add. I simply hate it, especially with its connection with the Catholic church, ugh!

Jimmy, for the last time as it turned out, came to stay with us through the summer holidays. Nothing sinister about that, it was just that he

In Spite of Everything . . . .

would start work next year. We were all growing up! Not too much to stop us playing boyish games, thank God!

We were all mucking about, having a pillow fight, when Uncle Pat walked in grim-faced. "How's Mum?" (Emma was in hospital).

"She's not in pain, anymore. Come into the kitchen, Jim, I want to talk to you alone."

We all looked at each other and Jimmy followed his dad down the stairs. We stopped mucking about! I heard the cry coming from the kitchen. Aunt Emma had died. She'd had TB and had been suffering for years.

It was very sad for Jimmy. Luckily, he had Nan around to comfort him. Jimmy was never down too long. I can hear him, now. "We're all in the same boat, now. No mum." Truthfully, I'd almost forgotten mine!

The summer holidays were now ended and it was back to school. I was now a second year student, which meant amongst other things, our playground football pitch was now further to the left.

Nan had received her letter from the farmer and had taken up her invitation to pick hops. We had all gone with her and, as usual, got her well settled in, but Eddie and I could only stay for a week, though Michael would be with her all the way through. We, once again, spent a couple of weekends with them. And had a great time. As it turned out, Nan was never on her own. Various members of the family spent time with her, which meant that I was totally relaxed and she made a bit more money (it was win-win).

Dad was still a bit of a will-o-the-wisp, only appearing for short periods. He sometimes didn't even come home to sleep. Aunt Betty was conspicuous by her absence and all mention of flats and marriage had ceased. As you can imagine, I wasn't that bothered (*status quo*).

I was plodding along merrily at school although, to be honest, I was struggling with a few subjects and the homework was becoming a problem. I had so many interests at my club. I had started running. This was initially taken up so that I could keep fit for football and it was an integral part of boxing training, but I had begun to enjoy it, for its own sake. Table tennis was another activity I enjoyed. In other words, I was too busy to be sitting indoors doing poxy homework.

I was able to get through a great deal of study during my journeys to and from school. This was all right for the problem-solving subjects, such as maths and physics, even to some extent, history and geography. However, essays in English meant that my handwriting was suffering. I decided to hardly bother with Latin, music and religious studies and French. This decision meant that I was now in constant conflict with certain teachers. The result being that I started to get detentions!

Now, these detentions were something else! Instead of writing lines, we had to learn poetry, line by line. I would sometimes have to learn thirty lines of this poetry, luckily five lines, at a time! When I was happy that I could memorise my five, the teacher in charge made me recite them to him. If they were right, then on to the next five. It was certainly good for the memory cells and, luckily, I had a very good photographic memory. I can't recall a single line now!

I skipped a few detentions and wound up getting the cane. The cane was something that filled some boys with dread but it really didn't bother me. Whenever I was given the choice of cane or poetry, I chose the cane! The Head of Year and the actual Head were getting a wee bit pissed off with me, however, and I had to suffer many a long lecture. Luckily, I was able to hold my own in class, mostly coming near the top in the important subjects, obviously absolutely shit in Latin, music and R.E.

I had been made captain of the school football team but I was under a great deal of pressure to improve my academic work rate. This was to be a conflict that would run and run.

The weather started to get very cold and there was snow before Christmas. This came on top of severe shortages of all kinds of food and fuel. The coal and coke ration was not very much and it was hard to keep warm at home. We started to go round to the bombed out houses and take floorboards up to use for firewood. The police would chase us off but we came back as soon as they were gone. We weren't going to freeze, were we?

The long queues for food and coal were pitiful. We'd get frozen half to death just standing in line.

Christmas came and went and, in spite of all the problems, we managed to have a nice time. Dad was around a bit more but, sadly, the hostility to him from some members of the family was becoming very evident. Luckily, he was as thick as thieves with Nathan and Johnny and a couple of their cousins. The upstairs kitchen still was in full flow. Sorry, I forgot Uncle Pat, he was deeply involved, as well.

That winter was probably the coldest I can recall, although the terrible shortages probably made it seem even colder. It's nothing to be proud of but we were better off than many other families because, on a regular basis, bags of coal and coke were dropped off down our alley. Sadly, black market trade, but I was certainly too young to fully appreciate how wrong this was. We did share some of this bounty with some of our neighbours. Added to this was the fact that Eddie, Michael and I were able to obtain a lot of wood.

Granddad would be the first one up out of bed. His immediate job was to light the fire in the kitchen, both for a bit of warmth and for cooking. The inside of our bedroom windows had ice on them and we had no carpets, just lino, bare boards and a couple of rugs. We had as many coats and overcoats over our blankets as we possessed, otherwise we'd have frozen. Picture this! We had only cold water to wash in but I swear it was warmer than the inside of the house.

Granddad was slowly finding it harder to cut the wood up into small enough pieces, in order to get the fire going quick enough. I could hear him swearing and cussing but he was also finding it harder to get his words out. That was that, then! I made it my job to get the fire going. I became quite an expert. Old newspaper, very thin, pencil-like twigs, a few lumps of coal and then slowly, very slowly, adding coke (we had twice as much coke as coal). By the time Nan was about, I had a roaring fire. It was only then that I got washed and dressed. There was a bonus, I had warmed up in front of the fire.

The bitter cold continued, which didn't help the grinding poverty. There were days that I couldn't get to school, like many others. The queues and shortages got worse. I think we survived on stew for most of the winter, that and porridge oats. Nan had a great pot of stew continuously on the go. She just kept adding to it. I am not complaining; it was lovely.

Things got that bad for the council to dig up many of the side roads that had been laid down with wooden tarry blocks. These were similar in size as modern stone block paving and, once laid, had been covered with a thick layer of tarmacadam. They were then taken to the council yard in Weston Street. Once there, they were issued to the people. There was a simple way to ensure fair ration. We had to take our own sack and could only have what you could carry over your shoulder, definitely no trucks or trolleys or prams.

Eddie and I would get in the queue with our sack and, after a while, Michael would turn up and spell us. We were lucky because almost opposite the yard, lived a relative of ours, so we were able to pop in for a warm. It is hard to describe the wretched scene. People of all ages, some with not much better than rags on their backs, and youngsters with just rubber Wellington boots on, all standing in about six inches of snow. The council boys had placed a couple of coke-filled drums, which people were able to huddle round for a bit of warmth. It made a pitiful scene. We were lucky because Dad made sure that Nan had enough money to buys us stout boots and socks to match, as well as heavy overcoats. One of Nan's cousins knitted us woollen balaclavas! Now these were a feature in themselves because wool was scarce, so she knitted them with different types of wool, very cleverly interlocked. They kept us warm, so what the hell!

When I hear people moaning about modern day problems, I always think, they don't know how lucky they are!

Once our sack was loaded, I used to heave it on Eddie's back and we then struggled across the road. Eventually, Johnny or Georgie would pass by after finishing work in Tooley Street. They took over!

Tarry blocks were brilliant for lighting the fire because I could chop them into thin matchstick-style slivers with each one having a tarmacadam end. They exploded into light, unfortunately giving off nasty fumes, probably poisonous, but we didn't care, we were warm.

The winter seemed to go on forever. The snow and ice just wouldn't go away. I missed quite a lot of school and what annoyed me was that our teachers moaned that I wasn't making enough effort. Fuck them, I thought! Half of them lived in and most of the rest lived locally. I didn't get any detentions so I could suffer a bit of earache.

Betty appeared from time to time and, to be honest, showed a lot of interest in us. I did notice that she and Nan had longer and longer intimate chats. What were they up to, I thought?

Eddie was going to leave school at Easter and Dad's brother-in-law, Bill, had secured him a nice job in the print. In those days, anything to do with the print was a well-paid job.

Things were very slowly improving. The weather was getting a little better, which was a good thing because there were the Olympic Games taking place in London.

It seemed that my life could never run smoothly. There I was, in the gym, having a very nice session, when I was called over to the side by a mate of mine. "You'd better go downstairs, Paddy. A few blokes have stuck your brother inside the vaulting horse and won't let him out."

I tore my gloves off and dashed downstairs. There were four of them, all laughing and enjoying themselves. I knew them all. They were flash bastards; all of them petty crooks. They thought they were hard. "Get off that fuckin' horse and let my brother out. What do you think you're fuckin' up to?" They slowly jumped off and I helped Michael out. "You alright, Mikey?" "Yeah, those bastards had a go at me." I turned to face them. "What the fuckin' hell you lot playing at? You know he's my brother. Now leave him alone."

One of the most arrogant spoke out, "We were only teaching him a lesson. He was a bit saucy to us. We didn't hurt him." I gave it some thought. "Listen to me and listen well. Leave him alone! If he's saucy, then one of you c . . . s come up and tell me! Mikey, stay away from them!" I went back upstairs and gave the heavy bag a right pounding.

It had to happen, just had to happen! The same mate, "Sorry, Paddy, they've only gone and done it, again. Now, calm down, for God's sake." Calm down, calm down. That was impossible. That was like stopping having a piss.

Fortunately, when I'm really mad, I manage to see things more clearly. I knew exactly what I was going to do. There they were, smirking! They jumped off and came towards me. A big mistake. I picked the loudmouth leader (John). He kept coming, overconfident!

I hit him with a beautiful straight right (the mug punch). His face exploded! I'd never seen such blood. He flew backwards, clutching his mouth and a strange choking sound came from him. I had knocked his front teeth right out of his gums. They were now in the back of his throat. His flash hard mates backed away.

There was total mayhem. A couple of instructors came rushing forward to John. He needed tending; he was bleeding badly. They covered his face with towels and took him away to the first aid room. The head man of the club appeared, in a very agitated state. "What the dickens was that all about? You know that fighting is forbidden. What did you hit him with, for crissake?"

"They were hurting my younger brother and just about to attack me. It was self-defence. And, by the way, I used my hands." I turned to the three, "Don't let me see you, again, or you'll get the same, you fuckdogs."

In Spite of Everything . . . .

"Now, now, less of that! I think it would be better if you got dressed and went off home. I'm sorry but I must give you a two-week ban and that includes football. Come on, everyone, the show's over. Back to whatever you were doing."

"Michael, come on. We're going home." On our way home, I told Mikey not to say anything to Nan. "What about Eddie?" "I'll tell him myself." "That was some punch, Paddy! I thought you'd knocked his head off."

It was a great punch, one of the best I had ever thrown. My knuckles were proof of that, some skin was missing and my hand was beginning to swell. "You're back early. Anything wrong?" That lady doesn't miss a trick! "No, not really, Nan. Just had enough tonight, ain't we, Mikey?" He nodded. Nan stared at me. She knew!

I told Eddie all about it and he was livid. He knew those people and, like me, had no time for them. They would never know how lucky they were that he was not around. I think he went to sleep still as mad as hell. My hand was throbbing!

I walked into the kitchen and could tell straightaway that I was in trouble. Nan was sitting at the table but so was Dad, both looking very serious. Dad went straight on the attack. "You don't stop, do you? You cause trouble wherever you go! You've really done it, now! That boy you hit last night has lost four of his front teeth and will have to have false ones made! Can you imagine that? False teeth at thirteen years of age. Your nan's had his mother up here threatening to call the police. This will have to stop, young man. Why the hell did you hit him?"

I felt like screaming at him. He was incapable of giving me a chance. How I never just walked away, I will never know. "Dad! Them fuckers," I got a smack round the head for that, "were having a go at Michael and they thought they could give me a good hiding," I paused. "What? So I can't protect Michael anymore?"

Dad's mouth dropped open. "There! I told you, Ted. I knew that he wouldn't just attack someone. He might be a bit short tempered, but he's no bully."

Good old Nan! "How's your hand, Paddy?" As I was telling my side of the story, Eddie walked into the kitchen. "I know those blokes, Dad. They're a nasty bunch. They only fight mob-handed[42]. They'd have given Paddy a good kicking if they'd had a chance! Wait till I bump into them!"

Dad turned to Eddie, "Son, I don't want you getting into trouble. It seems like he's taken care of things already." He then glanced at me. "Do you think it's finished, son? No danger of any comebacks?"

"I wouldn't think so, Dad. They looked shit scared of me." Another softer clip round the head. Nan said that she would go round to see Mrs Paisley and give my side of the story because it sounded like he deserved what he got. Nan actually knew the family. There were no comebacks and I never heard anymore about it . . . or, so I thought!

I could hear raised voices, very angry voices! Granddad was finding it harder to complete a full sentence, which sadly meant they almost always finished with effing and blinding (swearing). It was the frustration! "You've brought that woman round here, after bringing her all the way from Liverpool. You then introduced her to the boys, telling them you'd be getting married and you want to take them with you. Now you're fucking about with other women and living life like a single man. It's not good enough to just put money in for their keep, you've got to act like a proper father. The boys are growing up fast and they deserve better."

"You don't have to remind me of that! I wouldn't do anything to harm them but I must have my own life, as I see fit, and I don't need you shouting at me." I heard Nan's voice, a little softer, telling both of them to calm down.

Granddad, again, "Well, for the boys' sake, please make your mind up very soon and tell the boys what your plans are! Mark my words, you'll lose those boys if you're not careful. Young Paddy's not that happy at the moment. Be very careful, Ted! It's not your fault but we know them even more than you do. Their lives have been disturbed enough, don't you think?" (Never a truer word spoken! Paddy's not happy.)

I heard the kitchen door slam and someone hurrying down the stairs then the front door slamming loudly.

Dad didn't come up to bed that night. I whispered to Eddie, "Are you awake?" "Yeah, shush, be quiet. Mike's asleep. Wait there, I'm coming over."

He very quietly sat on my bed. "You know I've been going out with Dad these last few Sunday mornings?" "Yeah, of course, you've been going with him to have all those old gold watches repaired, ain't you?"

I don't exactly know where the old gold watches were coming from but there was obviously some scam going on, probably involving Uncle Nathan, no doubt!

"Yeah," a slight pause, "but he's been seeing another woman, Aunt Marie. I've been sworn to secrecy but she knows you and Michael."

"Well, I don't know her. I didn't know we had an Aunt Marie," (remember, I was only young and naïve).

"You silly sod, she's not a proper aunt, not like a relative. Dad just asked me to call her that, that's all! She's very nice and I know that she wants to meet you but Dad said not yet."

"What the fuck does she want to meet me for? I've had enough of fucking aunts."

"Shush, be quiet! That's why Dad won't allow it but, listen, will ya? Give your ears a chance. Betty turned up the other Sunday and they had a terrible row. It was quite funny because I could hardly understand what she was saying. She certainly wasn't very happy. She gave me a cuddle and said goodbye. She was in tears."

"She was here the other afternoon, having a real long chat with Nan. I bet that was what it was all about."

"Don't breathe a word to Nan or any of the others and, certainly, not to Michael."

"What do you think I am? Simple Simon?"

Eddie crept away and I could hear his heavy breathing. I couldn't get to sleep even considering going down to talk to Nan but I didn't.

Life returned to normal and before long Easter had arrived. The snow and ice had at last melted away and all the talk was about the Olympics. I was allowed back in the club, albeit with warnings about my future conduct. Now that I was playing regularly for two football teams, fitness was of the essence. That's where running came in. I wasn't very good over short distances but I found out that I had bags of stamina and good lungs. I could run for miles.

Let me explain. We used to run two, three or five bridges. Two meant leave the club, run over Tower Bridge, turn left and then back over London Bridge and then back to the club. Three was over Tower, bypass London then turn left over Southwark then back to the club. Five was same as the others but this time coming back across Waterloo Bridge then to the club (the five bridges: Tower, London, Southwark, Blackfriars and Waterloo).

The five was a real good test of stamina, something that was to be a very important asset for me, in the not too distant future.

Eddie had now ended his school days and was now starting work. It felt very strange and it was noticeable that Nan now treated him slightly differently. He was now almost a man and she acted towards him in a similar way as she did to Jimmy, Eileen and Johnny. I couldn't get it out of my head what Eddie had told me that night or the row that was

In Spite of Everything . . . .

going on. I don't know how I stopped myself tackling Dad about it (on those rare occasions, our paths actually crossed). I certainly didn't show my hand to Nan.

I jumped off the bus just before it turned the corner into Spa Road. This always annoyed the bus conductress but, come on, I was one of the lads, after all!

"Hi, Paddy, loov. Nice to see you. How've you been getting on? Don't run away, I've gorra have a word with you." There she was, across the road. Betty! She told me that she was going to see 'me nanna' but wanted to have a word with me first. Had I ever been out with Dad lately and did he take me to another lady? What a crafty cow, I thought! She seemed to be slightly relaxed when I let her know that I very rarely went anywhere with Dad, and that I didn't know anything about another lady. I thought I'd better add that I had so many things to do and couldn't find time to go out with anybody.

"Hi, Nan, there's a visitor to see you. Aunt Bet." Nan gave her a warm welcome, as did Granddad. I got changed and did a rare thing, homework. It got me out of the way!

She poked her head round the front room door. "Bye, bye, loov. See ya soon." A bit too friendly, I thought!

Even though Eddie was working, he still did his Saturday work for Kit and Michael. There was still a shortage of nylons and there were still thousands of Yanks in London. Nathan and friends had an unending supply of American produce, which was very fortunate because it was now becoming difficult, well, almost impossible, to smuggle the raw spirit from the bonded warehouses. Security was now very tight and added to this, the local coppers, who had been only too pleased to turn their backs, were now getting very difficult (and costly!).

"Nothing lasts forever, son. We'd better pack things up before we get our collar felt. It was nice while it lasted though, wasn't it?" These were Nathan's words, as he was dismantling the still. I had a few other irons in the fire, so wasn't that bothered.

I'd just got back from the Blue and was strolling down Tower Bridge Road, heading for the pie and mash shop. He crossed the road and showed out to me. It was Big Jimmy, a boy of my own age but, unfortunately, a bit simple. He was a large lump and a member of a large local family, most of who were villains. They liked to think that they were the local guv'nors. They didn't impress me or bother me or any of our family. As a matter of fact, most of their people were friends with various members of ours, although that's where it ended. We never got involved in their business!

He approached, smiling, then whack! I felt this thud against my cheek. It was like a hammer blow and I wasn't prepared. I was on the floor, a bit dazed, but a lot annoyed. He wasn't smiling now, the big bastard! It's funny how a reputation can work against you! Most people he'd hit didn't recover and, even if they did, there was the fear of the family. Now, all of this conspired against him!

He didn't realise it at the time, but he was now in a fight! Something he'd never had to do before.

I was up on my feet like a shot. It was then I realised I was bleeding, but, unfortunately for him, blood has never bothered me. I hit him, once, twice, three times and more! He couldn't fight! This was the first time he'd been hit back and I can assure you, I could dig[43].

He started bellowing and snorting like a wild horse, which brought it to people's attention. He was trying to ward off the blows but couldn't. He then made a grab for me, as all non-fighters seem to do. I was a bit concerned because he was stronger than me. (Thank God for that Peter all those years ago down hopping.)

I stepped inside of him and had him on the floor and he fell heavily like a sack of shit. He was almost finished but I wasn't. I leant over him and smashed him again and again, round the head. Then I heard the shouting.

"Waggie! Waggie! For gawd's sake, stop him before he kills him!" It was Aunt Anne, who was doing her shopping. Waggie had the wet fish

In Spite of Everything . . . .

stall. I felt his strong hands grab hold of me and pull us apart. Big Jim was actually crying, yes, crying! He had been taught a lesson. Sadly, although he never ever came anywhere near me or any of mine, he did carry on bashing other people up.

Aunt Anne called out for someone to give her a towel or something and one was produced. She wrapped it round my face, "Look at the state of you! Will you ever stop fighting? Come on, let's get you home. Nan will go mad! Look at the state of you!"

Once I'd been cleaned up, the damage showed! My upper gum had been split almost up to my nose and one of my front teeth was missing.

I spent the rest of the afternoon at Guy's Hospital and had to have several stitches. My face was as swollen as hell and it throbbed!

Why did he do that? That was what kept going through my mind! I was to find out the reason very shortly. The dopey sod had been put up to it by that cowardly bastard, John. He had kidded poor Jim that I was taking away his reputation. See, as I've already written, reputations can work against you.

Eddie and Johnny went round to see Big Jim's family and it all got straightened out. It was a fair fight with no villainy! Johnny (God bless him) used to say, many times over the years, "They don't like it, Paddy, but they don't know what to do about it!" They never did!

The odd thing is, our families were to remain friends for the rest of our lives, although now that I live away from London, I have lost touch. Throughout the years, with the many funerals, at least one member of that family showed up to show their respect. Big Jim never did although, to be honest, he was a bit simple. He never spoke to me again!

I had lost one of my front teeth and the shame of it was that if I'd taken it with me to Guy's, they could have fixed it back in place. Luckily, my

|341

top teeth were overcrowded, so it didn't take that long before the gap closed naturally.

As I approached the school gates, I saw the duty teacher staring at me. "Hey, you! Wait here a moment." He studied my swollen, gap-toothed face. "Stand outside the Head's office. You've been fighting. You're a disgrace."

I did as I was told; I wasn't that bothered. At least I'd miss the stupid morning assembly. I got some funny looks by passing teachers and staff and, in due course, the Head turned up with the head parish priest (they were a double act). They looked shocked upon seeing me. The priest just shook his head from side to side, making tut-tutting noises.

They entered their office and, after a short while, I was called in. I marched in, head held high, making sure that I looked them in the eye. After all, I'd done nothing wrong.

The Head opened, "I see that you have been fighting again, after I have expressly forbidden it. Will you ever learn to do as you are told? We are very disappointed because you have settled down very nicely into school activities. What have you to say for yourself?"

"I was attacked without warning and I had to defend myself. As I've told you before, sir, and Father, it is impossible for me not to defend myself. This happened in Bermondsey, where I live. I wasn't in school uniform and it was out of school hours, so I don't understand why I am in trouble."

"You are wearing the school uniform, now! And you are a disgrace. You are definitely not giving off the correct image."

They chatted quietly together. "You cannot possibly attend classes looking as you do. It will disturb the rest of your class. You will have to go home and not attend classes for three days. That should be sufficient for the swelling to subside. Here is a note for your parents." I took the note and was about to leave. "One moment before you

In Spite of Everything . . . .

go. I'd like you to go and see Matron. She may be able to help you. I assume that you have homework and textbooks with you?" "Yes, sir." "Good. Make sure you study and try to stay out of trouble. Be off with you, now."

Matron was very helpful. She gave me some cream to rub in my face and some aspirins for the pain. I never took the pills.

Nan was surprised to see me and a little annoyed. She thought the school were out of order but I just held them in contempt.

Granddad was sorting out his horse racing bets, carefully studying his paper. "Want me to write your bets out for you, Granddad?" "Yes, thanks, Paddy. That'll be nice. The old minces ain't what they used to be."

I carefully wrote down his "Philipadula" (nowadays called a Yankee). "Who's taking your bet?" "Your Uncle Terry." "Well, give us your money and I'll take it round for you. I know his pitch." "Thanks, boy."

Street betting was illegal but the police had a very relaxed attitude to this popular practice, although it was very unwise to openly shove it in their faces, therefore, it was all a bit furtive.

"Hello, Paddy, you look a bit of a mess. I heard all about it. You alright?"

"Yes, thanks, it's not as bad as it looks."

"What you doing round here?"

"I've got something here from Granddad." He gave me a nod, at the same time directing me down Valentine's Yard. A face that I recognised took my bet and gave me a slip of paper as a receipt. "See you later, Tel." "Yeah, be good and give your nan my best." I waved as I strolled away. I didn't know then but I would have a very close relationship with Terry in the not too distant future, thanks to my privileged education.

I returned to school without incident. A few of the boys were dying to know what had happened to me but the majority avoided me like the plague. I'd just finished dinner and was heading towards the playground, when I was buttonholed by one of the sports teachers. "Wait a moment, I'd like to have a chat with you." My immediate thought was, more trouble, but I was wrong!

"I understand you do a bit of boxing?" He was studying my face, "Although it looks like you needed some lessons in self-defence."

"Yes, sir, I do box and I love it." I pointed to my mouth. "I was jumped on without warning." Then with a twinkle in my eyes, "You should see the other boy."

"Do you know that we are forming a school boxing team?" "No, sir, I didn't." "We need a couple of boys from each year. Are you interested?" "Yes, sir, very much." "Good. Is there any boy that you could recommend?" There was one boy, Benson. He was a rough handful unlike most of the others, so I gave his name to the teacher. He thanked me and said he would be in touch.

I must say something for my school, when they did things, they didn't muck about. A part of the large indoor gymnasium was converted to accommodate boxing. There were bags, speedballs, ropes and light weights and a boxing ring. To be fair, every bit as good as my club.

When I told Nan, because I had to have parent permission, she said, "What with your football, cricket and now boxing, you'll never be home. You'll have to get Dad to sign that form." She smiled at me, "I'm glad you're happy, Paddy. You do know that I worry about you sometimes, don't you?" I studied those deep blue, sorrowful eyes. "Yes, Nan, I do. But, honest, I'm alright."

Dad signed the forms and, as usual, when one door opens, another smashes you in the face!! Dad called a meeting and then, with all three of us and Nan present, he sprang the news on us! He had secured a big, brand new, three-bedroomed flat, just off Red Cross Way in the

In Spite of Everything . . . .

Borough, and he and Betty were getting married. This would take place in August. We all looked at each other.

Nan, very hurriedly, butted in, "I think you're doing the right thing, Ted. Betty is a very nice woman. Congratulations! If you don't mind, I'd like to talk to the boys, alone." Her eyes were fixed on me. I could sense her saying, be quiet, don't you dare do anything! I got the message.

I could already feel the bottom dropping out of my life. The damned inner rage was beginning to take over!

"Now, you've got to remember, your dad is trying to do the best for you. Me and Granddad are sure of that. You boys have had a difficult life so far but you are growing up fast." She turned to Eddie. "You've started work already, so you should be able to help your dad." Then turning to me. "I can see it in your eyes, Paddy. I know that you are not happy (that was an understatement) but you have only got a couple of years at school before you go to work. They won't eat you and Betty is a very nice lady and will do her best for you. Please, please, have an open mind because I want all three of you to agree." I started to speak, "Tut-tut, let me finish! Michael, you're the youngest. How do you feel about going to live with Dad?"

"I'll still be able to see you, won't I, Nan?" "You silly sod, of course, you will. The Borough is only ten minutes walk away and, funnily, that's where you all came from."

"As long as Eddie and Paddy will be with me, I really don't mind too much. I like being with Dad."

"You know that we'll all miss you. The house will be very quiet once you've gone." She hesitated and looked at me, realising that she might have overstepped the mark. "I want you three to go away and have a talk amongst yourselves. You've got plenty of time but, remember, you must all stay together!" Again, concentrating on me, "Your dad may have made some mistakes. You won't realise it yet but he is a young man and he adores all three of you."

She got up and started to leave the room. "Paddy, I want to talk to you alone. Don't mind, do you, Eddie?" He knew. He was no fool. "No, Nan, that's alright." I followed Nan to the kitchen and there followed one of the most harrowing conversations I would ever have. You may find it hard to understand but the memory is so vivid, that I'm close to tears as I write it down! I not only didn't fancy living with Dad but, in my young mind, I thought I was deserting Nan and I knew that she would never desert me.

"Nan, I'm not leaving here. I don't care what the others do, I'm not going anywhere." Nan was close to tears herself, which made me even madder.

"Paddy, Paddy, please! You, of all the boys, must have noticed that Granddad (who was lying down at the time) is becoming rather ill." I butted in, "What's the matter with him, Nan?" "The doctor said that he's probably had a couple of small strokes and they tend to slow you down." I went to interrupt but she put her hand up. "He won't be getting any better and he'll take up more of my time. He's not very happy about the way things are turning out and stress is the last thing he needs, at this time. He is fully aware of your feelings but," a short pause, "if you boys break apart, it will kill him! You're an intelligent boy. We all have to do things in life that we don't like and you're brave enough to overcome your doubts." How she stopped herself crying, I'll never know. "I'm not leaving you, Paddy, and you won't be leaving me. I love you, you awkward sod! Come on, give us a kiss!" She gave me a hug and it was then that I knew I was beaten! [Apart from the awful moment when Michael told me that his new heart was being rejected, this was the most traumatic conversation I would ever have to endure!!]

She put some money in my hand, gave me a wink and nodded her head towards the window. I didn't need anymore hints. Off I trotted to get her some blind man's.

I was as mad as hell. I didn't know who with exactly but it would take me years to get over that conversation. In a strange way, I always felt a bit sorry for Eddie and Michael because they never shared such intense moments with Nan.

A few weeks later, I was walking home from the club, when Eddie called out, "Wait for me, I'm going home. I'll walk along with you." I didn't know where he'd appeared from but I was to find out later that he had been shadowing me for the past couple of weeks. He was making sure that I wasn't attacked as a reprisal for what had gone on earlier. He was a great big brother.

"I'll come and live with you and Dad. I'm still not very happy and probably never will be but it's for the best. Anyway, it's what Nan wants and that's all that matters." [That was one of the hardest and most harrowing decisions I was to ever make in my life!! But it was the correct one, even though it would cause me much heart ache]

"That's brilliant, Paddy. Mikey will be happy. He's a bit wary of you, you know that, don't you?" "No, not really. What's he got to be wary for? I'd do anything for him, surely he knows that?" "Of course, he does, you silly sod! He worries about how violent you can become. It scares him, that's all."

The school boxing team would not start training until after our summer holidays, which was just as well because my upper gum was taking a time to heal and I wouldn't have passed the medical anyway.

We saw more and more of Aunt Betty and everyone, including Dad, seemed a bit more relaxed. Nan had spread the news!

I knew that like me, she never fully got over that conversation. Sadly, she carried a feeling of guilt. For years to come, as I grew up, I used to make light of it by telling her that I was a bit of a wimp for making such a fuss. She used to give me a funny look.

It was a good summer. I played a lot of cricket and there were the Olympic Games but, unlike today, we had no television so it was purely by the big news features in the cinema that I followed it. I remember Zatopek and Fanny Blankers-Koen but not much else. My interest was the Ashes series against the Australians, I could listen to that on the wireless.

Cousin Jimmy and I went to the Oval a couple of times and we saw Don Bradman (sadly, he was out for a duck), Ray Lindwall, Keith Miller and, of course, our Len Hutton. That was a great time but whoa there! There were a few things going on before that!

A certain wedding!!

Because Cousin Jimmy still spent the summer holidays with us, Betty, who by now was a frequent figure, got to know him quite well. It would be the last we spent with each other in this house and he would also be starting work, early next year.

1948 turned up a few more surprises. The NHS was introduced and the school leaving age was raised to fifteen. This meant that my old school and, of course, Michael's current one, would be making fundamental changes. They would be amalgamating with St Joseph's Catholic School (you'll never believe it), situated in Red Cross Way, the Borough, which meant that he would transfer to St Joseph's because all pupils of eleven and older would be taught there, and the infants of five to eleven would be taught at our old school. Quite simply, it meant that there was now a separate senior and junior school.

Unlike Eddie and me, Michael was unable to progress to a higher level. He wasn't a dunce but his skills were in his hands. He could make anything, whether in wood or metal, and he would be able to make a good living for himself and his family in years to come.

There was (as seems normal) to be a sting in the tail because Michael would now be on his own amongst boys of up to fifteen. Many of these lads knew Eddie and me and there were few rough handfuls amongst them, some of whom despised us both. In truth, I never gave it a moment's thought but Eddie certainly did. Remember, he was the eldest and very protective, even more so in view of the impending changes, which were soon to come about!

Dad provided the money for us to buy new suits. Nan took care of Michael but Eddie and I went to the tailors on our own. Eddie had good taste so Nan thought it about time we looked after ourselves. I don't think she took that decision without good reason. She was ever so slowly letting go.

Dad took us all up to our new flat and, even though I wasn't keen, I had to admit it was very nice. It had three large, bright and airy bedrooms, a big lounge with a large veranda, kitchen, bathroom, toilet and hot and cold running water.

Dad gave us the choice and Eddie thought it a good idea for him and Michael to share the bigger of the bedrooms and I would sleep on my own. There was nothing sinister in this. It was quite simply that he figured that it would be Michael who could become more disturbed and he would be able to keep an eye on him and reassure him if it proved necessary. This proved to be a very wise move!

I could see now why Dad had chosen the holidays to get married and make our move. We would live on the third floor (of five) and we were able to help Dad move in the new furniture. He would bring nothing with him from Nan's, in spite of all her offers.

This was to be a decision which, sadly, went down badly with some of the family. Playing the devil's advocate, I later was of the opinion that whatever he did would be criticised by some!

He was without doubt in a no-win situation. In spite of everything, I did defend him at a future date. Remember he **was** my Dad, and although I criticized him, I would never allow anybody else that privilege. At this moment in time, I had problems of my own!

The wedding took place on a Friday. All three of us were there, as were most of Dad's sisters and their families, plus a contingent from Liverpool. They all knew Eddie and Michael, of course.

Nan came along (only for our sakes), as well as Eileen, Johnny and Uncle Nathan, plus some cousins and a few friends. The wedding took place in the Catholic church! Now, this is where my dad proved to be insensitive! It was in the same church that he had married our mum, not that many years previous and, here's the rub, he was annoyed that Granddad didn't show up to help him celebrate!

There would be problems over that one in a couple of years' time!

After the wedding, there were the usual photographs being taken. Now, honestly, I don't know why, but I refused to be in any of them. I kept Nan company.

We all went back to Aunt Kit's flat (they had just been awarded a beautiful flat themselves and it was just off Long Lane, which was a stone's throw away—one of my throws, anyway!). Nan and the rest didn't follow which really disturbed me.

It took me no longer than five minutes to work out false affection. There were all Dad's relations, the same ones who hadn't given a tinker's fuck about us throughout the war, all fawning over us, pretending we were the loves of their lives. I saw through it immediately. It was for Dad's sake (their big brother) and to cover their guilt. As far as the Liverpool mob went, well, I couldn't understand them and I didn't give a fuck for them anyway. I wasn't staying here!

Dad and Betty were going away for a week and it had been agreed that we would remain with Nan for a further fortnight. This would give Betty a chance to organise her house.

Eddie and Michael (bless them) were lapping it up and, looking at them, I sometimes wished that I could be like them but I wasn't!

I called Eddie over. "Ed, I'm pissing off. I'm not going through all those stupid goodbyes. I'm going back to Nan's."

"Listen to me, Paddy. You'd better go and tell Dad what you're doing. You don't want to upset him." "Yeah, okay, Ed. See you later." Dad seemed very happy with himself and, seeing me approach, changed ever so slightly. "What's that miserable face all about? Not enjoying yourself?" One of these days, he'll feel sorry for taking the piss out of me in public! "Nah, lovely day, Dad, but I've got to get home. I think Nan was a bit upset and Granddad ain't bin too well. I've got to do some things for them. Have a nice holiday. See you in a couple of weeks."

I about-turned and walked straight out of the room (no fuss). I was just about to close the front door behind me, when Betty grabbed my arm. "I can understand you being a bit upset but, please, don't go without at least giving me a kiss and wishing me luck. I love your nanna as well. She's a lovely lady and you are a credit to her. Come on, luv, it won't kill you." I did! It would be the last one!

When I got down the stairs, I took the flower from my buttonhole and chucked it into the corner. Nan was right, she was a decent woman.

Nan must have heard me coming up the stairs. "Is that you, Paddy?" There was a slight alarm in her voice. "Everything alright? Are the others with you?"

"No, Nan, they're staying for a bit longer. There's no problem, it's just a bit too crowded for me. You know what I'm like!" She certainly did! That's why she's worried. "Go upstairs and get changed. You don't want to spoil that nice suit."

Eileen, who was sitting round the table, chipped in, "You look real handsome in that suit, Paddy. You'll have all the girls chasing after you." I went red.

Johnny appeared, "Had enough, Pad? We were having bets on how long you'd stay." Nan turned to him. "What did I tell you?" "I'm only pulling his leg, Mum. You don't mind, do you, Pad?" "I don't give a fuck, John." Nan whacked me for that! I enjoyed the whack, unfortunately, there wouldn't be many more.

Because of all the turmoil, Nan had decided to give hopping a miss this year and Uncle Pat and family had taken up the offer. This would prove to be a complete disaster but would have a significant effect on Michael's life.

The return to school was looming and it was hard to take in that I would be starting my third year. It seemed to have come around very quickly and the summer holidays had whizzed by although, with all the goings on, it was not surprising.

Old Father Time waits for no one and the day I was dreading was almost upon us. Dad had some trouble getting some pieces of furniture and this had delayed the move. I actually returned to school for a week before we moved out. That Saturday lunchtime will stay in my mind forever, well, until I die!

Dad had managed to get one of his cousins to pick us up in a small van. We only had the clothes we wore and had been wearing. Everything else had already been taken to our new home.

Nan was nervously fussing about, as was Eileen. Johnny and Jimmy were out. I don't think they could handle it. Eddie and Michael made a big fuss of saying goodbye. Unfortunately, Michael started to cry. That alone must have broken Nan's heart but she certainly didn't show it!

"Nan, I ain't gonna say goodbye because I'll be back this evening, probably after our tea. I've got to put a few stalls away, so see you later! See you, Eileen!" Then I walked out of the house and didn't look back. If I hadn't done it just like that, I don't think I would have been able to leave. Thankfully I missed the tears.

By the time we'd whizzed up Long Lane and been purposely shaken up in the back, Michael was squealing with laughter. That made it more bearable.

We drove into the flats and stopped in the corner where our stairs were and, as we clambered out, Dad quickly showed us our bike shed. Eddie and I were given keys. The bike shed door opened easily, thankfully it was a large space and our three bikes fitted in easily.

Betty opened the front door and gave us all a hug. Her sister, Maureen, was there, as well. That meant more hugs. Betty fussed around and showed us to our bedrooms, which were well furnished and spotless. There was a built-in wardrobe in each room. Although Eddie's room was bigger than mine, because there were two beds in theirs, I had more room in mine. My school clothes were already hung up.

We all gathered, a bit nervously, in the big well-furnished lounge and that funny time, when nobody wants any silence, passed by. To be honest, these were nervous moments for everyone.

After a short while, Betty and Maureen decided to get some tea ready and disappeared into the kitchen.

"Dad, I'm going round Nan's after my tea. What time do you want me back?"

"What time does Nan usually want you in?" "About nine o'clock."

"Don't you fancy staying in with us tonight, son? You're staying in tonight, ain't you, Ed?" "Yes, Dad, I'll probably go out tomorrow night."

"Whilst getting ready to rife round to see Nan, Dad suddenly blurted out, "I don't think that it's a good idea to go round your Nan's every evening, you should stay in for a couple of nights." How I stopped myself I will never know, but I calmly replied, "You're not gonna stop me are you Dad??" He knew that he was on very thin ice, "Of course not you dopey sod, just thought you might give us a chance now and again." He hesitated, "Don't be late!!"

"I told Nan I'd be back and I've got to see Granddad to sort out tomorrow. I usually give him a hand and he's not been himself lately."

Dad looked glum. "Alright, son, be back sometime near nine o'clock. You've got your shed key, haven't you?" "Yes, thanks, Dad. That's a great shed, by the way." That brought a smile to his face.

Teatime was another very awkward occasion. We all managed to sit round the small kitchen table, a bit too crushed really, and although the grub was all right, there was something missing. It was all too neat and precise and everyone was much too polite and formal. I suppose, given the unusual circumstances, it wasn't surprising.

I couldn't get out of there quick enough. I was on my bike and, within ten minutes, climbing up the stairs.

Johnny looked at me. "Blimey, that didn't take long. Have you come back to aggravate us or have you been chucked out already?"

Nan butted in, "Leave him alone! You all right, son?" "I don't take any notice of him, anyway, Nan! Yeah, everything's okay." I hesitated for a moment. "Mikey's all right now, Nan." "Do you want anything to eat?" "No, thanks. I might do later but now I've got a job to do. See you after I've put the stalls away."

Kit was almost in tears when she saw me. Us leaving had really shocked her but once I'd assured her that everything was sweet[44], her smile returned.

Eileen was in when I returned. She looked up, "Everything all right? Not too bothered, are you?" "No, honestly, it felt a bit strange but no problems. Are you going out tonight?" "No, not tonight. A couple of friends are coming over. Why? Are you staying?" "Until nine o'clock then I'll have to go. Want to play some cards later?" "That'll be a good idea."

Nan gave me something to eat and once Eileen and two of her friends had settled down, we played some cards, whilst listening to AFN (American Forces Network) on the wireless.

"Paddy, it's nearly nine. You'd better be getting back." She never said 'home'. "Have you got lights on that bike because it's getting dark."

In Spite of Everything . . . .

"Yeah, of course, I have! I'll be off then! Thanks for the grub, Nan. See you tomorrow. Bye, Eileen. Oh, Nan, I almost forgot. Tell Granddad I'll see him in the morning. I'll go straight to his shed."

I didn't forget to say goodbye to Eileen's friends but I couldn't hang around. If I'd have stayed much longer, I don't think I would have been able to go. Nan fully understood.

I locked my bike away and climbed the stairs. Everything was new and cold. When I opened the front door, I was surprised to find the hallway in darkness but I could see light coming from the living room. "Hi, hi, anybody home?" There was a muffled reply then Eddie opened the living room door. "Ho, there you are. You've come home then!" He was joking. Dad and Betty were sitting on the settee. "Had a loovely time, son? How's ya nanna?" Dad seemed ever so slightly irritated and said nothing.

"She's okay, thanks, Aunt Bet. She sends her regards. Where's Michael?"

"He's just this minute gone to bed. I shouldn't think he's asleep yet."

"I'll go and say goodnight. Are the lights in the hall broken already?"

Dad answered, "No point in wasting electricity, lighting up the hall and kitchen if we're all in here. I want you to switch the lights off when you're not in a room. Do you think you can manage that?" [There he goes again, sarcastic fucker!] I ignored him!!

"You alright, Mikey?" "That you, Paddy?" He was already half asleep. "Yeah, you look comfy. It looks like a nice bed. Sorry to wake you, see you in the morning, nite, God bless."

I went back into the living room. It was probably my imagination but I felt like an intruder. "Mikey looks comfortable. I won't hang around. I'll get to bed myself. Nite, nite. See you in the morning." I gave Eddie a wave.

Betty spoke up. "You know where all your things are, don't you, son?"
"Yes, thanks. Thanks for everything."

It felt strange laying here in my new bedroom. Once I'd closed my bedroom door, I felt suddenly very alone and it was not a very nice feeling. I could very faintly hear the muffled noises coming from the flat next door because, as it turned out, my bedroom, which was in the corner of the block, backed onto their lounge. There was also the noise of people coming and going but no buses or trams.

These new noises were nothing to do with the fact that I could not sleep. My mind was so active that, at one time, I had to sit up or I think my head would have burst open. I must have made more noise than I thought because suddenly the door opened and Betty called out to me. She sounded very concerned.

"Are you alright, Paddy? You're not too upset are you? I know you miss your nanna but please don't worry, I'll do my best to look after you."

I hesitated for a second. Upset, worried, missing Nan? She obviously didn't know the first thing about me! "Oh, no, thanks for worrying but I've never been able to get to sleep. I'll drop off in a minute. Nite, nite." The darkness ,once she'd closed the door, was a comfort.

The morning was noisy and lively, all scrambling for our breakfast and all following each other getting washed and dressed. It was nice to have hot water on tap and the atmosphere felt more relaxed.

Betty spoke to me and tried to smooth things over. I looked her in the face, "If Dad ever stopped me seeing Nan, he'd never see me again." She knew that I meant it, and I never heard another word on that subject ever again!

I took the opportunity to catch up on some homework because I had a couple of hours spare before I needed to go and help Granddad. Betty, all dressed up, poked her head into the living room. I was seated by the window with all my papers strewn over the dining table. I looked up. "Hurry up and get ready or you'll be late!"

"Late? Late for what?" "Well, church, of course, you silly sod. Mass starts in about twenty minutes so you'd better get your skates on." I looked at her excited face. "I don't go to church." Then returned to my books. "What?! Don't be daft, you must go to Sunday mass! You just must!"

"I don't because I don't believe in it." The poor woman was gob-smacked. It was as though I'd hit her. I could hear the chatter coming from the kitchen. I could hear Eddie, Michael and Dad. Dad appeared, "Now, come on, son. You're upsetting everyone! It won't hurt you to go to church, will it?"

It didn't make the slightest difference to me that Dad never went to church. I hated the Church and certainly wasn't going to any mass.

"Dad, I don't want to upset anybody but everyone seems ready to upset me. If you make me go to church, I'll obey you but I will not, definitely not, go inside the place!"

Dad dropped his hands to his side. "So, you're happy for your brothers to go without you. I thought that you always stuck together!" I chose to ignore that stupid remark! Eddie butted in, "Dad, he's not gone to church since 1946. We understand!" Then jokily, for my benefit, "He's a nuisance, anyway, we're better off without him!"

Dad looked at me, shrugged and walked away. I heard them all going out except Dad, of course. Michael, all done up in his Sunday best, popped in to say goodbye.

"Mikey, when you come back, I'm going to give Granddad a hand. Wanna come round with me? He'll be pleased to see you." "I think Dad is taking me out but I'll ask him. Gotta rush. See you later."

That one incident was the first of many that were sadly to sour my relationship with Betty. She was, as I would find out, a very narrow-minded lady and she liked to impose her ideas on everyone. If ever two people were definitely not made for each other, it was us! [What's the opposite of two peas in a pod??]

I had already forgotten the latest confrontation and was busy finishing my homework, when Dad came into the room. "How's your work going, son?" "Okay, Dad, I've nearly finished." "With all that's been going on, I've not taken much notice of you lately. How are you getting on at school?" "I hold my own, thanks, Dad. But apart from the sport, I don't like the place very much." "Oh, I didn't realise that." "Dad, honest, it doesn't bother me one little bit." He half smiled, "Hmm, it wouldn't, would it? I'm just shooting out for while. When I come back, I'm taking Michael over to your Aunt Kit's. Want to come with us?"

"No, thanks, Dad. I'm helping Granddad with his fish stall. He needs a hand because he seems to be slowing up." (I just couldn't help it). "I think us moving out has affected him badly." That gave him something to think about! "See you later, son."

I heard them walking along the street. They seemed very relaxed and happy which made me feel good, as well. Eddie came in first. "You alright, Paddy?" "Yes, thanks, mate. Where's Mikey?"

"I'm here! What you want?" "I'm going to give Granddad a hand with his stall. Fancy coming with me?" Betty came in, by now very stone-faced. "We're all going to see your Aunt Kit. I thought you'd be coming with us."

"No, thanks, my granddad needs help. He's not very well." I looked at Eddie. "What you doing?" "I'm going with Dad but I'll pop round later."

She seemed very slightly irritated but she was concerned about Granddad. "Give your granddad my love. I like that man very much." (Well she should because without his pressure, I doubt if she would have got married to Dad). "In spite of what you've done this morning, and I still can't forgive you, you're a very good boy helping your granddad out. Bless you!" (Well, it was Sunday).

I finished my homework, packed it all away then got myself ready to go out. Betty looked at me. "You're off then?" "Yeah, I'm on my

In Spite of Everything . . . .

way, now." Then a teeny bit sarcastic, "Are you coming back for your Sunday dinner?" "Yes, of course, I am." She actually smiled. "Your dinner will be ready at one o'clock. Don't be late because we won't wait for you."

That'd be a bit of a rush because Nan always had dinner at half past two. This gave all the men time to get back from the pub (another thing Betty disapproved of).

The shed door was open and, as I jumped off my bike, Granddad came out into the small yard. He looked tired but his old face lit up with a broad smile. "I knew you wouldn't let me down, son. Nice to see you. How's things with you all? How's Mikey?" (Granddad pronounced it "my-kee"). He was his favourite but he would be, wouldn't he? He was the youngest and he was a very lovable boy (unlike his older brother).

"Everything's alright and Michael is settling in great. Eddie's going to pop round later. They've all gone out to visit one of Dad's sisters."

Granddad stopped for a few seconds. He looked me straight in the eyes, "And what about you?" "Nothing bothers me, honest." He chuckled to himself. "Let's get on with it, son. The pub's open in an hour's time." We both worked away in silence, nothing sinister in that, because I also preferred peace and quiet. I must have some of his genes!

The stall was now ready and it looked a picture, everything displayed in a clean and tidy way. We were both happy! The stall had only been set for a couple of minutes when I saw Eddie strolling down Melior Street towards us. "Here comes Eddie!" Granddad looked up and a big smile creased his face.

"How ya doing, Granddad? He's not been driving you mad, has he?" "Hello, Eddie, of course not. I know how to handle him. How are you, son? Still enjoying going to work?" "The work's not too bad, Granddad, but I like the money every week." The pub had just opened and a few of Granddad's mates had already gone in. There were also a few customers lining up. "I'll serve for you, if you like. That'll give you a chance to have a pint. I know that fucker won't do any serving for you." Eddie was dead right there! That's the only thing I wouldn't do for Granddad. I didn't mind getting ready for him and I would clear up but not serve!

Eddie was in his element. He was good with the customers and they loved him. Time flew by! "Paddy, we'll have to be on our way. It'll take us a quarter of an hour to get back and we can't be late on our first Sunday. That'll be rude."

"I'll go and get Granddad. I forgot you are on foot because I've got my bike. Fancy a back-saddle?" "Great idea but I'll pedal, you sit at the back." That was agreed then!

Granddad appeared, "Thanks, boys. Got to get back early, have you?" By now, I wasn't too happy. "Betty likes to have dinner at one o'clock on Sundays, I don't know what that's all about. You gonna be alright without us? "Yes, of course, I am. Don't be silly. Johnny'll be here soon. He'll take care of me." He said that last remark with a smile.

"Will I see you next week, boys?" "You'll see me tonight, Granddad." With that, I hopped on the saddle and Eddie peddled us home.

"Wow, that's good timing. I'm just about to put your dinners out." Then turning to me, "How's your granddad?" "Well, he's alright but he's slowing up a bit. I don't know how long he'll be able to manage that stall." I paused for a moment. Shall I? Shall I? "I didn't want to leave him on his own today because he has to stay until two o'clock. That's why Nan used to have dinner at half past two." There, I've said it! "I like to have dinner at a proper time that gives me time to clear away and have a nice afternoon with your dad."

Dad then opened his mouth. "Them's the rules, son." I only wish that he didn't have that sheepish grin on his face. It had probably escaped his memory that since he'd been home from the army, he'd only sat down and had no more than half a dozen Sunday dinners with us. He seemed very happy to let Nan and Granddad take care of us while he was pissing it up with his mates. What a fucking hypocrite!

The sad thing (as far as I was concerned) was that he was a very nice man and he thought the world of us three. I only wished he was a little bit different. Once again the food was all right, very basic. She wouldn't cook roast potatoes because it mucked up her oven so we had meat, boiled spuds and plenty of vegetables. It was all very bland. The kitchen was spotless because she washed and cleared away as soon as the cooking had finished. It all reminded me of eating in that canteen in Newcastle. It wasn't bad but so different from Nan's.

I would later find out that Betty was not a keen or good cook. She just went through the motions. On the other hand, we certainly didn't starve.

To be honest, we all spent a pleasant afternoon with Dad helping me build my Meccano and helping Michael with his model-making. He was good with his hands. That's who Michael took after although to be honest, we could all turn our hand to most things. It's in the genes!

"Alright to go out, ain't it, Dad?" He looked uneasy. "Do you have to? We thought you'd stay in tonight. Remember, school in the morning."

"I'm only going round Nan's. I haven't seen her today and I want to know how Granddad got on." I let that sink. "Why? You don't mind, do you?" I noticed the slightest of glances towards Betty. "No! No, son, of course. Be careful on your bike and don't be late home." Betty didn't look too happy. "What about yus tea?" "Oh, don't worry. Nan'll look after me, I'm sure. Thanks anyway, Auntie."

Nan was pleased to see me but Granddad had already gone to bed. "When you turned up today, you made your granddad's day. You know that, don't you?" I didn't but it made me very happy.

Uncle Jim was also indoors and, with him, his girlfriend, Marie. She was a real beauty and, like Jimmy, had really dark hair. They made a handsome couple. This was the first time I'd actually met her. She made me some sandwiches and they were the daintiest I'd ever had. She cut the bread very thin, actually resembling today's thin-cut bread. I will never forget the look on her face, as I demolished them, half at a time. We laughed about that many times in future years, especially when she came up against Eddie. He was a real fucker, because he would eat a whole round in one gulp!!

Nan always went over the pub on Sunday evening, where there were always friends and relatives. Sometimes her older sister, Mary, would be there. She was about ten years older and she would domineer her! It was strange to see because Nan was certainly no shrinking violet, but they were very close, being the sole survivors of a family of nine. They lost three brothers in the First World War; the rest had just passed away.

I walked Nan over to the pub. "Goodnight, Nan. Thanks for the tea. I won't see you tomorrow, I've got club. See you Tuesday night." She gave me a peck on the cheek. "Mind how you ride that bike. Goodnight, son." A slight pause. "How's Michael? No problems?" "No. Eddie takes care of him but he seems to be alright, anyway."

She waved and disappeared into the pub. As I rode home down Long Lane, my mind wandered a bit. I was surprised how little my life had actually changed and the fact that it all seems to have gone so smoothly. I was reasonably happy and Nan seemed satisfied with the outcome although these were early days. I did have a few worries about Betty because I knew that she was a good woman but, unfortunately, a bit like me. Domineering! This would create problems, which was a shame.

Getting to school was even easier because I could catch the tram just across the road, which took me direct to Vauxhall, where I caught my bus. This undisturbed journey gave me more time to revise, which was just as well because the lessons were getting harder. I had less than two years of schooling and was taking various 'O' levels, so had a lot of work to get through.

We all settled into a normal routine although a bit different from what had our lives had been, whilst living with Nan. Betty worked and didn't get home until after five and Dad, because he started at five o'clock in the morning, always had an afternoon sleep. This meant that Michael came home to a virtually empty house and, unless I had sports or detention, I was also home before Betty. This made for a very cold house. No warm greeting. It took some getting used to.

I did sometimes feel for Betty because, as soon as she got home, she had to prepare our tea and, as a consequence, everything was rushed. She relied on quantity and not quality. Dad was beginning to feel the financial strain of bringing up a family. Luckily for him, Eddie was now giving Betty housekeeping money (a practice which seems to have died out in my family, anyway!).

My week was divided up between going to my club and, on the off nights, spending time with Nan, Eileen and Johnny. I never stayed in. As I write this, my mind dwells on the point that this was a bit rude on my part but, at the time, I was a young teenager and through no choice of mine, my life had been torn apart. I desperately needed to hang on to the life I had become used to. It was no surprise, therefore, that my lifestyle would create tension and confrontation.

Besides playing football for the school team, I was deeply involved in the boxing. I received a bit of a knock back when the doctor, who examined us for fitness to fight, would not give me the go-ahead just yet. He was still unhappy with the gap in my front teeth and the scarring on my gum. There was one thing in my favour, being that my upper teeth were overcrowded and the loss of one gave the others a chance to spread out and close the gap. It was closing very quickly and, I mean, quickly. I trained with even more purpose but wasn't able to take part in the upcoming inter-school show. I helped out, acting as a second.

The weekend was soon upon us and all through Saturday, I had been thinking about Granddad. "Nan! You know tomorrow, will it be alright for me to have Sunday dinner with you?" She looked a bit startled. "Oh, Paddy, whatever for? There's no problems are there?" "No, Nan, course not. It's just that I had to leave Granddad to clear up on his own last Sunday because Betty gets dinner ready at 1 o clock. That's all, honest!" She thought for a few moments. "Make sure it's okay with your dad. I don't want you causing any trouble, young man. Ya folla?" "I'll make it sweet. Anyway, I'm off now, Nan. Don't forget to tell Granddad that I'll see him in the morning." A kiss and a cuddle then I was off.

"Blimey, bit early for you, ain't it? What? Your Nan got rid of you?" There it was again, that hint of sarcasm, mixed with ridicule. One day . . . one day . . .

"Hello, Mike, fancy a game of cards? I'll teach you to play cribbage, if you like." "Yes, please. I'll get the cards." "And the board," I reminded him.

Dad looked up. "Alright for me to join in? You can teach me, as well. It's strange but I never learned how to play that game." "Course, you can. What about you, Aunt Bet? Want to join in?" "No, thanks, Paddy. I don't like card games. Don't mind me, I've got some knitting to do and that'll keep me busy. Thanks for asking."

We had a very pleasant evening, although I did have some difficulty in explaining the scoring to Michael. Sums were not his best subject and 15-2, 15-4, etc were a problem for him.

Michael seemed very happy and it was then that it dawned on me that I had been ignoring him. I had been so caught up with my own issues, that I had not considered how he was feeling or how he was getting on in his new school and, with Eddie now at work, it was my duty to look out for him. This I would now make sure I did.

I started off asking Dad if he could join my club because he was now old enough. I promised I'd look after him and make sure we weren't home late. I also suggested that he should come with me to spend a little time with Nan and Granddad. Surprisingly, Dad agreed. I think the clincher was when I said that I would stay in with him from time to time. I felt a little happier even though I was still a little bit annoyed with myself for not thinking of this earlier.

They were all busy getting ready for church and I was surprised when Betty tried to persuade me to go with them. I point blankly refused, which made her very upset, shaking her head and huffing and puffing. She liked to get her own way!

"Dad, will it be alright for me to stay and help Granddad, like I used to? It'll mean that I won't be able to get back for dinner but Nan will do dinner for me, then I'll come back straight after. He is really finding it hard lately. He needs my help."

"You won't be able to do that every Sunday or you'll never have dinner with your brothers. Can't Johnny or Jimmy help him, sometimes?"

"I'll have a word with Johnny. He'll help." "You don't leave me a lot of choice, do you, son? I'll let Aunt Betty know."

"Thanks, Dad. I'll be away in a minute. See you later."

That Sunday went like clockwork. Granddad was very grateful for my help. I had a beautiful dinner at Nan's and Johnny was more than willing to take over from me. "Paddy, you don't have to worry about your granddad. I'm more than willing to help him every Sunday. You go and enjoy yourself." "John, I really want to help him. We'll do it on alternate Sundays." I couldn't help smiling as I said it. "Betty's a shit cook and it gives me a chance to have a proper Sunday dinner." We agreed but sadly our arrangement was short-lived.

I signed Michael in and he was remembered. The gymnastics supervisor was very happy. Michael fitted in like a well-worn pair of shoes. He was very likeable and brilliant at gymnastics. Eddie used to make a show, now and again, and it was great to have all three of us together. Whatever could go wrong?!

The past few months had passed in a blur and, in spite of my reservations, life wasn't that bad. I was getting used to the clinical aspect of everyday living. The food Betty prepared was just about edible but the flat was well furnished, clean and comfortable, and I was living with Eddie and Michael. Sadly, Dad and I were opposites and this could never change. I liked Dad very much but could never love him.

Granddad was slowing up but Nan and the rest of the family were good. Uncle Jim was now engaged to be married and he and Marie were getting wed in the spring.

Christmas was now upon us and luckily, for our family anyway, there was a bit more money about. This meant that things were a bit more festive although there was still rationing in force. With half our family working in the docks, we had access to more than most.

The markets were buzzing, which meant that Eddie and I were very busy, which enabled us to make a nice bit of pocket money. Thank God for the ladies and their insatiable desire for nylons, although God had very little to do with it. Uncle Nathan and the thousands of Yanks were our benefactors.

Michael had now taken over my old job of wheeling back the market stalls at close of business. This had double benefit because it meant that he saw a bit more of Nan, Granddad and family, and Kit with her Michael were thrilled to see him again.

This Christmas would unfortunately throw up another confrontation!

My present from Dad and Betty had been an addition to my Meccano set and I was now able to erect really complicated models. Eddie had bought me a wind-up electric motor, which meant I could make working cranes, for example. Dad was very helpful and we enjoyed ourselves and it all seemed like a nice family Christmas.

I can't remember whether it was Boxing Day or the day after, but Dad said that he would be visiting his older sister, Charlotte, and would like us to come with him. Since it was Christmas, I agreed to go along with him. I thought it a bit strange when we left the house without Betty and it was obviously prearranged.

As we strolled along, Dad seemed just a little nervous. I thought it may be over the quite-heated row that I'd had with Betty about not attending Christmas Day mass. But it had nothing to do with it!

We were about halfway to Charlotte's when Dad started out. "I've been wanting to get you boys alone because there's an important matter I want to ask you about." He paused for a while, obviously having difficulty getting his words out. "We've all been living together for the past four months and I hope you're all very happy." We *all* reassured him with a yes. Again, a small pause. "You all refer to Aunt Betty and this is becoming very embarrassing for me and her because, remember, we are married and it has become very awkward, as far as our neighbours are concerned. She is your step-mother after all." Another pause then the bombshell! "I'd like you to call her mum!"

I can't recall whether my first reaction was anger, hatred, pity or just numbness. Immediately, Eddie answered. "That's alright, Dad. Of course, I will," closely followed by Michael. "I do already, Dad. Well, sometimes, anyway." I walked on in silence. Why, oh, why does this shit seem to follow me all the time? Will it never end? Why does Dad always adopt that slight sarcastic tone when talking to me?

"You're a bit quiet. What? You lost your tongue?" I stopped and turned to face him. Eddie put himself very close to me.

"I ain't never gonna call her mum, or anybody else for that matter. She's not my mum! She died in the war, don't you remember?"

Dad went white and made a grab for me but, because of Eddie, missed.

"You spiteful, ungrateful fucker! After all she has done for you and that's all the thanks she gets? I might have known that you would be so fucking awkward." I stayed calm. "I'm not ungrateful and I do, very much, appreciate her hard work but Dad, she's not my mum and I swore to myself that I'd never mention that fucking word again!" How I stopped the tears, I'll never know. "I still miss our mum and I wish every day that she was alive but she's not! And every time I hear the word **mum** it breaks my heart", I screamed out. "Can't you fucking understand that!!"

I had never told anybody that before! I think Dad was almost in tears. Michael certainly was. "Sorry, Ed. Sorry, Mikey. I've got to go." I dashed away. Dad called out, "You don't have to run away, for God's sake. Will you be coming home?" I turned, "Yes, Dad, I'll see you later." They all looked a sad picture and I almost went back but Eddie called out, "Don't worry, Paddy. See you at home later."

"Hello, son. I'm surprised to see you this early." A pause. "Anything wrong?"

"No, Nan. Dad, Eddie and Mike are going over to visit Aunt Charlotte. I didn't fancy it. Hello, John. Hello, Eileen."

Nan looked at me. Unfortunately, she could read me like a book. "Paddy, come into the front room. I want to talk to you." I followed her. "Now, come on, son. What's the problem? You'll have to tell me, sooner or later. Get it off your chest before you start me worrying."

I was trapped and it didn't take me long to realise it. "It's nothing really, Nan." "Then why do you look so upset?" I didn't realise it was that obvious (I don't think I'd better take up acting!).

"Dad has asked me to call Betty mum." (That was hard to get out). Nan was motionless. "She *is* your step-mother now."

"Yeah, I know that but she's not my mum and I ain't ever gonna call her that and I don't care what happens." The door suddenly opened and Eileen came striding in. "Sorry, Mum, but I knew that something was up and I couldn't help but ear-wig. They've got no right to ask him to call her that." Even she couldn't bring herself to say the word mum. "Now, please, Eileen, I'll take care of it. You'll only make matters worse."

Eileen looked as mad as hell, which was very unusual. "Don't let Annie know. She'll go potty. You know what's she's like." She left us alone.

"Paddy, look at me. Don't be rude to your dad or Betty but you just do what you think best and what makes you comfortable. It'll all turn out for the best, you'll see." She seemed to relax a bit. "Now, forget it and come up to the kitchen. Johnny will start to get fidgety."

I didn't stay all afternoon but made my way home. Wonder what sort of reception I'll get? It was as though nothing had happened apart from Dad, who was slightly uneasy (it could have been my imagination). Betty seemed to be extra nice to me and the boys were as pleased as punch.

We spent a very happy day together.

That night, I had only been in a bed a couple of minutes, when there was a tap on my bedroom door and it opened very slightly. "Paddy, are you still awake?" I looked over and Betty was peeping through.

"Yes, what's up?" She crept in. "Are you alright, son? I know you got a bit upset earlier. Please, boy, I don't ever want to harm or upset you. I really do understand your feelings and if it makes you happy, please call me Betty, but please, not Aunt. You are probably too young to understand but it's very embarrassing for me, especially in front of our neighbours. Are you happy with that?"

"Yes, of course. Thanks for talking to me." "Goodnight, son. Sleep well. See you in the morning." She bloody well kissed me on the cheek before leaving!

Dad never spoke to me about it again. When I returned to school, by now wearing my brand new blazer, which Eddie had mostly paid for, I would received some very good news. The examining doctor had given me a clean bill of health, which meant that I could box again.

I think I should explain why Eddie had paid for my blazer. He didn't like the school issue because it didn't fit very well, so he paid the extra money to have a tailor-made, bespoke version. He reckoned that I looked the business in my new blazer. He was a good big brother. What did surprise me, however, was that Dad never became involved nor even commented.

I had been training hard and had been picked to box for the school in the upcoming competition, which was to take place at Latchmere Baths. Eddie was so excited that I thought he'd burst. The evening of the bouts was soon here and both Eddie and Johnny had turned up to watch.

What a surprise awaited me! I walked into the communal changing rooms and there, just a few paces in front of me, a group of lads all togged up for boxing. There, in their midst, the joker I'd given a belting to those couple of years ago. He caught sight of me and looked very hostile. "What you doing here, flash bollocks? I thought you'd run away." An official immediately jumped in. "Hey, you, I don't want any of that sort of nonsense in here. Wait 'til you're in the ring. Now, come on, be lively and get prepared and gloved up."

"See you in the ring, please God!" That's all I had to say before being ushered away. My instructor cornered me and reminded me that aggression was good but only when controlled and only in the ring.

Once we'd been weighed in and examined again by the tournament doctor, we received our list of opponents. I was praying that I would face "Loud Mouth". It was not to be, however. The lad I would be boxing looked a tough boy and he looked as though he had a bit of colour in him. He was obviously very friendly and well known by the gang of lads because they all kept pointing and laughing (what did they know that I didn't?).

I was fourth on and boxing from the blue corner. It was the noise that the crowd made that first struck me and, to be honest, it made me feel a little uneasy. I relaxed a bit during our introduction because I could hear Eddie's voice, above all others.

In Spite of Everything . . . .

The referee brought us together and it was obvious that my opponent was very popular. I couldn't wait for the bell! We met in the middle, touched gloves and then away we went.

I'm not going to go through round by round but I found it surprisingly easy. I landed punch after punch and could feel the counters were getting less and less and were hardly hurting at all. My opponent was becoming quite distressed and I was not enjoying myself. Thankfully the ref stopped the bout halfway through the final round (the third).

The seconds quickly got the boy (who I was later to find out called Joey) back into his corner and onto his stool. The ref held my hand up and congratulated me.

I immediately went over to see Joey, who had already recovered and we embraced each other. I could hear Eddie's voice.

I was examined again then allowed to shower and change. Another surprise awaited me. I was almost finished getting dressed when Joey and his pals (Loud Mouth being one of them), came over to me. Billy (AKA Loud Mouth) spoke out. "Er, mate, that was a great fight. We all thought that our Joey would give you a belting. Wanna shake hands and forget all that other nonsense?" Some officials were eyeing us intently. I stood up, smiled and stuck out my hand. "Thanks for the fight, Joey. Maybe we'll come up against each other another time." The lads burst out laughing. "Not fucking likely. You can piss off." Joey had a big, wide, bruised smile.

Our school lost six to four but my mate, Bunton, had also won his fight. Once I told my instructor that my big brother and an uncle were waiting for me, I was allowed to leave. "Well done, O'Donovan. You looked really classy in there. Those hands of yours are like greased lightening. See you in the gym."

Johnny was pleased but Eddie, he was over the moon. "Paddy, the way you took that bloke apart! Well, it was top class. I bet even you wouldn't fancy getting in the ring with him, would you, John?" Johnny just smiled. "He's a bit useful, that's for sure."

At the Borough, we went our separate ways. "Well done, Paddy. I'll let your nan and granddad know how you got on. See you later." We strolled up Marshalsea Road in silence. Eddie suddenly said, "Me and Mikey will never refer to Betty as mum when we're talking to each other, but we'll probably call her that. Are you comfortable with that? And give me an honest answer, not one that you think I want to hear."

"Ed, I really don't care what you call her. She's not a bad woman. She came in and spoke to me the other night and she's quite happy. You know what I'm like and, as long as us three are together," I hesitated, "I don't give a fuck!"

He put his arm round my shoulder, "Great fight, Paddy, great fight. I can't wait for the next one. I'm definitely gonna bring Mikey along."

Things were already buzzing around in my head. Things that would give Eddie a very big surprise! I didn't bother changing onto the bus at Vauxhall anymore. When the crowd of lads got on, there was now lots of waving and friendly chatter. I called out to Billy, "How's Joey getting on?" "Thanks to you, he's got a big headache and he's taking a couple of days off school. He'll be alright. He's a tough fucker. Thanks for asking. How are you?" "A bit bruised but otherwise okay." I went back to my homework.

As I pulled up and placed my bike against the alley wall, I cannot explain why, but I had an odd feeling. I let myself in, calling out as I climbed the stairs. It was too quiet and I immediately felt uncomfortable. The kitchen door opened. There was Marie with a worried look on her face. "Hello, Paddy. They said you'd be coming round. Now, don't worry, but your granddad has been taken to hospital. We think that he might have had a stroke. Your nan and all the others are at the hospital."

"Hospital? Which hospital? He's not gonna die, is he?" "Now, don't be silly. He's in the best place." "Marie! What hospital?" "Guy's but Nan said for you to wait here with me. Someone will be coming home soon."

In Spite of Everything . . . .

I about-turned. "I'm going up there. It'll only take me ten minutes." Marie realised that there was no point trying to stop me. "Don't go mad on that bike of yours. Your nan won't be happy if you hurt yourself." I only just heard the end of her words. I was off, pedalling like mad. That was a terrible bike ride; my mind was in turmoil.

I pulled into the main entrance and the first person I saw was Johnny. He waved frantically at me. "Paddy, Paddy, over here!" I headed towards him. "I've been waiting for you. We knew you'd show up. Who told you? Marie?" "Yeah. How is he, John?" "I won't lie to you, he's very ill but they think they've got him stabilised. Follow me and I'll take you to the ward." He glanced at my bike. "You'd better shift that thing out of the doorway before someone trips over it."

Eileen and Jimmy were seated in the corridor, just outside the ward. Eileen was the first to get up. "You won't be able to go in, Paddy, but Nan and Aunt Anne are with him and Granddad is conscious, which is a good sign. Come and sit down beside me." She and Jimmy brought me up to date and explained all that had happened.

"I told Nan the other day that he hasn't been his usual self on Sunday morning."

"Yes, I know you did. We were all aware of his condition but didn't ever think that it'd come to this."

I took them all by surprise when I suddenly jumped up and walked straight into the ward. The nurses looked startled but, being a small ward, I saw Nan and Annie straightaway. Granddad was propped up in bed with lots of tubes all over him. He looked very sick. Nan turned towards me with tearful eyes. She put her finger in front of her mouth (meaning, be quiet). As I reached the side of the bed, Nan took my arm. Out of the corner of my eye, I could see the ward sister bearing down on me but I kept my gaze firmly fixed on Granddad. I couldn't tell if he even recognised me, which was very upsetting. The sister whispered in my ear. "You'll have to come with me. Only two allowed and certainly no children." She never knew how fortunate she was (calling me a child). Nan beckoned for me to behave myself and follow the sister.

I was back in the corridor. Eileen said, "You're a sod. You're not allowed in the ward. You're getting us all in trouble." At least I'd made Jimmy and Johnny laugh! Eventually, Annie came out and Jimmy took her place. She planted a large kiss on my face. "I think he recognised you, Paddy. You certainly made him a bit restless."

I was ordered home by Eileen, telling me that I couldn't stay all night and that Dad would be getting worried (there were no mobile phones in those days). I reluctantly agreed and left them there.

As I walked into our flat, Dad immediately appeared in the lounge doorway. He looked very angry. "What sort of time do you call this? Where the blazes have you been till this time? We've all been worried sick. Eddie has gone out to look for you."

"Sorry, Dad, I've been up Guy's. Granddad has had a stroke and he might die. I lost track of time."

Betty appeared. "Jesus, Mary!! Is he very bad?" "I don't really know but all the family are with him. I just don't know."

Dad looked like he'd wish the ground would open up and take him. "I'm really sorry, son. I didn't know. Is your nan alright?"

"That's alright, Dad, I understand. You know what Nan's like, she just gets on with things but she looked worried."

That night, it took ages to get to sleep. Eddie had popped in to see me and ask about Granddad. He said he'd go to the hospital after finishing work.

I got up, as usual, dressed and had breakfast. The talk was all about Granddad, of course. I left the house to make my way to school but turned left, towards Guy's. I had to find out how he was.

In Spite of Everything . . . .

"Hello, Paddy, didn't expect to see you this early. No school today?!" "Hello, Uncle Pat. How's Granddad?" "He's had a good night and he's awake. Want to see him?" I was past him in a flash and through the ward doors. I got some alarmed looks from the duty nurses but I didn't take any notice of them. Granddad was propped up on a great pile of pillows. He had some colour back on his cheeks and even managed to give me a weak smile. "Mornin', Granddad. What do ya think you're doing in here? You can't stay here too long, you've got to open your stall on Friday night." Again, that very weak smile. It was only then that I noticed Aunt Anne half asleep in a chair, round the opposite side of the bed.

"You been here all night, Aunt?" "Hello, son. Not exactly all night but your nan wouldn't leave Granddad alone, so we made her go home for a while and I got here at about five o'clock." We were interrupted by a large staff nurse. "Young man, you just can't barge in here whenever you feel like it. There are prescribed visiting hours, especially for children."

"Sorry, nurse, but, firstly, I'm not a child and, secondly, that's my granddad lying there and I'll come and see him whenever I please."

I think she was taken off guard by my stare and determination. Uncle Pat put his hand on my shoulder. "Paddy, I know you're upset but don't cause a fuss in here. Besides your granddad, there are a lot of very sick men in here. Say goodbye to him and give him a chance to have some rest." He gave me a cheeky wink. "Staff is in charge and we must all do as we're told."

I said goodbye to Granddad and Aunt Anne, who had difficulty in keeping a straight face. "Bit of a fucking battleaxe, ain't she? She oughta be careful how she speaks to me! Anyhow, Granddad looks much better, don't you think?"

"Yeah, much, but you'd better calm yourself down, son. We certainly don't want any aggro in here!" "Yeah, you're right. I'll be on my way now to school. I'll probably get a bollocking for being late. See you later." "Oh, Paddy, before you go, I'm gonna run Granddad's stall for him while he's in here. Do you fancy giving me a helping hand to set it all up on Friday because you know the way he likes it?"

"Yeah, of course, I'll probably see you before then, so we can make arrangements."

I got some very funny looks, as I went through the school gates, but I quickly made my way to my classroom. I rapped on the door and went in. All eyes were on me. The tutor looked very angry. "What do you think you are doing, barging in here in the middle of my class? Get out and wait outside!"

I about-turned, closed the door behind me and hung around outside during the remainder of the lesson. I heard the tutor setting some homework, so I knew the particular lesson had finished. Very shortly, the door opened. "What sort of time do you call this? You're more than two hours late. I hope that you have a sound reason for your lateness."

"I've been up the hospital to see my granddad. He's not very well."

"Did you receive permission?" "No, sir, it was all very sudden."

"You must understand that you just cannot decide, willy-nilly, to take time off from school just to visit sick relatives. I am giving you a detention. Report to the detention room tomorrow night, after school has finished." He gave me a smirk. "You know where that is, no doubt." "Yes, sir." I could have killed him.

That evening, Eddie and I went to visit Granddad and, fortunately, he was improving rapidly. He was having difficulty speaking and, although they had him out of bed, one of his legs wasn't working properly but Nan had been told that there should be improvement but it would take time.

On the way back home, I broke the bombshell news to Eddie.

"I've decided that I'm not going to box anymore tournaments, Ed." He stopped dead in his tracks. "What?! What the hell do you mean? I can't believe you! What's the matter? You must be upset over Granddad. You'll get over it, you'll see!" "Ed, it's got nothing to do with Granddad, I promise you! I'd made my mind up straight after my fight the other evening. I didn't enjoy it, Ed. Unless I've got a very good reason, I don't enjoy beating someone's head in and even more than that, I ain't gonna do it for the pleasure of a crowd of people! I don't know. I'll still carry on training and sparring but no more tournaments."

"Well, I know that it's no point in arguing with you. It sounds like you've made your mind up but, nevertheless, it's a crying shame because you looked so good. We could hear other people talking about you but, more to the point, Dad was coming to watch your next fight. He'll be very disappointed." We carried on home in near silence, with Eddie shaking his head, murmuring, "What a waste. What a waste."

We got home and after Eddie had brought Michael, Dad and Betty up to date, he turned to Dad. "Paddy's got some bad news, Dad." Dad looked a bit startled.

"Leave off, Ed! It's not that bad. Dad, it's only that I'm not going to fight in anymore boxing shows, that's all!" Dad looked a bit puzzled. "Wh . . . why not, boy? Why not? I thought you enjoyed boxing." "I do, Dad, very much so but I don't enjoy bashing people for fun. I'm not an entertainer." He shook his head. "God help me, son, I don't think I'll ever, ever be able to make you out." With that, Betty chirped up, "Well, I'm glad. I hate boxing and think it should be banned. Good on you, boy!"

That next evening, I decided to ignore the detention. I thought it was unfair anyway and I wanted to get home and get up to the hospital. Fuck 'em!!

Granddad was continuing to improve. Nan was happy, I was happy, as were all the family!

After morning assembly, I was ordered to the Headmaster's office. Once in his office, I received a severe lecture about not obeying the school rules and making matters worse by not doing my detention. I gave my side of the story, ending by saying that I thought the punishment unfair. I might as well have been talking to thin air. I was given six strokes of the cane on my hand. I was given the choice of backside or hand but there was no way that I was going to bend over! No way! It stung a bit but I very soon got over that. At least that ended the matter!

I knew that the next day would be a bit awkward because I had boxing training and I was about to break the bad news to our trainer. I still badly wanted to carry on sparring and training but I was worried about his reaction. He and the other trainers and the rest of the boys were totally shocked and disbelieving but I wasn't about to change my mind!

"I can't pretend to understand you, O'Donovan, but I respect your decision. It's a crying shame though! Of course, you can stay with us, you don't mind getting into the ring and sparring, do you?" "Thank you, sir, thanks very much. Yes, sir, I'd love to spar with the boys but I'll hold my punches a bit. Is that gonna be alright?" "Yes, of course. You can teach a few of the younger boys a few tricks."

That was one of the happier moments at my school. I didn't realise it then but I would benefit in years to come. The training I did, where I threw very few punches but made sure I never got hit, was a real benefit for our school team and good for me. I was offered a chance to help out in the corner during competitions but I politely refused. I hated the screaming audience! Supposedly, 'fight fans'!

A couple of weeks passed by in a flash but, luckily, Granddad kept improving and Nan was given the good news. He could leave hospital and come home, unfortunately, he was unable to walk properly. His right arm was very weak and, added to all this, he was finding it hard to talk. He would need a lot of care and, as an unexpected bonus, Nan would have plenty of time to help him, all because we three were no longer living with them. It's funny how sometimes things do turn out for the good. There would be another slice of good fortune coming my way, as well!

I'd shown Uncle Pat the ropes and helped him set up Granddad's fish stall but he naturally wanted his two sons, Jimmy and Patsy, to help him on Sundays. I didn't mind that much because it gave me extra free time.

"Mike, I want to have a chat with you. Got a minute?" "Yeah, course I 'ave. What's the problem?" "Granddad's having trouble rolling his cigarettes and you know how fussy he is? He always wanted you to roll them, remember?" "Yeah, of course." "Well, now that he's not very well, you're gonna have to get round there a bit more often and take care of things for him. It always makes his day when he sees you, anyway."

"No trouble, Paddy. I'll ride round there straightway." I don't want to give the impression that Michael wasn't close to Nan and Granddad (much the reverse actually) but he was a bit young and, sometimes, didn't think too deeply (unlike yours truly!) but he didn't need to be told twice!

This would be my last full year at school. The year, in fact, when I could legally leave but Nan had promised that I would stay on and take my 'O' level exams. Something that I had been reminded of, by the school, on many occasions.

They need not have bothered. I would keep Nan's promise without fail! Things were about to conspire against me in the coming months, which would certainly put a strain on that promise.

Once I'd put out Kit's stalls and helped stock it, both Tower Bridge Road and the Blue Anchor, I would help Granddad write out his horse racing bets. He was settling down now although still needed help coping with the stairs but, now the weather was improving, Uncle Jim had arranged for a wheelchair, which was put outside in the alleyway. This allowed him to get some fresh air and meant that he could be wheeled over to the pub. He still had difficulty speaking although, in his frustration, he would swear and cuss quite a lot. He managed to get those words out but we all understood! His hands were still very unsteady.

He liked to have multiple bets, i.e. doubles, cross doubles and accumulators (Phillip-a-do-lah). This meant that for a relatively small wager, he had lots of horses to follow.

I used to run his bets over to our Uncle Terry (no betting shops at that time) and I knew that this type of betting caused him nightmares but, to be fair, very profitable because they rarely won.

On Sunday mornings, I used to go through the paper with Granddad, studying the results and every now and again, some of his doubles and trebles would come up. Granddad used to love it. When I reckoned out exactly what he had to come, I then had to go round and collect his winnings, straightaway, no hanging about! I was sworn to secrecy, never to let Nan know what he'd won (or lost).

I always gave Terry's settler the betting slip and the exact amount due. He soon realised that I never made a mistake. "Er, Paddy, give us a minute before you dash off. How's Uncle Pat (my granddad) getting on? They been offered that ground floor flat, yet?"

"Yeah, as a matter of fact, Nan's only just received a letter from the council and there's a nice ground floor place, available in six weeks' time, and thanks for asking. They're all okay. See you later."

"Hey, whoa there a minute! There's something else I want to talk to you about. You seem to be able to reckon those complicated bets out. What about giving me a hand on Sunday morning, helping old Charlie out and doing some settling for me? We can get very busy and the punters can get a little bit impatient and it's taking the piss a little out of the plod, if a crowd is left hanging about. I'll pay you well. It's a nice little earner. You interested?"

I gave it about two seconds thought. "Yeah, love to. When do you want me to start?"

In Spite of Everything . . . .

"What about next Sunday? Nine o'clock. Meet me here." "See you at nine. Wait till I tell Granddad." "Give them my regards and tell them I'll pop in to see them during the week. Be lucky!"

They were all up and about when I got back with Granddad's winnings and I couldn't wait to give my good news. Johnny was amazed that not only was I able to handle that particular job, but also had the confidence to take it on. Nan didn't quite understand it but she was ever so proud.

"I'm popping over to your stall, Granddad. Do you want me to bring anything back for your tea?" Nan gave me a list. "You gonna write it down, Paddy?" "No need, Nan. I'll remember what you want. See ya."

Cousin Jim was pleased to see me but I felt that he was a bit embarrassed. I put him at ease straightaway. "Thank God you've taken over this job, Jim, because I would have been in trouble juggling my Sunday mornings because I've got a job with Uncle Terry. You know? The bookie?"

I explained what had gone on to Uncle Pat and that put everyone at ease. I pulled their legs a bit. "Make sure you get your display laid out properly. I'll tell Granddad if you don't." I hung around for a while, mainly chatting to Jimmy, because now that he was at work, I didn't see that much of him. Uncle Pat parcelled me up Nan's order and just as I was about to ride off, Uncle Nathan and a couple of his pals pulled up.

"Hey, Paddy. A word in your ear." I dropped my bike and went over to him. "Where're you off to, son? "Now that Uncle Pat's running the stall, they don't need me and, anyhow, I've got a new job."

Nathan was a very precise man so I had to explain every little detail from start to finish. He looked pleased. "Good on you, son. I always knew you had a sharp brain in that head of yours. He's a nice man, that Terry. He'll look after you. Eddie looking after you?" A bit of a wink. "Getting your share?" "Yes, thanks." "Before you go, there's a couple of things I need to talk about." He suddenly got serious. "Haven't had any comebacks over that big fuck, Jim, have you?"

"No, not a titter." "Good. Do me a favour? Make sure that Jimmy over there," he nodded towards Cousin Jim, "keeps his eyes and ears open and his mouth shut! He worries me at times. I know that he means no harm but, as I've told you many times, you can't trust anybody."

"Don't worry. He's been properly worded!" I dropped Nan's fish off and made my way home but just before I was about to leave, Nan said, "You can have dinner here, if you like. You don't have to rush off."

Over the last few weeks, whilst Granddad had been in hospital and since he'd been home, I had been going home and having dinner with the rest of them because I didn't want to give Nan any extra work.

"No, thanks, Nan. I've already told Betty that I'd be home for dinner. Bye for now. See you in the week."

I would regret that particular decision on that certain Sunday. There would be a whole lot of shit heading my way!

We had our dinner, plain and functional, and I told Dad all about my new job. He was impressed although Betty, true to type, wasn't in favour of gambling. I did explain that I was not exactly gambling but she wasn't convinced. I really didn't give a fuck, anyway!

I stayed in that afternoon (what a mistake!). There was a ring on the doorbell, which Betty answered, and in strolled the local priest! In those days, the priest would pop round various households for tea and a chat.

I hardly knew him and, of course, he, in turn, hardly knew me. I was very polite and respectful but the subject soon came up about my absence from Sunday mass.

It started to get a bit heated, much to the alarm of Betty, but the priest became very angry and aggressive. I held myself together but very firmly tried to explain to the stupid man that I had the right to my own opinion and that I did not believe in God. In my opinion, for me to go to church would make me a hypocrite and that if there was indeed a god then he would understand. The priest was having none of this and tried his best to bully me into going to mass. He was wasting his time. He left, very frustrated, shaking his head from side to side. He'd done his best and, in his mind, what was his divine duty and I didn't have a problem with that. My only wish was that he could be able to consider my view but sadly that was not in a Catholic priest's makeup (well, not in those days, anyway).

Betty never spoke to me for the rest of the day. A silence that would be repeated over many years to come. That Sunday would prove to be very significant indeed and there would be stern challenges ahead, as a consequence.

I was up early that next Sunday, ironically having breakfast and getting ready at the same as Betty, Michael and Eddie (although I'd noticed that Eddie wasn't too keen anymore).

I told Betty that I'd be having dinner at Nan's. She thanked me for letting her know but I felt that she wasn't too sad about that arrangement. I think she was dreading the arrival of the old bag of yeast[45].

Terry showed me into a little front parlour of a house in Valentine's Yard, where Charlie was already seated. There were all the SPs (starting prices) from yesterday, and a few from Friday, pasted on a board. Eventually, people appeared clutching their betting slips and we went to work. Charlie was very surprised when I was able to work the bets out even quicker than him. In truth, I even surprised myself. The figures just used to jump out at me. Terry was as pleased as punch because it came out in conversation that old Charlie was shortly moving away to one of the new estates in a place called Downham. He knew that he had a new settler and one he could trust!

Besides the money, there was an added bonus in working for a local bookmaker. My street cred had risen to new heights. This was very nice but, as always, there would be drawbacks. A great many of my friends were delighted but a few of the local herberts were very jealous and probably envious. There were problems on the horizon.

I walked through the door and knew straightaway there was a problem!

"That you, Paddy?" Came Eddie's voice from the front room. "Yeah, what ya want?" "Come in here. You'll see." I hurried into the room. Michael was sitting on an armchair, looking very sorry for himself. Eddie was pacing up and down like one of those caged lions in the zoo. "Sorry, Paddy," murmured Michael. "Sorry? Sorry? What the fuck for?" "Eddie butted in. "Why're you so late home?" "I've been boxing training after school. What the fuck's going on?" I was beginning to get annoyed. Eddie began, "A couple of those bastards over there," nodding towards Red Cross Way, "have pulled Michael about and given him a slap." I went rigid. "Now, calm down a minute and listen to what I'm gonna tell you. You already know a couple of them but there are others you don't. Michael said that he was going to tell you," he hesitated, "but they just laughed." "Where are they now?" "Like I just said, calm down! One of the ringleaders is round the back of the block waiting for you. Ya fancy it? Because he's your age, otherwise, I'd have hurt him already."

I threw my gear on the floor, alongside my jacket. "Come on then. Where are they?" We flew down the stairs, three at a time. "Be careful, Paddy. I think he's a bit useful. I'll make sure no one interferes."

There, standing at the rear of our block of flats, was a crowd of boys and girls, all laughing and joking. They noticed us heading towards them. The laughing stopped. "Which one of you c@#?s hit my young brother?"

"Me! He deserved it. He's a saucy fucker. Why? What you gonna do about it?" "Put your stupid hands up and you'll find out." I'll always remember the shock on his face, as I walked straight up to him and hit him a big right-hander followed by a left, which caught him smack on his jaw, a millisecond before he crashed to the floor.

I'm not proud of it but I was about as mad as I'd ever been before in my life! I calmly stood over him and before he had a chance to recover,

I kicked him in the head. It made a sickening noise and he was out cold.

Eddie realised the danger signs and, before I knew it, he dragged me away. I was screaming at the now very subdued crowd. "If anyone goes near my brother again, I'll fucking kill you."

It took Eddie a good half hour to calm me down and as soon as he was comfortable, "I'm just shooting out to make sure that bloke is alright. You might have really hurt him. I won't be long."

When he got back, he was all smiles. "He's still a big groggy but he'll be alright. I don't think he'll be troubling us again and he's not going to the old bill. They're a big family but one of his older brothers knows Johnny very well, so there's no fear of any comebacks." He turned to Michael. "Stay out of their way whilst you're in school. It won't be long. They'll all be leaving shortly."

Unfortunately, there was more to come. A couple of weeks had gone by when, once again, I was greeted by Eddie and, this time, by Dad as well. Michael's face was bruised and swollen. He had been bullied again. This had now become a direct challenge to me and Michael was being used as the scapegoat. I was furious!

Dad spoke this time. "You're gonna have to have a fight, son. A boy your age has given Michael a bashing and Eddie has already made the arrangements." Dad didn't know about the other fight!

I think it worthwhile explaining why things were arranged in this way. The local tearaways mistakenly thought that because I went to a 'posh' school, I had become soft and somehow scared of them. Nothing could be further from the truth!

As before, same place, an even bigger crowd. The only difference being, I knew the lad who had hit Michael. His name was Terry and he was no mug[46]. He was reputed to be the top dog in school. I never quite understood why or how but this actually calmed me down and made me concentrate.

I thought, why not? We faced each other, both ready for a fight. I threw the big mug punch. A right hand cross. It landed square in the side of his face. I knew then that he was not a good boxer but he was big and strong. We waded into each other, exchanging punch after punch. He hurt me and I knew I was hurting him. I landed punches on him at a two-to-one ratio and it slowly started to show. He was blowing hard by now and his face was cut. My nose felt like it had been dislocated but I was determined.

He dropped his hands and made a grab for me (fucking wrestling again!) and he was a strong fucker but, thanks to my old mate of many years ago, Peter, I turned the tables and he was on the floor. I remember Eddie's shout, "Don't, Paddy, don't!" I snarled at Terry, "Get up, you cowardly fuckdog, and fight properly, you fucking dog!"

He was no coward! He got up and took a vicious amount of punishment. I was very fit and could fight ten rounds in training. He was bigger and heavier than me and I was unable to knock him off his feet but there was very little coming back. It was like punching a heavy bag and I was merciless.

I heard Dad's shout, "Eddie, stop him now before someone (someone? That's a laugh) gets hurt!"

Eddie stepped between us. "That's enough, Paddy, leave him alone. It's all over." He looked at the crowd. "Any of you know where he lives?" A voice said, "I do."

"Well, make sure he gets home. Now, fuck off the lot of you, before I start." Dad never said a word but I knew he was as proud as a peacock. He even made me a cup of very sweet tea. "For replacing all that energy you've just used up." There was a bit of a commotion going on outside on our landing then a loud banging on our front door. Dad went to answer it. "What the fu . . . ," he muttered.

When the door opened, there was a man and a screaming woman outside. "Let me get my hands on that fucking bastard. Have you seen what he's done to my boy?"

Well, Dad didn't fuck about! He grabbed this bloke by the throat and virtually lifted him of his feet. He rammed him against the wall and shook him like a rag doll. Very calmly, he said, "It was a fair fight. Nobody interfered. Your boy lost good and proper and, anyway, he's a big bully because he hit my youngest son, who's nearly three years younger. If he ever does it again, he'll get more of the same. Only, next time, I won't put a stop to it." The man was gasping and the woman was in shock.

Dad threw the man away like a piece of rubbish. "If you ever come knocking on my door, again," Dad pushed his face forward, "I'll throw you down those two flights of stairs! Now, piss off, the both of you."

Thankfully, that would be the end of things. Michael was left alone although he had plenty of fights but only with boys of his own age. Some he won, some he lost.

To close this little episode in our lives, many years later, about 30, in fact. I was having a drink in a pub just off Borough High Street with my cousin Seamus, when we were approached by this fellow. "Hello, Terry," Seamus said. "How are you?"

"Hi ya, Sham! It can't be, can it? Is that you, Paddy, you fucker?" He was smiling and friendly. I stood up. "Well, I'll be fucked. I haven't seen you for years. I didn't know you knew Seamus. How are you?" He laughed and looked at Seamus. "Did you not know what this bastard did to me, all those years ago?" He smiled at me. "Fuck you, Paddy. You didn't 'arf hurt me. You didn't have to go that strong, you fucker!" "You should have given up and gone down and stayed down! Now, sit down, I'll buy you a pint."

We had a really nice chat about old times and how all our lives had turned out. He was keen to know all about Eddie and Michael. I jokingly said, "You wouldn't want to fuck about with Mike, now. He's a really big, strong bastard but I'll give him your regards. One thing I can tell you is that my hands hurt me for the best part of a month. You were a tough bastard." Sadly, Terry is no longer with us. He died.

All three of us showed up that day! Nan and Granddad were moving to their new ground floor flat and although it was only a few hundred yards away, there was a lot of furniture to move. Kit had given permission for us to use her market stalls and with the help of Johnny, Nathan and Jimmy, plus Nan, of course, we soon had the job done.

Kit and Michael had been fussing around, making tea and cakes for everyone, but you could see that they were very sad and a few tears appeared when it came time for Nan to finally say goodbye.

Eddie took care of Granddad and pushed him (via the pub, of course) to his new home. I can remember feeling quite sad myself, which was very out of character, but I had very, very fond memories of Tower Bridge Road and although we had moved out earlier, somehow while Nan still lived there, it felt like my true home.

The tight bonds were slipping!

My life was going through a settled and routine stage. My Sunday job was working out real well. I continued with my market activities although Michael had taken over the stalls. There was still a bit of business with Uncle Nathan but this was dropping off slightly. There were fewer Yanks around nowadays and ever so gradually, the shops were getting fuller.

Whenever I wasn't playing cricket or boxing training at school, I would be at my club either training, playing table tennis or billiards. I was never interfered with by anybody and, more to the point, neither was Michael. True peace!

It just couldn't last!

School assembly was coming to a close when the Head made a final announcement. "Father O'Brien (the parish priest) wants to say a few words." He did and I knew straightaway that it was a set-up.

"It has come to my knowledge that some of you boys have missed Sunday mass." There was a slight gasp. "I would like any boy that did not go to mass on Sunday to please stand up." I realised that our local priest had found out from Betty what school I was attending. My chair made a terrible scraping sound as I stood up. There must have been about five hundred pairs of eyes gawping at me.

The priest continued, "I find it hard to believe that any Catholic boy could possibly fail to complete his sacred duty. What is your excuse, boy?" There it is again, that aggressive and self-righteous, pompous attitude.

I had been pushed into a corner, which left me no choice. "I didn't go Sunday or any other Sunday, Father." I was always polite and respectful. "I just don't go to church." The entire school gasped. The priest was taken off guard and unable to control himself. The Headmaster took over.

"Quiet, quiet! O'Donovan, report to my office at once. The remainder, make your way to your classrooms, in your usual orderly way. Assembly dismissed."

I made my way over to the Head's office and waited outside. I could hear murmurings coming from the office, when suddenly the door opened and I was told to enter.

Whilst I'd been waiting, my brain had been in overdrive. I had not broken any of the school rules and I was beginning to get a bit pissed off with my treatment.

The Head was seated and a grim-faced priest was standing alongside him. The school secretary, who had let me in, also remained.

The priest started to lecture me and remind me that, as a Catholic, I was duty bound to attend mass and that I was committing a mortal sin by not so doing. He instructed me that I must follow him, right now, to the church and take confession. The Head nodded!

I ignored the priest and spoke directly to the Headmaster. "Sir, I haven't broken any school rules and I have kept up with my studies.

What I do outside of school is my own personal choice! I don't wish to be rude or disrespectful, but," I now faced the priest face on, eye to eye. He wasn't comfortable. "Father, I will not go to church with you. I'm sorry if that causes you any distress but my mind is made up, whatever the consequences."

I heard the secretary gulp! The priest and Head were both stunned into silence but not for too long. "You ridiculous boy. Get out of this office and back to your classroom at once."

I returned to class and got on with my studies. At lunchtime, I was mobbed by my classmates, one or two of them said that they had also missed mass and couldn't understand why I hadn't remained seated, like them. "I don't go to church but there's no need to lie about it."

The week went by and I noticed a very cool attitude towards me from most of the teachers and, certainly, the teaching monks. They looked at me like they'd seen a strange animal. Even some of the more religious pupils gave me a wide berth, like you would a leper.

Even I couldn't believe it when, once again, Monday morning assembly, the same priest plus two others. A stupid repeat of last Monday's shenanigans.

In the Head's office once more. "This has to stop. You are causing unrest in our school and beginning to disrupt your fellow pupils. Why you insist in your stupid and sinful ways, I fail to understand. You have already let down your boxing team. What will happen next? Why you bothered to come to a Catholic college is beyond me. What have you got to say for yourself?"

"I earned the right to come to this college, sir, and it was actually my grandmother's choice. Not mine. I did not let the school boxing team down. That's a downright lie. I help the team considerably. I just refuse to fight for other people's pleasure and, with respect, sir, it is your insistence in making me stand up in front of the entire school, over which is a private matter," I stressed the word 'private', "that is turning me into some sort of weird hero. Something I do not want and think is unfair."

I don't think he was prepared for that clarity of argument but it was their fault for educating me too much. The Head paused for a moment. "I see here that you would be able to leave, come next term. Is that your preferred option?"

"That would mean that I would miss my 'O' level exams, sir, and my grandmother promised you that I would stay at school, in order to complete my studies. I will leave as soon as my exams are finished, sir." The secretary was busy taking notes and the priests were shaking their heads. The Head continued, "The school year ends in a couple of weeks. I need time to think this one out. You're dismissed. Get back to class."

That lunchtime, I went over to the gym and emptied my locker. There was an instructor standing in the corner, eyeing me up, but keeping his distance. "Sorry, sir, I won't be coming back. I've finished with the club." He made no comment.

The summer holidays came and, strangely, I found them a bit boring. I hung around with mates, some new ones from the Borough and Waterloo, and some of the older ones from Bermondsey. I played a lot for cricket over Southwark Park but I think I missed the company of Eddie and Jimmy, who were both now at work.

Nan and Granddad had settled in nicely and it was so nice for Granddad because he was able to sit in his wheelchair, just outside his front door, where there were many passers-by. Sadly, his old legs never improved.

It used to make me both sad and angry as I saw him crumpled up in that chair. There he was, the man who had looked after all of us throughout those terrible years, now a weak old man. Those hands that had clawed at debris until they bled, trying to rescue people, now permanently trembling. It seemed unfair to me. His old face used to lighten up as soon as he clocked[47] me. Not quite as much as when his Mikey appeared, but enough for me.

For yet another year, Nan was unable to go down hopping but Uncle Nathan and Aunt Anne drove her down there a couple of times. She enjoyed that because she had many hoppin' friends.

Jimmy, Uncle that is, and Marie had married during the summer and had set up home together. They were a handsome couple. This just left Eileen and Johnny at home with Nan. With everyone pitching in, this meant that Granddad was being well looked after.

I had spoken to Dad about my unhappiness with my school, sparing him all the sordid details, and asked his opinion and possible permission to leave. His reply was, sadly, a bit predictable. "Where do you think you'll wind up? In some old secondary school? What do you want to become? A dustman? Anyway, I thought you always said that your nan wanted you to go to that school. You've only got another nine months to do. It can't be that bad. Just get on with it!"

"Okay, Dad, I will! I only asked!"

We returned to college midweek and, of course, I was now a senior. The new intake looked so young and small and as I saw them excitedly lining up for classes in their bright new uniforms, I thought, that was me four years ago.

During our first morning assembly, I waited. I had made up my mind as to what I would do should any problems arrive but, luckily, none did. But sadly, I would receive some bad news later in the day!

A meeting had been called in one of the sports halls for all the members of the school football teams. Being both a senior and last year's second year captain and senior vice captain, I made sure that I sat right in the front. I could see that the head sports master was accompanied by one of the brotherhood (Catholic teaching monks) and I sensed that I was the topic of their whispered conversation. Once things had settled down a bit, the sports master, very discreetly, beckoned me to the far side of the hall. Then very quietly, and a touch nervously, he informed me that I was seen to be a bad influence on the rest of the school and, therefore, I would be stripped of my vice captaincy and, obviously, could never be school captain. He did offer a small olive branch. He would welcome me as a team member.

I knew then about the smallness and pettiness of man. I smiled at the coach, thanked him and shook his hand.

"No, thanks, sir. Thank you for all your help and support over the years but I'll not take up your offer. I will never represent the school again." I'm sorry but I just couldn't help myself. "Anyway, I'm now playing enough football with my Church of England Young Man's Club. Let Brother Christopher know, will you?"

With that, I left the hall. So that's how they're gonna play it, were they? They were wasting their silly time! That Thursday night, I spoke to one of the club trainers and told him that I would be available to play for the team on Saturday mornings from now on and I was welcomed with open arms.

Michael was now able to take over all my Saturday jobs (everyone's a winner). That Sunday morning, I had a word with Uncle Terry, offering my services on Saturday afternoon or evening. He said that he would probably be able to use me, from time to time.

I was quite chirpy and happy with myself that first Monday morning. I now knew exactly where I stood and I liked things to be that way. I had made my plans!

Now that I was a senior, we were seated at the rear of the morning assembly and I made sure that I had an end of aisle seat. Sure enough, as I thought, the priest suddenly appeared alongside the Head. The normal speeches were made and, as usual, finishing with a short morning prayer. The very second that the prayer had finished, the priest took hold of the microphone.

They weren't ready for this!

I just got off my seat, turned my back on the platform, and walked straight out of the assembly, making my way to my new classroom and I waited outside the empty class. I heard them approaching, pupils first, closely followed by our year tutor.

"Outside the Head's office immediately." There I was, once again, waiting to be called in. I didn't have to wait too long.

"How dare you leave assembly without permission. Are you going to obey any of the school rules?"

"Yes, sir, of course, I am. I thought that after prayers, assembly had ended but, to be honest, sir, I didn't think I should suffer any more humiliation from the Father."

"In future, you just wait until you're dismissed. Is that quite clear?"
"Yes, sir!"

"I'm now going to punish you. Hold out your hands, one at a time."

He gave me, what they called, six of the best and he really laid that cane on hard. It hurt but I didn't show it, which made him even madder because he'd done as best he could (and he knew that I knew it). "Get out of my sight and return to your class."

We were now studying 'O' level history and geography and, by some quirk of fate, we were being taught by none other than Brother Christopher, who could hardly disguise his loathing of me. Unfortunately for him, these were subjects that I loved and, probably as a consequence, were extremely good at. I achieved top marks, which meant that although he would never praise me, he was unable to find fault.

He was obviously a sportsman but he was also a spiteful and cruel man. He would clip lads around the head and rap knuckles with a large wooden protractor. I could tell that he was dying to have a go at me. There was a boxing mate of mine in my class and he did tend to struggle a bit and, to be honest, was a bit loud from time to time.

In Spite of Everything . . . .

This morning, he overdid it and he was ordered out front and told to hold his hand out. That man did lay into him, whacking him across the hands with that big stick. To my complete surprise, my mate burst into tears from the pain. I couldn't believe it because I thought that he was tougher than that!

Once class had finished, I went over to his desk. "You shouldn't have cried like that. I thought you wouldn't let him get to you."

"I heard that O'Donovan. Watch yourself or you'll get some of it and then we'll see who cries." He was still in the class and I turned to face him. "I haven't done anything wrong, Father." I knew that would annoy him because he wasn't a priest!

"I'm not Father, as you well know. Call me Brother!"

"Sorry, Brother." I levelled my deep blue eyes at him. "You could never make me cry." I then just strolled right past him, as though he didn't exist.

I was now getting seriously pissed off with most of the other pupils, and they in turn, became wary of me.

As I've said before, life has a funny way of chucking up bonuses if you're sensible enough, that is, to recognise them.

I no longer played football at break or lunchtime, and because of my seniority, I was able to go outside the school, going for long walks, sometimes to the park and sometimes to the river. That was lovely as long as the weather was half decent. This is England and the weather can be bad! On the rainy days, I took to going to the school library, where there was a very large selection of books. I enjoyed reading the classics: Dickens, Steinbeck, etc. There was always a small group of boys playing chess and this was a game I had never played or seen played. I had just started to show some interest in the rules and the various moves, when I was invited to take part in a game. Luckily, the boys were very patient but it didn't take me that long to get the hang of it. It did however take me quite a while to record my first win.

I have enjoyed chess all my life and I made sure that I taught my children to play. I was even able to teach my dad, sadly only towards the end of his life, but he enjoyed it and this has left me with good memories.

There you are! Because of the bigotry and small mindedness of some members of my old school, I have an appreciation of good books and the knowledge of a wonderful game. Bonuses!

So, remember, by doing someone a bad deed, you could wind up doing them a favour! Now, there's a thought!

Dark clouds were looming!

Granddad was becoming weaker and weaker and, during November, he was admitted to hospital. I was now legally able to leave school but was now determined to take and pass my forthcoming exams. I took no part in any school activities and it looked like the priest had actually given up on me. I was also able to drop religious studies, due to my coming 'O' level exams. We all visited Granddad on a regular basis and, whenever I visited, there were always family members gathered around. Unfortunately, he seemed to sleep a great deal nowadays.

Christmas was fast approaching and thankfully rationing was all but over. Sadly, for Nan, this would be a drab old Christmas. She didn't much fancy decorating her flat, not with Granddad lying in hospital.

It was Christmas Eve and I let myself into Nan's flat (she had given me a key straight away). "Oh, oh! Anyone in?" "I'm in here, Paddy." As soon as I saw Johnny slouched in his chair, I knew. "What's the matter, John?" "You're not gonna like it, Pad! Granddad's on his last legs. We're gonna lose him."

I wasn't that surprised but still shocked. "Where's Nan?" "She's at the hospital with him." I about-turned and headed out. "I don't think you should go up there, Paddy. Why don't you wait here for a while? There's nothing you can do." "I'm going up there, John!"

In Spite of Everything . . . .

It didn't take me long to pedal round to the hospital and, as usual, most of the family were there. Eileen and Annie had swollen, tear-stained eyes and the men were grimfaced. "Where's Nan, Uncle Pat?" "She's in with Granddad. You wanna go in?" I was already halfway there. I didn't need fucking invites!

Nan looked up at me with those very familiar sad eyes. "He's asleep, son, you won't be able to wake him, I'm afraid." He looked peaceful but was hardly breathing. "You better say goodbye to your granddad. He can't go on much longer." I was truly choked. My old mate was going to die!

"Don't get too upset, son. He's had a good innings and he'll be out of pain soon. Now, give him a kiss and say goodbye." I had always found it difficult to actually kiss anybody, let alone a man, but I went up to the top of the bed and planted a large kiss on his forehead. I swear to God that his eyes opened and there was a faint smile! Nan noticed it.

"He knew you, Paddy, he knew it was you! Now, please do as you're told and go home."

I never saw him again.

I was too upset to hang around making small talk, so I just walked away. They let me go without a word.

I was almost home and it was just getting dark, when I saw Eddie and Michael. They were headed towards the hospital. Eddie called, "Have you been up to see Granddad?" "Yeah, you'd better hurry up. He ain't got much time left. Nan's with him."

Dad and Betty asked me how he was. "I don't think he's got much longer. He's very weak."

There was a rat-tat-tat on our front door. I knew it wasn't Father Christmas! "Hello, Ted, Merry Christmas." It was Uncle Nathan. "Sorry to give you bad news, this early on Christmas Day, but the old boy died last night. What a Christmas present for the old gal. Will you let the boys know? Sorry but I've got to shoot off. See you soon. Bye everyone."

I walked into the hallway where Eddie and Michael were already comforting each other. Michael understandably was very upset. Betty looked at me. "Are you alright, son?" "Yes, thanks. It's not a surprise but I shall miss him. I'll go and see Nan in a minute."

"Don't go too early. She must have been up till late last night and she could probably do with a lay-in, bless her. I really thought a lot of your granddad. He was a straightforward, honest man. Do you fancy coming to church this morning to say a prayer for him. It is Christmas Day, after all." "Sorry, but no." She just shrugged.

I didn't feel like opening Christmas presents but we made the best of the situation. I'd known Granddad all my life and now he was gone (does everyone go?).

"Hello, Paddy. How are you? It's a sad old day and that's for sure." Eileen's eyes were red and swollen. "Oh, don't worry about me. How's Nan?" "I'm in here, Paddy. Come in and see me." Nan was sitting up in bed, looking no different than usual. "He's at peace now, Paddy. You may not fully understand but he's suffered enough over the past year. I'm glad you were able to see him before he went. He definitely recognised you and when he saw his Mikey, he actually smiled. The last smile he ever made. Make sure you let Michael know, won't you?" "Yeah, of course, I will."

"Now, away with you. I want to get dressed." Eileen, Johnny, Uncle Pat and a few of Granddad's cousins were all sitting around in Nan's front room. The mood was very subdued, which was very unusual once that crowd were together.

"Fancy a cup of tea, Paddy?" "No, thanks, Eileen. I won't hang about. What you all doing for your Christmas dinner?" I don't know why but that thought just struck me.

Nan came in. "Why? Do you want to stay? We've got a nice chicken and a leg of pork. Eileen and me are just about to start getting ready now. You lot will have to get out of my way. Go for a walk or something." Nan was as strong as a lion. She just would not be down for too long.

"I'd better not, thanks, Nan. That would certainly upset Betty. Oh, by the way, she sends her regards. I'm going now. See you tomorrow." Nan planted a kiss on my cheek. "Bye, son, Merry Christmas!"

It didn't matter what we did to enjoy this Christmas time, but a shadow hung over nearly everyone. The funeral arrangements had been made and Nan offered me the chance to skip the proceedings. I had politely insisted that I would be there. She, in turn, insisted that Michael should stay away, saying that it would upset him too much. This was agreed and Eddie would have the job of telling him.

Nan seemed overly nervous about mine and Eddie's presence at the funeral, and this surprised me but I was to find out why!

It was a couple of days before the funeral when, as I popped into Nan's, I heard part of a conversation going on in the kitchen between Nan and Aunt Anne. "Are you going to tell Paddy or not, Mum? He'll have to know. You know that, don't you?" Tell me what? I thought.

"Hi, Nan, anyone in?" The chatter stopped dead. "Is that you, Paddy? I'm in the kitchen with your aunt. Be out in a minute." Annie, as usual, made a grab for me but I was alert and squirmed away from her. "Give us a kiss, you handsome sod."

"Leave him alone, Anne. You know what he's like. We were just talking about the funeral and all the arrangements. There's going to be an awful lot of people and the cemetery's a long way off."

"Why's that, Nan?" I couldn't help think that there were quite a few cemeteries fairly close. "I haven't got time to explain why, just yet, but I'll probably tell you tomorrow. The main thing is that you wear black shoes, a white shirt and a black tie. You've got a nice dark blazer, haven't you? "Yeah, but I haven't got a black tie. Where can I get one?" "I'll have one for you tomorrow and for Eddie as well, so let him know."

I sensed that they wanted me out of the way, so I said my goodbyes and off I went. My mind was still buzzing. Tell me what?

That next afternoon, Nan was as good as her word. Two black ties. This would be the first time that I would wear a black tie but, sadly, certainly not the last.

I could feel it. "Paddy, I need to talk to you. Come into my bedroom." She looked very serious and ever so slightly nervous.

"Now, listen to me, son. We are burying your granddad in a cemetery over the other side of London, at a place called Kensal Green." "Why that far away?"

"Paddy, please, don't interrupt. The reason for that is that during the war, we didn't have any choice where to bury the dead. We were told where to go. Kensal Green is a Catholic cemetery." She hesitated and put her hand on my shoulder (this is serious). "And it is where your mum is buried!" That hit me like a bombshell. I wasn't prepared for that!

"We thought it would be nice to have Granddad alongside her and, one day, so shall I." I was lost for words. I bet that's why she didn't want me at the funeral. "That's alright, Nan. It's a brilliant idea. I'll be alright, honest!" She seemed mightily relieved. "Does Eddie know?" She nodded.

The day of the funeral brought more shocks! Dad had gone to work, as usual. He wasn't coming! He had been very quiet about things but I never doubted that he would be making a show. He didn't.

I could, sadly, never forgive him although in later years, I did come to understand things more clearly, but I couldn't forgive. Never!!

In Spite of Everything . . . .

When we arrived at Nan's, there was a large crowd of people standing outside the front door. I knew most of them, being relations, of course. Uncle Jim was the first to speak. "Hi, boys, want to go in and see your granddad?" He had been brought home the previous afternoon and remained laying with an open coffin during the night. He would have had at least one member of the family alongside him all the time. Members of the family and friends would have been expected to show their last respects. There would be, and was, a fair bit of drinking.

We went in, straight into the front room, which was crowded by black-clothed relatives, both men and women. I made a beeline for Nan and gave her a hug. "You all right, Nan?" "Yes, thanks, Paddy. Nice to see you and Eddie. You both look very smart. Your granddad would have been proud of you." Eddie gave her a big hug, as well. "He's in Johnny's bedroom. Do you want to go in and see him for the last time? He looks very peaceful."

I wasn't too keen on that. "No, thanks, Nan. I can remember him just as he used to be. That's all right, ain't it?" "Of course, it is. Whatever you prefer, son."

Eddie made his way in and he got himself very upset. I think I made the right move! The undertakers turned up with a big black hearse and three big Rolls-Royces. They started proceedings by entering the house and inviting family members to see Granddad, before closing down his coffin.

Uncle Pat, Dave, Jim and John carried Granddad out of the house and placed him in the hearse. The rest of us then followed. This last sight brought many of the women to tears, as well as a few of the men.

Uncle Jim had a list which told the undertaker who would be sitting in each car and there was a strict pecking order. I was most surprised when my name and Eddie's were called for the first car alongside Nan, her older sister, Mary, Uncle Pat (the eldest son), Aunts Anne and Eileen. Apparently, Nan had insisted that she wanted it done that way.

Quite a few people were unable to get any form of transport to get them to Kensal Green but not Uncle Nathan! He had borrowed a big V8 Pilot (in black, of course) and he managed to squeeze the remaining close relatives in.

It took ages to get to the cemetery, having first, very slowly, toured Bermondsey, driving right past our old house and Granddad's old haunts and, although we did speed up a bit, it was a long, sad journey.

Nan's sister, Aunt Mary, was a very daunting lady. She looked like the old Queen Victoria and she didn't give the rest of us time to talk. She was in charge.

At the cemetery, the men of the family carried the coffin all the way to the graveside and lowered him down into the ground. It was very moving and very final.

There was a priest in attendance and he gave his blessing and said the necessary words. We then, one by one, shook earth onto the coffin. This was the first funeral I'd ever been to and, unfortunately, would not be the last. I would, sadly, be visiting this particular graveyard many times in years to come.

Nan approached Eddie and me. "We're going to lay some flowers on your mum's grave but I must warn you, that because of the war, she is in a communal plot."

"I'm not going anywhere near that fucking place, Nan. Sorry but I'll meet you at the gate." Eddie gave me a clip round the ear. "Stop swearing!" "Leave him alone, Ed, I understand. Off you go, you know the way, don't you?" I was already on my way and gave Nan a wave.

I could see the cars come to a rest and everyone get out. Some carried flowers. This was as close as I'd dare be. It was as I looked at my family, my mind began to wander right back to that day in church when that fat Eileen had a go at me. What did she mean? *"Your mum wasn't killed by the bombs."* Well, what the fuck was she buried alongside all those others for? I could feel myself getting angry. Hurry up! Let's get away from this place. I had to get these thoughts out of my mind or my head would burst.

On the way back, there was a slight incident. It will always amaze me that some people find it hard to stay out of other's business. She, fat Aunt Mary, couldn't keep her mouth shut. "You should be ashamed of yourself not paying respects to your mother. I've never seen anything like it."

Nan shuddered and it went deathly quiet. I could have ripped her tongue out! "Mind your own business, it's got nothing to do with you. If I want your opinion, I'll ask! I don't, so shut up!" She looked visibly shocked. Nan leaned over and put a calming hand on my shoulder. Aunt Mary tut-tutted but never opened her mouth again. Uncle Pat caused many a laugh in local pubs with that story.

Dad didn't even ask how the funeral went or how Nan was. He carried on as though nothing out of the ordinary had occurred. I could never work that one out! Or ever forgive!!

I returned to school and concentrated on my forthcoming exams, still keeping myself to myself, and only taking part in the bare essentials of school life. There seemed to be a sort of standoff between me and school principles. I could tell that they were not entirely comfortable with my attitude but I barely broke any actual school rules but, as usual, the storm clouds were brewing.

Now that on most lunchtimes I went away from the school, I started to become acquainted with other senior students from other local schools, some of them being girls! A couple of my closest mates became very interested in this situation. We used to hang around the local market and stroll together in the park. A few of the boys and some girls had started to smoke. This was in those days a sure sign of adulthood, but I didn't like the taste or smell of tobacco, therefore, I didn't smoke and never have to this day.

We strolled through the school gates and were confronted by the duty teacher. "You three report to Head, at once." I was gobsmacked.

"What for, sir?" "You've been reported for smoking and you know that's strictly against school rules." I narrowed my eyes towards him and spoke very slowly and precisely. "I do not smoke, sir." "You'll have to talk to Head. Now, do as you're told." My mates were shocked. "How did he find out?" I looked at him. "We're all wearing school blazers, you dopey fucker. I bet it was one of those nuns. They gave us a funny look, remember?"

We stood in the corridor outside the Head's office. A place well known to me but not for my mates. "What do you reckon will happen, Paddy? Do you think he'll call us all in together? What shall we say?" I was now getting a bit impatient with these two clowns. "Listen, I don't know and I don't care. Look after yourselves. You'll find out soon enough."

The school secretary appeared and took our three names then disappeared into the Head's office. I had already decided on my action and kept it to myself.

The door opened and one of the boys was called in. There was a sound of muffled conversation then the unmistakable swoosh of the cane and the sickening slap on bare flesh. There were six of these accompanied by a painful yelp towards the end.

My other mate, who by this time was a trembling wreck, followed. "He really laid that on, extra hard. My hands are burning." "Wipe your eyes, you prick. Don't let him know that he's hurt you." He looked ashamed! The whole procedure was repeated but, this time, the clown was actually sobbing, yes, crying, like a big girl! When he came out, I completely ignored him.

My turn! I walked smartly into his now familiar office and stared at the Head. "Yes, yes, just as I thought. So no doubt you are the bad influence on those boys." He hesitated for a couple of seconds. "What have you got to say for yourself?" He was enjoying this! "I don't smoke, sir, I never have and probably never will and, sir, I definitely do not try to influence anybody. I'm not at all interested in what others do."

"You were seen by Sister Boneface. Are you telling me that the Holy Sister is telling lies?" "No, sir, definitely not. She must have simply made a mistake. I do not smoke and I do not tell lies."

"You were in the company of those other boys, the ones who have admitted smoking, weren't you?" "Yes, sir, I was!" With that, he got up, cane in hand. "You are part of the blame, therefore, I intend to punish you, also." A short pause. "Hand out, you know the drill."

I squared up to him, now being taller and broader, looked him in the eyes. "No, sir, I will not accept the cane from you. I have done nothing wrong." He was, at first, startled, which quickly turned into rage. He raised the cane in a threatening way and I thought for a moment he was going to lash out at me. I took a step towards him and in a cool, calm voice, "Don't do that, sir, whatever you do, don't hit me with that thing." I try never to make threats and I already had my plan ready. If he struck me, I would lay him out. Thankfully, he saw the danger and common sense took over (or so I thought). He went into an uncontrollable rage and he was white with anger, actually jumping up and down. He started screaming at me. "Get out of my office and get out of my school." The side door opened and the secretary poked her head round. She looked alarmed. "Is everything alright, sir? Is there anything I can do to help?"

"You can show this student the front door. I want him out of my sight." I about-turned and walked out of his office, quickly followed by his secretary. "What did you do to the Head? I've never known him so mad." "He was wrong and I wouldn't accept the cane. That's all." She shrugged. "I think you had better do as he said. I'll talk to him later and get a letter sent to your parents. I'm sorry." "I'm just off to my classroom to collect my things. I'll be back in a couple of seconds." "I don't know if you should really but please be quick or else I'll be in trouble."

I knocked on the classroom door and entered. "Sorry, sir, I've only popped in to collect my books and bag." The teacher seemed a bit confused. "I've been expelled, sir." There was a gasp from the class.

The secretary was very pleased to see me and quickly ushered me through the school gates.

Was that the end of my school days?

Sitting in the tram, I had time to mull over the day's events. It did bring a smile to my face. The sheer stupidity of it all. The complete bigotry of that stupid headmaster, who had found me guilty and sentenced me without a shred of evidence and his childish ranting. It could hardly be taken seriously! But, then again, what about my exams. He had no right to deny me my chance! What would Nan say about it?

I decided to change at St George's and call in to see Nan but I wouldn't tell her anything about what had just taken place.

I called out, as I opened Nan's door. "It's only me, Nan." "What, no school today, Paddy? "Just a half day today, Nan. How are you? Hello Aunt Anne, where were you? In the kitchen?"

"Hello, boy, nice to see ya. Come on, give us a kiss." She never altered! I did give her a very small peck. "I've just put the kettle on. Fancy a cup of tea and some biscuits?" It was a sure sign that Uncle Nathan was up to his old larks—biscuits!

I didn't hang around too long. I was never fond of nattering with women, so I gave Nan an extra big hug and even kissed Annie again, and then I was off. I knew that Eddie finished work early on Wednesdays, so I made my way up to the Brick and wandered down New Kent Road.

I think he saw me before I saw him. He looked a bit alarmed. "What's up?" "Nothing to worry about, Ed. There's no aggro. I'll tell you all about it on the way home. How are you, anyway?" He called out to some of his workmates, "This is my younger brother. You know? The one I've told you about." There was lots of waving in my direction.

I gave Eddie the full account, leaving nothing out. "He was out of order, Pad. Do you want me to go and see them?" "No, thanks, Ed. I'll try to sort it out. If I need help, you know I'll ask."

"Are you going to tell Dad?" "Of course, I'll have to. They will be writing to him, anyway. So he'll get the true story from me first." I had to stop for a moment. "But, Ed, I don't think he gives a flying fuck about me, so I don't expect a lot of support." "Oh, come on, Pad. You are a bit hard on him, ya know. Just give him a chance."

Immediately we got indoors, I went into the lounge where Dad was reading a book. "Hi, Dad." "Hello, son." "Dad, I need to talk to you." That got his attention. "I've had serious trouble at school." I told him the whole story.

"You must have done something wrong. You probably deserved it. Anyway, you wanted to leave school a few months ago, well now you can." Eddie was in the room and even he was a bit surprised. "Come on, Dad, didn't you listen to what Paddy just told you?" I didn't give him time to reply. "They were wrong, Dad, and I'll only leave school on my own terms, not when anybody else decides. I'm going back in the morning. Thanks, anyway!" I looked at Eddie and shrugged.

I went to my club that evening and I told Michael about all the goings on. "I heard Dad talking to M . . . Betty, so I wondered what had happened. Would you have hit the teacher if he'd whacked you?" "I'd have smashed his fucking face in."

I showed up at the school gates the next morning and the teacher on duty wasn't sure what to do. He asked me to stand aside and wait for a moment. He popped quickly into the front office. He came out followed by the school secretary. She smiled at me. "Good morning, O'Donovan. I'm sorry but you have been expelled. I have a letter here which you might as well take with you. It explains everything. I'm truly sorry. Goodbye."

I got a lot of curious looks, as I made my way against the ever-increasing stream. Most avoided my eyes.

So that was that then!

The letter had been addressed to Mr and Mrs O'Donovan. I didn't open it and decided to give it to Betty.

That evening, much to my surprise, Betty discussed the letter with me. The basics were that I had been caught smoking, was a bad and disrupting influence on other pupils, had refused punishment and had threatened the Headmaster.

A complete pack of lies!

Dad, as I had predicted, believed every word written in the letter. Again, surprisingly, Betty had her doubts. She certainly knew that I didn't smoke, that was for certain!

We talked and broke the letter down, sentence by sentence, and came up with a plan.

1. I did not smoke, therefore, not even Jesus Christ could have seen me with a cigarette in my mouth.

2. I was not, nor ever had been, a bad influence on any pupil. I recalled my asking not to be made to stand in front of school, for that very reason.

3. I had not refused punishment. I had refused corporal punishment but had been given no alternative.

4. I thought the Headmaster had become very heated and was about to strike me with the cane. I politely told him not to do that!

5. The school secretary had obviously been concerned because she made an appearance.

"Do you want me to take this up with the LCC school board, or do you just want to leave and start work?"

"I just want a chance to take my 'O' level exams and I don't care where I take them. The Head is out of order and has no right to expel me. Can you help me get back into that school?"

Betty was clearly upset and very annoyed and determined.

"You've been badly treated, son, and although we've got a few issues between us, I'll do my best to get you back in school." And she did!

She visited the school board and had to practically bully them into getting involved because I was over the school leaving age and they had many other problems on their hands. Nevertheless, I was visited at home and interviewed and we were promised that some action would be taken.

I had a lovely couple of weeks, spending my days either hanging around The Cut in Waterloo or with Uncle Nathan in the Borough Market. Nathan and his pals were very interested in my row with the school and he encouraged me to go all the way and not take it lying down. I asked him not to say anything to Nan because she'd only worry and that was the last thing I wanted.

Bookie Terry had a different opinion. He thought that I should forget the school and go to work. He had an in-law called Joe, who was a Wharf Superintendent. "I'll have a word in his ear, he'll find you a nice job. With brains like yours, you'll have no trouble." I thanked him but my mind was made up. I wasn't going to give in. "I understand but, if you don't mind, I'll still give you a mention. It won't do any harm, will it?" "Thanks, Terry."

A letter finally arrived from the LCC. It was addressed to Betty, so I didn't open it. They had arranged a meeting between ourselves and the school but they promised nothing.

The day arrived and Betty and I set off to our meeting. Her instructions to me were fairly simple: be polite and don't lose your temper, whatever the outcome. I was by now getting used to not going to school and it was a great temptation to tell them all to go fuck themselves but then I thought of Nan.

The meeting was set up in the dreaded office. There was the Head, his assistant and the secretary. There were two people from the council and us two. The place was crowded.

The discussions took place mainly between the Head and the council officials. I was delighted because they argued the exact points I had made.

I didn't want to appear smug but the Head was plainly losing the argument. The main thrust being that he had not considered the reported sighting and hadn't given a fair judgement to my side of the argument.

The only time I was asked to speak was to refute his argument that I had threatened him. I only told the Head, "not to do that". That was when I thought there was a danger that he was about to strike me with the cane. I also clarified that I had never refused punishment, however unfairly, I had only refused the cane i.e. corporal punishment. I noticed the lady official shudder as I said that. She was obviously one of a new breed against all forms of physical punishment.

The meeting came to an end and we were asked if we would mind waiting outside for a short while. "You did very well in there, son. It's obvious that you were wrongly and badly treated." "Thanks for your help."

The secretary appeared and asked if we would like to come back into the office. The Head offered no apology but said that in view of the exceptional circumstances, and my desire to finish my studies and sit my exams, he would allow me to return to school. He gave me a high handed and pompous lecture as to my future behaviour but wished to bring the whole matter to a close. I was to return to school the very next day.

We thanked them all before leaving. Betty was justifiably pleased with herself and although I did appreciate her hard work, we were sadly destined to have a very fiery future.

We were both headstrong, opinionated and stubborn people and held differing views on many things. Religion being the main cause of frustration for both of us.

It was all plain sailing from now on. I had returned to school now even more isolated because I no longer wanted anything to do with any of the other students. I would now wander over to Battersea Park where the work was going on, setting up the funfair for the coming Festival of Britain. I mixed with other students but avoided any from my own school. I was still very unhappy that those two mugs never told the Head that I wasn't smoking. They were shit scared!

The exams were now upon us. I would be taking English, maths, physics and history. The bare minimum. I regret not taking geography because I found the subject very interesting but I had done all the studying of that subject and that was enough for me.

I have always been blessed with a good memory and I literally sailed through the exams. It's worth mentioning the physics exam. I read the paper through and the answers were as clear to me, almost as though I had the textbook in front of me. It felt like cheating. I finished my paper, checked it over and sat back. The examiner came over to me and asked if I was having difficulties. He was very surprised when I told him that I had finished. He advised me to check my answers once more. I made a show of rechecking then got up and handed my paper in. I got 94% pass!

My last exam was history, a particularly interesting period (1832-1936). I polished off my paper, handed it in to the examiner, collected my jacket and bag and said goodbye to him. I walked out of the school, never looked back and never said any farewells.

My schooldays were over!!

Chapter 11

I thought it better to wait for my exam results before attempting to start work, even though Uncle Terry had spoken to his in-law and there could be an interesting opening for me.

The Festival of Britain was going on at the South Bank in Waterloo, so I spent a great deal of time over there. Aunt Anne and Eileen helped run an ice-cream van and I managed to get some work helping them. Uncle Nathan didn't let this opportunity pass by. He sold balloons, toffee apples and even took people's photographs. I sometimes took their money, names and addresses although there wasn't really much point because he rarely had film in the camera. We had to be on our guard because the place was crawling with police, but there were thousands of people from all over the country and from around the world. Thankfully the weather wasn't that bad either. Fortunately he never got our "collar felt" but had to be on our toes from time to time.

The fun was over and it was time to go to work. My 'O' level results had turned up in the post and I had passed all four with flying colours. I also received a very frosty letter from the school, reminding me that all textbooks were the property of the school and should be returned. I had left everything in my desk so didn't bother replying.

Dad had been getting a bit agitated with my delay in starting work, muttering that he couldn't keep me forever. I decided to go and see Terry's in-law, Joe. I got a really warm reception and felt very comfortable and at ease with this man, even though he was the superintendent. I gave him a brief history of my education and of my exam results and he offered me a job as a trainee tally clerk. It sounded very interesting. I would have to complete a full application form and my employment would have to be confirmed by the Hay's Wharf Head Office, but it would just be rubber-stamping. The job was mine! The forms would be sent to me in the next few days. He told me to make sure I filled them in properly. "What you doing now?" "Well, nothing planned." "Fancy a walk round the wharf with me? I have to make myself seen and I can show you where you'll be working." "Yes, thanks, that'll be great."

We strolled together through Cotton's Wharf and Fennings. I saw many, many people I knew and who knew me and there was plenty of waving and shouting. It was a very busy place. I was taken to a dockside office and introduced as the new trainee. It was a little bit embarrassing but I received a warm welcome and I felt comfortable already.

When I gave Dad the good news, he was very pleased and I know he did it to annoy me, "Your mother will be happy with the extra money coming in." I couldn't comment.

Eddie was delighted with my news and Michael was ever so slightly jealous. He hated school with a vengeance and couldn't wait to start work but his eyes brightened up when I told him that I'd find some pocket money for him.

I'd filled the application form in, as requested. It was nice to be able to put down on paper my qualifications. I didn't bother with the post since I was only a ten-minute walk away from the head office, St Olaf's House so I handed my papers in by hand. A few months ago, I visited St Olaf's House. It's now a private hospital. Unfortunately, Ryan had snapped his Achilles and was treated there. He has fully recovered, thankfully, but it was indeed strange to revisit my old stamping ground after almost 60 years.

I must admit that I was a bit anxious as I tore open the letter. It was good news. I had been offered the job. I was given a telephone number to call in order to arrange an interview where my duties would be fully explained and a start date agreed. We didn't have a telephone so to avoid mucking about, I presented myself at St Olaf's and eventually spoke to the right person and we arranged a suitable date. I would be back in less than two weeks.

My first day of work had arrived. I was a little bit excited but not nearly as much as Michael. He was jumping around in his usual way muttering all the time that he could hardly believe that I was starting work.

The start time was eight o'clock and, as what was to become a habit of a lifetime, I was early. I knew where to report for work, it was the office on the quayside at Cotton's Wharf. At that time, Tooley Street was teeming with life. There were hundreds of dockers streaming through the dock gates with lorries and horse and carts, all jostling for position. The dockers were a noisy lot, shouting and joking amongst themselves. There were lots of faces that I recognised, and then I heard my name being called out so I turned in the direction of a voice that I knew very well. It was my Uncle George. He bundled his way toward me. "Mornin', Paddy. Are you starting today?" "Hi ya, George. Yeah, I thought you knew." "I knew that you'd got a job. Joe told me but I wasn't sure when. Do you know where to go?" "Yes, thanks, see you around." He gave me a wink and went on his way but stopped suddenly and turned around. "Uncle Dave works on this wharf. I'll let him know you're here. By the way, any problems, come and find me. Be lively, son."

I was given a very warm welcome by the men in the quayside office and the man in charge told me that I wouldn't be going out today because he wanted to show me how things worked and what would be expected of me. I was comfortable with that.

I was taken through the tally cards and shown things like ships' plans and bills of lading, etc. It was explained that there was a strict plan to unloading a fully laden ship. You couldn't just unload it in a haphazard fashion because cargo would slip and possibly injure the stevedores, who were working the holds, or the ship may actually capsize. I was taken onto a couple of boats that were being unloaded and whilst I was peering down into the hold, I spied a very familiar face, Uncle Dave. The top man (that was the man responsible for giving instructions to the crane driver, all of these being given by hand signals. No mobile phones in those days) yelled out, "Davey, look who's here. One of your nephews." Dave looked up and waved. "Hi ya, Paddy, nice to see ya. We'll have a chat at dinnertime. Wait for me, won't you?" I gave him the thumbs up. This was an entirely new world and I felt very comfortable.

I hung around once the hooter was sounded and, eventually, Uncle Dave appeared. He was beaming and he put his big arms around my shoulder. He was a big strong man but a gentle giant. A very nice man and one I was very fond of. "We all knew you had a job here, you lucky sod. You know that you've landed once of the best jobs in the docks, don't you?" "Well, I never knew it was that! Good! How's Aunt Sarah?"

"She's lovely, thanks, son. Wait till I tell her about you. Anyway, do you know where Davey works?" I knew that my cousin, Dave, worked in the docks somewhere but I didn't know exactly where, and although he was a few months younger than me, he had left school and started work before I had.

"Follow me, I'll show you where he is but he's probably gone off to have his dinner. You know what a guts-ache he is but no worries, I know what café he uses. Lively, now, we've only got an hour."

I found Davey sitting alongside a couple of blokes of similar age and his eyes nearly popped out of his head when I walked into the café. Uncle Dave went on his way.

Davey introduced me to his mates, Bill and Mick. They seemed like nice fellas. I was obviously unaware at that first meeting that it would be through my friendship with Bill that I would eventually come to meet Rosie.

The food in the café was brilliant and cheap and I would spend many, many dinner hours in this place. Bill was a real chirpy sort of bloke and very easy to get on with. Mick, who was a bit older, was a very good boxer and I would spend many rounds of sparring with him, in the coming years.

I felt as though my life was changing direction and it felt very comfortable. I had definitely fallen on my feet.

I now started work in earnest. It hadn't taken me very long to fully understand what my job entailed even though for the first couple of weeks, I worked alongside an experienced tally clerk. The main goods that were being unloaded were dairy products from Holland and Denmark, consisting of butter, cheese, pork and eggs, as well as tinned luncheon meat, brawn and ham. It also soon became evident that there was lots of thieving going on or "ullages", as we were to describe these shortages on our report for the various merchants.

Each morning, I would be given my defined area of work, for example, bacon. These came wrapped in a sort of mutton cloth, each being one side or half a pig. They would be brought out of the ship in large slings or nets. They would then be placed onto a platform and the dockers would load each individual side on their sack barrow and walk them past me. Each side would be weighed and numerated. This was carefully recorded by me. They would then be taken either straight to be loaded on waiting transport or to a chilled storage area.

The dockers were on piecework, which meant that they were paid according to the amount of goods they unloaded. Their only delay was me, therefore, the quicker I was able to record or tally, the more they earned. I had an incentive because the fourteen-man gang would all put in a shilling a day to keep me sweet. Everybody was a winner.

Then there was an added perk. With a wink and a nudge, the odd side would bypass me and disappear into the dark warehouse. That evening, I would take home a very decent cut of pork. I like all my new colleagues; was very well looked after because they needed my help and permission.

In Spite of Everything . . . .

What really amused me was that the meat was always nicely wrapped and portioned so that it could be hidden under clothing. There was security at the dock gates but just a few local blokes against hundreds of streaming dockers. Their little huts would always contain a few parcels, so everybody was sweet.

Dad and Betty were very happy with this extra bounty. I always wondered whether Betty would confess her sins? It was my job to write up the final report, comparing my tally with the merchant bills of lading. We blamed the shortages on those thieving bastards in Rotterdam.

Much the same procedure went on with the cheese and butter, although the butter arrived in large frozen barrels. They would be smashed open and large chunks hacked away, right at the end of a shift, of course.

The tinned produce was a bit more difficult because they were very large tins, which was impossible to hide. You certainly couldn't completely take the piss out of the security. Also there was always a sprinkling of coppers hanging around in Tooley Street but these dockers were very crafty. They had large tin openers and the meat could be removed and divvied up. This practice gave me extra work because each crate had to be itemised (each ullage crate, that is). I was very well looked after for my troubles. No wonder Uncle Dave had said that I had the best job in the docks.

Now that both Eddie and I were putting money into the house, a few luxuries appeared. We had agreed to help Dad buy a television and a radiogram, which meant we were able to start buying records. Michael was also happy because we both gave him a bit of pocket money, but he was always skint. He couldn't hold on to money. Luckily, I was getting more money than Eddie and, possibly Dad, a fact I didn't advertise, but it was Michael who got the benefit!!

Christmas was on us in a flash and the extras increased considerably. We worked until dinnertime on Christmas Eve then there was a mad dash to the local pubs. I was much too young for alcohol but a group of dockers insisted that I come with them for a Christmas drink. The landlord didn't seem to worry too much. They got me blind drunk to the point where they laid me out on some chairs and propped me under a table. I never did know how I got home that evening. I do know that I felt like shit next morning! Betty was as mad as hell and Dad wasn't that happy either. I could hardly eat my Christmas dinner.

That evening, still feeling very woolly, I went round to see Nan and the family. Nan already knew all about my shenanigans. She wasn't very pleased and Johnny was really annoyed. "They took a liberty with you, the bastards. They should know better. Wait till I meet up with them." I thought that if those blokes had known about Johnny, they wouldn't enjoy their Christmas!

I started to feel a bit better and we had a nice quiet Christmas. Remember, it was the first without Granddad. Apparently, Uncle Pat had walked into the pub on Christmas Eve and had given out a severe bollocking. It was he who had taken me home.

After Christmas, it was straight back to work and, following lots of apologies from many of the offending dockers, life now settled into a daily routine.

There were many perks working for a large corporation such as the Hays Group. They had a large and varied, well-run sports section and I got involved with a vengeance.

There was football, of course, but I found it very difficult at my age to get into any of the senior teams. The men were not only good but just too strong. Even Davey (AKA Tarzan) found it difficult, as did Bill, and he was the best amongst us. It would be another year before we would make an impression.

There was a thriving table tennis section and I was able to hold my own. However, the crème de la crème was the big gymnasium at Mark Brown's Wharf and I soon got settled in there. The husband of Dad's sister, Tony, was a very good boxer and although I hadn't had that much contact with him, he welcomed me with open arms. It was here that I sparred many rounds with Mick, who had many amateur awards to his name. He was a bit smaller than me but very slippery.

It was whilst Tony was watching us in the ring that he was the first to mention that I had quick hands. Mick had already found that out. "Paddy, I'm being serious, you could go a long way in this game. Why won't you box for our club?" We stopped sparring and Mick said, "I've been wondering the same thing."

I gave it a moment's thought. "I can't see the point and I can't stand the fans. They scream and holla like a bunch of wild animals and most of them haven't even had a fight. I'm not a fucking circus act!" I got out of the ring and took my gloves off. Tony came over to me. "I hope I haven't upset you, Paddy. I'll never mention it again. Anyway thanks for helping out with Mick. We both appreciate it." "Yeah, that's okay. See you next Wednesday. Bye, Mick, see you tomorrow." I smiled at him. "Don't forget, keep that left up."

The year had started well but it would turn out to be very traumatic.

Chapter 12

The news spread like wildfire, "The King Has Died". It's strange how in an area where most people were left wing and didn't have much time for the establishment, the old King was well respected and admired. The general feeling was one of deep sadness. There was many a pint drunk to his memory on the day. We were now to have a queen just as in Victorian times. Then the thought struck me that Nan had witnessed two queens. Our new Queen wasn't even in the country which must have been sad for her, not being beside her dad as he passed away.

I was to receive more startling, close to home, bad news. Uncle Dave, who had been off work for a while, had been diagnosed with an illness called leukaemia. This was something I'd never heard of before and it was very, very serious. It was even more surprising because Uncle Dave was the biggest robust member of the family and I could never imagine him being ill.

In no way being unpatriotic, but the death of the King had little meaning to us. We had our own problems because Dave was going downhill fast and there didn't seem to be any cure.

He eventually wound up in the Brompton over the river, where they tried everything to make him better. At one time, they asked all close family members to donate some blood but, following tests, out of more than two dozen of us, only two were suitable. One being me and the other being one of his cousins. Johnny, Patsy and the rest were mortified, unable to understand why they were unable to give blood to their brother. Even though the doctors explained the reasons, they were still unhappy. Sadly poor Johnny never got over that disappointment and it changed his life completely.

Terry and I (yes, another Terry) gave blood on two separate occasions and although it prolonged Dave's life for a few more weeks, he sadly passed away.

I remember looking at Nan at that sad funeral and admired the way she held herself with dignity. She was very sad and deeply shocked. She was losing her family, one by one, and I knew (yes, really felt it), that one day, the same would happen to me. I walked over to her and held her tightly, tighter than ever before. I was relieved that this funeral took place at Hither Green and not that bastard place, Kensal Green.

There are many things you could say about dockers, that they were lazy, disruptive and dishonest, some of which might have a ring of truth about it but, and a big but, they were certainly generous!

Uncle Dave was a well-liked and respected man and upon hearing of his death, the whole of the pool (the dockland area between London and Tower Bridges, arranged a collection for his widow, Aunt Sarah). You must be made aware that the benefits available in those days were very meagre. We took care of our own. (This is where I get on my high horse. How can a so called civilised country like ours have so badly looked after the very people they called on to defend our land and yet, nowadays, lavish benefits on so many lazy and disloyal layabout slags??)

The amount of money collected was quite outstanding for those days. It topped £800. It may seem small change now but you could buy a decent semi for around £2000, so work that out. This money was given to Aunt Sarah and allowed her to look after young Maureen and Terry. Davey, of course, was at work.

They also arranged a charity boxing show at Manor Place Baths and I was duty bound to take part. I boxed three exhibition rounds with a lad from the Fisher Club, who was London ABA champion at the time. I reckon I could have taken him in a real competition. He had a bad habit of throwing too many rights and left him open to a left hook counter to the ribs. The adrenalin wasn't pumping that hard but I could still feel his body shudder from time to time. We got a standing ovation and nubbins (that's money chucked into the ring). It all helped for Aunt Sarah.

A couple of Johnny's best mates were among the audience and they later embarrassed me with their praise. They said that I "had style".

One of the earlier junior bouts had a young lad called John fighting and he was a real terrier in the ring, he threw lots of leather. I was to become a warm friend of his in the future when I would know him as Butch.

There were plenty of old fighters in the audience. The likes of ex-lightweight champion, Tommy McGovern (my dad's cousin), Tommy Daley and some up and coming lads, the Cooper twins.

Yet again, after all the Xs (expenses) were taken care of, a few bob went Aunt Sarah's way.

Johnny just couldn't seem to cope with Dave's death. He took to drinking badly, which caused further problems because he became very violent in drink and he was an extremely powerful and dangerous man. He hurt and upset many "faces" and it was very difficult for the family to keep the lid on it.

Sadly, his relationship with Aubrey, who he was engaged to, was becoming very strained and it was to come to an end, when in a drunken rage, in the middle of a popular local pub, he took offence over a pretty dress she was wearing and tore if off her body and ripped it to shreds. Luckily, his older brother, George, was also in the pub and I don't know how, but he managed to get Johnny out of the pub before anyone else interfered. Because that would have been a disaster

They never saw each other again and although throughout the years that followed, Johnny made light of their relationship, I knew that he had a lifetime of regret. He never married therefore never had children of his own, probably the reason he was so fond of Eddie's, Michael's and mine and so proud of their achievements. It's very sad because he was a very intelligent and humorous man and would have made a wonderful husband and father. But that was not how it was written. He had a drink problem all his life but was able to somehow control it but more about him later.

I had to find a way to get some of my ill-gotten gains on to Nan's plate but I knew that she would have nothing stolen and she would have been very upset with me and I certainly was having none of that.

There's always a way! Uncle Nathan had opened a fruit stall on London Bridge Approach and I was in the habit of hanging around the stall on my way home from work and sometimes during my dinner hour. He loved my company and I would even give him a hand serving his customers as they rushed to catch their trains home from the City. There used to be literally thousands of City gents making their way home and they had to be served quick.

One lunchtime, we were chewing the fat[48] and I hit on the idea that if I gave him some of my whack[49], he could get Aunt Anne to give it to Nan, letting her think that Nathan had bought it real cheap. The plan was foolproof or so I thought. I can still hear him now in that authoritative tone, "Son, you're putting yourself on offer. Those thieving, conniving bastards are using you. If they're tumbled, they'd grass you off because they couldn't get away with it without you being involved. They're taking fucking liberties with you, son. How many times have I told you? Trust no one. Don't let them know what you know." He hesitated for a moment. "You'll have to put a stop to it now. I know it won't be pleasant but you're not a grass. Just let them work out how to do their thieving without your help." He hesitated again. "Now, please promise me you'll take care of it?" I was disappointed but I trusted Nathan. "That's it, that's the finish. I'll get hold of the ganger (head man) and give him the bad news."

That next morning, I was in early and offered to handle the bacon. No one objected because it was one of the toughest details. I made a beeline for the ganger. "Tim, we need to have a chat. Can you give me five minutes?" "Mornin', Paddy, what's the problem?"

I very carefully explained my concerns and told him that from now on, everything that's unloaded would be tallied and weighed. If there were to be any thieving, it would have to be done out of my area and out of my sight. "I'm not a grass, Tim, or a company man, but I want no part in any funny practices. Do we understand each other?" He looked a bit shocked and was put completely off guard. "Sorry to hear that, Paddy, but you'll have no trouble from me. I'll let the rest of the gang know. See you on the quayside."

I go some very odd looks from the rest of the gang but, as the morning wore on, things were just about returning to normal (minus the winks, of course). A couple of the men seemed to be a bit annoyed because I overheard some funny comments, but I ignored everything and got on with my job. There is always some bastard who will spoil the party and, sure enough, he was about.

There was this younger big bloke, well, fat really, and he kept slamming his trolley into the weighing platform in a very aggressive way, at the same time making silly comments. I tried to ignore the mug but I just couldn't stand it too much longer. I told him to be careful with his trolley, telling him that he'd fuck the scales up if he wasn't careful and that could bring the job to a halt. He chose to ignore me. I even noticed other men having a quiet word in his ear but he just shrugged them away. For about the fifth time, I asked him to be careful but he just blared at me then as he walked away, I heard him call me a c***.

I wasn't standing for that! "Oi, tubby, ain't anybody told you that if you call anybody a c***, you'd better be ready to have a fight?" He didn't even turn round, just gave me a 'V' sign. Old Arthur, he was the docker who put the bacon on the scales and then back on the trolley, put his hand on my shoulder. "Take no notice of him, son, he's a Connaught[50]. Anyway, we'll take care of him, he won't be here tomorrow." I was seething!

Here he came again, crash bang wallop. Arthur glared at him as he hoisted the bacon side onto the scales then, without warning, the tub of lard pushed me very hard in the chest. He was a strong fucker and sent me reeling backwards, nearly putting my spine out. I don't think he reckoned on what came next.

In a flash, I dropped my papers and hit him square on the side of his face and, because he was coming towards me, it was a mighty blow. He yelped and put his hand up to his left eye. I'd never seen anything like it before, or since, in my entire life. All hell broke loose and people came running over but, as he took his hand from his face, it was as though an egg had been stuck below his eye. The swelling was awesome and getting worse. His eye was now completely closed

I was gently guided away and told to cool down and I heard someone tell him to go to the first aid station immediately. His eye was seriously damaged.

Although I had landed a near perfect punch, I think that because he carried too much fluid, that was the cause of the rapid swelling. He did as advised and hurried off to the medics. I never set eyes on him again. He apparently came from the north of the river and had only got a day's work at our wharf.

There was a short delay but after about ten minutes, normal service was resumed. Nobody crashed into the scales, anymore.

I was just leaving the dock's gates to meet Davey and Bill for dinner, when a voice called out for me to "be-lay" (stop). It was the Superintendent, Joe. "Hold on, son, I want a word with you. I know we're no angels down here but you just can't go around bashing people round the head. What on earth did you hit him with and why?" I was a bit confused. What did he mean by that? "He called me a c*** and I hit him with this." I held up my right hand. "What? Did he say that I hit him with something?" Joe looked surprised. "He didn't but I didn't think a punch would cause all that damage." He half smiled and shook his head. "Remind me not to upset you, Paddy. Now go and have your dinner break and, by the way, your union rep will be around to see you later. Enjoy your dinner."

The news had spread like wildfire, always exaggerated, as usual, and it filled our dinnertime conversation.

Everything had settled down and the afternoon shift was going along nicely. Tea break arrived and Uncle George appeared. He was a union shop steward. The gang were up on their feet explaining to my uncle, in very concerned voices, that they had not been part of it and telling him exactly what had occurred. I could see that Uncle George was not happy and, beside him being a union man, he could get very violent. It was obvious that these men did not want to get involved in any problems with our family and I knew that a few of them were very concerned about Johnny's reaction, even though I had tried to reassure them.

Uncle George sorted it all out and declared the matter over. We then returned to work. "Don't rush off after work, son. I want five minutes with you. See you in your office." I nodded and went to work.

"So, tell me why this all happened? There must be a good reason." There was just Uncle George and I alone in the office, so I told him everything, and I mean, everything! He took it all in and gave it some thought. I got a bit of a bollocking for allowing myself to become involved and praise for being sensible enough to put a stop to it. "I don't give two fucks what they get up to but you must promise me that you won't give them a helping hand. Just keep your mouth shut, eyes open and let them sort themselves out. I'll be having a quiet word with a couple of the gang so you'll hear no more about it. See you around, Paddy." He left me in the office but poked his head round the door with a big smile on his face. "Nice punch!"

On the way home, I stopped by and had a chat with Uncle Nathan and gave him a detailed account of the day's ruckus. He nodded a lot and, like Uncle George, praised me for what I did.

Eddie had a bit of important news to tell me. He had received his national service call up papers but, much to Dad's disgust, he threw them in the dustbin. He wasn't going to take any notice of them and had decided not to report for his medical. For once in our lifetime, I wasn't the bad boy.

I continued to go to my club and to spend a lot of evenings at Nan's house but we were all getting older and meeting new friends, which would have an effect on my lifestyle.

There was a mobile coffee stall at the Borough, adjacent to the large church, and most evenings the local tearaways hung around, drinking coffee and noshing meat pies and hotdogs. I would stay around until the early hours and made quite a few new mates, as well as keeping in touch with the old ones. Many of the boys were now petty criminals but they were fully aware that I wasn't the least bit interested. I was pleased that I was accepted by these types of lads because some of them were local characters. But they were all very aware that I could handle myself.

One of the likeable rogues became very friendly with me and asked if I was interested in buying a car with him. To be honest, I'd never been that interested in motors but I had money and this didn't seem a bad idea. The fact that neither of us had a driving licence, or that we were not yet old enough, never occurred to me.

"What kind of motor is it, Ted?" "A Humber Super Snipe. You interested then?" "Well, why not? It's bound to be a bird puller, ain't it?" He was now very excited. "It's in a lockup under the railway arches at Waterloo. How about we meet next Saturday afternoon and have a look at it? You happy with that?" "Yeah, I'll see you before that and we'll make a meet."

We went to see the car; had a drive! That was a laugh, driving instructions on the hoof!! It was an enormous black car with massive running boards and the driving area was separated from the back. It was a real beast. We argued for hours over the price but what really sealed the deal was the off-street parking that came with it. We parted with £20, a cockle[51] apiece!

With much crunching of gears and bashing into pavements, we taught ourselves to drive but we didn't take too many liberties because although there wasn't a great deal of traffic control around in those days, we couldn't take the piss. In actual fact, Eddie, who also had no driving licence, used to borrow it from us and he and his mates had a fine old time. My mate, Ted, didn't mind because Eddie used to treat him.

It was a bird puller and we had a long list of girls who were gagging to be driven around. Naturally our mates were envious and our "street cred" soared.

There was great excitement in London and, I suppose, all over the country but at the time I was only aware of London. Our new Queen was about to be crowned and London was buzzing. There were some street parties and most of the pubs were ablaze with flags and bunting. It was like the end of the war again.

Everything was completely calm and relaxed at work and the dockers seemed comfortable with me. The pilfering was still going on, of course, but not in my sight and not on my shift. I had learned that Uncle Pats, who was now the labour master at New Fresh Wharf, had tried to find the bloke who had caused me trouble but he was unsuccessful. He had put out a warning that if he was seen anywhere near Tooley Street, he would be seriously hurt. He couldn't have been that stupid because he was never seen again. I was really pleased over that because Johnny was raving mad and that bloke could have been hurt bad.

The cricket season was in full swing and Davey had arranged for us to have a trial for the dock second team. They had a lovely ground just outside Sidcup, Kent. I was very surprised when the captain turned out to be my Uncle Tony. We were picked for a coming match and, after a short while, Tony tossed the ball to me. We sorted the field out and I asked the keeper if he would stand up to the stumps because I was only medium paced. He did and in no time at all, I'd taken my first wicket and went on to take five in all. That would be the first and last game for the second team, because I was transferred to the first team. Tony was a bit upset but thought that I would be better off in that league.

It took a while to settle in because I was so young but I quickly earned respect, from the rest of the side, through my batting and bowling. I played most of the remaining matches and had a very pleasant summer.

There was an uneasy peace in our house. Betty and I would never see eye to eye but we tried to avoid confrontation and arguments. I made sure that my housekeeping was given to her on Friday evenings and she washed and ironed for me and kept my bedroom clean. Her cooking never improved but I either ate round Nan's or in the many local cafes. She wasn't very happy with that arrangement but hard luck.

Dad and I didn't have that much to do with each other. We had different interests and now that I was working, whatever little control he had over me was now a thing of the past. I could not forgive him over Granddad and failed to understand why he'd never been to see the old gal (Nan), but he was a nice, kind man in his own way so I tolerated him. In truth, we tolerated each other.

Michael was getting real excited because he was finishing school soon and he'd got himself an apprenticeship with a top class heating and ventilating company (the RR of the trade). It was because he was so good with his hands, he was chosen out of hundreds of applicants. We were all so proud of him. Eddie and I decided to pay for a new suit and I think we must have shamed Dad a bit because he put some money in.

Eddie took charge and they chose a nice light-coloured material. It's funny because all through their lives, they both preferred light colours, whereas I always only ever had dark suits. So it was a good thing that Eddie took over because I'd have talked him into a dark one.

Eddie hadn't heard any further from the call up and he was having a nice old time. He had always been a very good singer (as was Michael) and so he started going from pub to pub, entering singing competitions and there were many pubs taking part. The bigger competitions paid out very good prize money but there was a catch, an entrance fee! Eddie had a bit of a problem here because he knocked his money out almost as soon as he got it. He was very generous, was my big brother!

This is where I came to the rescue. I would stake him and he would give me a share of the winnings. Now, this wasn't as much of a gamble as it might sound. Eddie was very rapidly becoming a star performer and he won nine out of ten. Now that's a very good odds and I knew what I was talking about.

It was only on rare occasions that I actually saw him sing because I was still underage for pub going and some of the publicans were a bit nervous about underage drinking but, anyway, I spent most of my evenings at my club and messing about with my own mates, pushing our old car to get started. We used to offer all the lads a ride round the manor but many, many times we had to be jump started so there was lots of moaning and groaning, which soon turned to joy once we'd got started. Girls, as well, by the way!

I also enjoyed going to the pictures (the cinema) and often went with Johnny over the West End to see the new releases. Johnny wouldn't queue and, in those days, there used to be massive long ones.

We used to stand out in front of the main doors and Johnny would make a show (a small nod of the head). Once the cinema was open and the queue started moving forward, the doorman would slide a couple of tickets into John's hand in exchange for a couple of shillings (10p in today's money). We would then stride into the cinema in front of most and get a decent seat. There used to be the odd grumble but that was all. We saw some great films in that fashion, half-price and no long queuing.

Eileen was also a very keen picture-goer with different taste to Johnny. She preferred the musicals and there were plenty of them. If she didn't have a date, I would keep her company because a lady couldn't go alone. Even in those days, there were the odd marks about. I loved Eileen's company anyway so everyone was a winner.

These were lovely times. What could possibly go wrong?

As soon as I walked in the flat, I sensed an atmosphere. Betty just grunted, "He's in there," nodding towards the front room. I thought who's in where? What the fuck's going on?

Eddie was talking to Dad and they both looked a bit glum. "Hi, Ed. Hi, Dad. What's wrong?" Dad stared at me. "We've had the police up here. Your mum . . . ," (there he goes again. I wanted to scream at him, "She's not my fucking mum!" But I kept my cool because I was a bit concerned. My immediate panicky thoughts were Michael and that sent shivers down my spine.) " . . . is very upset." Fuck her, I thought. "Is Mikey alright?"

Eddie realised straightaway. "No, no, you silly sod. It's me. I've got to sign on for the call up otherwise I'll be nicked."

I let out a gasp of relief. "Never mind, mate. You've had a decent run and that Korean War is nearly over." I had to lighten the atmosphere. "Anyway, a wimp like you might not pass the medical." He jumped up and grabbed me. Some wimp! He was a real charmer, was my older brother, and he soon had Betty eating out of his hand, even making her laugh! That pleased Dad, crisis over!

He very shortly had his medical and was passed AI (of course) and was now waiting for his call up papers. They arrived shortly before Christmas and he had been assigned to the Royal Navy (his first choice) and had been ordered to report to Plymouth. It will be strange not having Eddie around but we all had to grow up and go our separate ways. Michael wasn't very happy because he hated change.

The cricket season was coming to an end and the nights were drawing in again. I would try to make one of the football teams but if not, I still had my club side.

I had completely settled in at work and had a renewed confidence. I stood no nonsense from anybody and did my job very efficiently.

Because of all my interests, I found that I was struggling a bit working for Terry, the bookmaker. So I had a nice long chat with him, telling him that if he could get someone to take over from me, then I'd quit. He fully understood. "I bet you've got something going on down those docks, you crafty sod. What about putting me in something?" I told him the story about what went on and he gave me a deep, thoughtful nod. "You done the right thing, Paddy. If there's any thieving to be had, do it yourself trained private and don't involve anyone else." Then with a wink, "Unless they're one of your own!"

It took him a couple of weeks before he found a replacement for me. So, sadly, there ended our association, or so I thought.

His words kept ringing in my ears because, of course, I was always thinking of different ways to make an extra bit of money.

Uncle Nathan now ran his fruit and veg stall virtually full time. He had a partner (in reality a 'go-for') so that actually they ran two stalls a couple of yards apart.

As I've said before, I was in the habit of spending part of my dinner hour hanging around and chatting and I also hung around after work before going home. He seemed to like my company and I certainly liked his because he was such a character (a real geezer).

We used to sometimes have a coffee together in the Italian restaurant opposite and the seeds of a nice little earner were planted.

Nathan fully understood the mechanics of my job and he, of course, knew that some tasty produce came under my control. "Tell me exactly how it all works, Paddy, every little thing. Don't miss anything out, it could be very important." He wanted to know how the goods got out of the docks, legally!

I explained that a proportion went straight on to cartage and some was stored in the name of the importer. I knew where the goods were stored and in whose name they were registered and, more importantly, the proper appropriate storage reference.

Vans, lorries, horse and carts would turn up and would have varying collection notes, but they must bear the name of the company actually paying for the storage and the main reference number and, just as important, the location. Some of the paperwork was a bit scrappy but all the relevant details had to be correct or they would be sent away.

The various drivers used to appear in their hundreds to a main delivery office and the clerical staff were run off their feet so, as long as everything matched, they would stamp the collection note and allow the vehicle through.

What made everything more chaotic was the impatience of the drivers. They would bully the poor clerks to get their orders stamped and get loaded as quickly as possible. First thing in the morning, it was manic.

Nathan took this all in. "Let me think this over for a couple of days, son. I think I've got a good idea. You might have hit on pay dirt!" He looked up. "Don't say a word to another soul. Your cousin, Dave, works in the quayside, don't he?" "Yeah, but he's not involved." "Good. Keep it that way! Got to go, work to be done. See you tomorrow." As he left, he put his index finger up to his mouth and smiled.

Without causing any fuss or bringing undue attention, I started to bring up the subject of lorry drivers and collections because both Davey and Bill worked in one of the traffic offices, where they arranged for the loading of lorries, etc. They both laughed and told me of the impatience and confusion that was all around them. We made quite a joke about it. There was a couple of odd times, when I had half an hour or so to spare, so I wandered over to their quayside office and witnessed the activities first hand (very casual, of course). "You surely don't allow a collection down to this scrap of paper, do you?" It was a handwritten collection order for some cheese. "As long as it's got stamped by the main office, we don't give a fuck." Bill continued, "Sometimes, they turn up with bits of paper like this. What's happened is that they've taken instructions over the phone from their guv'nors but as long as the reference numbers tally up, then it's hunky dory (okay)." I just laughed.

My plans were complete!

I made the second team, as did Davey and Bill. We were the new kids on the block and although we lacked a bit of strength, well, Bill and me, Davey (Tarzan) had no problems. Bill used to play on the wing and was probably the best player amongst us but we more than held our own.

In those days, we worked Saturdays up to midday and we would have a great big dinner at our favourite café then meet at 1.30pm at the bottom of Duke Street Hill, where a coach would take us to Sidcup (our home ground) or further afield.

We were well organised with managers and trainers and our own first aid man. Our kit was always cleaned and ironed, therefore we looked very professional. I played in what is now called central mid-field (the engine room) and I was what they called a mud magnet, probably because I never shirked a tackle. There was always tea and loads of sandwiches at the end of the game, and that was an added bonus.

Bill and Dave used to make their own way home, if we had played at Sidcup, because they both lived at St Paul's Cray, which was only a couple of miles away. Once I was dropped off at Duke Street Hill, I would stroll up to Uncle Nathan's stall where he was usually just finishing off.

In Spite of Everything . . . .

"Hi ya, Paddy, had a good game?" "Yes, thanks. Had a good day?" "Not bad, son, not bad." He wouldn't give too much away. If he'd just got hold of the crown jewels, he'd keep it to himself (don't educate anyone). I gave him a wink. "We need to talk. Remember that business we were chatting about? Well, I've got it sussed[52]. He stopped what he was doing. "Not now, son. Come up and see me in the week . . . on your own." "Yeah, will do. I'm off now. See ya later."

Eddie was tarting himself up as I went indoors. Michael, Dad and Betty were sitting in the front room, watching our new telly. We were the first family in our block to get a television, only because Eddie and I shared the total cost with Dad. Michael jumped up and asked how I'd got on. "We won 4-2." "Did you score?" "No, I'm a defender but Cousin Dave got two of the goals." Dad piped up, "What? Is Davey an attacker? I would have thought that anyone his size would be in defence." No, he's our centre-forward and you wouldn't fancy him running at you." Dad just ummed and returned to his telly. Betty looked up. "There's some sandwiches for you on a plate in the kitchen." "Ta very much but I've gorged myself already at the football club. I don't feel hungry. Thanks for your trouble though." She looked away.

I got myself all dolled up and stuck my head into the lounge. "I'm off out now. See you later. See you in the morning, Mikey." Dad couldn't resist calling out. "Try not to be too late, son." I ignored that last remark.

Ted and few other mates were hanging around at the top of Red Cross Way and we had a short chat. We'd decided to get the motor out and go for a spin. There was about eight of us and we noisily made our way to Waterloo and our lockup. A miracle! Ted got the old motor started straightaway so we had a bit of whip round and made our way to the nearest petrol station. We bought a pound's worth, which was over four gallons (it's nearer seven pounds a gallon, as I write this).

Our world was to come crashing down!

I had taken over the driving and we were prowling around, windows open, shouting and yelling at any girls we came across and at any mates we knew when, Ring! Ring! There, right up our daily[53] was a black Wolseley (the old bill). I pulled up sharply. "You lot in the back, keep quiet and behave yourselves!"

I got out of the car and two coppers got out of theirs and approached me. Ted had also got out and was standing beside me. "This your car?" "Yeah, why? I ain't done nothing wrong, have I?" "Well, you're making a lot of noise, for starters! Have you got any documents with you?" "What documents do you mean?" "Don't try to be funny, young man. Driving licence, insurance and owners logbook." The other copper chipped in (he'd been wandering round the car). "And road tax. This one's out of date." They took me back to their car and took note of my name, address and date of birth (I gave Eddie's). Then they gave me a slip of paper with instructions to produce my documents at Stone's End police station within five days. Then (unlike today, I'm sure), they let us drive away with a warning to be a bit quieter.

We'd put the car away by now and were now hanging around the coffee stall. "Where's our logbook, Ted?" "I've got it indoors. My dad has been telling me that we should register it in our name at County Hall. Do you know what to do?" "No, but I know someone who will. I'm playing football in the morning. Will it be alright for me to pick it up on my way out, about half past nine?" "Yeah, I'll be up." "We'll find out about road tax as well, but the insurance might be a problem, but I'm sure my uncle will have some ideas. Leave it to me." I didn't mention the lack of driving licence!

I picked up the logbook and went on to play a game for my club. It was considerably easier because most players were about the same age as me, although a little quicker.

I made my way round to Nan's straight after the game and felt the atmosphere the moment I stepped through the door. There was no music! Nan was sitting quietly in the corner and I could see that she'd been crying and it takes a lot to make her cry. My heart was in my mouth. "What's the matter, Nan?" Then Eileen's soft voice called me from the kitchen. "In here, Paddy." As I walked into the kitchen, it was obvious that she'd also had some tears. "What's the matter?" "Nothing to worry about. Sit down and I'll explain everything."

She began to explain but my mind was numb. I had trouble taking it all in because I was deeply shocked. I knew that Eileen hadn't been too well for a long time, but this!

She had contracted TB but hastened to add that it was considered mild and in its early stages. She would be going away to a sanatorium in the country at a place called Haslemere. It didn't matter how much she tried to reassure me, I knew that TB was a killer. "When are you going and how long will you be away?" "I'm off tomorrow and I might be away for a year." My heart sank. The mere thought of losing Eileen filled me with dread. For possibly the first time in my life, I felt fear. Utter, useless fear and there was nothing I could do to help. Eileen obviously noticed. "Now, come on, liven up. I promise you that I'll get better and, anyway, you will be able to get down to see me. For gawds sake don't let Mum see you like this. You'll frighten the life out of her."

That did the trick!

I was fearful of touching Eileen because I didn't know whether I would be able to stop myself from crying and that would have certainly put the wind up Nan! I pulled myself together, rose from the chair and gave her a crushing cuddle. I somehow thought that I might be able to transfer some of my strength into her. "Come on, Paddy. Let's go and see Mum. Chin up."

I knew that Nan trusted my opinion (remember, I went to college) and I assured her that Eileen's condition would be cured. I don't think she was fully convinced but we both tried to make light of it.

Poor Johnny was unable to cope with this latest piece of bad news and would no doubt go on the piss. I gave that matter a little thought. "Does Uncle Pat know this piece of bad news?" "Yes, he's known about it for a couple of weeks." I thought, they've kept that quiet.

"Does he know that you're off tomorrow?" "No, not yet. Why?" "Well, I was just on my way over to the stall to see Jimmy. Do you want me to tell him?" "I think you'd better, don't you, Mum?" Nan just nodded.

As I was about to leave, Nan suddenly livened up. "Are you coming back for dinner? I've got a nice roast on." That was Nan for you. She wouldn't be kept down for long!

"Is the Pope a Catholic? See you later." I walked down Bermondsey Street like a zombie. I just couldn't get Eileen out of my head. That terrible turmoil was going on inside me and, as before, I thought my head would burst open. I felt so alone and helpless. If I lost Eileen, I don't know how I would cop but, by the time I got to the fish stall, I'd got myself together."

Jimmy was serving. "Hi ya, Paddy. You look serious. Have you lost a pound note or something?" I smiled. He was always a cheery, happy-go-lucky bloke. "Get on with your job, bollocky. Has your dad had enough of you?" "No, he's in the pub with Uncle John." All my cousins referred to Johnny and Eileen as uncle and aunt, but because I had been brought up with them, I didn't. I was relieved that he was with Johnny because, as his eldest brother by nearly twenty years, he could control and influence him and Johnny would certainly need that now.

I walked into the pub and spied them straightaway. They showed out, then Johnny said, "Have you been round home?" "Yeah, but I wish I hadn't." "So, you know, then?" "Yeah." Uncle Pat looked at me. "Do you want a pint, son?" "No, thanks, Unk. I'll give Jimmy a hand. Thanks, anyway."

Jimmy didn't want to talk about Eileen, which was no surprise. He lost his mum to TB. "This ain't wartime anymore, Jim. They'll get her better. You'll see."

Uncle Pat came out and took over. "Have you told Paddy our news?" "Just about to, Dad." He had plenty. He had decided to sign on for the army for three years because that way, he would be able to choose his regiment and, in his case, learn a trade. He chose the Royal Signals to train as a wireless operator. His reason being that he would be called up anyway, so, why not? But there were other issues, as well.

Uncle Pat had taken up with another woman and would get married shortly and they had been offered a brand new house at a place called Merstham, about 20 miles from London. Jimmy worked in Shoreditch so that would be a problem.

There was a lull in trade and Uncle Pat came round to see me. "Has he told you?" "What? About the army and your moving and things?" "Unfortunately, son, I won't be able to run this stall, anymore." I hadn't thought about that! "It was always a temporary thing but I know you used to help your granddad. You're alright about it, ain't you?"

What the fuck is going on? There couldn't be any more bad news, could there? "I'll certainly miss the old stall but nothing seems to last forever. Will somebody be taking it over?" He explained who it would be and I knew him, he was an old friend of the family. That somehow softened the blow!

I felt the logbook in my pocket. This is a very peculiar day but there are always bonuses. The car problem now seemed insignificant!

The dinnertime was now over and I helped Jimmy and Uncle Pat clear down the stall and put it back in the lockup. I felt a little bit sad not because of the actual stall but the memories of Granddad (nothing lasts forever). Jimmy and I made arrangements to meet over Christmas because both he and Eddie would be going off into the Forces.

Nan, as usual, put out a wonderful, tasty roast dinner. Uncle Pat and Jimmy had both come to visit and she even had sufficient for them to have a bit of meat and potatoes. Johnny was half-drunk and getting all emotional but that was Johnny's way.

I hung around for a while, not really wanting to say goodbye, but eventually I gave Eileen a big kiss and a cuddle, promising to see her as soon as possible. Nan would take care of all the visiting arrangements. Sadly Eileen was being picked up in the morning by an ambulance.

Before I left, Nan explained that because I had been in close contact with Eileen over the years, I would receive a letter from the hospital arranging an appointment for a test to make sure I hadn't any infection. The same applied to Eddie and Michael.

I couldn't go straight home. I was too upset wondering whether I would ever see Eileen again, even though she'd impressed on me that what she had was mild (but TB was a killer).

I gave the news to Michael but played it down, telling him that she'd be home in a couple of months. Betty seemed more upset than Dad but, to be honest, Dad didn't show much emotion. Betty asked me to give Eileen her love and wished her better. I explained the testing we were to have and that sparked a bit of interest in Dad.

I didn't get much sleep that night, laying awake in the dark, because I just couldn't get Eileen out of my mind. Then I woke up.

I made sure that I took the logbook with me to work and, as soon as I'd golloped down my dinner, went off to see Nathan.

"I'll buy you a cup of coffee, son. Look after things for me, Jim. I'll only be ten minutes. Got a bit of business to do." He gave Jim a wink and off we went. "I've figured out a foolproof way to get goods out of the wharf but, before I explain, I've got a problem." I pulled out the logbook and proceeded to tell him, chapter and verse. He frowned but eventually started to smile. He knew a man who, for a few quid, would take care of the insurance. He explained how to get the road tax. This entailed queuing up at County Hall. There was nothing he could do about the driving licence. "You'll have to put your hands up to that one, son. It'll only be a fine but you'll probably have to go to court." He smiled and put his hand on my shoulder. "You silly sod, but you're only young once." He then carefully explained which pub I could meet 'The Professor' in and said that he would see The Prof first thing in the morning. "Now, very, very carefully, give me some education." I did, making sure not to leave out anything. He was very interested!

"Get your motor sorted out tomorrow then pop up and see me on Wednesday. I've got a lot to think about. Now, piss off, I've got a living to get."

I called in to see Teddy straight after work and explained what had to be done. Ted's dad seemed a bit pissed off but his mum was a fucking nightmare. She ran the house and both Ted and his dad did as they were told. In the end, I'd had enough. "I'm the unlucky one. It's me who's been nicked, not your Teddy." I explained that we both owned the motor and shared all the costs. She wasn't happy with the motor being registered in my name, after I'd explained that we couldn't register joint owners. "Once I've got the insurance sorted, in both our names, you take it up to County Hall and register it in your name, Ted." They all seemed happy with that! Ted wasn't a bad lad, but his parents were greedy bastards.

I met The Prof, next day, in the Queen's Head and he was easy to spot. He stood out like a sore thumb, having a 'City Gent' written all over him. Nathan had straightened him and he signed me a backdated cover note that tallied with the date Nathan had put on the transfer of ownership part of the logbook. He had even signed it! The Prof wouldn't take any money off me. "Nathan has taken care of me, old boy. Remember, that's only for one month and two weeks have gone already. See you in a couple of weeks, young man."

That night, I dropped the cover notes in at Ted's, making sure I showed his mum that *both* our names were on it. "Once you've got the tax disc, Ted, let me have it and the cover note because I've got to show them at the nick and I've only got a couple of days. See you round the stall later. Bye."

I didn't bother going home but headed straight for Nan's. Even though I was still obsessed over Eileen, I couldn't help smiling to myself. That Nathan has got more strokes than Big Ben.

I had a nice dinner, as usual. For some reason, Nan had been expecting me to come round tonight. She was obviously worried about Eileen but continued to reassure me that all would turn out all right. Johnny, on the other hand, was hopeless. As I've said before, he couldn't handle bad news!

I sat around chatting but, once Nan had got herself ready to go over the pub, for her couple of Guinnesses with her mates, she took my arm and over the pub I took her. I gave the publican enough money for her drinks then, once she'd settled down, gave her a kiss and went on my way.

There was the usual crowd of lads hanging around the stall and, once I turned up, there was the usual banter and skylarking. Eventually, Ted showed up with one of his cousins, Freddie. "Hi, Ted. Hi, Fred. Alright?" They both showed out. "How did you get on at County Hall? No problems, were there?" Ted looked uneasy. "Sorry, Paddy, but I couldn't get over there today." He could see the look on my face. "For fuck's sake, don't get annoyed. You know what my mum's like. She went apeshit about me taking the day off work." He held his hands out. "I promise I'll take care of it this coming Saturday morning, honest!" "Ted, listen to me! You know that if I don't produce by Thursday, I'll be nicked. It'll cost me more than a poxy day's work!" Ted was genuinely upset. "Sorry, Paddy, it's the best I can do." "Well fuck you!!"

Nathan had proved right, once again ("You can never trust strangers, only your own). I had already decided that I would not be able to drive around once the police knew that I didn't have a licence, therefore, there wasn't much point in owning a car (or half).

I shrugged. "Make sure you get it taken care of on Saturday, mate. I'll take care of the old bill." Fred bought the coffees and the meat pies and normal business resumed.

"Ted, I want out of the motor. Shall we try and sell it?" "Ah, leave off. I love that motor. 'Aven't upset you, have I?" "Ted, I've got to hold my hands up. I've been caught bang to rites. If they do me again, they'll throw the fucking keys away! If you want to keep the car, then buy me out. Listen, we gave £20 for it. I'll take a cockle."

Ted gave it some thought. "I'm a bit short at the moment." He turned to his cousin. "Do you fancy getting involved, Fred?" Now, Fred was a cunning fucker, so didn't commit one way or the other but I couldn't allow things to get out of hand. "Fred, if you slap my hand right now, you can buy my share for a neves (seven pounds)." It took Fred all of three seconds. "Done! I'll pay you Saturday afternoon. Will you be up The Cut?" "Yeah, about two o'clock onwards." Then we slapped hands, deal done!

Ted was a careful (tight) sort of lad, so he was gutted that he'd shit out on a bargain. I would have liked to have been behind him when he told his greedy mum!

Sitting opposite Uncle Nathan, having a coffee in the Italian, I told him chapter and verse. "How much do I owe you for the insurance?" "Get yourself out of trouble first then we'll sort it out." He took a long sip. "Now, educate me, again!"

The weekend soon came around and I was sitting in the coffee bar at the top end of The Cut, when Freddie strolled in. "Hi, Paddy, seen Teddy, yet?" "No, he's probably still in a queue over there." I nodded my head in the direction of County Hall. "Here you are, a neves, wasn't it?" "Yeah, thanks, Fred." He handed me seven crisp pound notes. We shook hands. Half a dozen or so of our mates, plus a few girls, began to appear and we proceeded to drive the owner mad. We had him running about like a blue-arse fly. All very light-hearted though. A few of the boys had their morning papers and were trying to find possible winners of the afternoon races. They used to ask my advice but I tried, time and time again, to explain that I understood odds and the betting but I didn't bet on the horses myself. (Uncle Terry had a very nice car but his punters had bikes, if they were lucky. QED.)

Ted turned up, all flustered, and whinging about the amount of time it had taken to register the motor and get a tax disc. He was such a tight bastard that he couldn't handle the fact that all vehicle tax starts at the beginning of the month and here we were near the end.

"Ted, for fuck's sake, stop moaning. Want a nice coffee? Fred's in the chair! Have you got the tax disc?" "Yeah." "Let me have it and the cover note so that I can get the old bill off my back. I've been weighing it up, Ted, and if I take care of the insurance, you can take care of the tax. How does that sound?" Ted wasn't silly. He knew that the insurance was dearer! "Yeah, that's okay. Has Freddie paid you, yet?" I patted my pocket and smiled.

He passed me the papers and, after a short while, we all made our way over to the Pie and Mash shop in Lower Marsh.

If you've never tasted pie, mash and liquor, I feel sorry for you. It is delicious, especially when followed by stewed eels (it makes my mouth water, as I write).

The pie shop was run and owned by Italians and they were always pleasant people. "Don't often see you in here Saturday dinnertime. I thought you always played foota-ball?" "Yeah, I normally do, but we didn't have a game this afternoon and I had a bit of business to take care of. Double pie for me." He smiled. I had an enormous appetite and just having a single would irritate me.

Many years later there is a wonderful and almost unbelievable tale, centred around the Pie and Mash shop, but I mustn't get ahead of myself.

I turned up at the nick and produced the ticket given to me by the traffic. There was a lot of turmoil going on with coppers rushing to and fro. The duty copper produced a great big book and plonked it down on the desk in front of me. After a lot of umming and aaring, he found what he was looking for. Other coppers kept asking him questions and he was obviously getting a little bit pissed off. "You're two days late. These documents should have been shown by Thursday. Do you realise I could nick you just for this alone?" I said I was sorry but my mate had the logbook and he was working away.

That seemed to do the trick but, in truth, I think he just wanted to get rid of me (you see in those days, they didn't like spending time on traffic incidents because the beat coppers and the new traffic didn't get on with each other).

"Just giving me extra work," he mumbled. After studying my papers, he made a few notes and then, to my utter amazement, gave me back the documents and told me that he was satisfied and I was in the clear. I was gobsmacked but got out of there as fast as my legs could carry me.

That was my lucky day. I wasn't asked to produce a driving licence. The answer came when I looked at the ticket given to me by the traffic and, by a piece of luck, they hadn't put a tick alongside the driving licence!

I was walking on air as I made my way up Long Lane and, as I was going past Terry's pitch, he called out, "How's Eileen, Paddy? Have you had any news, yet?" "Hi ya, Tel. I'm on me way to Nan's right now. I'll let you know if there's anything to report. How ya doing, anyway?" He smiled. "Betting over a hundred, son. Be good!"

Nan was in the kitchen. "Hello, darling. Fancy a cup of tea?" I gave her a kiss. "Yes, thanks, Nan. Heard from Eileen, yet?" "There's a letter on the mantelpiece." She seemed happy. "Aunt Anne was round earlier and she read it to me. You have a read, anyway."

She described the place and it sounded really special. A great big house with acres of grounds. She was sharing a room with three other ladies and she seemed relaxed (well, she would, wouldn't she?). "Sounds very nice, don't it? I notice that you'll be able to visit her in a couple of weeks. Who'll be going with you?" "Aunt Anne has offered and so has Uncle Jim." She had already read my mind. "You'll have to come next time, probably be after Christmas. Sorry, son." "Don't be silly, Nan. That's alright."

Then my name was called out. It was Johnny from his bedroom. This would become his trademark. Whenever any of us came round and, of course, he was laying about in his bedroom, he would summon us in for a chat. "What you been up to?" "Only hanging around with some mates. Why?" "Haven't had any trouble at work, have you?" "No, it's all quietened down. Everything's sweet." He shrugged. "Good! Have you read Eileen's letter?" I nodded. "Seems like a nice place, even though it's a hospital." "A sanatorium, John! There's a difference. They make you better!" He didn't argue. "What do you think of Mum? Does she seem alright to you?" "Alright? Alright? Of course, she is. She's as strong as a lion. I don't think we need to worry about Nan! You going out with your mates tonight?" "Yeah, we're going to see Eddie sing in the King's Arms. It's the final tonight, so we'll all give him loads of support even though I don't think he needs it, do you?" "No, he'll piss it. The shame is that he won't be doing many more comps for a while, not where he's going." Johnny chuckled.

"Don't worry about him. He'll look after himself." Before leaving, I asked Nan what she was doing for Sunday dinner. "Roast beef, you cheeky sod. Doesn't Betty feed you?" I gave her a cuddle. "She can't cook like you, Nan! See you tomorrow. See you, John. Give Eddie a big cheer."

There were a few of the lads hanging around the tea stall outside Waterloo station, taking the piss out of the paraffins[54]. They told me that Teddy and Fred were tearing around the area but it was beginning to get a bit boring. We decided to go over the Bridge (Waterloo) and have a stroll road the West End and see if we could pick up some skirt (girls). We had a laugh but, sadly, no girls (this time).

It was now Friday and I hadn't been up to see Nathan all week. I don't know why. "Hello, stranger, where've you been? I thought I'd upset you or something." He gave me a sly wink. "Order the coffees. I'll be with you in a minute."

The moment he sat down, he pressed a nice bundle of notes in my hand. "Put that away. Count it later. There's an apple[55] for you! Happy?" Happy? You bet I was! At that time, a bank manager earned that kind of money per week.

"It all went smoothly then, did it?" "As smooth as a baby's bottom. My man is over the moon. We only took ten cases, as agreed, there's no need to get greedy. That's how you get your collar felt. Paddy, I know I've been through this with you before, but you did get rid of that bit of paper that had the details on it, didn't you? Because I don't want your handwriting on anything." "Yes, of course, I did just as you said and burnt it. Don't worry."

"Now, you don't need to know who the driver was or where the stuff was sold and they certainly know nothing about you." He got a little bit closer and serious. "This is between the two of us. Don't breathe a word to anyone." He paused and stressed. "*Anyone.*" I put my finger over my lips! As I was about to go, he whispered in my ear, "I've made arrangements that when your Nan does her weekly grocery shopping, she'll get a bit extra, at no cost. She will never work it out, I'm sure of that. I thought that'd make you happy. See you later, son."

On my way back to work, I think I worked out who Nathan's customer was. There were a couple of local ex-boxers, who ran a cut-price grocery business in Tower Bridge Road, and I knew that Nathan had done business with them during the war years and the ongoing rationing and they had always looked after our family. I shrugged to myself, at the same time, fingering the wad of notes in my pocket (ignorance is bliss).

Another Christmas was upon us again but this was a time of plenty. For us anyway! With all of us at work, there was no shortage of money and even Betty splashed out. She was still a rotten cook but she tried.

This Christmas morning, all four of us, i.e. Dad, Eddie, Michael and I got smartened up and went to have a drink with Dad's brothers-in-law. He was as proud as a peacock. They were all quite jealous of his three fine young sons. We would repeat this tradition on many occasions, during the coming years, but this would be the last time that we would all be together for the next four years.

All three of us went round Nan's that Christmas night because, without Eileen, we thought she needed our support. That was probably the first time in our lives that we were able to pay Nan back, in a small way, for what she had done for us. I know that she appreciated us and we made her very proud.

Uncle Pats, George, Jimmy, as well as Aunt Anne and Nathan, were all there, plus the usual cousins and friends. The news from Eileen was encouraging. She was actually getting a little stronger. The party got into full swing.

I couldn't wait to get back to Nan's the next morning. It was that little bit of the devil in me. I knew there would be many, many hangovers and I just loved making lots of noise and winding everyone up. I couldn't repeat some of the names I was called!

I managed to have a nice chat with Jimmy, not knowing when we would see each other again. Like Eddie, he was away in a few days' time. Our lives were changing and would never be quite the same again.

It had arrived. Eddie's last night of freedom. I actually bit the bullet and had dinner with them all. Betty had pulled out all the stops but she just didn't have that magic touch, probably because she ate like a sparrow and wasn't really that much interested in food. But in spite of her shortcomings, we had a pleasant time. "Dad, hope you don't mind but after I've had a couple of pints with you, I'll be going round to see Nan. Will it be alright with you if Michael comes with us?" "Of course, son. I never doubted that you would want to see your Nan. It'll probably be the last time she sees all three of you together for a few years, at least, but, Ed, don't be too late. You know how bad Mikey is getting up in the morning and not too much drink. Remember, he's still underage."

We all went round to a local pub in Flat Iron Square (you'll never find it on any map but it's at the end of Union Street as it joins Southwark Bridge Road) including Betty. Dad's brother-in-law, Bill, met us in there. We had a couple of pints with them then the three of us made our way to Nan's place, Dad and Betty telling Eddie that they'd see him in the morning.

Nan was overjoyed to see us. She loved it when the three of us were together (well, she would do, wouldn't she, after all the trouble she went through to keep it that way). Nan got herself ready then off we went. She was on Eddie's arm with us close by. Johnny was in the pub with a few of his mates, as well as some of Eddie's friends. Eddie, naturally, was the centre of attraction and he loved it. Why not?

Nan sat with a couple of her lady friends and we made sure they were well looked after. Nan was proud to bursting because the three of us were running the show. Her face was beaming. We were a job well done. She had done her duty and, boy, did she milk the moment!

Time to go! Eddie gave Nan an enormous hug and got a little upset but Nan had said many goodbyes in her lifetime. She handled it very well. Eddie promised to write.

The three of us had a lovely chat on our way home. We stopped off at the coffee stall and had a meat pie apiece (Eddie had two). I had arranged a morning off and told Eddie that I would see him off from Waterloo Station. He was a bit surprised.

I could hear Dad moving about and I heard him give Eddie a wakeup call. I was up in a flash, got washed and dressed before the others. Eddie was busy finishing off his packing and, as usual, Michael had buried himself under the sheets. He was hard work, getting him off to work and with Eddie not about, that would be my job, no doubt!

Eventually, just Eddie and I were left in the house. "Ready to go, Ed?" "Yeah, about as ready as I will be! Come on then, let's go!"

Waterloo Station was as busy as usual although now seemed slightly smaller than the last time I was standing on a platform. Eddie sorted out his train which was going to Exeter then changing for Plymouth.

"Time to go, bruv. Thanks for being here." His eyes began to moisten. "Leave off, Ed. None of that!" He dropped his case and gave me a hug (that was alright). "Make sure you look after Michael. I'll write." "I will, Ed, I will! Goodbye, bruv. I'm going now. I'm not gonna stand here waving like some old tart. Goodbye!" I turned and walked away, resisting the temptation to turn round although I *knew* that Eddie would.

As I walked down the great steps of the station, my mind started to wander. This was the first time we had been parted. Life moves on! Naturally, my thoughts settled on Nan! I'd go and see her tonight!

It felt really strange not having Eddie around, even more so for Michael. He'd never slept in a bedroom on his own before. No matter how I tried, conflict was always round the corner, sort of creeping up on me.

With Eddie's money missing from the family budget, I was asked to pay in a bit more. Now this I didn't mind too much but Betty wanted to take more off Michael, as well. He was an apprentice and didn't earn very much. When he told me, I was very annoyed.

"Dad, it's a bit of a liberty asking Michael to give up more of his pitiful earnings. He'll hardly have any spending money. Can't you and Betty (not 'Mum') put in a little extra and the three of us can make up Eddie's couple of quid. Surely that'll be fairer?" "It's easy for you to talk but I don't earn very much nor does your mother." I glared at him but kept in control. "She has to take care of the house and that's what she's decided." I was gobsmacked. "Alright then. How much more do you want to from Michael? "Another ten shillings." "In that case, I'll now give Betty three pounds a week and that will take care of Michael's bit. Happy with that?" "As long as you can afford it, son." "Dad, I wouldn't have offered if I couldn't. One other thing. How much did Eddie put towards the telly?" "Two shillings a week." "I'll give you that, as well! I know Michael loves his telly so we don't want to lose that do we?"

I gave Michael the good news and he was as happy as a punter when his double comes up.

It may be me but I just couldn't get out of my mind how greedy my dad and Betty were. They were ruthless, not much charity about those two. I would have to keep a very keen eye on Michael coz he was now my sole responsibility.

I never breathed a word to anyone regarding this latest incident but Michael did. He told our Aunt Anne all about it, which was a silly thing to do because she was a bit fiery, was our aunt, especially over anything to do with us three. She tackled me about it but I calmed her down and reassured her that I was fully capable of taking care of things because I was making good money. The way she looked at me made me think that she knew more than she should (well, she was Nathan's wife!). "Look after him, Paddy, won't you?" I just gave her a wide smile. No need for words!

I had some very interesting information to tell Nathan about, so I stuffed down my dinner and left the rest of the lads in the café. Over a cup of coffee, I explained that we were receiving large quantities of tinned ham, as well as the other usual goods. He was very interested. "That would make a nice little earner, my boy! Now, you're sure that you're completely covered? Nothing can be traced back to you?" "No, for sure! The details I'm passing on to you are known by at least thirty people. There wasn't a problem, was there?" "No, no, son. It all went like clockwork. My man is over the moon." He took a deliberate sip. "But, we mustn't get greedy! Greed is what gets people catched."

I nodded in agreement. "I'll get you the info and you decide the rest." "Good boy! Oh, before you go, I was having a drink with your guv'nor, Joe, the other night. He knows that pilfering goes on all the time but it's not his concern. He's probably got a little something going on, anyway! Not a peep in our direction and I know he'd have marked my card, if necessary. See you soon, son. I'm off to try and make some money."

The thing with Nathan was that he would have known all about the Michael incident at home but he would never comment unless asked.

The crafty Italians had probably guessed that Nathan and I were up to something. It was quite funny because I could tell they were dying with curiosity!

"Everything's sweet, my boy!" He must have noticed that I had been studying the 'I-ties'. "Whatever you do, son, never trust those greasy fuckers. They may seem nice but they are not our own and not to be trusted. Anyway, to business. Have you got deep pockets?" He smiled. "Don't look surprised but I've got a nice and nifty[56]." It was hard to hold myself together. This was a serious load of dosh! "I don't think it wise to carry that sort of cash with you into those docks, just in case you got a tug (searched)". Which did happen now and again just so that the security could justify their existence. "I'll have it here with me, so call by and see me once you've finished." He gave me a pat on the back. "Nice one, son, very nice indeed."

That afternoon, I got through my work in a daze. I was on autopilot. That was more than two months' flat wages. I picked up my money and, as I was about to go, Nathan got all serious. "We'll give it a rest for a couple of months, son. Mustn't get greedy, must we?!" He held his hands together as though handcuffed. I nodded and went on my way. I was walking on air!

It's funny how we soon got used to not having Eddie around and, apart from the very difficult task of getting Michael out of bed, things took on a normality. Our dad was a saver with his precious savings book, so I used to get some amusement out of the fact that he'd have had a fit if he could see my stash hidden away in my bedroom. I didn't trust the Post Office.

Amongst the many sports and pastimes I enjoyed was playing billiards and snooker and now that I was old enough, I started spending some time in the billiard hall at the Elephant and Castle. There were quite a few local villains and tough lads hanging around that place and because of this, most of my mates gave it a wide berth, but I got on very well with most of the clientele, which meant I made a few more mates. Some had jobs and went to work and some were criminals but that was their choice. I was never influenced one way or another.

In Spite of Everything . . . .

Now that I didn't own any wheels, either took Shanks's Pony (walked) or relied on mates to give me a lift. There were a group of lads who also hung around the coffee stall at the Borough. They were mainly well-dressed fellas and they would drive up the Locarno Dance Hall most Saturday nights. They were keen to take me with them mainly for some help should they get in any trouble (although I had made it crystal clear that if they cause trouble, I would not help out). I was never a dancer but the place was teeming with girls!

Nan gave me the good news that on her next visit to Eileen, I could go with her. It was a difficult place to get to, needing a train from Waterloo and then a long bus ride.

It was now late February and it was very cold and as soon as we got out of the London, there was snow on the ground and quite a lot of the stuff. All the fields were white.

The three of us (Aunt Anne was also there) soon found the bus and the conductress knew exactly where the sanatorium was and it didn't take that long either.

The snow must have been over a foot deep and as we made our way along the driveway (luckily cleared), the sound of laughter and screeches of excitement could be heard coming from the rear of this enormous mansion. We presented ourselves at the reception and the nurse on duty seemed to remember Nan, giving her a warm smile. "Nice to see you again. I hope the journey here wasn't too bad." "My grandson has taken care of me, thanks." That made me feel very proud. "You're a lucky lady. Anyhow, Eileen is actually playing about in the snow with some of our other patients. Come through here and see for yourselves." We followed her down a large corridor, which opened out onto the large back garden. I spied Eileen immediately and she looked the picture of health with big red rosy cheeks and, although well wrapped up, I could tell that she'd put on a bit weight.

I yelled out to her, much to Nan's horror! Eileen turned towards us, waved and came running over. She was beaming and gave us all the biggest of hugs.

We had a lovely afternoon with Eileen and it was so good to see her again! And, looking so healthy! I felt so much easier because although it was explained to us that she wasn't out of the woods yet, it was obvious that she was on the mend.

We had to drag ourselves away but visiting time was finished and it was now dark and very cold. We chatted away non-stop all the way home, me doing my best to convince Nan that Eileen would be home soon.

There was a big crowd of us milling around, chatting and skylarking, eating meat pies and sipping coffee, doing our best to keep warm. That night, amongst many others, there was a bloke called Phil. At one time, we had gone to school together, actually sat next to each other, during the war years. Now, Phil was a particularly nasty bastard. He always carried a chiv (razor) and had used it on many occasions. He'd already served time behind bars. We got on fairly well with each other although I'm not very keen on people who use 'tools' but we went way back.

Not many people fancied mixing it with Phil because he was a bit of a maniac, even some of the very tough families steered clear of him. So, there was always an uneasy edge about things when he was about.

I, as well as Eddie and Johnny, had warned him never to pull his blade out to threaten us, or any of our family, and he was left in no doubt as to what would happen to him if he did! We never had a problem with him and he would always make sure that should he meet Nan in a pub, he would buy her a drink and be very respectful. She actually thought that he was a very nice boy.

I don't know how it all started but the talk got round to Phil who was proudly going on about how he'd striped (cut) a local face and how he'd run away screaming. I didn't join in the celebrations.

"What's a matter, Paddy? Don't you approve?" I turned to face him, making sure my hands were free. "You're not taking the piss, are you? You know that I don't give a fuck what you do or who you do it to."

I paused. "As long as it's not to any of mine." You could have cut the atmosphere. He smiled. "Leave it out, Paddy. We're mates, ain't we? I didn't mean to upset you. I love you and your family." We shook hands and normal order was resumed. For the time being, anyway.

In those days, the use of drugs, in our circles anyway, was very rare and mostly unknown but I'd often wondered about someone like Phil because he often acted a bit weird.

This particular night was one of those times. He kept jabbering along about his exploits with his chiv and how he was both feared and respected locally. He was surrounded by hangers-on. Then the subject eventually got round to me, with Phil explaining why he would never attempt to cut me.

"Paddy, just for a laugh and I really mean it, just for a laugh, do you reckon I could get my chiv out of my pocket before you could land one on me? Remember, I've seen you box many times."

"Phil, Phil, for fuck's sake, what's got into you? Please drop it, you're making me nervous." "Come on, it's only a joke! Not scared are you?" People drew away from us. I had to make my mind up very quickly. What was on this psychopath's mind? He definitely seemed a bit high, therefore, very dangerous.

"Remember, Phil, this is not my idea but since it's for a laugh, come on then, hands down by your side." I got within range of him and noticed that his eyes were a bit wild. I'd better concentrate.

His right hand came up and quickly disappeared into his jacket. My left hook crashed into the side of his mouth and he yelped in pain and crashed backwards into the side of the stall, sending cups and plates flying everywhere and then collapsed in a heap on the floor. His hand was still inside his jacket. I quickly stood over him and pressed my right foot very firmly into his chest, making sure that he couldn't get up or remove his hand. He was a bit dazed but I hadn't knocked him out because, as I've said before, I didn't possess a knockout punch.

"Phil, listen to me and, for fuck's sake, listen very very well!! As you said, it's only for a laugh so when I let you get up, make sure your hand is empty then let's shake on it. You understand, don't you?" He was pulling himself together by now and smiled. "You didn't have to hit me that hard, you bastard. Still friends, ain't we? Give us a hand up, will ya?"

He offered me his "empty" hand so I gave him a help up. Phil looked around and laughed out loud. Then he winced with pain and very tenderly rubbed the blood from the side of his face. He then turned to George, the stall owner. "Sorry about that, George. Only having a bit of fun. Do I owe you anything for the broken cups and spillages?" "Nah, that's alright, Phil. No trouble."

Things returned to normal but I never took my eyes off Phil (and never did) and that would prove to be the right thing to do, as events in future years would prove!

Apart from the continuing drama, trying to get Michael out of bed and off to work, things at home had settled down with all of us getting on with our differences, which lead to a calm and peaceful period.

I was getting on very well in my job and fully enjoying the sporting activities, even taking up a new pastime. Shooting! There was a .22 rifle range on the top floor of Mark Brown's Wharf and I took to it like a duck to water, very quickly reaching a very high standard. I was even asked to be in the rifle team but with my football, table tennis, boxing and running, not to mention snooker, hanging around with the boys and chasing all the girls, I gave it the thumbs down. I didn't know then but in the very near future, my shooting skill would come in very handy.

A couple of months had passed by and Nathan thought it time for a little bit of business. I agreed and supplied the vital details. Nathan suggested that we give the tinned ham a miss so I gave him details of luncheon meat and brawn. Then burned my notes, as instructed.

In Spite of Everything . . . .

One lunchtime, whilst hanging about and chatting to Nathan, he suddenly got a little serious. "I heard that you gave that slippery cutthroat a slap the other night. What was that all about?" I told him the whole story. "Keep any eye on him, son. He's a nasty bit of work. I think he's a bit of a nonce[57]. I know George and he's terrified of him."

"Nathan, he knows that even if he cut my arm off, I'd still break every bone in his fucking body." "Hmm, yeah, but watch him!" "Have you heard from Eddie, yet?" "As a matter of fact, we got a letter from him only the other day. He's finished his basic training and volunteered for the marines and he's been accepted but will have to pass the course, which is supposed to be seriously hard." "Well, if anyone can pass, I'm sure your Eddie can. He's a fit, hard fucker! Sorry, Paddy, but I've got work to do. See you in a couple of days." He winked. "I've got a bit of something for you." He gave me a big thumbs up. "See you later. Thanks for the advice!"

Summer was now approaching and my life was tripping along effortlessly. I was making good money and enjoying myself and for the time being, at least, no aggravation.

I came in from work and Betty was in the kitchen. "Hi, son, there's a letter here for you. A big brown one!" She seemed rather pleased with herself. Yeah, it was big brown letter with OHMS printed all over it!

In truth, I was expecting it but it was still a bit of a shock. I tore it open and, as I thought, it was my call up papers, instructing me to present myself for a medical. Shiiiit! I thought to myself.

I read through the documents very, very carefully and decided to apply for an exemption on the back of an apprenticeship. I was fairly certain that I wouldn't be able to get away with it but it was certainly worth a try. There were the beginnings of political rumbling about the abolition of National Service, so I lived in hope. Things were going so sweet for me that it would be a shame to spoil them because they might never return again! I posted off my application.

"Do you fancy coming with me to see Eileen, next week?" "Yes, please, Nan. Who else is coming?" "Just us two and Johnny."

I had already worded one of my mates and he had offered to drive me to the sanatorium on my next visit because I'd told him what a shitty journey it was, trains and buses. I'd laid it on a bit thick and added Nan to the picture. I'd done him a few favours via the Prof and he knew how protective I was over Nan. I hadn't said anything to Nan about a possible lift because I needed to straighten it first.

Nan was pleased as punch as she got into the back of the big Pontiac and Johnny was a bit impressed, as well! We found our way to Haslemere with no trouble, me navigating and my mate, Jozza, doing the driving. "Where to now, Paddy?" "Fucked if I know, oops, sorry, Nan. Look, there's the train station over there. Pull over and I'll jump out and ask that bus driver." It was easy to find from the directions the driver gave me and, in no time at all, we were driving up to the front entrance.

I was amazed by the difference since the last time I was here. There were trees and bushes in full bloom, lovely lawns and the most beautiful flowers everywhere. Jozza looked amazed. "What a gaff!"

"Thanks, Joz, but you know that you can't come in with us, don't you? We'll be a couple of hours, so what you gonna do?" I gave it a moment's thought. "Whatever you do, don't start eyeing up any of those big houses. You'll wind up getting nicked." He laughed back at me. "I'll behave myself. Promise! See you back here in a couple."

Nan was a bit puzzled over Jozza! "You were a bit hard on that nice young man, don't you think?" "Don't worry, Nan. He's used to me. We're alright."

Eileen looked as bright as a button and we had a lovely afternoon with her. There was still no news about when she'd be coming home but it was as plain as the nose on your face that she was getting better by the month.

In Spite of Everything . . . .

I brought her up to date with Eddie and she was delighted to know that Mikey had settled in at work. I made her laugh until she had tears running down her face, telling her how hard it was getting him out of bed in the mornings. After I told her about my call up, she wondered how he'd make out once I wasn't there! I hadn't thought about that! We had to drag ourselves away but visiting time was over. I promised to keep her up to date with everything, especially my imminent call up.

There was Jozza, waiting patiently. Johnny asked me what he did for a living. "He's a thief! Him and his mates do a lot of drummin'[58]. I know that it's not very nice but I don't get involved and, as you can see, he'll do me a favour when I need it. He's not a bad bloke really, in his own way!" Johnny just grunted because, like me, we had no respect for housebreakers even though they obviously picked big rich houses to rob.

It was a pleasant drive home with Nan, so noticeably pleased to see Eileen in such good health. Then we pulled into a nice pub on the way home, just outside Croydon, and that put the cherry on the cake.

I brought Michael up to date regarding Eileen and made him laugh repeating the story about his laziness. He promised that he would make sure to visit Eileen if and when I was called up, that is, if she was still away. I hoped not!

We were sitting in the restaurant and Nathan had already weighed me in (paid) and I was giving him the news on Eileen's progress. "She'll be home soon son, you see."

Nathan was very interested in my possible call up and I suggested that we had better step up on our activities because it could all come to an end soon. "Nothing lasts forever, son. We must still avoid getting too greedy but as long as you're absolutely sure that nothing can come back to you, we'll go to work." Just then the door opened and Jim pointed this bloke towards Nathan. "That's him, over there."

The man was holding a letter in his hand and was obviously very nervous. "Excuse me, Nathan, isn't it?" "Yes, son, what do you want?"

Nathan was very aggressive and the poor man was shaking. "Sorry to barge in on you like this but I wonder if you can help me?" Nathan stared at him. "I'm the manager of Waltons, the fruit and flower shop on the station, and I've received a written complaint about bad fruit that our rep on London Bridge Approach has supplied." This story will need some explaining! Nathan never paid full price for anything. Most of his fruit was second grade, apart from the carefully chosen items that made up his display.

He would lay out his apples, pears, oranges and tomatoes in carefully prepared sections but would serve from the back, where all the shit was. He would scream at anybody who had the nerve to dare touch his precious display. Remember, he was a very tough man was Nathan and most of his customers were nice gentle City workers (no match for him).

As I've already mentioned, he never paid full price for anything, and this went for his brown paper bags. He bought them crooked from a bloke who worked in Spicers, the big printing firm in Union Street, and they supplied Waltons. These bags were all nicely printed with Waltons' name all over them in nice big shiny letters. He used other companies bags as well.

"Give us that letter, son, and for fuck's sake, sit yourself down. You're making the place untidy." This poor man did as he was told. He was nervous! Nathan read the letter and burst out laughing. "Paddy, you gotta read this fucking letter. It's priceless!" The poor man didn't know whether to laugh or cry! It was a great letter and we should have framed it! It was so well written and the reference to their 'representative' was hilarious. They had also demanded their money back. Now, there's a laugh on its own! Getting money out of Nathan was like pulling teeth. His pockets were like fish hooks, only designed to go one way.

I tossed the letter back to the manager. "Tell him to go fuck himself." That remark didn't do much for the bloke's confidence but then again, it wasn't meant to!

"Come on, Paddy, calm down. This man is very nice and polite." He turned to the white-faced, terrified man. "Sorry about the little hiccup, son. I don't want you to get yourself in any trouble with your head office. I promise that I won't use any more of your bags." He hesitated. "I'll tell you what I'll do. Come over to my stall and you can take any that's got your name on them. Now, I can't be no fairer than that, can I?"

The manager's face was a picture. He was now relaxed and smiling. "Thank you. I'm really sorry to have troubled you." He gulped in some air and very quietly asked the question, "What about the refund?" Nathan growled at him. "I've had to pay money for those bags and I'm giving them to you for nothing, ain't I? Take it out of that." There was no argument and Nathan was as good as his word.

I can tell you that story caused many a laugh for years to come.

We received good news from Eddie. He had passed his marine course with flying colours and was now a full marine. He posted a picture of himself in his full new uniform. He looked very smart and I could not wait to give Nan and the rest of the family the news. Nan, of course, was very proud, even though, bless her, I don't think she actually fully appreciated what Eddie had achieved.

I was walking through Cottons Yard on my way to Fenning's Wharf, when I heard a familiar voice call my name. It was the Superintendent, Joe. "Hold up a moment, son, I need to have a quick word in your ear." For a quick moment, I thought I was in trouble but he was smiling. "Hello, guv. What's the problem?" "No problem, son. Just letting you know that Head Office, [as I thought], have chucked out your request to support your deferment. Sorry, boy, but you're captured!" "I'm glad it makes you laugh!" "Don't worry, son, your job will be here when you get back." I couldn't help smiling. "Thanks a million. That makes me feel much better. Gotta rush. The ship's waiting for me."

So that was that then! The army life for me! Always assuming that I pass the medical and I didn't hold up much hope of failing that (my fucking ears were fit!).

The postman never let's you down, does he?! There it was, lying on the carpet. OHMS. I was instructed to attend a medical at an address in Blackheath. They even enclosed a postal order for the bus fare. I threw that in the dustbin. I didn't want any charity. My mate, Jozza, would take me.

I didn't say anything to Nan at first but kept Johnny informed, also Uncle Nathan, which meant Aunt Anne would also know. As I'd planned, I got a lift to the medical centre and took my place in the queue. We all stripped down to our underpants and, like an assembly line, shuffled from one doctor to another, separated by small screens. There was a serious lack of privacy but it didn't bother me in the least because I had become used to communal changing rooms. It was all over in a couple of hours and I thought I would be told the result straight away but I was informed, very stiffly, that I would get a letter in a couple of weeks or so.

Good old Jozza was patiently waiting for me. "How'd ya get on? Did they chuck you out?" "Sadly, no. Thanks for waiting, mate. I owe you." We got on our way and Jozza started to speak. "Funny thing, Pad! I wanted to have a chat with you. I know that you have some tasty relations and me and the others (his thieving mates) are having trouble getting rid of some of the more valuable bits of contraband. Is there anybody you know that might be able to help?" I gave it some thought. Of course, I knew someone but there was no way I'd educate those stupid fuckers! "As a matter of fact, Joz, I might be able to help. Leave it with me for a couple of days. I'll let you know." My mind was buzzing. "Anyway, exactly what sort of stuff are we talking about?" "There's always silver ornaments and cutlery and, if we're a bit lucky, some tasty tom[59]." "I think I can help, Joz."

I could see Nathan setting his stall up with his mate, Jim. I gave them a show (wave). "How'd you get on with ya army medical, son?" "I won't know for a couple of weeks." Jim smiled at me. "Paddy, if you don't pass then no one will. Look at ya! You're as fit as a fucking fiddle." He started humming the tune to the old song, "You're in the army now." I playfully grabbed him in a headlock and hoisted him off his feet. He screamed like a girl. "Fuck you! Nathan, tell him to let me go.

He hurts!" I didn't need any telling. Jim gave me a couple of playful jabs in the stomach. I laughed and looked at Nathan. "Got time for a chat?" "Get the coffees in. Won't be long, Jim."

I gave Nathan the fully story and he was pleased to know that I hadn't put his name up. "I've had a good education, remember!" Nathan was very interested because I knew that he already handled a lot of stolen goods. "The rules are these, son. They must not know who I am and they must never meet me. You will have to act as a go-between. They hand you over what they've got, you bring it to me and, if I'm interested, I'll offer them a price. There's no haggling. They take it or leave it. Is that clear enough for you?" "Yeah, I'll put it to them but where do I get my bit of bunce?" "As usual, if I do well, then so will you. Also, make sure that those scoundrels look after you. They needn't know about our arrangements." He took a sip of his coffee. "In actual fact, the least they know, the better!"

A couple of nights later, I bumped into Jozza and mates at the stall and gave them the good news. They seemed happy with the arrangements, apparently that was the normal way of doing things.

"Don't waste my time and try to pass of a load of shit, will ya?" They said that they'd only involve me with the tasty bits. "Another very important thing, you must make sure that you only fence goods that are stolen way off the manor. We don't want anything that's nicked locally. You folla?" They promised me that where they did their thieving was miles away.

I now knew that there was a strong likelihood that this would be my last cricket season for a while and gave our captain the bad news. He and most of the team were very disappointed because I'd had a very successful season with both bat and ball. The more knowledgeable players had seen it all before and weren't surprised by my call up. They all wished me the best.

What a way to spoil a decent summer! My official enlistment papers arrived and I was instructed to report to the RAOC army training camp, Hilsea Barracks in Portsmouth. Once again, my train fare was enclosed. I had a couple of months of freedom left and when I showed the papers to Dad, he explained that the RAOC were responsible for supplying everything the army needs and that it was a vast outfit. My experience in handling goods was the obvious reason I'd been assigned to this particular branch of the army. Dad said that I was lucky because it was cushy posting and, with my experience, I would have no trouble settling in.

At tea break that next morning, I went along to see Joe, the Super, and showed him my papers. He shrugged his shoulders. "Never mind, Paddy. Your job is here once you return. You've fitted in well and do a nice job. I'll let Head Office know and remember to call by and say goodbye before you leave us. Good luck, son!"

Mick, Bill and Cousin Dave had already been called up and were no longer around and although they had been replaced by a younger set of lads, it wasn't the same for me. I did eat dinner with them but didn't hang around. I was off to tell Nathan the bad news.

"You could go on the run and tell them to stick the army up their arses but I would think you wouldn't be able to carry on your work down there." Nathan nodded towards Tooley Street. "Looks like you'll just have to make the best of it, son." I gave him some vital information, which he quickly copied down, making sure to give me back my notes. "Paddy, my boy, I know that it's only natural for you to want to make a killing before you leave, but we must be a bit careful. Things will come to a sudden grounding halt and I'm worried that there could be even the slightest suspicion over you. We'll have a couple of nice bits and then leave it alone for a clear month. You happy with that?" "Yeah, of course, I am. You're talking sense, as usual." We made a nice few bob over the next month.

The days were flying by so I gave Nan the news and the date that I would be leaving. She just gave me that rueful smile of hers followed by just one question. "How's Michael getting on at home and how's his job?" I was able to look her in the eye and assure her that everything was "sweet". She seemed satisfied with my answer. I thought it a bit strange at the time but she didn't seem to be concerned about me. I do know now that she considered me fully grown up and able to look after myself. She'd done a good job!

I was desperate to see Eileen again because it was obvious that she wouldn't be home before I had to go in the army and, luckily, there was a visit planned for the coming weeks. Aunt Anne and Nathan would be going therefore I could go with them. That evening, I went round to see Annie. They lived in Kennington. She was surprised and pleased to see me, as were her four children because besides Walter, now a teenager, and Seamus, she now had a lovely daughter, Doodie, and a toddler called Wil. They were all great kids. The boys idolised Eddie and me, partly down to the fact that we sorted out the local gangs who gave them grief, and partly because we were much older cousins.

Nathan was sitting alone in his favourite armchair. "Hello, son, didn't expect to see you. Thought you'd be out with your mates" "I'm meeting some of them after. I've just popped in to tell Aunt Anne about my call up and to cadge a lift with you to see Eileen. Will that be alright?" "Course it will, son. We'll be glad to have your company. You'll be able to tell your aunt all your news."

I spent a nice hour with them and eventually went on my way. My mates were a bit shocked when I told them my call up date. It wouldn't be long now. I noticed Jozza and his closest pal, Chisel, having a private chat, glancing in my direction from time to time. I heard Jozza say, "Not just yet, wait till we're on our own." I had a shrewd idea what they were after!

I'd got it in one! Later that evening, whilst sipping coffee at the Borough, they told me that they had had a tickle and thought my man could be interested. "I'll go and see him tomorrow and make the necessary arrangements. Meet me here tomorrow." I pulled them closer to me. "I only want to see you two, nobody else. You clear on that? If anybody else shows up then all bets are off!" I stressed that point very clearly (Nathan's words were ringing in my ears. "The more people there are involved, the more chance of being grassed). "No trouble, Paddy, you've got it!"

This was proving to be a busy time for me and I kept thinking that this was no time to be going in the fucking army but I didn't have much choice. I certainly didn't fancy doing porridge because Nan would be heartbroken!

So, I'll just have to take it on the chin. Nathan gave me precise (and from him 'precise' was a valid description) instructions on how I should handle the business. I would meet my two friends in a nearby pub and I would drive their motor round to Nathan's lockup. He'd value the booty, offer a price and I would return to my mates and give them the good news. "Don't forget, son, drive away in the opposite direction. They're bound to give their eyes a chance."

It all went like clockwork. Nathan viewed the haul and after a mixture of tut-tuts and appreciative noises, finally said, "Right, son, leave this stuff here, go back to you mates and offer them a monkey (£500)." I gasped because that was a serious amount of money those sixty years ago, a serious lot of cash!

I just couldn't help myself but the look on their faces when I told them that they would get a 'three-a' (three hundred pounds), well, it was priceless.

Jozza didn't know what to say but I knew that Chisel was a bit more forward. "Fuck me! Is that all? He's a bigger thief than we are!" I chose not to react too strongly to his outburst. "You don't know what the fuck you're talking about. Clocks are a very dodgy thing to get rid of and some of that silver will have to be melted down because it could be traced. There's a lot of work to be done." Chisel soon realised that he was getting a little bit too outspoken then Jozza spoke up. "We understand all that but what about that bit of tom. There were diamonds amongst that lot." "Sorry, Joz, but the same applies. It'll all have to broken down because the old bill will have photos of that type of tom." I let them get their stupid heads round that for a couple of minutes more then broke into a wide smile. "Just pulling your legs! I can get you a monkey!" I knew that £500 was a bit keen but they now seemed much happier. Chisel didn't leave it at that. "You, fucker. You had us going there. I still think that it's a bit short but it's all profit.

Thanks, Paddy." He stuck out his hand and I shook it. Chisel didn't know it, at that time, nor me either, but that handshake would get him out of a fair bit of bother in years to come.

I handed over the car keys. "I'll have your money in a couple of days. Here's a one-er (£100)." They eagerly took that from me.

Nathan was right, the one-er was the clincher. He had also told me not to come back, regardless! They would have to wait a couple of days to get their stuff back. He'd read their minds exactly!

It was two days later before I went up to see Nathan and he was a very happy man. I knew that he'd never pass me on any details but it was obvious that he'd done very well out of the recent deal. He didn't stop smiling and whistling. We made arrangements for the remainder of the money and I in turn, met up with the boys and weighed them in. They passed me over a score (£20). Not bad for a half-hour's work!

"What you gonna do when you go in the army, Paddy? Can you take us to meet your man. We'll behave ourselves."

"Sorry, Jozza, that can't happen. My man knows all about me going into the army and he'd like to help but there is definitely no way he'll deal with you direct. No way at all." He knew by my tone that there was no point in taking this line any further.

The trouble with people like Jozza isn't that they might grass but take him as an example. He doesn't go to work and drives around in a big flashy American car. Not exactly invisible, is he?! There's plenty of money to spend and this is mostly spent in local popular pubs. The law are not a silly as some people think. In no time at all, Jozza and friends will become known to the local force. They actually grass their stupid selves. I didn't give a fuck (education has to be paid for).

Time was galloping on. My departure getting ever closer!

I had informed my club that I wouldn't be able to play a full season, so there wasn't much point in my signing on for this year's football.

There was a strict limit to the number of registered players and my leaving would have left them a player short. The club thanked for my efforts over the past years and allowed me to use all the facilities up until my departure.

I had just finished a very hectic session in the gym and had several rounds sparring with an up and coming lad. The trainer was very grateful. "You certainly kept him on his toes and he now knows what it feels like to get hit! I've heard that you're soon off to the army, is that right?" "Yeah, in a couple of weeks. You were in the army, weren't you?" In those days, a majority of trainers had served in the forces, many as PTI instructors. "Yes, you'll get on very well in the Forces. A good boxer like you will soon get into a regimental boxing team and that will get you many privileges, you'll see!" I just grinned and nodded at him. Those words set my mind working. I'd better keep very quiet about my boxing because there's definitely no way I'm gonna do any boxing for the army (Nathan's words came to mind, "Don't ever let anyone know what you know!).

I had a lovely journey bouncing about in the back of Nathan's van because I had to let Aunt Anne sit in the front seat, didn't I? Once again, lovely Eileen looked the picture of health and she had some even better news. She had been given the all clear and would be coming home before Christmas. I felt a bit horrible with myself for being disappointed that I wouldn't be around but soon got those selfish thoughts out of my head. I knew that Nan and the rest of the family would be having a wonderful Christmas. Her getting over that terrible disease certainly made my going away easier.

We said our goodbyes, with Eileen hanging on to me a wee bit longer, but she knew that I didn't like too much fuss.

"Uncle Nathan," I always called him 'Uncle' when in the company of Aunt Anne. "Can you drop me off round Nan's. I want to give her the good news." "Of course, I can. Tell your nan that we couldn't hang around. Annie's got to get back for the kids."

In Spite of Everything . . . .

Nan's face lit up when I gave her the news and Johnny nearly jumped out of his armchair. "Gotta have a pint on that, Paddy. Gonna have one with me?" "Course, I will. Hurry up though, I want to get home and tell Michael before he goes out."

We had a couple together and I left him in the pub. He would be there for the rest of the night. That was his way.

I gave the good news to Michael and, of course, Betty and Dad. Michael was even livelier (if that was possible). Betty seemed genuinely pleased but Dad, as usual, didn't seem to show that much enthusiasm or was it my imagination? I knew that I was ultra critical, which was wrong, but I just couldn't help myself.

The time had arrived! It was my last day at work because, even though I wasn't due to report to the barracks until Wednesday, I had to finish on a Friday.

I was working this day in Cotton's Wharf, which was one of the biggest, and I was getting fed up with the endless handshakes and backslapping and, of course, the horror stories about the Kate Karnie (army).

I broke one of my golden rules and had a couple of drinks at dinnertime (a practice that most of the dockers did). It's hard to imagine that being allowed these days! I followed this up with a few drinks with my fellow tallymen and wound up half-pissed. It was a special occasion, after all! "See you all in a couple of years' time. Keep my seat warm."

The dinnertime drinking just has to be described because I doubt very much that you will ever witness its likes again.

The pub in question was Moonies, an Irish-run pub in Duke Street Hill, although there was a lower entrance opposite Wilson's Wharf. The bar staff would commence pouring something like a hundred pints of Guinness and they would fill them about halfway and then let stand in long rows. They would then be topped up and any excess head was scraped off with a wooden spatula until perfect. This whole process took the best part of an hour.

The men poured in at a couple of minutes past midday and greedily devoured the beautiful dark and creamy beer. All that would be left were empty glasses. They then returned to a somewhat hazardous job.

No! I don't think you'll witness that ever again (health & safety!!).

That whole weekend went by in a haze, what with the drinking and saying goodbye to various girlfriends and most of my mates.

It's worth mentioning why a lot of my mates never went into the Forces and the answer is quite simple. They were either unfit, simply because many of them had never bothered with any sporting activities, preferring to hang around smoking or they didn't have a job or a fixed permanent address, some having been chucked out by their parents and some coming from broken homes. Therefore, the authorities couldn't trace them. Records weren't as sophisticated as they are now. Many of these lads would eventually get nicked and serve time in prison and the Forces didn't want them anyway!

Michael and I spent our last Monday together at our club. We didn't train or anything like that but just played some table tennis and billiards. I wanted to have time to have a final chat with him.

I was concerned about his work and the fact that he was so bad at getting out of bed, but he assured me that he would improve and he had actually asked Betty to make sure he got up, even going as far as telling her to chuck water over him (and she did!).

I reminded him to make sure and visit Nan more often. He got slightly annoyed about that but although he loved Nan as much as me, he did forget to go round as often as I would have liked. I reminded him that he was my younger brother and therefore must do as I ask! (He did.)

Finally, money! I had saved a fairly substantial amount of cash and I had made a false back in the lower drawer of my chest. Michael's eyes

In Spite of Everything . . . .

nearly popped out when I told him. He didn't ask where it had come from which was just as well because I wouldn't have told him. I think he knew that anyway. "If you get stuck for cash, open it up and take a couple of quid but don't be fucking greedy. I want some left when I get back." That made him laugh. I knew that as an apprentice, he didn't earn much and Betty and Dad were merciless, even more so now that both Eddie and I were away. "Don't make yourself become a scruff. If you need a new suit or shoes or a nice shirt, then just take the money." I let that sink in. "It's not for fags or booze!" He'd had enough. "Fuckin' 'ell, Pad! You're worse than the effing priest!" He was laughing. "But I know what you mean and I'm really grateful. Thanks! I'd give you a kiss but you'd probably give me a right-'ander!"

We went straight home after finishing at the club. Again, lots of handshaking and farewell pats on the back.

Dad had gone to bed and Betty was about to go. "My word, you're home early. All the girls gone home?" I smiled. "Well, I had to get him home early. You know what he's like getting up! I hear that you've got the job!" That stern face returned. "Yes and I'll make sure that he does, the lazy sod. Nite, nite, both of you."

I showed Michael my stash and I think he was even more wide-eyed when he actually saw the amount of cash. "Ain't you taking any with you?" "Just a few quid. You never know what goes on in the army. I've heard some funny stories and I don't think I could control myself if anyone turned me over[60]. See you in the morning, Mike."

Two hours lying awake in the dark, as usual, my mind going over everything. Then I heard Betty calling Michael, she didn't leave off but it worked. I heard him get up. She was much better than an alarm clock.

I gave it a few minutes then got up and went into the kitchen. "I didn't expect you would be up this early. The tea's made. Not going to work today are you?" "No, not anymore. I've finished. I woke up because of him." I nodded towards the bathroom. "I'm sorry that I got you up." "Don't be silly, I was awake already. Nice job, by the way." Again nodding towards the bathroom.

Sadly, Betty couldn't see the funny side of things which made her seem so severe and serious and this was shame because she was basically a good woman.

They both went off to work and I washed, dressed and had breakfast. I then popped out to the corner shop and bought a morning paper. I had planned my day out so I came home and read through the paper. I was going to stroll over to the Borough Market and meet Nathan but I knew that he didn't get there until late. Remember, he only bought the unsold shit!

There they were, Nathan and Jim, eating toast and sipping tea in the market café. Nathan saw me and waved me over. "I keep forgetting you've finished work. Sit down and have a tea and toast. It's lovely." Jim gave me a wink. A market trader stuck his head in the door. "Nathan! All your gear's ready. In your own time, mate." I couldn't stop laughing. "What ya smiling at, son?" "Nothing, really. It just amuses me the way you've got everyone straightened up." "Well, it's no point getting older if you don't get a bit wiser, is it?" He was a character.

We finished our tea and made our way to the market stall where his van was parked and there was a great stack of crates of various produce. I was surprised by the big pile of grapes. "I didn't know you sold grapes. I've never noticed them on your stall." "What them? No, I buy them for the Italians in the restaurant across the road. I can't understand why but they can't get enough." He shrugged his shoulders. "It's good business so I ask no questions. Come on, give us 'and to load up."

I watched him and Jim set their two stalls up and again marvelled how Nathan managed to get such a lovely show out of the old crap that he bought. The atmosphere amongst the various market traders was always good humoured and I was well known to all of them, so I had to spend a bit of time hanging around each stall bringing them up to date with my news. Most of them were eager to be part of the fold because Nathan was the guv'nor.

It was time for me to leave them because I'd made a meet with a couple of lads in the Milk Bar in The Cut. Nathan asked me if I was going out tonight and I told him that I would be having a drink with Nan and Johnny. "Me and your aunt will be coming round for a pint with you, son. See you later!"

I shook hands with Jim then yelled out to the others and then I was gone. When would I see this place again?

I had a bit of dinner whilst chatting with some of my scoundrel mates, with them, once again, trying to persuade me to put them in touch with 'my man'. They had about as much chance as trying to sell a load of sand to the fucking Arabs! Eventually, we all drifted apart with just the odd "See ya" but that's how I liked it.

Dad was sitting in his armchair, reading the newspaper and biting his nails, as usual! He put the paper down. "Had a good day, son?" "Yes, thanks, Dad. Said goodbye to a few mates and hung around with Uncle Nathan for a while." "How is he, nowadays?" "Same as ever. I'll be seeing him tonight because he's having a drink with me and Nan. You're welcome, you know?" "It'll be a bit late for me, son. I have to get up very early for work, remember?" Then much to my surprise. "But, I'll have a couple with you, a bit earlier, if you like."

There it was, that almost natural barrier between us. He just wasn't sure about me and it showed. "That'd be lovely, Dad! About seven o'clock be okay?" I knew that he always had a couple of hours' sleep in the late afternoon. "I'm gonna have a little kip now, so see you later."

I went out again just before Betty got in from work, only to save any conflict, because I was headed for my favourite café in Borough High Street. I chose the roast beef dinner. It was beautiful. When the owner's wife cleared my plate away, she asked me if I wanted any afters. I gave it a bit of thought and chose the roast lamb dinner. The owner burst out laughing when he saw the shocked look on his wife's face. The portions were very generous so as to avoid any worries she had, I explained that I had an enormous appetite and didn't have a sweet tooth. The owner had seen it all before.

When I got back home, Dad was up and having some tea alongside Betty and Michael, who had just got in from work. "Do you want something eat, son?" "No, thanks Betty, I had a big dinner earlier on (a little white lie). I just want to have a nice wash and get changed. We're going out a bit sharpish for a farewell drink." Before I could get in another word, she blurted out. "I've got a bit of a sore back and I really don't fancy going out tonight. That'll be alright, won't it, son?" "Course it will, don't be silly. Anyway, I'm just having a couple with Dad then going off to see Nan."

Dad and I were ready and waiting for Michael in the front room. I had a nice surprise in store for Dad. We had a television which cost 7s 6d a month and we all put money towards the cost. Eddie was no longer putting his share in and now neither would I. I knew that they all enjoyed their telly including Michael and I was a bit worried that they might not be able to finish the payments. I had given it a great deal of thought.

"Dad, please don't think I'm being flash but I received a very nice bonus from work (another white lie) and now that I won't be putting any money in, I want you to take this," I held up an envelope, "and finish off the payments on the television." He was completely lost for words. I continued very quietly so that Betty wouldn't hear. "There's thirty quid in there, Dad. That should be enough, shouldn't it?" Dad spluttered. "Oh, son, you don't have to do that. I'll manage." I got off the settee. "Please, Dad, take it. I won't need it where I'm headed. I'd probably get it nicked, anyway." Just then, Michael popped his head round the corner. "What you two up to? You look like you've seen a ghost, Dad. He ain't been annoying you again, has he?" Michael had that cheeky grin on his face. Dad got up and put the envelope in a drawer. "No, son, he's not annoying me. Come on, boys, let's have a drink."

I had already suggested that we have a drink in the little pub closest to us. Just across the road, in fact. I didn't want to walk up to Union Street to the pub that Uncle Bill always drank in because I wasn't that fond of Bill, who was a virtual stranger to me anyway, and I didn't fancy spending my last night drinking with him and by doing so, let him get the idea that he held any importance in my life. I am not suggesting in any way that he was a bad man, just that I wasn't in the least interested in him or his friends. I think that Dad had got the message.

The three of us had a very pleasant private hour, with Dad giving me advice about how to handle myself in the army. I took note of everything he said because he'd had plenty of first hand experience, after all! He advised me to be calm and not overreact to things and he was sure that I'd make a good soldier.

It was now time to be on our way and poor old Dad, very self-consciously, gave me a tentative hug. He thanked me once again for what I'd done. It's strange but we were naturally distant from each other. He would be off to work long before I needed to be out of bed, so this was our goodbye. Dad did say to me that he would make sure and look after Michael. He fully understood how concerned I was but I was not to worry. He'd be okay. I had enjoyed the couple of drinks we'd had, because we hadn't spent that much time together like that!

"Hi, Nan, are you ready?" "Hello, Paddy. Hello, Mikey. I won't be long. Are you two walking me over? Johnny and Nathan and a couple of others are already in the pub. They were fed up waiting for you."

"We had a couple with Dad. He sends his regards." "There you are! I told them that's where you'd be. Michael, help me on with my coat, please." She gave him that fixed stare. "You're not going to drink too much, are you? Remember your age." Michael laughed. "Nan, I can drink more than him," pointing at me.

The pub was buzzing and a quiet cheer went up as we stepped into the bar. Aunt Anne and Uncle George and Lil were all there, as well as Uncle Jim who, as usual, was in charge of the whip.

We had a very nice time and even the landlord got into the swing of things and he laid on a few sandwiches and snacks. I think I recognised the meat filling on the sandwiches and gave Uncle Nathan a crafty wink. He touched his head in recognition.

Time was called and it was time to go even though I knew that Johnny and his mates would stay for afters[61]. I didn't fancy hanging around any longer. I was already half-pissed and talking nonsense, plus I was supposed to be looking after Michael. But in actual fact, I was more worse for wear than he was.

I started my goodbyes. There was plenty of warm hugging and kissing going on, with Aunt Anne making sure that she got a chance to give me an enormous lingering hug and kisses. She did it, in part, because she knew that I wasn't comfortable and she had a wicked sense of humour but, also, because that apart from her own children, she loved Eddie, Michael and me unreservedly.

Someone said that I should watch out for myself but Nathan couldn't stop laughing. He growled, "Don't be fucking silly, I wouldn't fancy meeting the bloke who could get the better of him."

Well, it had to come to it! It was time to say goodbye to Nan! It wasn't something that I was looking forward to. All eyes were on us. She was sitting on the bench seating so I sat down beside her and put my arm around her, pulling her close to me. We smiled at each other and I noticed a couple of small tears in the corner of her eyes. "Come on, Nan, none of that. You'll have the whole place in tears." I gave her my broadest smile. "I'm only going in the army and there's no war on, so I'm not in any danger. It'll be a piece of piss." With that, she gave me a playful slap. "No swearing!" "Sorry, Nan!" I looked deep into those blue eyes of hers. "Nan, I'm going to give you a kiss then I'm getting up and walking straight out of the pub. You understand?" "Of course, I do, son. Don't you think I know you by now?" She got an extra hug for that.

I got up, looked straight at Nan, bent down and gave her a kiss on the forehead then turned away and strode out of the pub, waving and shouting out my goodbyes. I never looked back.

The bar door closed behind me and it was suddenly dark, cold and quiet. I had only gone a couple of steps when the pub door opened and Michael called out, "Hold it, Pad, wait for me." He was beside me in a flash.

In Spite of Everything . . . .

"Mike, I fancy walking down Bermondsey Street and going past our old house and school. You alright with that?" "Anything you say, bruv."

It was strange following our old school journey and walking past the ruins that once were the custard factory and the Guinness buildings then round the corner past Granddad's old pub and the empty spot where he had his fish stall. Our old house was no longer there. Just an empty space. I couldn't help but remember the happy days we had there nor could erase the terrible ones.

We two chatted away to each other all the way home past the church then through Maize Pond, Newcomen Street then Red Cross Way. We were home.

The flat was dark and quiet. "See you in the morning, Mike. Nice singing, by the way." Following the norm, towards the end of our drink, the singing had started. Nan, as usual, was in good voice and after considerable pressure, Michael had sung a couple of songs. He had a lovely voice, very similar to Eddie's but the difference was that Michael needed pressurising, whereas Eddie just loved to entertain. I didn't bother!

I lay there in the dark with just the odd sound filtering through the half open window. Sleep would not come. My mind was buzzing. The odd thing was that the army was the last thing on my mind! My thoughts drifted way back. The war, the loss of our mum (what did that cow mean, she wasn't killed by the bombs? Why did everybody carefully avoid the subject? Why? Why? Why?), the memories of Devon and Newcastle then the years of conflict at school then the docks and all the fun I'd had.

I wondered how Eddie was getting on and how Michael would handle being on his own, then there was Eileen. She must, must get better. I tried stupidly to concentrate my brain on curing her illness. It was like being a kid again; I thought my brain would explode. Only now, there was no one to go and play cards with! And I wasn't a frightened little kid any more!!

I heard a light tapping on my bedroom door then Dad's head appeared. "Sorry to wake you, son, but I had to say goodbye. Don't mind do you?" I must have fallen asleep. "No, that's alright, Dad, glad you woke me. What time is it?" He grinned. "Five o'clock. Sorry! Anyway, goodbye, son, and good luck. I suppose it's a waste of time asking you to write." He waved and was gone.

I managed to slide back into the land of nod. Betty woke me up, gently tapping on the door. "I've made a cup of tea for you. Do you want me to bring it in to you?" I had to pinch myself to make sure I was awake and not dreaming. I'd never received this kind of treatment before! "Er, no, thanks. I'll get up. Leave it in the kitchen, please." I never drank or ate in bed. It just never felt comfortable.

"Thanks for the tea. Is he awake yet?" Nodding towards Michael's room. "Well, he was a couple of minutes ago but you know how he is. You'd better look in on him. I bet he's gone back to sleep." He had. His mug of tea lay on his bedside table, untouched.

"Oi, wake up, you lazy fucker. I've got to be on my way in half-hour's time." That was a lie. I didn't need to leave for a couple of hours. The trick certainly worked because he sat bolt upright and started to drink his tea. I laughed, "Don't choke yourself. We've got loads of time." "You, bastard."

"You've got him up then? Paddy, there's clean underwear and socks in the airing cupboard and a couple of clean, ironed shirts hanging up. I've got to get off to work now, son. Give us a kiss before you go." I gave her a soft cuddle and a peck on the cheek. It just didn't seem right to overdo it. That would have been hypocritical but she was a nice, fine, upright woman. "Thanks for everything and I really do appreciate what you've done for me. I know that I haven't been the easiest person to get on with but I just can't help myself. Thanks, once again for everything and oh, by the way, tell Dad that I probably won't write." I shrugged my shoulders and grinned. "You know what I'm like!" With that, she gave me a friendly nudge and kissed me on the cheek. "Look after yourself, son." Then, as she was about to shut the front door, she turned. "I'll say a prayer for you on Sunday. Cheerio,

Michael. See you at teatime." He was still in his bedroom and called out, "See you later, Mum."

I packed a small case because we had been advised not to bring too much civilian clothing. It wouldn't be needed!

We strolled up Union Street and crossed Blackfriars Bridge Road into The Cut. Michael had insisted that he carry my case. I knew that Michael was ever so slightly pissed off with me because I kept going over and over again: "Make sure you get to work. Don't lose your job. Keep an eye on Nan and remember the money, if needed, but don't take it all!" He did manage to see the funny side of it. "You're like a fucking old woman. Don't worry, I can look after myself. I'm not a kid anymore but seriously, thanks, Paddy."

We were closing in on Waterloo Station. It was teeming with people, as usual, but this time, no steam engines! I turned to Michael. "Mikey, when we say goodbye, I don't want any fuss. Just one hug and I'm history. I won't stand for any girly silliness. Okay with that?" He smiled. "I've known you all my life. I understand."

We sorted out my platform and made our way to the gate. One big hug, "Goodbye, bruv, see you whenever." Then I was through the gate and striding up the platform. That's when I noticed other blokes of my age carrying small suitcases.

I did not want to look back but, in the end, gave in. He was at the gate, waving away. I gave him the thumbs up then opened the carriage door and boarded the train. When would we meet again? What surprises were in store for me? I put my case in the luggage rack, sat down and smiled!

I heard the key in the front door then the call, "Hi, luv, where are you?" "I'm in here!" (That used to drive her made!)

"Where's here?" "In the conservatory! Did they catch the train on time?" Charlie and Daisy had been staying with us for a few days and now Charlie was taking her home to her mum. "Yeah, they were

|479

okay." She bent over and gave me a kiss. "I thought you'd be writing. Had enough for the day?"

"No, in actual fact, I've finished the first book. I've stopped just as I'm about to go in the army." "You are only barely halfway through your life story. You are going to carry on, aren't you?" She seemed concerned.

"Of course, I am. This is where my life changed forever and I've got to meet you, haven't I? I've had a chat with Ryan. Claire and Louise have just got back from Holland. Lou done really well. She finished midway and, remember, that was against much older girls." Louise had been representing Great Britain in rollerdance against the Continental teams. How proud do you think I am with that?! One of my grandchildren in the Great British team!

"Make us a cup of coffee, luv. I've got another book to write!

---

[1] Oxford = oxford collar = dollar, five shillings
[2] greedy =
[3] jacket = vest = pest
[4] straightener = fair fight, one-on-one
[5] hop the wag = not go in
[6] manor = local area
[7] collar felt = getting arrested
[8] burk = Berkshire bull = fool
[9] S.P. = starting price = the facts
[10] carrot cruncher = local farmhands
[11] townie = what they called Londoners
[12] nipper = youngster
[13] Nelsons = Nelson's Eddies = readies = cash
[14] sky = skyrocket = pocket
[15] kettle = kettle on the hob = fob = watch
[16] tin-tack = sack = fired, dismissed
[17] button-'ole = talk discreetly, secretly
[18] your own = the family, only family!
[19] Rosie = Rosy Lee = tea
[20] barney = heated friendly rows
[21] livener = hair of the dog, a pint of beer
[22] plod = police
[23] straightened = got them on your side
[24] worded = had a strong talk, informed
[25] give your eyes a chance = have a good look around
[26] do a runner = go away without permission
[27] tasty = very hard, able to fight
[28] put them in it = give a share of the scam
[29] verbal = jeering, piss-taking
[30] tumble = understand, work it out
[31] brassic = brassic lint = skint, no money
[32] blind man's = blind man's bluff = snuff
[33] petrols = petrol tanks = Yanks, Americans
[34] porridge = prison term
[35] Joanna = piano
[36] firm handed = a big group
[37] a pull = confront, face-to-face

[38] hooks = all dockers were issued with a large metal hook with a wooden handle. It was so that they could grab a varied amount of cargo
[39] nit-nit = be quiet
[40] a face = very well known locally
[41] life of Riley = enjoying yourself in a carefree manner
[42] mob-handed = in a gang
[43] dig = a hard punch
[44] sweet = going smoothly, no problems
[45] bag of yeast = priest
[46] mug = idiot, fool, softie
[47] clocked = noticed, saw, spied
[48] chewing the fat = having a chat
[49] whack = share
[50] Connaught = Connaught ranger = stranger
[51] cockle = cock and hen = ten
[52] sussed = worked out
[53] daily = Daily Mail = tail
[54] paraffins = paraffin lamp = tramp
[55] apple = apple core = score (20)
[56] nice and nifty = £50
[57] nonce = one who practices nonsense, a pervert
[58] drummin' = house burglaries (drum-house)
[59] tom = tom foolery = jewellery (or as spoken "jewlery")
[60] turned me over = stole from me
[61] afters = after hour drinking, now called a 'lock-in'

CPSIA information can be obtained at www.ICGtesting.com
Printed in the USA
LVOW110802100412

276950LV00002B/16/P

9 781467 883955